Using Information Technology Advancements to Adapt to Global Pandemics

Efosa C. Idemudia
Arkansas Tech University, USA

Tiko Iyamu
Cape Peninsula University of Technology, South Africa

Patrick Ndayizigamiye
University of Johannesburg, South Africa

Irja Naambo Shaanika
Namibia University of Science and Technology, Namibia

A volume in the Advances
in Information Quality and
Management (AIQM) Book Series

Published in the United States of America by
IGI Global
Engineering Science Reference (an imprint of IGI Global)
701 E. Chocolate Avenue
Hershey PA, USA 17033
Tel: 717-533-8845
Fax: 717-533-8661
E-mail: cust@igi-global.com
Web site: http://www.igi-global.com

Library of Congress Cataloging-in-Publication Data

Names: Idemudia, Efosa C. (Efosa Carroll), 1970- editor. | Iyamu, Tiko,
    editor. | Ndayizigamiye, Patrick, 1979- editor. | Shaanika, Irja Naambo,
    1989- editor.
Title: Using information technology advancements to adapt to global
    pandemics / Efosa Idemudia, Tiko Iyamu, Patrick Ndayizigamiye, and Irja
    Naambo Shaanika, editor.
Description: Hershey PA : Engineering Science Reference, [2022] | Includes
    bibliographical references and index. | Summary: "This book provides
    insights and understanding on how companies and organizations are using
    advances in IT to adapt to global pandemics such as COVID-19, especially
    harnessing the power of various digital channels such as big data
    analytics and artificial intelligence to better serve their customers
    and business partners"-- Provided by publisher.
Identifiers: LCCN 2022007254 (print) | LCCN 2022007255 (ebook) | ISBN
    9781799894186 (hardcover) | ISBN 9781799894193 (softcover) | ISBN
    9781799894209 (ebook)
Subjects: LCSH: Information technology--Management. | Technological
    innovations--Management. | COVID-19 Pandemic, 2020-
Classification: LCC HD30.2 .U85 2022 (print) | LCC HD30.2 (ebook) | DDC
    658.4/038--dc23/eng/20220329
LC record available at https://lccn.loc.gov/2022007254
LC ebook record available at https://lccn.loc.gov/2022007255

This book is published in the IGI Global book series Advances in Information Quality and
Management (AIQM) (ISSN: 2331-7701; eISSN: 2331-771X)

British Cataloguing in Publication Data
A Cataloguing in Publication record for this book is available from the British Library.

All work contributed to this book is new, previously-unpublished material.
The views expressed in this book are those of the authors, but not necessarily of the publisher.

For electronic access to this publication, please contact: eresources@igi-global.com.

Advances in Information Quality and Management (AIQM) Book Series

ISSN:2331-7701
EISSN:2331-771X

Editor-in-Chief: Siddhartha Bhattacharyya, RCC Institute of Information Technology, India

MISSION

Acquiring and managing quality information is essential to an organization's success and profitability. Innovation in information technology provides managers, researchers, and practitioners with the tools and techniques needed to create and adapt new policies, strategies, and solutions for information management.

The **Advances in Information Quality and Management (AIQM) Book Series** provides emerging research principals in knowledge society for the advancement of future technological development. This series aims to increase available research publications and emphasize the global response within the discipline and allow for audiences to benefit from the comprehensive collection of this knowledge.

COVERAGE

- Application of IT to Operation
- Electronic Commerce Technologies
- Emerging Technologies Management
- Human and Societal Issue
- Web Services and Technologies
- Knowledge Management
- Supply Chain Management
- Business Process Management and Modeling
- E-Collaboration
- Decision Support and Group Decision Support Systems

IGI Global is currently accepting manuscripts for publication within this series. To submit a proposal for a volume in this series, please contact our Acquisition Editors at Acquisitions@igi-global.com or visit: http://www.igi-global.com/publish/.

Titles in this Series

For a list of additional titles in this series, please visit:
http://www.igi-global.com/book-series/advances-information-quality-management/73809

Library and Media Roles in Information Hygiene and Managing Information
Collence Takaingenhamo Chisita (Durban University of Technology, South Africa & University of South Africa, South Africa) Alexander Madanha Rusero (University of Johannesburg, South Africa) Ngoako Solomon Marutha (University of South Africa, South Africa) Josiline Phiri Chigwada (Chinhoyi University of Technology, Zimbabwe) and Oluwole Olumide Durodolu (Department of Information Science, University of South Africa, Sout Africa)
Information Science Reference • © 2022 • 268pp • H/C (ISBN: 9781799887133) • US $215.00

Mass Communications and the Influence of Information During Times of Crises
Mohammed Nasser Al-Suqri (Sultan Qaboos University, Oman) Jamal Mattar Alsalmi (University of Nizwa, Oman) and Obaid Said Al-Shaqsi (Media Training Centr, Oman)
Information Science Reference • © 2022 • 307pp • H/C (ISBN: 9781799875031) • US $215.00

Social Justice Research Methods for Doctoral Research
Robin Throne (University of the Cumberlands, USA)
Information Science Reference • © 2022 • 397pp • H/C (ISBN: 9781799884798) • US $215.00

Encyclopedia of Information Science and Technology, Fifth Edition
Mehdi Khosrow-Pour D.B.A. (Information Resources Management Association, USA)
Engineering Science Reference • © 2021 • 1966pp • H/C (ISBN: 9781799834793) • US $2,145.00

Handbook of Research on Managing Information Systems in Developing Economies
Richard Boateng (University of Ghana, Ghana)
Business Science Reference • © 2020 • 695pp • H/C (ISBN: 9781799826101) • US $295.00

For an entire list of titles in this series, please visit:
http://www.igi-global.com/book-series/advances-information-quality-management/73809

701 East Chocolate Avenue, Hershey, PA 17033, USA
Tel: 717-533-8845 x100 • Fax: 717-533-8661
E-Mail: cust@igi-global.com • www.igi-global.com

We dedicate this textbook to all those who passed away because of COVID-19-related illnesses.

Editorial Advisory Board

Table of Contents

Preface.. xiv

Chapter 1
Smart Technology For Addressing Pandemic Disruption: Impact of Social
Media Influencers on Brand Awareness During the Pandemic............................1
    Kaneez Masoom, Babu Banarasi Das University, India

Chapter 2
How Can I Help You Today? The Rise of Virtual Assistants in Human
Resources Management 21
    Dragos Vieru, Teluq University, Canada
    Simon Bourdeau, Université du Québec à Montréal, Canada
    Mickaël Ringeval, Université du Québec à Montréal, Canada
    Tobias Jung, Deloitte Consulting, Germany

Chapter 3
Adaptation to Pandemic Through Universal Access to Innovative
Technologies: ICT Access for Future Pandemics 47
    Abiodun Alao, University of Johannesburg, South Africa
    Roelien Brink, University of Johannesburg, South Africa

Chapter 4
The Role of Information Technologies to Adapt to a Global Pandemic:
Digitalization Disruption in the New Renaissance 66
    Julia Puaschunder, Columbia University, USA

Chapter 5
How Can Advancement in Information Technology Help College Students
During the COVID-19 Pandemic? Evidence From the Video Game Industry..114
    Reza Gharoie Ahangar, Lewis University, USA

Chapter 6
Supply Chain and Warehouse Management Systems: A Case Study From an
International Company..129
    J. Zambujal-Oliveira, University of Madeira, Portugal
    Carolina Rodrigues, University of Madeira, Portugal
    Maria Pereira, University of Madeira, Portugal
    Martinho Freitas, University of Madeira, Portugal
    Daniela Freitas, University of Madeira, Portugal

Chapter 7
Technological Growth in Religious Organisations: Exploring Social Media
Through System Dynamics...148
    Courage Matobobo, University of South Africa, South Africa
    Felix Bankole, University of South Africa, South Africa

Chapter 8
Sustainable Quality Education During the Pandemic and Beyond: Challenges
and Solutions for Higher Education Institutions..177
    Hakan Islamoglu, Recep Tayyip Erdogan University, Turkey

Chapter 9
Teleworking: The "New Normal" in Response to a Pandemic..........................199
    Leigh Nathan Breda, University of Cape Town, South Africa
    Michael Kyobe, University of Cape Town, South Africa

Chapter 10
The Online Education and Virtual Collaboration Model...................................226
    Efosa Carroll Idemudia, Arkansas Tech University, USA

Compilation of References 238

About the Contributors 269

Index...273

Detailed Table of Contents

Preface xiv

Chapter 1
Smart Technology For Addressing Pandemic Disruption: Impact of Social
Media Influencers on Brand Awareness During the Pandemic 1
Kaneez Masoom, Babu Banarasi Das University, India

Social media's emergence as a communication platform for consumers to interact with or about brands has significantly altered brand-consumer relationships. Companies are increasingly investing in influencer marketing, or hiring digital influencers to endorse their brands, as social media marketing becomes more advantageous. Influencers are changing the way brands create content, as well as how users consume and share it. The role of social media influencers in raising brand awareness, particularly during extraordinary times such as pandemics, is still in its early stages. Despite technological advancements and an increase in the number of online influencers, many challenges remain for businesses to connect with consumers during pandemics. The impact of social media influencers on brand awareness during a global pandemic is discussed in this chapter.

Chapter 2
How Can I Help You Today? The Rise of Virtual Assistants in Human
Resources Management 21
Dragos Vieru, Teluq University, Canada
Simon Bourdeau, Université du Québec à Montréal, Canada
Mickaël Ringeval, Université du Québec à Montréal, Canada
Tobias Jung, Deloitte Consulting, Germany

The pandemic context has fast-tracked the digital transformation of many organizations that pursued to dramatically change their organizational processes to survive in a global digital economy. While virtual assistants (VA), a specialized artificial intelligence-based chatbot, such as Alexa or Siri, have penetrated our private lives, many organizations are still trying to understand and evaluate why and how to integrate these technologies into their employees' workday. The study explores whether VAs can be used to support human resources (HR) trainee management software in a German organization and how it can be done. Four key HR areas of self-service, onboarding, training, and knowledge management were explored. Interviews were conducted to analyze which VAs' functions can be reused to support trainee management software in these four areas. The technology affordances and constraints theory were used to analyze data collected. The results showed that a VA's functions can support trainee management software especially in the areas of self-service, onboarding, and training.

Chapter 3
Adaptation to Pandemic Through Universal Access to Innovative
Technologies: ICT Access for Future Pandemics 47
    Abiodun Alao, University of Johannesburg, South Africa
    Roelien Brink, University of Johannesburg, South Africa

The implementation of information technology into the healthcare sector is inevitable to prevent future pandemics, as COVID-19 had a huge impact on healthcare services and humanity. Therefore, universal access to technologies in managing unforeseen pandemics is necessary. The objective of this study is to examine how healthcare institutions use innovative technologies to address future pandemics. The study reflects on one of the targets of Sustainable Development Goal (SDG) 9, which is to significantly increase access to IT and strive to provide universal and affordable technology access to global citizens by 2030. This is to obtain the vision to work towards building an open, inclusive, and digital network for a secure future. This study used discourse analysis to critically analyze the use of innovative technologies like AI systems, machine learning, the internet, mobile phones, mobile computing, and other technologies adopted to manage the global pandemic. This study recommends to policymakers the importance of universal access to innovative technology to address pandemic issues.

Chapter 4
The Role of Information Technologies to Adapt to a Global Pandemic:
Digitalization Disruption in the New Renaissance 66
    Julia Puaschunder, Columbia University, USA

The outbreak of the COVID-19 pandemic has exacerbated the rise of AI, robots, and algorithms in the economy, which is expected to completely disrupt employment patterns. With the advancement of technologies, employment patterns will shift to a polarization between AI's rationality and humanness. Robots and social machines have already replaced people in a variety of jobs. Almost all traditional professions are prospected to be infused with or influenced by AI, algorithms, and robotics in the future. AI and robots offer the luxuries of affordability and democratization of access to services, as they will be—in the long run—commercially more affordable and readily available to serve all humanity. Also, the longevity potential of machines outperforms any human ever having lived. These new technologies also come with the price of overpopulation problems and the potential for misuse and violent action. Just like many other technologies, robots could be misused. This chapter discusses the current trend of digital disruption and its wider societal implications.

Chapter 5
How Can Advancement in Information Technology Help College Students During the COVID-19 Pandemic? Evidence From the Video Game Industry..114
    Reza Gharoie Ahangar, Lewis University, USA

A revolution in information technology advancements has been started in recent years. A part of these technology advancements is happening in the video gaming industry. This study investigates the effect of video games on college students' performance during the COVID-19 pandemic. The authors examined the impact of video games on students' academic performance from the lens of time spent on video games and their effects on students' well-being and personal life during the COVID-19 pandemic. This study proposed a conceptual framework that highlights the positive impact of video games on students' mental health and academic performance during the COVID-19 pandemic.

Chapter 6
Supply Chain and Warehouse Management Systems: A Case Study From an International Company..129
    J. Zambujal-Oliveira, University of Madeira, Portugal
    Carolina Rodrigues, University of Madeira, Portugal
    Maria Pereira, University of Madeira, Portugal
    Martinho Freitas, University of Madeira, Portugal
    Daniela Freitas, University of Madeira, Portugal

The underperformance of an international company was based on the following major problems: the information technology and the inventory management system used in the group (several distinct channels that did not interact with each other) and the company's external environment (devaluation of the Russian ruble and decrease in purchasing power). To approach these issues, the chapter presents solutions to implement a new retail system, a redesign of the technology system used by the company, and some recommendations on external factors. Recently, the company has focused on a closer relationship with consumers, making available several services that simplifies the whole process of buying a product.

Chapter 7
Technological Growth in Religious Organisations: Exploring Social Media
Through System Dynamics 148
 Courage Matobobo, University of South Africa, South Africa
 Felix Bankole, University of South Africa, South Africa

Membership growth is an important aspect in religious organisations. Yet, the manner in which several religious organisations attract their membership has changed due to the adoption and use of social media. This study explores how technological factors influence the growth of religious organisations during and in the aftermath of the pandemic. Using the Seventh-Day Adventist Church (SDA) membership data, the research employed system dynamics. The findings from the quantitative data showed that the commitment of church members, good computer skills, age, and availability of resources contributed to the successful use of social media towards church membership growth. In addition, the qualitative data reveals that online evangelism is key to the growth of religious organisations. The results of the findings conclude that the growth of religious organisations can be improved by intensifying the level of online evangelism, improving commitment from members and utilisation of multichannel social media.

Chapter 8
Sustainable Quality Education During the Pandemic and Beyond: Challenges
and Solutions for Higher Education Institutions 177
 Hakan Islamoglu, Recep Tayyip Erdogan University, Turkey

Information technologies are an indispensable part of modern business, education, and personal lives. However, the COVID-19 pandemic has shown everybody around the world the insufficiency of available information technology infrastructures and the importance of establishing strong infrastructures for citizens from all backgrounds and geographic locations. The challenge has been especially hard for educational institutions because very few were truly prepared for an emergency transition to distance education. This chapter aims to explain the main components of a modern university information technology infrastructure and offer guidance in establishing a strong infrastructure for sustainable quality education.

Chapter 9
Teleworking: The "New Normal" in Response to a Pandemic 199
 Leigh Nathan Breda, University of Cape Town, South Africa
 Michael Kyobe, University of Cape Town, South Africa

This chapter intends to understand how telework pre-adoption perceptions differ from post-adoption realized benefits during the COVID-19 pandemic, and whether an organization will continue the use of telework once the pandemic subsides.

Literature was examined and a hybrid framework incorporating components of the perceived value theory and expectation confirmation model (ECM) was used. The perceived value theory focuses on the perceived business value of Telework pre-adoption and ECM focuses on continued use post-adoption. Resistance by managers to allow employees to telework is evident in surveys conducted as recent as 2019. While surveys conducted initially in 2020 during the pandemic indicated that at least 74% of CFOs intend to implement more telework in their organization and 60% of employees would opt to remain teleworking after the pandemic despite possible health implications, later surveys suggest that after continued use of telework, 59% of the employees now no longer prefer to telework into the future due to constraining factors such as isolation and blurred work lines.

Chapter 10
The Online Education and Virtual Collaboration Model....................................226
    Efosa Carroll Idemudia, Arkansas Tech University, USA

Worldwide, tech spending was approximately $4 trillion in 2019. In 2020, all successful global universities are using a wide variety of information systems platforms to adapt to the global COVID-19 pandemic. Universities are using the rapid constant changes in information technology to alleviate the COVID-19 crisis. During the COVID-19 pandemic, almost all universities in North America, Europe, Australia, and New Zealand conducted classes through online and virtual instruction. Unfortunately, most universities in Nigeria/Africa are not able to adapt to the global COVID-19 pandemic, and universities in Nigeria in 2020 were completely closed for classes. To help address this issue, the authors conducted their research. In addition, using the stakeholder theory, they developed the online education and virtual collaboration model. The model provides insights and understanding on how to develop online courses and classes effectively and efficiently in Nigeria/Africa. The study has significant research and practical implications.

Compilation of References 238

About the Contributors 269

Index 273

Preface

THE IMPORTANCE OF THIS TEXTBOOK TO ACADEMICIANS, PRACTITIONERS, RESEARCHERS, GOVERNMENT OFFICIALS, AND STUDENTS

The current global pandemic (COVID-19) has prompted many organisations to resort to technologies to adapt to the pandemic. For the past two years, global companies, organizations, and universities are using a wide varieties of information technology platforms to adapt to the global COVID-19 pandemic (Idemudia, 2020a, 2020b). Worldwide these companies, firms, organizations, and universities are using information technology advancements to adapt to the global pandemic. For example, stakeholders in the healthcare industry are using a wide range of information technology platforms to test, track, monitor, keep records, and treat patients with COVID-19. Data scientists/analytics are using information technology to create and develop a comprehensive database to alleviate the COVID-19 crisis. In addition, data scientists are developing mathematical models to gain insights and knowledge from COVID-19 database for better decision makings relating to pharmaceuticals, vaccines, drugs, and to predict the spread of the virus. Thus, there is a need to understand how various technologies have been used in the context of adapting to COVID-19 and the lessons that could be learnt that could inform future implementations of technologies in the advent of future pandemics.

Gartner, Inc states that "Worldwide IT spending is projected to total $4.4 trillion in 2022, an increase of 4% from 2021"[1]. The rapid constant advancements in a wide variety of information technology platforms are positively influencing global companies, universities, and organizations' operations. To date, and during COVID-19, global firms, companies, and universities are using advance information technology platforms to improve profits, sales, market shares, exceed customers' expectations, and improve strategic competitive advantages. Technology sector dominates the top ten largest companies by market capitalization[2]. The 100 Fastest-Growing Companies are using a wide range of information technology to make better decisions and competitive advantages[3,4]. In 2020, 2021, and 2022 during the global COVID-19 pandemic, most universities globally were forced to conduct classes and lectures through online and virtual instructions. Indeed, the COVID-19 global pandemic has changed the paradigm on how companies, firms, organizations, and universities operate. This textbook helps to provide insights and understanding to academicians, practitioners, researchers, government officials, and students on how to use advanced information technology to make better decisions and achieve competitive advantages. Some of the important concepts in this textbook are: (1) technical background of IT interventions to adapt to the pandemic, (2) strategic IT decision making, (3) criteria and priorities for technological projects, (4) the use of IT to better understand customers and competitors, and (5) solving real-world problems. This textbook aims to strategically help students, managers, faculty, practitioners, and government officers to make better decisions and to successfully adapt to the global pandemic. This textbook also presents how a wide range of information technology platforms have positively and significantly affected all companies, firms, organizations, universities, and business, most especially during 2020, 2021, and 2022 (i.e. COVID-19 global pandemic). Information technology platforms can help to reshape products, services, and create competitive values that exceed customers' expectations. Some of the benefits of a wide variety of information technology platforms are: (1) improve value chain, (2) create new products, (3) create new services, (4) target global buyers and customers, (5) deliver products and services, (6) better understanding of customers and competitors, (7) provide infrastructures that exceed expectations, (8) support products, (9) support services, (10) support market shares, (11) reduce cost, (12) differentiate products, (13) understand stakeholders better, and (14) support sales and profits. To date, because of COVID-19, global companies, firms, organizations, and universities are implementing a wide range of information technology platforms to improve infrastructure, virtual classes, meetings, workshops, conferences, online classes, product design, customers' services, employees' loyalties, inventory management systems etc. In addition, Information technology has a positive influence on logistic functionalities relating to supply chain management, just-in-time deliveries, operations, and services activities.

In essence, this book provides insights on multiple facets of technology implementation in the context of dealing with challenges and opportunities brought about by the pandemic. Thus, this book is timely for many reasons. Firstly, as the pandemic was mostly anticipated, many organisations resorted to technology as a survival option. Thus, there are many technological solutions that were implemented in a rush, haphazardly without thorough planning. Hence, this book will provide a sense of what worked or did not work based on the various contexts in which the technology was implemented. This is particularly important as it will guide future technology implementation in the advent of future pandemics.

Secondly, it is equally important to understand how various users (people, entities, and processes) utilized various technologies to circumvent the challenges related to the pandemic. This book will therefore help technology designers to develop user-friendly interfaces. It will also help build technologies that can adapt to the changing nature of various ecosystems.

Moreover, it is of paramount importance to be cognizant of technology enablers to devise adequate strategies to implement successful technology-driven interventions. The insights provided through the various chapters in this book will help identify context-specific enablers that can inform future technology-driven interventions.

ORGANIZATION OF THE BOOK

The book is organized into 10 chapters. A brief description of each of the chapters follows:

Chapter 1 presents updated technique, approach, trends, challenges, and perspectives relating to smart technology for addressing pandemic disruption: impact of social media influencers on brand awareness during Pandemic. Also, the author presents the concepts of the conceptual framework as a long term SMM strategy to create brand equity, and the effect of covid-19 on consumer behavior/business.

Chapter 2 discusses impact of how I can help you today? the rise of virtual assistants in human resources management. The analysis in Chapter 2 are virtual assistant and HR processes, self-service, onboarding, training, managing knowledge, and modern digital innovation management theories. In addition, the authors provide insights and knowledge on the difficulty in understanding the challenges, vital aspects, and opportunity of virtual assistants in human resources management.

Chapter 3 presents opportunities and challenges for adaptation to pandemic through universal access to innovative technologies: ICT access for future pandemic. The chapter provides insights and understanding to appraisal of technologies for pandemics, computer games, mobile phone messaging, telecommunication information dissemination, use of mobile computing, effective technology connectivity, satellite technology, and mobile internet capabilities. Also, the chapter present the advantages and disadvantages of advanced technologies in the healthcare institution.

Chapter 4 discusses and identify the role of information technologies to adapt to a global pandemic: digitalization disruption in the new Renaissance. The chapter provides insights and understanding relating to challenges of digitalization and economic growth, digitalization measured in interconnectivity and Artificial Intelligence, Artificial Intelligence in the age of COVID-19, Artificial Intelligence and contemporary growth, inclusive growth in the digital century, and big data ethics.

Chapter 5 provides an overview, challenges and opportunities relating to how can advancement in information technology help college students during the COVID-19 pandemic?: evidence from the video games industry. The author discusses proposed framework of IT-Pandemic and hypotheses development. In addition, the author discusses the relationships among covid-19 pandemic, sleep aid, video games, academic performance, remote learning due to covid-19, and time spent on school works.

Chapter 6 reviews supply chain and warehouse management systems - a case study from an International Company. The authors present a case evolution and state of the art, and the influence of the macro environment. In addition, the authors present a theoretical framework for supply chain and warehouse management systems.

Chapter 7 discusses the technological growth in religious organizations: exploring social media through system dynamics. The authors present the growth of religious organizations, and system dynamics. In addition, the authors present updated model and algorithm relating to the development of the church growth causal loop diagram.

Chapter 8 presents sustainable quality education during the pandemic and beyond: challenges and solutions for higher education institutions. The author presents updated techniques and methodology for hardware infrastructure, network and Internet infrastructure, software and service infrastructure, online meeting and web conferencing, online examination and proctoring, licensed software and auxiliary services, and technical and instructional support.

Chapter 9 discusses the Teleworking - The "new normal" in response to a pandemic. The authors present pre- versus post-adoption in a pandemic, telework literature review, perceived usefulness and trust of technology, telework in a pandemic.

Chapter 10 addresses the online education and virtual collaboration model. The author presents updated theories and techniques relating to university information technology applications model, university IT competitive advantages model, and online course contents/components model. The chapter explores the online education and virtual collaboration model.

Efosa C. Idemuda
Arkansas Tech University, USA

Tiko Iyamu
Cape Peninsula University of Technology, South Africa

Patrick Ndayizigamiye
University of Johannesburg, South Africa

Irja Naambo Shaanika
Namibia University of Science and Technology, Namibia

REFERENCES

Idemudia, E. C. (Ed.). (2020a). *Handbook of Research on IT Applications for Strategic Competitive Advantage and Decision Making*. IGI Global. doi:10.4018/978-1-7998-3351-2

Idemudia, E. C. (Ed.). (2020b). *Handbook of Research on Social and Organizational Dynamics in the Digital Era*. IGI Global. doi:10.4018/978-1-5225-8933-4

ENDNOTES

[1] https://www.gartner.com/en/newsroom/press-releases/2022-04-06-gartner-forecasts-worldwide-it-spending-to-reach-4-point-four-trillion-in-2022

[2] https://www.gfmag.com/global-data/economic-data/largest-companies

[3] https://fortune.com/100-fastest-growing-companies/

[4] https://innovativezoneindia.com/top-10-company-in-the-world/

Chapter 1
Smart Technology For Addressing Pandemic Disruption:
Impact of Social Media Influencers on Brand Awareness During the Pandemic

Kaneez Masoom
Babu Banarasi Das University, India

ABSTRACT

Social media's emergence as a communication platform for consumers to interact with or about brands has significantly altered brand-consumer relationships. Companies are increasingly investing in influencer marketing, or hiring digital influencers to endorse their brands, as social media marketing becomes more advantageous. Influencers are changing the way brands create content, as well as how users consume and share it. The role of social media influencers in raising brand awareness, particularly during extraordinary times such as pandemics, is still in its early stages. Despite technological advancements and an increase in the number of online influencers, many challenges remain for businesses to connect with consumers during pandemics. The impact of social media influencers on brand awareness during a global pandemic is discussed in this chapter.

DOI: 10.4018/978-1-7998-9418-6.ch001

INTRODUCTION

As a growing number of consumers shop online, the COVID-19 pandemic has resulted in significant growth for internet-based businesses (Abidin, C. 2015). The global e-commerce market is expected to grow by 27.6 percent to $4.28 trillion USD by 2020 (Al-Debei 2013). In recent years, organisations have been subjected to the introduction of digital technologies, which have transformed organisations, interactions with consumers, and value creation (Aral S et al., 2014). Online shopping has made it easier for consumers to compare products, and they can easily select the products that best meet their needs (Awad et al.,). Young consumers have largely shifted to online shopping, influencing how businesses must operate because young consumers are more likely to shop through social media (Bailey et al.,). At the same time, the global pandemic has shed light on the power of so-called social media influencers (SMIs), also known as "micro-celebrities." Influencers have been identified as an effective and strategic marketing channel for products and ideas (Klassen et al., 2018). In 2019, it was predicted that by 2022, brands would spend $15 billion on influencer engagement globally. (Schomer, 2019)

As countries around the world went into lockdown, businesses cut back on operations, and marketing budgets were drastically cut, some observers predicted that the social media influencer industry would be 'killed off' (see e.g. Hamdan, 2020; Tsapovsky, 2020). COVID-19 appeared to have signalled the end of influencer marketing as we know it, as the emphasis shifted from economic prosperity and personal gratification to public health and, to a lesser extent, environmental protection. However, as the world adjusted to life in the midst of a pandemic, it became clear that many commercially driven influencers would thrive, implying that because people are hungry for online content, influencers have become even more important as a channel for the marketing of ideas and products (Stephens, 2020). According to statistics, social media use has skyrocketed during the lockdown, with engagement increasing by 61 percent over normal usage rates in a survey of 30 markets (Holmes, 2020). While some influencers have clearly struggled to adapt to changing market conditions and rapidly shrinking commercial opportunities (Elliott, 2020), others have capitalised on public confusion and disorientation to increase their power, reach, and, ultimately, post-COVID marketability and market share (Ewens, 2020).

With the vast majority of the world's people staying at home, social media platforms have evolved into a communication channel to remain in touch with friends and family, as well as for interaction with brands (Dias et al., 2020). Brands have chosen social media to remain relevant during this time. Social media was also used to raise brand awareness and to assist the consumers in coping by providing positive messaging in order to overcome the current difficulties (Dias et al., 2020). In order to adapt, many brands have had to change their marketing and communication strategies. (Enberg, 2020). Social media platforms such as Instagram have been used by brands to communicate with followers, disseminate information, make donations, and create content masks and sanitization products (Dias et al., 2020).

Influencers, according to Argyris et al. (2020), are ordinary people, not celebrities, who have amassed a large number of followers on social media sites by posting engaging and appealing content presenting their habits, lifestyle and preferences. Influencers are known to post self-centred selfies, appealing group photos, and glamorous outfits. They also post Portraits taken at various events, product/brand promotion, views about fashion, beauty, travel, interior design, and food, and photos wearing the brands to persuade the general public (Jin et al., 2020). This marketing strategy is based on followers' positive perceptions of influencers, which makes their messaging highly effective, resulting in the desired brand impact (Tafesse & Wood, 2021). According to Tafesse and Wood (2021) research, 42 percent of marketers use influencer marketing as a long-term strategy rather than a one-time tactical campaign.

BACKGROUND

Social media has evolved into a user-centred realm where customers obtain knowledge, engage with other consumers, and share their opinions. Generally businesses attempting to sell their products are perceived as unwelcome (Berger, J. 2013). As a result, firms must work hard to build favourable brand equity in order to survive in the competitive internet market [1,12]. However, it is unclear how the COVID-19 outbreak has influenced how businesses must build long-term brand equity through social media marketing while also adapting to rapid changes and rising competition in digital platforms. Furthermore, many businesses still struggle to explain the benefits of a brand and accurately assess brand equity (Bhattacherjee, A. 2001). "Understanding Information Systems Continuance: An Expectation-confirmation Model." MIS Quarterly 25 (3): 351–370.

Uses and Gratifications theory investigates why people use certain media, as well as the pleasure they derive from its use and availability (Luo, Chea, and Chen 2011). This theory is based on the idea that media selection and usage is a deliberate and motivated action (Katz and Blumler 1974); users actively strive to meet their needs through a variety of means, and their individual needs and desires make use of a variety of media (Rubin 1994, 2002). U&G is frequently used in research. queries about a user's 'how and why' media usage Ku, Chen, and Lee 2013; Zhang). Ku, Chen, and Lee (2013); Zhang). Chua, Goh, and Lee (2012); Ku, Chen, and Lee (2013); Zhang). The level of enjoyment experienced by users in relation to active media use (Stafford, Stafford, and Schkade) 2004.

According to U&G, users' media consumption is primarily motivated by the fulfilment of personal needs. The components that shape their individual requirements, on the other hand, were not well understood. Katz et al. (Katz and Blumler 1974) established a U&G agenda: the social and psychological foundations of needs that generate expectations of the mass media or other sources, resulting in unequal patterns of media behaviour, need gratifications and other outcomes. As a result, conceptually extending U&G to explain users' CCCB makes an important contribution to the field. Existing research on the COVID-19's business implications has discovered some factors that may influence how firms and consumers build brand equity online. COVID-19.

MAIN FOCUS

In today's competitive economy, branding is a critical aspect of competitiveness because it distinguishes comparable goods and services provided by different enterprises in the minds of consumers. Brand awareness is important for businesses to differentiate themselves from competitors. International corporate decision-makers should design and adjust communication activities to increase favourable attitudes toward the organisation (Dacin and Brown, 2002). The introduction of social media as a communication platform for consumers to interact with or about brands has significantly altered brand-consumer relationships. In a social media environment designed to accommodate consumers rather than businesses (Berger, J. 2013). the consumer is now more powerful, creating barriers for businesses to intervene in this environment where they are considered uninvited to the conversation (Berger, J. 2013).

The uses and gratifications theory (U&G) and the social influence theory (SIT) are used to investigate CCCB in this paper (SIT). The following are the justifications: (1) U&G is a traditional theory of user mass media use that explains why users choose one media outlet over another. According to this theory, media consumption is a deliberate and motivated action (Katz and Blumler 1974). U&G provides theoretical power in explaining why users choose specific social media platforms and frequently create content in order to understand users' CCCB.

According to Hwang et al. (2021), three dimensions of gratification influence how consumers gather information and make purchasing decisions on social media: process, content, and social gratification.

The term "progress gratification" refers to the satisfaction gained from the use of social media and the information provided on social media platforms. The content gratification study specifically looks at the gratification that people feel when they view content on social media. Finally, social gratification refers to the ability to interact with other users via social media platforms, as well as the extent to which it satisfies the need for social interactions. These forms of gratification have a positive impact on the adoption of social media as a source of information to make purchasing decisions; social media reduces risks by providing more information than other platforms and the presence of social feedback, such as reviews and descriptions provided by others, which assist users in finding the information needed to make a decision (Hui et al 2017).

In this chapter, we present an integrative framework that draws on previous research, classifies and synthesises the role of social media information systems with reference to the impact of online influencers in creating and raising brand awareness.

PROBLEM

New marketing communication reality presents new challenges and opportunities for companies as purchase decisions are increasingly influenced by social media interactions. People rely more than ever on their social networks when making those decisions. Nevertheless, outcomes of social media activities are still disputed in practice. The effects of social media campaigns on consumers' perception of products and brands as well as the effects on purchase decisions have yet to be better understood. This study therefore investigates how social media influencers' activities, affect the awareness of brands, and ultimately influence the purchase decision process of consumers, especially during extraordinary times like pandemic. From a theoretical standpoint the results of this study contribute to understanding of the value-enhancing potential of social media campaigns and demonstrate how the awareness and perception of brands is influenced through this new communication channel of social media influencers. For brand managers this study is of value, as it shows that social media activities do have a positive influence on brands as they support their management of the purchase process.

The rapid growth of social media development results in a plethora of brands promoting their products or services. One of the many methods is to use social media influencers to promote your business. Recently, it has been discovered that companies that use Influencer marketing continue to grow because this method is considered to be quite effective in increasing brand awareness.

The effectiveness of an influencer on the social media depends upon the reach, the degree of the person's sposition in the social network and persuasiveness. These factors are linked to the relevance of the content the person creates online (Labrecque et al. 2013).

The impact of social influence on the adoption and use of information systems (IS) has been extensively researched. However, the majority of existing research on social influence takes the perspective of social normative compliance into account, such as the substituted measurement of subjective norms (Venkatesh et al. 2013; Ku, Chen, and Zhang 2013), thus ignoring the processes of social identification and internalisation influence. Interactions between content creators and readers have a significant impact on their contribution behaviours. Individuals' content contributions, in particular, are influenced by the number of followers they have. Followers are no longer simply a total number of users who receive information from the influencers other users, but they also have the ability to influence the behaviour of contributors. As participation in social media can take place anywhere and is not limited to a physical meeting, users have more opportunities for online participation (Hester, A. J. 2011). Furthermore, new digital technologies provide benefits to consumers such as convenience, enjoyment, information richness, and time and money savings (Hossain et al).

Numerous studies have been conducted to investigate users' content contribution intentions in online communities (Bo and Li 2015; Jin et al. 2013; Li, Yang, and Huang 2014; Furthermore, users' behavioural intentions do not significantly influence real-world continuation decisions (Hossain and Quaddus 2012).

According to U&G, users' media use is primarily motivated by the fulfilment of personal needs. However, the factors that shape their personal needs were not well understood. Katz et al. (Katz and Blumler 1974) established a framework for U&G: the social and psychological origins of needs, which generate expectations of the mass media or other sources, which result in differential patterns of media behaviour, resulting in need gratifications and other consequences. Most existing U&G studies on social media began with observed gratifications and attempted to reconstruct the needs that are satisfied. These studies focused on individuals and thus ignored the interrelationships between individuals and the media.

COVID-19 is a recent phenomenon, therefore, little has been published of its impact on social media marketing behaviour. While influencer marketing was already a hot topic in academic research, the COVID-19 pandemic, combined with trends in youth media consumption habits, has given it even more clout. Prior to the COVID-19 pandemic, there was much debate about the effectiveness of influencers in an advertising/promotion context. A major study conducted in 2018 by the Association of National Advertisers (ANA) for example stated that while 75 percent of consumers engaged in influencer marketing, only 25 percent believed It to be effective, according to 36% of those polled.

However the world went for a transformation with a global pandemic in 2019. Indeed, COVID-19 has resulted in people spending more time at home, which has resulted in more internet time and less social interaction for many. A survey of 1000 influencers conducted by A E (not to be confused with the television network) influencer marketing experts Amra and Elma Beganovich discovered three trends favourable to the growth of influencer marketing during COVID-19. The first of these trends is increased participation during the COVID-19 with only a minor price increase. One of the main reasons for this trend is that many influencers' lives were not disrupted by COVID19 because they typically prepare and record their online content at home.

Abidin (2015) defines social media influencers as "everyday, ordinary internet users who accumulate a relatively large following on blogs and social media through the textual and visual narration of their personal lives and lifestyles, engage with their following in digital and physical spaces, and [who] monetise their following by integrating "advertorials" into their blog or social media posts." SMIs gained followers' trust because they were perceived to be genuine and 'people like us' (Abidin and Ots, 2016). SMIs have strategically positioned themselves as reliable sources of information (and entertainment). This work offers potential explanations to generate new knowledge, resolve any inconsistencies, or develop a conceptual framework by synthesising existing knowledge. Furthermore, a literature review allows for the formulation of future research paths, which is especially valuable in this context, where knowledge about a specific topic is insufficient but literature on the topic is available. A literature review has many advantages over a narrative review, including being unbiased, objective, efficient, transparent, reproducible, and rigorous. In this chapter the approach aims to develop theory, i.e. the conceptual framework. Existing literature is analysed, through the theoretical lens of the uses and gratifications theory (U&G) to discover key constructs and develop a conceptual framework based on prevalent themes and new developments (Shao, G. 2009). We outline a brief strategy and relevant stakeholders that can assist businesses in building a foundation for their SMM strategy that is adapted to changing technologies, consumer behavior, and markets as a result of the pandemic. These results also function as a building block for future research regarding the creation of brand equity in the digital marketing sphere.

SOLUTION

Companies focus on raising consumer awareness in the context of marketing in order to elicit the desired responses from the audience. Keller (2003) defines brand awareness as a "personal meaning about a brand stored in consumer memory, that is, all descriptive and evaluative brand-related information", which relates to a brand's cognitive illustration. It is concerned with the likelihood and ease with which a brand will come to mind.

BRAND AWARENESS

Brand awareness is made up of two components: brand familiarity and brand recognizability (Keller, 1993). Consumer awareness of the company or brand can be identified as a stepping stone in the customer purchasing process. A higher level of awareness can increase the likelihood of a consumer purchasing a product or service. A higher level of awareness can increase the likelihood of a consumer purchasing a product or service. It has the potential to provide the company with a long-term, sustainable competitive advantage. Social marketers focus on raising public awareness in order to influence attitudes, associations, and beliefs about a specific organisation or brand (Foroudi et al., 2014). In general, brand awareness is a broad and nebulous concept that is intuitively recognised by individuals in most businesses. It can be defined as a tool that focuses on defining and increasing the familiarity and recognizability of a target audience with a specific brand (Foroudi et al., 2014, 2016). Consumer awareness is a tool used by businesses to influence consumer attitudes toward a brand or company by creating associations and beliefs among a target audience.

To determine the success of a consumer's attitude toward a brand or company, it is necessary to create favourable brand association and brand belief. Brand awareness can be defined as a customer's ability to distinguish and recognise a brand in a variety of contexts. Perceptions and attitudes can be influenced by awareness. Brand awareness reflects the brand's salience in the minds of customers. According to Aaker (1996), brand knowledge is important because it not only strengthens and makes the brand effective, but it is also an important factor that influences consumer attitudes toward the brand by creating a source of belief and association.

They came to the conclusion that raising awareness is critical for influencing behaviour in purchase situations. Higher levels of consumer brand awareness elevate the brand, increasing the likelihood that the brand will be remembered in purchase situations (Yasin et al., 2007). Given the widely accepted relationship between brand awareness and brand attitude (Macdonald and Sharp, 2000), it can be suggested that raising awareness can have significant behavioural consequences. Raising awareness about a cause or initiative may eventually result in positive and desirable changes in brand attitude. The attribute that is typically perceived as satisfying, which can result in a more favourable attitude toward the brand. According to Macdonald and Sharp (2000), customers prefer to buy products they recognise because products that are familiar are frequently preferred.

USES AND GRATIFICATION THEORY

The theory of Uses and Gratification investigates why people use specific media and the gratification derived from usage and access (Luo, Chea, and Chen 2011). This theory assumes that media selection and use is a deliberate and motivated action (Katz and Blumler 1974); users actively seek to meet their individual needs and desires through a variety of uses (Rubin 1994, 2002). U&G is frequently used to investigate the 'how and why' of media usage from the perspective of the user (Chua, Goh, and Lee 2012; Ku, Chen, and Zhang 2013). Gratification is commonly defined as a type of satisfaction felt by users as a result of their active use of media (Stafford, Stafford, and Schkade 2004).

U&G is a time-honored media use theory that has been used to investigate the use of mass media (Kang and Atkin 1999; Towers 1987), the Internet (Ruggiero 2000; Stafford, Stafford, and Schkade 2004), and now social media (Chen and Chan 2017; Ku, Chen, and Zhang 2013; Li, Guo, and Bai 2016; Luo, Chea, and Chen 2011). In particular, Luo et al. (Luo, Chea, and Chen 2011) discovered that U&G provides a better explanation of usage by explaining the direct effects of intrinsic and extrinsic needs on both content and the process of web-based information service usage when compared to the motivational model. U&G is also appropriate for explaining the continuous adoption of media services; according to Ku et al. (Ku, Chen, and Zhang 2013), individual users will continue to engage with SNSs if such tools meet their gratifications and needs. As a result, U&G has important implications for the current study, in which we define gratification as the personal needs that social media influencers meet (Ku, Chen, and Zhang 2013).

Users on social media primarily follow others because they are interested in other people's lives and have a desire to learn about them. Their attitude toward a specific subject is established by their knowledge of that subject and the professionally generated content. (K. Masoom,2022). Marketing through the social media influencers is not a new form of marketing, yet it has emerged as the most strategic option and grown in popularity in the aftermath of the global pandemic (Dias et al. 2020). This type of advertising has become a way for brands to increase brand awareness while actively promoting their products and services with influencers who are aligned with their target audience and value (Casaló et al., 2020).

Influencers are critical to increasing brand awareness and remaining relevant to millions of users worldwide (Casaló et al., 2020). Influencers cultivate a personal relationship and bond with their followers by cultivating a genuine online persona and sharing personal content (Tafesse & Wood, 2020). Users who have a positive perception of the influencers they follow can benefit greatly from social media marketing (Tafesse & Wood, 2020). Because the brand is leveraging the trust and connection between the influencer and follower, this would result in the desired impact (Tafesse & Wood, 2020).

Prior to the pandemic, brands used social media influencers to raise brand awareness (Campbell & Farrell, 2020). Influencers are important players in the social media landscape and influence marketing (Dias et al., 2020).

Influencer marketing entails extending brands' reach and impact on social media by leveraging the trust and connection that influencers have built with their followers. Influencer marketing, like native advertising, is a type of hidden advertising in which paid content is disguised as organic. While this has significant benefits for sponsoring brands, it is a double-edged sword because of the risk of misleading followers, who may mistake paid content for genuine, unpaid posts (Dhanesh & Duthler, 2019). While consumers generally appreciate the less intrusive nature of this type of advertising, negative reactions are possible if followers become aware of its covert intent (Dhanesh & Duthler, 2019). According to Argyris et al. (2020), influencers are ordinary people, not celebrities, who have amassed a large number of followers on social media sites by posting visually appealing content that highlights their lifestyle and merchandise preferences. Influencers typically post selfies, appealing group photos, glamorous portraits taken by others, product/ brand photos (style, beauty, travel, interior, and food), and frequently post photos wearing the products, which persuades viewers at large (Jin et al., 2020). This type of marketing is based on followers' positive perceptions of influencers, which makes their messaging highly effective in creating the desired brand impact ((Tafesse & Wood, 2021).

According to Tafesse and Wood (2021), 42 percent of marketers use influencer marketing as an on going strategy rather than a one-time tactical campaign. The global market for influencer marketing reached 148 million in 2019, an increase of 8% from 2018, and this figure is expected to exceed $373 million by 2027. (Tafesse & Wood, 2021). Brands that want to maximise the significant benefits that influencer marketing can provide should seek out suitable partners who have a large number of followers and the ability to influence them (Campbell & Farrell, 2020).

Social media reduces risks by providing more information than other platforms and by allowing users to find the information they need to make a decision using social feedback, such as reviews and descriptions provided by others (Wang C et al.). This has empowered consumers because social media allows them to educate themselves and each other, increases their ability to choose what they prefer from available options, and organise themselves as consumers in support or opposition to a specific brand or event. Kietzmann et al. (2011) identified seven functionalities to make sense of how functionalities shape the social media environment. Each functionality examines an aspect of the social media user experience and its implications for businesses aiming to build a community on social media plate forms.

The first social media functionality is the identity displayed by users, which refers to the extent to which they expose their identities within social media settings. This refers to objective identity information, such as name and gender, but it also aims to represent a broader spectrum of subjective identities rooted in various forms of self-expression, such as thoughts, feelings, and likes. Online self-disclosure increases user satisfaction but can be problematic if the user spends a significant amount of time online to keep up with the engagement they receive from their social circle. Regardless, even though consumers willingly share their identities online, they are still cautious about their personal information. As a result, when attempting to communicate with customers, businesses must pay close attention to their privacy.

, As consumers communicate their identities, they also engage in conversations with other users and groups, forming social media's second functionality. Within the conversational use of social media, users have different goals; they either have a specific goal, such as meeting like-minded people, or a broader goal, such as making an impact in debates on current issues. When people can share overlaps in their identities with others through conversation, they have more opportunities for self-expression and are more motivated to participate in discussions and movements that are important to them. To take part in these conversations the brands must understand the "conversation velocity, the rate and direction at which the conversation changes. Then they must understand when to manipulate consumer conversations; brands that understand when to participate or not participate in the conversation will give consumers the impression of a caring brand that is a positive addition to the existing conversation.

Sharing, the third functionality of social media, refers to the extent to which individuals exchange, distribute, and receive content; social media connects people over a shared object and functions as a form of interaction that can result in conversing or building relationships." businesses must first consider the content and frequency of content publication among users when attempting to intervene in conversations.

The fourth functionality, presence, describes the degree to which users are aware of the presence of other users. The factor of presence is inherently linked to other functionalities such as conversations and relationships; businesses must consider the importance of user presence and location and adapt their communication style to the manner in which consumers engage with one another. Peer reviews, which represent the presence and experiences of other consumers in the context of e-commerce, have a significant, positive effect on the evaluation and purchase intention of products or services; this effect is amplified when reviews provided by those in close proximity to the consumer are also present.

The fifth social media functionality, forming relationships, is defined by the association between users, which leads to them conversing, sharing content, meeting each other, or listing them as a friend; how these users define their connection also defines the content exchange with one another. Users can form groups either within their social network or through groups that connect based on their experiences or interests in a specific topic. Users can use virtual connections to find niche groups to which they can belong within a larger online community. As a result, when attempting to engage with customers, businesses must understand how to build or maintain relationships with them.

Reputation is classified as the sixth functionality and a determining factor in determining the standing of oneself and others within the realm of social media; trust in others, their expertise, and their content are frequently leading in social media environments, though technologies are not yet adequate at assessing the trustworthiness of content. Within the realm of Web 2.0, reputation is viewed as the currency with which businesses deal in order to position themselves, and the role of public relations is becoming increasingly important in reputation management. As a result, in order to determine the exact reputation, brand reputation among users must be measured using a preferred metric that fits these factors and is identified by the business, as well as a corresponding evaluation tool.

The seventh and final functionality is group formation. When users form groups, it is advantageous to allow these communities to label users as members or non-member relations without the members' knowledge in order to further their agenda, grow the membership, and so on. Aside from the primary goal established by the group, groups can provide individuals with secondary benefits that improve their well-being, such as recognition, valuable social contacts, and a sense of belonging to something larger than the group in question. Businesses must be aware that groups are more than just a certain number of users; they also function as independent segments within the realm of social media, with their own set of rules and structures.

INFLUENCER MARKETING DURING PANDEMIC

As consumers were confined to their homes, marketers have been forced to adapt and expand their online marketing strategies (Enberg, 2020). Dias et al. (2020) discovered that most brands were confronted with challenges to market and rethink strategies to remain relevant for their consumers while contributing to pandemic preparedness. The pandemic has also had an impact on the influencer marketing industry, with most influencers facing the challenge of creating organic and authentic content while still promoting brands (Enberg, 2020). Budgets have been significantly reduced, as noted by Enberg (2020), leaving brands with less money to spend on digital marketing. The scarcity of funds has also influenced influencers' willingness to work for free with brands (Enberg, 2020). As the pandemic worsens, influencers and brands have begun to shift their messaging away from products and services and toward values (Enberg, 2020). The brand enlisted the help of trusted advocates, giving them creative licence to add value to people's new realities (Enberg, 2020). These trends are not new; they have simply accelerated pre-pandemic changes such as the rise of "everyday influencers" (Enberg, 2020).

The most recent research on this topic focuses on the use and effectiveness of influencers, as well as influencer marketing for brands. Brands have had to broaden their methods of connecting with current and potential customers (Dhanesh & Duthler, 2019). They have begun to place a greater emphasis on communication and demonstrating their values (Dhanesh & Duthler, 2019). This type of marketing assists the brand and influencer in remaining relevant and popular among their customers and followers (Ha et al., 2019). Influencers serve as opinion leaders because their followers trust them more than brands (Ki et al., 2020). Influencers are thought to share more intimacy with their followers, making them feel more valued (Casaló et al., 2020).

This marketing creates brand awareness, which in turn creates a differential image in the minds of the consumers. Thus it can be stated that by raising brand awareness through social media influencers brand equity can be created. Keller defined brand equity as, "the differential effect of brand knowledge on consumer response to brand marketing," where brand knowledge is divided into two dimensions: brand awareness and brand image. These elements aid in attracting new customers, reminding them of products or services, and establishing an emotional brand connection (Chen, Y et al 2016). The overall quality of the brand relationship influences the likelihood of brand engagement in terms of willingness to purchase, intent to remain a member of a specific group, and intent to create electronic word of mouth.

According to Keller (1993), managing brand equity is a six-step process. To effectively improve consumers' brand knowledge, marketers must first determine the directions and goals for all marketing activities. Second, marketers must decide what image they want to project in the minds of their customers. Bruhn et al. (2012) distinguish two kinds of brand image: functional brand image (based on specific attributes of a product or service) and hedonic brand image (unrelated to product or service attributes). Business-created social media content has been shown to positively influence brand awareness and functional brand image, whereas user-generated content has been shown to positively influence hedonic brand image (Hajli et al.). Third, marketers should think about potential strategic options for creating value in the minds of consumers. The creation and integration of value in all business activities is a critical foundation for the further development of an SMM strategy. Increased time spent on social media and interactions with the brand boost brand awareness, which in turn boosts customer value (Islam et al.). SMM has been shown to positively influence brand equity and its two dimensions: brand awareness and brand image when executed correctly. Brand equity has a positive impact on customer responses, and investing in brand equity has a positive impact on the outcomes of SMM activities. Fourth, marketers must develop long-term strategies, particularly in the context of brand equity, where brand awareness and brand image change as a result of previous marketing activities. Fifth, it is critical to continuously measure consumer knowledge in order to detect changes and determine whether these are related to the effectiveness of current marketing activities. Because users are already spending time on social media, businesses must incorporate the information they learn about their customers through social media into their SMM strategy in order to build positive brand equity among a desired target group. Finally, marketers should evaluate viable extension prospects for profitability as well as potential brand image feedback.

THE EFFECT OF COVID-19 ON CONSUMER BEHAVIOR AND BUSINESSES

The COVID-19 pandemic has resulted in a significant increase in e-commerce, as many consumers continue to shop online (Carter, D. 2016). Since the start of the pandemic, businesses have seen significant growth in their online customer base, with the markets with existing high conversion rates continuing to grow (Arora et al.2019). This sudden aversion to shopping in physical stores could be attributed to cognitive responses to the COVID-19 pandemic, specifically fear and hope. These factors have been found to mediate the relationship between a consumer's ability to cognitively assess the threat and their behaviour, so those who are fearful and perceive the situation to be very threatening will stay at home and shop online. Although many consumers indicate that they will continue to shop online even after stores reopen (Shao, G. 2009), consumers who prefer to shop in physical stores are also being forced to adapt to online shopping. This shift in consumer behaviour is challenging for businesses, as they must find new ways to reach and engage with all online shoppers. When examining consumer adaptability to new purchasing methods during a pandemic, research shows that increased consumer adaptability weakens consumer resilience while increasing purchase satisfaction (Wang et al.2020) emphasise that a company's marketing decisions should be based on the company's characteristics in order to determine which strategy is most appropriate and beneficial.

THE CONCEPTUAL FRAMEWORK AS A LONG TERM SMM STRATEGY TO CREATE BRAND EQUITY

To begin, businesses should gain perspective on their SMM strategy's current state in order to take proactive steps in the future. Businesses must consider the shift in consumer expectations, as they now expect seamless, integrated, and holistic experiences. Within this process, social media is a viable tool for increasing customer understanding, competition, and international business contacts. This implies that social media marketing should be an even more integrated part of the marketing strategy than it is now. When using social media platforms as part of a marketing strategy, a more comprehensive understanding of customer engagement behaviour can provide greater value (Phua et al 2017).

Second, businesses should assess their current branding elements and prioritise approaches and channels that appeal to the greatest number of customers. Marketers should adapt these elements to the current situation or other externally influential factors while keeping customer attitudes toward their product in mind, and present products and services with empathy and transparency. In this case, social media can be used to expand one's reach by sharing the adapted brand elements, i.e., advertising, in order to create a strong brand image and boost brand equity. These brand elements also serve as a reflection of the brand image.

Third, marketers must postpone or adapt the timeline of their planned marketing activities based on the business's current situation. Furthermore, businesses should incorporate a periodic evaluation of brand value levels as a new business practise to identify areas for improvement and develop appropriate strategies to increase brand value. The importance of brand, trust, and reputation is growing, and maximising perceived brand value positively influences consumer preferences and choices (Pervin et al 2013.). Consumers are better prepared, more aware, and critical of technologies and brands as their use of digital channels and technologies grows, as does their knowledge of these elements.

Fourth, businesses should quickly adapt their messaging to demonstrate empathy toward their customers and provide relevant information about consumer purchases as well as measures the company is taking to keep both employees and customers safe. Following that, brands should implement new methods of selling products and providing services. Brand awareness, brand image, brand experience, customer trust, and consumer satisfaction created through social media have been shown to positively influence purchase decisions, demonstrating that a social media strategy can not only assist consumers in their decision-making process, but also provide them with support or information. Furthermore, the brand should be associated with positive elements. Firm-generated content, such as product videos, brand fan content, and user-generated content, has been shown to positively influence brand passion creation. Marketers play the roles of communicator and promoter when it comes to effectively transmitting messages and eliciting positive feedback from customers. A challenge in this step could be the growing expectations among both employees and customers about how a company contributes to environmental and societal causes. According to the literature, businesses may be more sustainable post-crisis if they adapt to business models based on environmental awareness.

CONCLUSION

Influencer marketing has emerged as a viable method for brands to communicate with and engage with their customers. According to the research, the relationship between influencers and brands can be mutually beneficial.

According to this study, younger social media users, those aged 18 to 24, are more likely to follow influencer accounts. This demographic is well aware of the connection between those influencers and the brands they promote. Furthermore, these respondents value and seek influencers who are open and honest about product and brand advertising. There appears to be a link between perceived sharing of interests, characteristics, and behaviours with influencers and followers imitating those behaviours. We can speculate that the more a person feels similar to the influencer, the more trust they will have in the influencer, and the more credible the influencer will be perceived to be.

As a result, the more trust a person has in an influencer, the more likely they are to purchase a recommended product or brand. The more an influencer demonstrates their sincerity, the more people they can reach and persuade to buy the products they are promoting. According to the findings, more brands used influencers to market their products during the pandemic. Many brands have also had to change their promotional strategies, advocating the use of masks and social distancing.

The purpose of this chapter was to provide an answer to the question of how businesses can adapt their SMM using the influencers to create and raise the brand awareness adapting to the effects of the pandemic. According to the literature review, having a long-term vision will result in the best outcomes during and after the pandemic. A four-step conceptual framework with relevant stakeholders was identified from the literature. Before taking additional steps to improve their SMM strategy, businesses should first gain a clear understanding of their current SMM strategy. Governmental entities and financial institutions can also participate in this process by providing businesses with options, such as funding, to adopt SMM. Second, it is critical to evaluate current branding elements and adapt them to the situation.

When looking at the developments that have emerged during the pandemic, there are a few that are worth noting in order to create an understanding of the future of

SMM. The first is the growing impact of digital technologies on business practises. As stated in both the theoretical framework and the findings of this literature review, technologies are rapidly evolving, and businesses must adapt to and keep up with these developments in order to provide optimal solutions to consumers. According to research, young consumers buy online more frequently, accounting for a sizable proportion of total e-retail consumers.

This means that businesses must focus on creating conscious products and enhancing brand equity through online channels in order to communicate with customers and connect them to their brand. Although nothing can be guaranteed, it is clear that many businesses that converted to online channels during the pandemic will remain online or even expand their current online market share in order to stay connected with consumers.

DISCUSSION QUESTIONS IN CLASSROOMS

1) What is Social media information system?
2) How does brand awareness helps a business?
3) Who is a social media influencer and what do they do?
4) What are areas of concern with transition of marketing from traditional to digital?
5) How can a business find new ways for communicating with customers during times like a global pandemic?

REFERENCES

Abidin, C. (2015). "Communicative Intimacies: Influencers and Perceived Interconnectedness." Ada: A Journal of Gender. *New Media, and Technology*, 8(1), 1–14.

Al-Debei, M. M., Al-Lozi, E., & Papazafeiropoulou, A. (2013). Why People Keep Coming Back to Facebook: Explaining and Predicting Continuance Participation from an Extended Theory of Planned Behaviour Perspective. *Decision Support Systems*, 55(1), 43–54. doi:10.1016/j.dss.2012.12.032

Aral, S., & Walker, D. (2014). Tie Strength, Embeddedness, and Social Influence: A Large-scale Networked Experiment. *Management Science*, 60(6), 1352–1370. doi:10.1287/mnsc.2014.1936

Arora, A., Bansal, S., Kandpal, C., Aswani, R., & Dwivedi, Y. (2019). Measuring social media influencer index-insights from facebook, Twitter and Instagram. *Journal of Retailing and Consumer Services, 49*, 86–101. doi:10.1016/j.jretconser.2019.03.012

Awad, N. F., & Krishnan, M. S. (2006). The Personalization Privacy Paradox: An Empirical Evaluation of Information Transparency and the Willingness to be Profiled Online for Personalization. *Management Information Systems Quarterly, 30*(1), 13–28. doi:10.2307/25148715

Bailey, J. E., & Pearson, S. W. (1983). Development of a Tool for Measuring and Analyzing Computer User Satisfaction. *Management Science, 29*(5), 530–545. doi:10.1287/mnsc.29.5.530

Berger, J. (2013). *Contagious: Why Things Catch On.* Veghawaii Org.

Bhattacherjee, A. (2001). Understanding Information Systems Continuance: An Expectation-confirmation Model. *Management Information Systems Quarterly, 25*(3), 351–370. doi:10.2307/3250921

Carter, D. (2016). Hustle and Brand: The sociotechnical shaping of influence. Social Media þ. *Society, 2*(3), 1–12.

Chen, Y., & Zahedi, F. M. (2016). Individuals' Internet Security Perceptions and Behaviors: Polycontextual Contrasts between the United States and China. *Management Information Systems Quarterly, 40*(1), 205–222. doi:10.25300/MISQ/2016/40.1.09

Hajli, N., Shanmugam, M., Powell, P., & Love, P. E. D. (2015). A Study on the Continuance Participation in On-line Communities with Social Commerce Perspective. *Technological Forecasting and Social Change, 96*, 232–241. doi:10.1016/j.techfore.2015.03.014

Hester, A. J. (2011). A Comparative Analysis of the Usage and Infusion of Wiki and Non-wiki-based Knowledge Management Systems. *Information Technology Management, 12*(4), 335–355. doi:10.100710799-010-0079-9

Hossain, M. A., & Quaddus, M. (2012). Expectation– Confirmation Theory in Information System Research: A Review and Analysis. *Information Systems Theory, 28*, 441–469. doi:10.1007/978-1-4419-6108-2_21

Hui, L., Weiguo, F., & Chau, P. Y. K. (2014). Determinants of Users' Continuance of Social Networking Sites: A Self-regulation Perspective. *Information & Management, 51*(5), 595–603. doi:10.1016/j.im.2014.03.010

Islam, A. A. (2016). Development and Validation of the Technology Adoption and Gratification (TAG) Model in Higher Education: A Cross-cultural Study between Malaysia and China. *International Journal of Technology and Human Interaction*, *12*(3), 78–105. doi:10.4018/IJTHI.2016070106

Masoom, K. (2022, February). A Study of Influencers' Marketing and its Impact on Brand Engagement. *IJRESM*, *5*(2), 49–51.

Pervin, N., Fang, F., Datta, A., Dutta, K., & Vandermeer, D. (2013). Fast, Scalable, and Context-sensitive Detection of Trending Topics in Microblog Post Streams. *ACM Transactions on Management Information Systems*, *3*(4), 1–24. doi:10.1145/2407740.2407743

Shao, G. (2009). Understanding the Appeal of User-generated Media: A Uses and Gratification Perspective. *Internet Research*, *19*(1), 7–25. doi:10.1108/10662240910927795

Tafesse, W., & Wood, B. P. (2020). Followers' engagement with instagram influencers: The role of influencers' content and engagement strategy. *Journal of Retailing and Consumer Services*, *58*, 102303. doi:10.1016/j.jretconser.2020.102303

Wang, C., Jin, X. L., Zhou, Z., Fang, Y., Lee, M. K. O., & Hua, Z. (2015). Effect of Perceived Media Capability on Status Updates in Microblogs. *Electronic Commerce Research and Applications*, *14*(3), 181–191. doi:10.1016/j.elerap.2014.11.006

ADDITIONAL READINGS

Matin and Khoshtaria, International Journal of marketing.(2022). The Impact of Social Media Influencers on Brand Awareness, Image and Trust in their Sponsored Content: An Empirical Study from Georgian Social Media Users

Susanto et al. Applied system innovation.(2021). Revealing Social Media Phenomenon in Time of COVID-19 Pandemic for Boosting Start-Up Businesses through Digital Ecosystem.

Jindhal and Gambhir. (2021). *Marketing in a Pandemic*. IGI Global.

Amina.I et al. IJOM. Strategic Adaptive Leadership and Emerging Approaches to Online Marketing of a US Small Business Real Estate Firm in Response to COVID-19. IGI Global.

Kentle and Audin. Qualitative market research. (2022). Impact of the pandemic on social media influencer marketing in fashion: a qualitative study.

KEY TERMS & DEFINITIONS

Social Media Information System: Social media information system (SMIS)- is an information system that supports the sharing of content among networks of users.

Influencer: A person with the ability to influence potential buyers of a product or service by promoting or recommending the items on social media.

Brand awareness: The extent to which consumers are familiar with the qualities or image of a particular brand of goods or services.

Social media marketing: Social media marketing is the use of social media platforms and websites to promote a product or service. Although the terms e-marketing and digital marketing are still dominant in academia, social media marketing is becoming more popular for both practitioners and researchers.

Consumer Behaviour: Consumer behavior is the study of individuals, groups, or organizations and all the activities associated with the purchase, use and disposal of goods and services. Consumer behaviour consists of how the consumer's emotions, attitudes, and preferences affect buying behaviour.

Digital Marketing: Digital marketing is the component of marketing that uses the Internet and online based digital technologies such as desktop computers, mobile phones and other digital media and platforms to promote products and services

Brand: A brand is a name, term, design, symbol or any other feature that distinguishes one seller's good or service from those of other sellers.

Product: A product is the item offered for sale. A product can be a service or an item. It can be physical or in virtual or cyber form. Every product is made at a cost and each is sold at a price.

Brand impact: Brand impact means significantly influencing a person's perception of a brand to the extent where they're engaging with them on an emotional level.

Social media environment: Social media environments refer to online spaces where individuals establish and maintain virtual social interactions with others.

Online persona: Internet identity (IID), also online identity or internet persona, is a social identity that an Internet user establishes in online communities and websites.

Influencer marketing: Influencer marketing is a form of social media marketing involving endorsements and product placement from influencers, people and organizations who have a purported expert level of knowledge or social influence in their field

Chapter 2

How Can I Help You Today?
The Rise of Virtual Assistants in Human Resources Management

Dragos Vieru
 https://orcid.org/0000-0001-6769-093X
Teluq University, Canada

Simon Bourdeau
Université du Québec à Montréal, Canada

Mickaël Ringeval
Université du Québec à Montréal, Canada

Tobias Jung
Deloitte Consulting, Germany

ABSTRACT

The pandemic context has fast-tracked the digital transformation of many organizations that pursued to dramatically change their organizational processes to survive in a global digital economy. While virtual assistants (VA), a specialized artificial intelligence-based chatbot, such as Alexa or Siri, have penetrated our private lives, many organizations are still trying to understand and evaluate why and how to integrate these technologies into their employees' workday. The study explores whether VAs can be used to support human resources (HR) trainee management software in a German organization and how it can be done. Four key HR areas of self-service, onboarding, training, and knowledge management were explored. Interviews were conducted to analyze which VAs' functions can be reused to support trainee management software in these four areas. The technology affordances and constraints theory were used to analyze data collected. The results showed that a VA's functions can support trainee management software especially in the areas of self-service, onboarding, and training.

DOI: 10.4018/978-1-7998-9418-6.ch002

INTRODUCTION

After two years of pandemic, there is a widespread agreement that digital technologies have made our lives easier while global economy is becoming more digital as businesses are being more and more affected by digital technologies such as the Internet, mobile connectivity, cloud computing, big data, artificial intelligence (AI), Internet of Things, predictive and data analytics and other emerging digital technologies (Soto-Acosta, 2020). The COVID-19 context has accelerated the digital transformation of organizations and entire industries such as retail and education. Digital transformation is about radically rethinking how an organization uses technology, people, and organizational processes to fundamentally change its performance (Kane, 2019). Moreover, the pandemic impact on organizations has provided opportunities for new business models that are based on a combination of AI tools and traditional business models.

The field of Artificial Intelligence (AI) has gained more and more interest over the past 10 years as the underlying technologies are now able to fulfill the requirements to process large amounts of data (Io & Lee, 2017; Liao et al., 2019). Artificial Intelligence typically indicates a broad class of information technologies that allow a computer to execute tasks that normally require human cognition, including decision making. By identifying and learning reoccurring patterns in large sets of data, AI-based software tools or chatbots, understand, process, and answer user queries in textual or vocal form (Saukkonen et al., 2019).

A Virtual Assistant (VA) is a specialized chatbot that serves a specific purpose, that is, supporting users (Battineni, 2020). Virtual Assistants can be seen as a Digital Innovation as they fulfill the three criteria of Digital Innovation stated by Nambisan et al. (2017). First, VAs have a so-called innovation outcome, as they enable new services within the company (Tambe et al., 2019). Next, VAs use digital tools (e.g., data analytics and deep learning) to enable desired innovation outcome, and finally, the innovation outcome can be used and adapted to different contexts, for example, healthcare or Human Resources Management (HRM) (Laranjo et al., 2018; Tambe et al., 2019).

In the field of HRM VAs have not made as much progress yet compared to the other areas (Tambe et al., 2019). One of the main reasons why AI in general is rarely used in HRM is that some HR functions or some HR activities are unstructured, including recruitment, training, and maintenance (Jantan et al., 2010). For instance, it is not easy to measure what constitutes a "good employee," assuming that most of the time "job requirements are broad, monitoring of work outcomes is poor, and biases associated with assessing individual performance are legion" (Tambe et al. 2019, p. 21). Factors such as "constraints imposed by small data sets, accountability questions associated with fairness and other ethical and legal constraints, and possible adverse employee reactions to management decisions via data-based algorithms" (Tambe et al., 2019, p.15) make it more difficult to use AI-based tools in the HR function that in other organizational areas. However, recent advances in cognitive AI technologies triggered opportunities for VAs to increasingly be used for different tasks in HRM (Liao et al., 2019) and will increase in the next 5 years (Saukkonen et al., 2019).

Within the field of HRM, scholars have proposed different areas where VAs can be used, for example, recruitment (Asher, 2017; Soutar, 2019) or training (Koeva et al., 2016; Sekhri & Cheema, 2019; Mohan, 2019), but to our best knowledge, no studies could be found on how VAs can be used in the area of the unique German dual vocational training apprenticeship.

Organizations and educational institutions cooperate to teach trainees expertise and train them on how to apply this knowledge within the companies. The dual vocational training apprenticeship concept, firmly established in the German education system, is based upon a combination of on-the-job training within a specific company and classroom-based training provided by a vocational school to apprentices also called trainees (German Federal Ministry for Economic Affairs and Energy, 2017). Every organization that uses this approach needs to coordinate and monitor its trainees to keep track of their learning process as well as their upcoming tasks. This coordination and monitoring are usually done by HR employees using a trainee management software. Virtual Assistants could be used to automatically perform these tasks. Considering that some of these tasks are repetitive while other are unstructured, could potentially a VA handle them in the same manner as a HR employee in the context of the post-pandemic realities?

To fill the gap in this literature we advance two main research questions:

1. *Can Virtual Assistants be used in trainee management software?* and if so,
2. How can Virtual Assistants be used to support trainee management software?

Since the use of VA to support trainee management software represents a new avenue of exploration, the Technology Affordances and Constraints Theory (Majchrzak and Markus, 2012) was chosen because it can help to "[…] explain how and why the same technology can be repurposed by different actors or has different innovation outcomes in different contexts" (Nambisan et al. 2017, p. 8). This theory was used to analyze the innovation outcomes of VAs used to support trainee management software.

Data were collected via a single case study. This research design was selected because the phenomenon of interest differs from every other occurrence as the usage of VAs differs from the everyday usage of trainee management systems (Yin, 2018). We performed nine interviews with HRM experts working for the organization

DigiSol (not the real name) and five interviews with employees from four of their organization clients. DigiSol is a 200-employee German IT services providing HRM software called Magellan to their clients in the aviation and banking sectors, which includes a trainee management module.

Recent studies have shown that many organizations are still not ready to use AI in HRM as processes, jobs, and technologies will have to change with the introduction of the AI (Jia et al., 2018). By showing which HRM tasks can be supported by VAs, organizations may be better informed when considering the usage of a VA in their trainee management system. The main contribution of this research is that a new, relatively unexplored field is analyzed, which can lead to a better understanding of the current AI-based technologies and how they can be used in a post-pandemic global economy. This might provide a solid foundation for more research in this field.

VIRTUAL ASSISTANTS AND HR PROCESSES

It has been suggested that the best choice for an information system (IS) that supports HR processes is a decisions-support system (Cao, 2010). Recently, it has been shown by several scholars, that many of the tasks accomplished by HR managers using decisions-support systems can now be automatically achieved by VAs (Buzko et al., 2016; Tambe et al., 2019; Sekhri & Cheema, 2019). For instance, HRM-related tasks, such as providing a service point for employees (Buzko et al., 2016; Klopfenstein et al., 2017), identifying recruitment performance assessment, onboarding, training (Tambe et al., 2019; Sekhri & Cheema, 2019) as well as gathering and managing knowledge can all be executed by VAs (Tambe et al. 2019). Thus, VAs can execute four key HR tasks: supporting employees in daily HR tasks, onboarding, training, and managing knowledge.

Self-Service – Supporting Daily Tasks

Virtual Assistants can provide support to employees during their daily tasks (Singh et al., 2018). Virtual Assistance consists of different supported tasks. For instance, executing search queries on employees in an efficient way so that the HR employee can work with the results more quickly than searching for it by themselves (Birzniece, 2011; Meyer von Wolff et al., 2019). Khurana et al. (2017) show in their study how a VA that was programmed to answer HR-related Frequently Asked Questions, was able to reduce the number of questions asked per day by 83%. By answering nearly all HR-related questions, VAs free time for HR employees and reduces repetitive work (Asher, 2017) and increase productivity (Brandtzaeg & Følstad, 2017).

The proactivity of VAs is another reason for increased efficiency. Virtual Assistants would show relevant information proactively to the users by realizing a prescreening of received resumés, gather a wide range of data, for example on the applicant's experience, and request for HR selection representative to start the process of application analysis (Nawaz & Gomes, 2019).

Onboarding

Onboarding represents the HR process of providing the necessary information and knowledge that are needed for a new hired employee to successfully start in the new job (Westberg, 2019). Organizations often think that onboarding happens automatically and naturally because an employee connects and exchange with other employees over time. Thus, several organizations do not make onboarding a priority (Hu, 2019). This can be problematic as a recent study showed that 25% of the new employees leave before they finish their first year because of a lack of understanding and guidance (Harpelund (2019). A well-planned onboarding process that includes a mentor (Asher, 2017) results in about 50% more productivity from the new employee (Harpelund, 2019). A common problem in onboarding is that new employees do not get a good first impression of the organization during their first days (Westberg, 2019). Virtual Assistants can be used to support the onboarding process by (1) providing relevant information to the new employee during a question and answer (Q&A) session, and (2) disseminating information about the new employee across the organization more quickly, which may lead to a faster welcome in the organization (Nawaz & Gomes, 2019).

Training

It has been shown that the use of AI during the training process, can significantly decrease the number of resources needed to provide support during and after training (Buzko et al., 2016). Using AI for training employees enables more efficient knowledge transmission via a personalized teacher (a chatbot). The chatbot communicates with the student and teaches different learning materials during the chat session (Winkler & Söllner, 2018; Mohan, 2019). Student's responses during the chat are analyzed by a VA that generates feedback to the trainee on whether the answer was correct or not (Koeva et al., 2016). Thus, VA can provide automatic, direct, and instant feedback to the student helping him/her to learn and accelerating the training process. After the learning objective is completed, the VA can generate a test that must be answered by the trainee to verify their knowledge (Koeva et al., 2016).

Managing Knowledge

Managing organizational knowledge requires the ability to capture new knowledge, share it, and reuse it in various contexts by various employees or AI (Tsui et al., 2000). A Virtual Assistant represents a potentially major source of precious knowledge for organizations. By asking the users about new information, new processes, or new systems in its organization, a VA can collect an important quantity of data and hand it over to experts, who can create new knowledge out of it (Meyer von Wolff et al., 2019). Another feature of a VA is its ability to quickly redirect a user to another human if a question cannot be answered. In this case, the answer of the human becomes new knowledge and should be saved and integrated into the VA (Massaro et al., 2018; Verleger & Pembridge, 2018). Furthermore, a VA can also help creating better social environment in organizations by analyzing the underlying social structures using data collected from the organizational social media or conversations between employees (Tsui et al., 2000; Tambe et al., 2019).

In conclusion, VAs can be used to support different HRM tasks, namely onboarding, training, and managing knowledge. In addition, VAs can be used as a self-service point (Sekhri & Cheema, 2019). Being able to answer questions on various topics quickly and doing this faster than humans, VAs constitute a viable option for supporting employees during their daily workday (Meyer von Wolff et al., 2019).

THEORETICAL DEVELOPMENT

Modern Digital Innovation Management Theories

During the last decade, the research in digital innovation management theories progressed by analyzing in more detail several aspects of digital product and service innovations (Nambisan et al., 2017). Some researchers began to identify the dilemmas that come with the management of digitalization (Tilson et al., 2010), and more and more researchers started focusing on the outcomes of digital innovations, on the required conditions for digital innovation to emerge, and on the problems which can be solved by digital innovations (Nambisan et al., 2017). According to Nambisan et al. (2017), the three fundamental questions when it comes to innovation management are: 1. "How do innovations form/evolve?", 2. "How should actors/entities organize for innovation?", and 3. "How [do] the nature of innovation and the organization of innovation interact?" (Nambisan et al., 2017, p. 224).

To analyze digital innovations and answer these questions, Nambisan et al. (2017) suggest to use the theory of the Technology Affordances and Constraints theory as a conceptual tool. This theory can be used to analyze the innovation outcomes of an existing digital innovation in a new context (Majchrzak & Markus, 2012; Nambisan et al., 2017) as well as to compare innovation outcomes in already known contexts (Nambisan et al., 2017). This theoretical lens focuses on the technology affordances, which according to Majchrzak & Markus (2012) are "[…] what an individual or organization with a particular purpose can do with a technology or information system" (Majchrzak & Markus, 2012, p. 1).

Affordances reflect the potential usages that come with the use of an IT artefact. Examples of the outcomes of potential IT affordances are, for instance, sharing information or increasing productivity (Majchrzak and Markus, 2012). IT affordances are then matched with the users' needs in a specific context to understand the relationship between the technology features and the users (Nambisan et al., 2017).

VAs Affordances

We conducted a literature review on human resource management and AI to identify and analyze which affordances may become available with the implementation of a VA into a trainee management software. Altogether, we identified ten affordances and we labelled them by following authors' recommendations[1].

The first affordance identified is **Increase Efficiency**, which means that a user needs less information to complete a task without increasing the time they need to complete it. As shown by different studies, the employees work more efficiently when they use VAs to search for something rather than searching for it on their own (Birzniece, 2011; Meyer von Wolff et al., 2019).

With an increase in efficiency often comes an increase in productivity, which is the second identified affordance: **Increase Productivity**. It represents a decrease of time needed to complete a task while not increasing the information needed for it (Brandtzaeg & Følstad, 2017). Productivity can also be increased in the training process when the VA is also available on mobile devices, which increases connectivity between the teacher and the student (Gonda et al., 2018). The third affordance identified is **Reduce Needed Resources**. Khurana et al. (2017) have shown that their VA was able to reduce the number of questions handed over to the HR department by 83%, which reduced the resources needed in the HR department significantly. Employees tend to forget where to find needed information, which can result in a waste of time and resources, something that the VA can easily prevent (Westberg, 2019). Besides reducing the needed resources, VAs can reduce the workload of employees (Asher, 2017), resulting in the fourth identified affordance: **Reduce Workload**. This can be achieved by using the suggestions for alternative solutions feature of a VA, which can result in less workload (Brandtzaeg & Følstad, 2017; Yawalkar, 2019). The workload can be reduced even further by using the VA to obtain an overview of unstructured information, so employees do not need to summarize this information (Meyer von Wolff et al. 2019).

Being able to solve the tasks with less workload, resulting in less stress during the day, leads to the fifth affordance: **Enhance Working Atmosphere**. As shown by Asher (2017), the implementation of a VA reduces repetitive work, which lowers employees' frustration by the monotony of their job and results in overall increase of happiness at work. Also, during the training process, employees will be less likely to become frustrated when working with a VA, as the AI tool can generate questions based on the learner's interests and provide tips if the learner cannot solve a problem. The help and support provided by the VA results in more motivated employees (Oudeyer et al., 2016; Winkler & Söllner, 2018; Ruan et al., 2019).

The sixth affordance identified as **Increase Information Availability**, would enable a user to access more information. As shown by Klopfenstein et al. (2017) and Meyer von Wolff et al. (2019), VAs are accessible at all times within the environment in which they are installed and are not bound by space or time, so users can obtain the needed information anytime they want. The seventh identified affordance is **Increase Information Sharing**. This affordance is enacted via different VA-supported functions that provide users with information without having the user search for them. In addition, proactively sharing information about a task that a user is currently working on (Nezhad, 2015) leads to better-informed employees overall (Nawaz & Gomes, 2019). The eighth affordance identified is **Increase Communication**. This affordance is enacted by feedback functions of VAs which collect feedbacks from employees, summarize it, and hand it regularly over to managers (Mohan, 2019; Nawaz & Gomes, 2019). The same strategy can be used in training where VAs can be used to gather feedbacks from the trainee and enable the teacher to enhance their lessons based on them (Winkler & Söllner, 2018; Gonda et al., 2018).

The last two affordances are not only enacted by VAs function but also flow from the implementation process of a VA. The ninth identified affordance was **Generate Knowledge**. This affordance results mainly from the implementation process as the existing knowledge in an organization must be collected and structured in a practical way to generated pertinent training data for VAs (Tambe et al., 2019). Here, every possible data point is collected and organized, which may lead to the discovery of new knowledge (Tambe et al., 2019). Also, the existing knowledge must be maintained to prevent it from becoming outdated which leads to the last affordance: **Maintain Knowledge**. Using the feedback function of VAs, the users themselves can maintain the knowledge by giving feedback on whether an answer was helpful or not (Cao, 2010; Singh et al., 2018). To address the two main research questions, we propose five research propositions (see Table 1) that were tested on the data that were gathered from the case study.

Table 1. Research propositions and related identified affordances

#	Research Proposition	Related Affordances
1	Virtual Assistants (VAs) can be used to increase the efficiency and productivity of organizations using trainee management software.	Increase Efficiency, Increase Productivity
2	The implementation of a VA into a trainee management software can be used to reduce the workload of an HR employee and the resources needed for a specific task.	Reduce Workload, Reduce Needed Resources
3	VAs supporting trainee management software can be used to enhance the working atmosphere and increase the communication in an organization.	Enhance Working Atmosphere, Increase Communication
4	VAs can be used to increase the amount of shared information and to remind employees and thereby increase the information availability overall.	Increase Information Availability, Increase Information Sharing
5	VAs can be used to manage knowledge by enabling more options of generating and maintaining knowledge.	Generate Knowledge, Maintain Knowledge

METHODOLOGY

An explanatory case approach (Eisenhardt, 1989) was adopted to identify relationships between an "observed state of a phenomenon and conditions that influence its development" (Avgerou, 2013, p. 428). Following Eisenhardt's (1989) methodological recommendations, we anchored our problem definition and preliminary construct specification in extant literature and crafted our data collection instruments accordingly.

The selected organization was DigiSol (not the real name), a German IT consultancy firm with 200 employees that develops and sells banking and HR management software called Magellan consisting of different modules. Besides developers, the organization employs several consultants - HRM specialists, that analyze DigiSol's clients HR processes and provide recommendations on how to improve them. One of Magellan's modules, called Training, is dedicated to the management of trainees. It is used to coordinate and oversee the management and to plan and review their tasks at different worksites and their educational objectives. At the time of the writing (February 2022), DigiSol was still in the process of testing a Virtual Assistant for their Training module.

Interviews were the main method of data collection and were based on a protocol made from the extant literature and research. Two types of informants were selected: based on the recommendations provided by the heads of HR Department and the Development Department, we first selected several key stakeholders involved in the VA development – managers, developers, and consultants. Overall, nine interviewees were selected. Then, based on the firm consultants' recommendations, we contacted six client organizations that were participating in the VA testing process. Four organizations (called here Client organization 1, 2, 3, and 4) were interested in our research and five interviews were carried on. The five interviewees were involved in at least two VA test sessions in their respective organizations. Thus, overall, fourteen interviews (see Table 2) were conducted via Zoom that lasted between 35 to 75 minutes.

Table 2. Interviewees OVERVIEW

Organization	Position	Time in this position
DigiSol	Head of Digitization Department	2 years
	Customer Support Consultant	3 years
	VA Project Manager	2.5 years
	VA Software Developer	5 years
	Head of the HR and Organization Department	14 years
	Consultant for the Solution Integration	3 years
	HR Systems Consultant	10 years
	Head of Development, Product Owner	1 year
	Consultant for the Solution Integration	2 years
Client organization 1	Trainer of the IT Department	10 years
Client organization 2	Personnel Officer	18 years
Client organization 3	Trainer	27 years
	Trainer	3 months
Client organization 4	Training Coordinator	13 years

Following Yin's (2018) recommendations, we triangulated the interviews with archival sources, including project documentation, organization documents (wiki boards, management presentations, communication plans, and emails). The archival documents were used in two ways. First, emails and management presentations were used to formulate and refine interview questions and second, reports were used to validate interview reports. Phase 1 of the coding process consisted in creating a list of categories based on the definitions of the ten identified affordances during the literature review. In Phase 2, the interview transcripts were introduced into a database, read carefully and relevant portions highlighted. The highlighted portions were then keyed into the database into a field called "evidence" as chunks of rich text.

All the transcripts, starting with the first interview, were coded using the preliminary set of codes. The development of the coding scheme was an on-going process throughout the transcription of each of the interviews. The goal of the coding was to identify patterns. Usually a pattern, in collected interview data, "at minimum describes and organizes the possible observations and at maximum interprets aspects of the phenomenon" (Boyatzis, 1998, p.4). In our case, we were looking for chunks of text that would relate to any affordance that has been defined in section VAs Affordances. Patterns may be generated inductively from raw interview data or generated deductively from theory or prior research (Patton 2002). We chose the latter approach. We followed Patton's (2002) two-stage analytic induction: first, we selected and coded pieces of texts (mostly from the transcripts of interviews and archival documents) and then we analyzed the resulting data to determine whether the findings support our five research propositions. The analysis of the three data sources yielded 616 patterns to one or more of the 10 affordances.

FINDINGS

Proposition 1: Increase Efficiency and Productivity

The first research proposition is based on the affordances **Increase Efficiency** and **Increase Productivity**. It is the second most referenced research proposition with 188 distinct patterns referencing it. The first affordance, Increase Efficiency, is referenced 69 times either directly or indirectly during the interviews.

"Firstly, you don't need a person to answer your questions and secondly, you have an answer immediately, and you have it at any time" (HR systems consultant, DigiSol); "From a business point of view, the organization could save millions of euros from now on. Firstly, because knowledge is not lost and secondly, because the search is concentrated at one point, and I don't have to run around a thousand times to gather my information." (Personnel officer, Client organization 2).

The second affordance mentioned in the first research proposition is Increase Productivity. There were 72 patterns referring to it in the DigiSol interviews, 19 in the archival documentation, and 28 in the client interviews.

"It is able to remind the trainee, for example, that he/she has to maintain the report book, that he/she has to go to vocational school tomorrow, that his/her certificate is still missing, and it needs to be uploaded." (Consultant for the Solution Integration, DigiSol); "Definitely higher productivity. There are time advantages when a VA is optimally introduced and used." (Trainer, Client organization 3)

The analyses of all three data sources show that both Increase Productivity and Increase Efficiency affordances are supported by the data. While the Increase Efficiency affordance is the third most referred to affordance, the Increase Productivity affordance is the second most referred in every data source. Hence, the data provide some evidence to support the relevance of Proposition 1.

Proposition 2: Reduce Workload and Resources

The second research proposition is based on the affordances **Reduce Workload** and **Reduce Needed Resources**. Both affordances together are referenced by 69 distinct patterns. Data analysis identified 42 patterns in the DigiSol interviews. Across all data sources affordance Reduce Workload is supported and it is the sixth-most frequently referenced one (38 patterns).

"This is a key aspect in addition to reducing organizational hurdles during the onboarding process. With the VA, the trainee has someone on his side to support him. The VA could therefore ensure that time and money can be saved in the background." (Head of Development, DigiSol); "From a business point of view, the organization could save millions of euros. Firstly, because knowledge is not lost and secondly, because the search is concentrated at one point, and I don't have to run around to gather my information." (Trainer, Client organization 3)

While the affordance Reduce Needed Resources is mentioned in 25 patterns in the interviews with the DigiSol employees, only 5 patterns in the archival documentation and 1 pattern in the client interviews were found. We believe that this lack of patterns in the client related data is due to the similarity between the two affordances in terms of practical results. Notwithstanding this, we consider that overall, the patterns found in the three data sources provide some evidence to support the relevance of Proposition 2.

Proposition 3: Enhance Working Atmosphere and Communication

The third research proposition is based on the **Enhance Working Atmosphere** and the **Increase Communication** affordances. We found 93 distinct patterns that refer to this research proposition, with 52 of these patterns being identified in the DigiSol interviews. As mentioned earlier, Enhance Working Atmosphere affordance covers everything that makes employees enjoy their work more, makes them feel more welcome, or allows them to feel more appreciated. DigiSol interviews showed great support for the Enhance Working Atmosphere affordance (the fifth most frequently identified pattern), and no pattern could be identified that would state that the working atmosphere would deteriorate if the VAs were used. Additionally, the analysis of the other two data sources has shown that this affordance is supported by the evidence.

"I believe that one of the benefits will be that the trainees are better informed, because I believe that at some point when a trainee has had many questions, he no longer dares to ask a question and then thinks: 'Somehow, I'll be fine by'. And then the trainee may not be as well informed as if he could simply ask five times without anyone noticing." (Head of HR, DigiSol); "The fact that I can ask the VA questions is of course convenient, that I don't have to put myself in the position of asking the trainer the same question five times during the training session." (Trainer IT department, Client organization 1)

The other affordance, the Increase Communication may overlap with the Enhance Working Atmosphere affordance because a better communication can also result in an enhanced working atmosphere. Overall, 33 patterns refer to this affordance, with 20 of them being extracted from the DigiSol interviews, 4 from the archival documentation, and the rest from the client data.

"VA can be used to create a platform on which the trainees can exchange information. They can virtually meet and exchange ideas. An advantage would be that the VA could be configured to moderate the platform. From time to time, it could send notifications to the users that they should exchange more information with each other." (Customer support consultant, DigiSol); The trainees often have the problem that they don't know whether they have read everything about a certain topic and a VA would be a great help here. For example, considering a specific topic, the VA would notify you 'communicate with this or that employee, because he or she is dealing with the same topic'." (Trainer IT department, Client organization 1)

The analyses of all three data sources show that both Increase Communication and Enhance Working Atmosphere affordances are supported by the data. Thus, the data seem to also provide some evidence to support the relevance of Proposition 3.

Proposition 4: Increase Information Sharing and Availability

The fourth research proposition is based on two affordances: **Increase Information Availability** and **Increase Information Sharing**. With 224 distinct patterns (133 from the DigiSol interviews, 67 from the client interviews, and 24 from the archival documentation), it was the most frequently referred to research proposition. The analysis of the DigiSol interviews yielded 100 patterns referring to the Increase

Information Availability affordance. It is the most referred to affordance over all data sources.

"One aspect about VAs is exciting: the availability of information. The HR employee goes down the stairs to interview, let's say, Jan a potential new employee. The VA can instantly give him the information about the school the candidate finished, what kind of teacher and grades he had" (VA Software Developer, DigiSol); "For the instructor, it is good that he could say 'Give me an overview of the trainee', so that he can intervene in time if grades are not right and not wait until he can't make up for the gap anymore" (Trainer, Client organization 3)

While somehow similar to the Increase Information Availability affordance, the Increase Information Sharing affordance is focused on functions that proactively provide information to the trainee.

"VA would ensure the procurement and sharing of information. For example, one could tell the VA that an appraisal should be arranged for specific trainees in the third year of the apprenticeship and the VA would send it out immediately." (Head of the HR, DigiSol); "I think it is very difficult to follow the conversations during the training sessions because of data protection. By tracking conversations, then filtering and sharing the information, the VAs would be great tools." (Training coordinator, Client organization 4)

Since both affordances were identified in patterns of data in all data sources, the relevance of Proposition 4 seems supported.

Proposition 5: Generate and Maintain Knowledge

The fifth and final research is based on the **Generate Knowledge** and the **Maintain Knowledge** affordances. With 42 distinct patterns referring to this research proposition, it is the least frequently referred to research proposition. The overall support for the Generate Knowledge affordance is low compared to the other affordances. Five of the nine DigiSol interviews do not contain any pattern that supports this affordance, but all have at least one pattern that does not support it. As more than half of the DigiSol and client interviews and the archival documentation do not support this affordance, the Generate Knowledge affordance is categorized as not supported by the data.

"When it comes to generating knowledge, it definitely depends on the amount of data that the VA has available. If the VA has dealt with a quiz or a question 80 times, he

has a lot of data available and may also be able to draw conclusions about similar problems, but at least for the moment, it will not be able to generate new knowledge." (*Head of Development, DigiSol); "VA can help a trainer collect knowledge and avoid having to do it several times. However, the human must have a kind of control whether the knowledge is useful." (Personnel Officer, Client organization 2)*

The last affordance that was analyzed was Maintain Knowledge. We identified 21 patterns in the DigiSol interviews, 2 in the archival documents, and 8 in the client interviews that refer to this affordance.

"The VA will be able to check the quality of the answer [from a trainee] by using a feedback function if the trainer has searched or asked for something. While the VA is not yet able to generate new knowledge, it can check the existing knowledge for quality." (VA Software Developer, DigiSol); I think that the VA could be used as an evaluation system, for example, I think it's a very good thing that the VA would evaluate if any of the answers [from a trainee] are not helpful and provided feedback on how to improve them." (Trainer, Client organization 3)

Overall, all three data sources indicate support for the Maintain Knowledge affordance. However, as Generate Knowledge affordance was not supported by the data, Proposition 5 is categorized as partially supported by the data.

DISCUSSION

Our research is based on the view that technology artifacts, in an organizational setting, are understood and appropriated in the context of specific practices (Orlikowski, 2007). Likewise, this study views VAs not only as a sum of their material functionalities but also in terms of the affordances they offer their users (Faraj & Azad, 2012). A technology affordance represents the "potential for action that emerges out of the interrelationships among the technical features of a system, people's ability and predisposition to use these features in certain ways, and the organizational context within which this takes place" (Gal et al., 2014, p. 1372). Thus, affordances are neither an objective property of the technologies, in our case the VAs, nor a subjective trait of the people who use them (Leonardi, 2013).

First, our analysis reveals that in the case of the DigiSol interviewees, VAs affordances become associated with different functionalities and meanings based mostly on the individual's background and previous experiences in the HR management software field. The analysis of this data source shows the emergence of a cognitive interpretation of the constraints and affordances of the VA technology.

Second, the data analysis of the client interviews reveals that clients' perceptions about the technology are closely interwoven with their perceptions about the nature of the HR tasks. Hence, during the test sessions they developed representations about the VA technology that were influenced by their backgrounds and previous experiences accumulated during traditional training session.

Clients' perceptions of potential affordances might have also been influenced by what Carter et al. (2020) call it a strong IT identity. IT identity represents a set of significances an individual confers to the self in relation to IT and emerges as a product of individuals' personal histories of interacting with IT (Carter & Grover, 2015). From this viewpoint, a strong IT identity can be described as "positive self-identification - use of the target IT is integral to my sense of self (who I am)" (Carter et al., 2020, p. 1315). All 5 interviewees from the client organizations were trainers therefore, we surmise that these individuals were influenced in their perceptions of technology affordances by their past experiences as training professionals.

Our analysis has shown that the first four research propositions seem to be supported, whereas the last one seems partially supported by the data. Our research propositions are based on the affordances enacted by the VA's functions as resulted from the literature review. As four research propositions are fully supported by the data, we can answer to our first research question positively. Thus, it can be suggested that there are several ways a VA can be used in a trainee management software.

We will try to answer the second research question, how can a VA be used in a trainee management software, by discussing our findings with respect to the four key HR tasks identified earlier: 1. Supporting employees in daily HR tasks (Self-Service); 2. Onboarding; 3. Training; and 4. Managing knowledge.

Concerning the Self-Service task, our analysis suggests that VAs may enable affordances that yield the following outcomes: identify and provide information proactively, offer an overview of unstructured information, provide file access, and point out contact persons. In terms of the HR task of Onboarding of trainees, our data analysis shows a strong perception of several practical affordances of a VA when the technology is used to support the onboarding of newly hired employees. However, some client organization interviewees thought that some in-person communication will be lost if a VA is included into the onboarding process despite its advantages, such as automatic welcome messages, the capacity to start the onboarding process at any time, spread information about new employees.

All interviewees perceived that the task of Training can be fully supported by a VA. This is due to its perceived affordance to act as a personalized teacher (in the specific context of the German dual vocational education apprenticeship system), who can talk to the trainee on daily basis, answer to any of the questions a trainee may ask and offer feedback. The interviewees also perceived the VA as being able to also challenge the trainee by providing tips to improve trainee's performance.

Finally, regarding the fourth task, Managing Knowledge, our analysis shows limited support for the research proposition that suggests VA can be used to efficiently manage knowledge. Mixed results show that interviewees' perceptions of a VA implemented with currently available technologies is not useable to generate new knowledge automatically in the context of trainee management. Generating knowledge can be divided into two parts: first, the manual data collection part that comes with the implementation of a VA and second, the automated part where a VA tries to generate knowledge. Interviewees' perception is that organization internal databases can be used to generate knowledge but only for the manual data collection process. Moreover, based on interviewees' current understanding and interpretation of VAs, it is not possible to access and analyze these information sources automatically. Moreover, the knowledge that is required to support the trainees is, in most cases, too specific to be generated automatically. Another function that the literature suggests is that the VA can ask employees to provide information about new topics in the organization. However, our data analysis suggests it would be too much work for the HR employees to ensure the quality of the knowledge, and thus, the interviewees see this as a constraint of the VA technology.

CONCLUSIONS AND FUTURE RESEARCH

The goal of our article was to show whether a VA can be used to support trainee management software, and if it can be supported, how it can be supported by identifying several technology affordances. To our best knowledge, we did not find other empirical studies to analyze this topic. Thus, a literature review was conducted to identify the HR tasks that can be supported by a VA. The identified tasks were Self-Service, Onboarding, Training, and Managing Knowledge. Each area was then checked for functions that may also be used in trainee management software. To analyze if and how VAs can be used to support this type of software, we adopted the Technology Affordances and Constraints theory, as suggested by Nambisan et al. (2017). Based on the technology affordances identified in the current literature, five research propositions were advanced that were tested for relevance on the data collected from a single case study (Huberman and Miles, 2002; Yin, 2018).

The main contribution of this article is to the literature on Virtual Assistants and HR management. By proposing five research propositions, this study provides a more in-depth explanation of a relatively unexplored field, which improves our understanding of how AI-based VA technology might be used in the context of HR management in a post-pandemic global digital economy. By using the Technology Affordances and Constraints theory it was found that VA technology, in an organizational setting, is understood and appropriated in the context of the specific practices of HR. For practitioners, this study also provides insights on what could influence VAs adoption, use, and ultimately success in the context of HR training. To a certain extent, it doesn't really matter what functionality the technology offers, but how the users perceive its affordances.

Our work has two limitations. The main limitation of this study is that it provides generalizability of the conclusions from empirical statements issued from the case study to theoretical statements (Lee and Baskerville, 2003). To offer statistical generalizability (Yin, 2018), our findings need to be validated against a variety of organizations in process of implementing VA technology in an HR context. The second one is related to the lack of consideration of the data security aspect when the functions of the VA were analyzed. Because the data protection laws in Europe are strict, some of the presented affordances may be useable in theory but not when the data protection laws are taken into consideration.

The results of our research offer potential for several future research avenues in trainee management and VAs in the context of an increased utilization of AI-based tools for digital transformation. Technology artifacts such as AI-based VAs can be described as information systems (IS) agentic tools that can assume responsibility for tasks with ambiguous requirements (Hill et al., 2015). There is a need for better understanding of the relationships between humans and agentic IS artifacts (Baskerville et al., 2019). A first future avenue for research would be the application of the IS delegation theoretical framework (Baird and Maruping, 2021) in the context of HR VAs to identify and analyze different decision models of how to delegate human-VAs tasks. The framework stresses the importance of the IS agentic tool "attributes relevant to delegation (endowments, preferences, and roles) as well as foundational mechanisms of delegation (appraisal, distribution, and coordination)" (Baird and Maruping, 2021, p. 315).

The results of the data analysis suggest that trainers and trainees must complete different tasks that only exist in the training management. While the data collection has revealed some functions, it was focused on analyzing how VA functions of other HR-related areas can result in technology affordances in trainee management. Thus, a second avenue for future research would be to identify if there can be more tasks specific to the trainee management process that a VA can support and eventually generate specific affordances. Finally, the interviewees perceived that a VA cannot be used to generate knowledge automatically as today's VA technology is not yet able to extract complex information from different data sources, but some interviewees also expressed that in case it would be possible, automating the process would be a great addition to the VA's functionality. Hence, the third proposal for further research would be to study the possibility of automating the process of extracting information from different data sources to generate new knowledge for the organization.

REFERENCES

Asher, N. (2017). *A Warmer Welcome: Application of a Chatbot as a Facilitator for New Hires Onboarding* [Master Thesis]. Linnaeus University.

Avgerou, C. (2013). Social mechanisms for causal explanation in social theory based IS research. *Journal of the Association for Information Systems, 14*(8), 3. doi:10.17705/1jais.00341

Baird, A., & Maruping, L. M. (2021). The Next Generation of Research on IS Use: A Theoretical Framework of Delegation to and from Agentic IS Artifacts. *Management Information Systems Quarterly, 45*(1), 315–341. doi:10.25300/MISQ/2021/15882

Baskerville, R., Myers, M., & Yoo, Y. (2019). Digital First: The Ontological Reversal and New Challenges for Information Systems Research. *Management Information Systems Quarterly, 44*(2), 509–523. doi:10.25300/MISQ/2020/14418

Battineni, G., Chintalapudi, N., & Amenta, F. (2020). AI chatbot design during an epidemic like the novel coronavirus. *Health Care, 8*(2), 154. PMID:32503298

Birzniece, I. (2011). Artificial intelligence in knowledge management: Overview and trends. *Computer Science, 46.*

Boyatzis, R. E. (1998). Transforming qualitative information: Thematic analysis and code development. *Sage (Atlanta, Ga.).*

Brandtzaeg, P. A., & Følstad, A. (2017). Why People Use Chatbots. *Proceedings of the International Conference on Internet Science*, 377–392. 10.1007/978-3-319-70284-1_30

Buzko, I., Dyachenko, Y., Petrova, M., Nenkov, N., Tuleninova, D., & Koeva, K. (2016). Artificial Intelligence technologies in human resource development. *Computer Modelling and New Technologies, 20*(2), 26–29.

Cao, Z. (2010). Research on the Intelligent Human Resource Management Information System. *Proceedings of the International Conference on E-Product E-Service and E-Entertainment*, 1–4. 10.1109/ICEEE.2010.5660205

Carter, M., & Grover, V. (2015). Me, My Self, And I (T). *Management Information Systems Quarterly, 39*(4), 931–958. doi:10.25300/MISQ/2015/39.4.9

Carter, M., Petter, S., Grover, V., & Thatcher, J. B. (2020). IT Identity: A measure and empirical investigation of its utility to IS research. *Journal of the Association for Information Systems, 21*(5), 1313–1342. doi:10.17705/1jais.00638

Eisenhardt, K. M. (1989). Building theories from case study research. *Academy of Management Review*, *14*(4), 532–550. doi:10.2307/258557

Faraj, S., & Azad, B. (2012). The materiality of technology: An affordance perspective. In P. M. Leonardi, B. A. Nardi, & J. Kallinikos (Eds.), *Materiality and Organizing: Social Interaction in a Technological World*. Oxford University Press. doi:10.1093/acprof:oso/9780199664054.003.0012

Gal, U., Blegind, J. T., & Lyytinen, K. (2014). Identity Orientation, Social Exchange, and Information Technology Use in Interorganizational Collaborations. *Organization Science*, *25*(5), 1372–1390. doi:10.1287/orsc.2014.0924

German Federal Ministry for Economic Affairs and Energy. (2017). *The dual vocational training system in Germany*. Available online at https://www.bmwi.de/Redaktion/EN/Downloads/duales-ausbildungsprogram.pdf?__blob=publicationFile&v=3

Gonda, D. E., Luo, J., Wong, Y., & Lei, C. (2018). Evaluation of Developing Educational Chatbots Based on the Seven Principles for Good Teaching. *Proceedings of the 2018 IEEE International Conference on Teaching, Assessment, and Learning for Engineering (TALE)*, 446–453. 10.1109/TALE.2018.8615175

Harpelund, C. (2019). *Onboarding: Getting New Hires off to a Flying Start*. Emerald Group Publishing. doi:10.1108/9781787695818

Hill, J., Ford, W. R., & Farreras, I. G. (2015). Real Conversations with Artificial Intelligence: A Comparison between Human - Human Online Conversations and Human - Chatbot Conversations. *Computers in Human Behavior*, *49*, 245–250. doi:10.1016/j.chb.2015.02.026

Hu, Y. (2019). *Do People Want to Message Chatbots? Developing and Comparing the Usability of a Conversational vs. Menu based Chatbot in Context of New Hire Onboarding* [Master Thesis]. Aalto University, Finland.

Huberman, M., & Miles, M. B. (2002). The Qualitative Researcher's Companion. *Sage (Atlanta, Ga.)*.

Io, H. N., & Lee, C. B. (2017). Chatbots and conversational agents: A bibliometric analysis. *Proceedings of the IEEE International Conference on Industrial Engineering and Engineering Management (IEEM)*, 215–219. 10.1109/IEEM.2017.8289883

Jantan, H., Hamdan, A. R., & Othman, Z. A. (2010). Intelligent Techniques for Decision Support System in Human Resource Management. *Decision Support Systems*, 261–276.

Jia, Q., Guo, Y., Li, R., Li, Y., & Chen, Y. (2018). A Conceptual Artificial Intelligence Application Framework in Human Resource Management. *Proceedings of the 18th International Conference on Electronic Business (ICEB 2018)*, 106-104.

Kane, G. (2019). The technology fallacy: People are the real key to digital transformation. *Research Technology Management, 62*(6), 44–49. doi:10.1080/08 956308.2019.1661079

Khurana, P., Agarwal, P., Shroff, G., Vig, L., & Srinivasan, A. (2017). Hybrid BiLSTM-Siamese network for FAQ Assistance. *Proceedings of the 2017 ACM on Conference on Information and Knowledge Management*, 537–545. 10.1145/3132847.3132861

Klopfenstein, L. C., Delpriori, S., Malatini, S., & Bogliolo, A. (2017). The Rise of Bots: A Survey of Conversational Interfaces, Patterns, and Paradigms. *Proceedings of the 2017 Conference on Designing Interactive Systems*, 555–565. 10.1145/3064663.3064672

Koeva, K., Nenkov, N., & Dyachenko, Y. (2016). Artificial Intelligence Technologies for Personnel Learning Management Systems. *Proceedings of the International Conference on Intelligent Systems (IS 2016)*, 189–194.

Laranjo, L., Dunn, A. G., Tong, H. L., Kocaballi, A. B., Chen, J., Bashir, R., Surian, D., Gallego, B., Magrabi, F., Lau, A. Y. S., & Coiera, E. (2018). Conversational agents in healthcare: A systematic review. *Journal of the American Medical Informatics Association: JAMIA, 25*(9), 1248–1258. doi:10.1093/jamia/ocy072 PMID:30010941

Lee, A. S., & Baskerville, R. L. (2003). Generalizing Generalizability in Information Systems Research. *Information Systems Research, 14*(3), 221–243. doi:10.1287/ isre.14.3.221.16560

Leonardi, P. M. (2013). Theoretical foundations for the study of sociomateriality. *Information and Organization, 23*(2), 59–76. doi:10.1016/j.infoandorg.2013.02.002

Liao, Q. V., Wen, T. W., Shmueli-Scheuer, M., & Yu, Z. (2019). User-aware conversational agents. *Proceedings of the 24th International Conference on Intelligent User Interfaces: Companion*, 133–134.

Majchrzak, A., & Markus, M. L. (2012). Technology affordances and constraints in management information systems (MIS). In E. Kessler (Ed.), *Encyclopedia of Management Theory*. SAGE.

Massaro, A., & Maritati, V., & Galiano, A. (2018). Automated Self-learning Chatbot Initially Build as a FAQs Database Information Retrieval System: Multi-level and Intelligent Universal Virtual Front-office Implementing Neural Network. *Informatica (Vilnius)*, *42*(4), 515–525.

Meyer von Wolff, R., Masuch, K., Hobert, S., & Schumann, M. (2019). What Do You Need Today? - An Empirical Systematization of Application Areas for Chatbots at Digital Workplaces. *Proceedings of the 25th Americas Conference on Information Systems*.

Mohan, R. (2019). The Chat bot revolution and the Indian HR Professionals. *International Journal of Information and Computing Science*, *6*(3), 489–499.

Nambisan, S., Lyytinen, K., Majchrzak, A., & Song, M. (2017). Digital Innovation Management: Reinventing Innovation Management Research in a Digital World. *Management Information Systems Quarterly*, *41*(1), 223–238. doi:10.25300/MISQ/2017/41:1.03

Nawaz, N., & Gomes, A. M. (2019). Artificial Intelligence Chatbots are New Recruiters. *Artificial Intelligence*, *10*(9), 1–5.

Nezhad, H. R. M. (2015). Cognitive Assistance at Work. *AAAI 2015 Fall Symposium*, 37–40.

Orlikowski, W. (2007). Sociomaterial Practices: Exploring Technology at Work. *Organization Studies*, *28*(9), 1435–1448. doi:10.1177/0170840607081138

Oudeyer, P. Y., Gottlieb, J., & Lopes, M. (2016). Intrinsic motivation, curiosity, and learning: Theory and applications in educational technologies. *Progress in Brain Research*, *229*, 257–284. doi:10.1016/bs.pbr.2016.05.005 PMID:27926442

Patton, M. Q. (2002). Qualitative Research & Evaluation Methods. *Sage (Atlanta, Ga.)*.

Ruan, S., Tham, B. J., Murnane, E. L., Jiang, L., Qiu, Z., & Brunskill, E. (2019). QuizBot: A Dialogue-based Adaptive Learning System for Factual Knowledge. *Proceedings of the 2019 CHI Conference on Human Factors in Computing Systems*. 10.1145/3290605.3300587

Saukkonen, J., Kreus, P., Obermayer, N., Ruiz, Ó., & Haaranen, M. (2019). AI, RPA, ML and Other Emerging Technologies: Anticipating Adoption in the HRM Field. *Proceedings of European Conference on the Impact of Artificial Intelligence and Robotics*, 287–296.

Sekhri, A., & Cheema, J. (2019). The new era of HRM: AI Reinventing HRM functions. *International Journal of Scientific Research and Review*, *7*(3).

Singh, M. P., Agarwal, P., Chaudhary, A., Shroff, G., Khurana, P., & Patidar, M. (2018). Knadia: Enterprise Knowledge Assisted Dialogue Systems Using Deep Learning. *Proceedings of the 34th IEEE International Conference on Data Engineering*, 1423–1434. 10.1109/ICDE.2018.00161

Soto-Acosta, P. (2020). COVID-19 pandemic: Shifting digital transformation to a high-speed gear. *Information Systems Management*, *37*(4), 260–266. doi:10.1080/10580530.2020.1814461

Soutar, K. (2019). *How chatbots can be used to re-engage with applicants during recruitment* [Master Thesis]. Aalto University, Finland.

Tambe, P., Cappelli, P., & Yakubovich, V. (2019). Artificial intelligence in human resources management: Challenges and a path forward. *California Management Review*, *61*(4), 15–42. doi:10.1177/0008125619867910

Tsui, E., Garner, B. J., & Staab, S. (2000). The role of Artificial Intelligence in Knowledge Management. *Knowledge-Based Systems*, *13*(5), 235–239. doi:10.1016/S0950-7051(00)00093-9

Verleger, M., & Pembridge, J. (2018). A Pilot Study Integrating an AI-driven Chatbot in an Introductory Programming Course. *Proceedings of the IEEE Frontiers in Education Conference (FIE 2018)*, 1–4. 10.1109/FIE.2018.8659282

Westberg, S. (2019). *Applying a chatbot for assistance in the onboarding process: A process of requirements elicitation and prototype creation* [Master Thesis]. Linköping University, Sweden.

Winkler, R., & Söllner, M. (2018). Unleashing the Potential of Chatbots in Education: A State-Of-The-Art Analysis. *Academy of Management Annual Meeting*, 1-41. 10.5465/AMBPP.2018.15903abstract

Yawalkar, V. (2019). A Study of Artificial Intelligence and its role in Human Resource Management. *International Journal of Research and Analytical Reviews*, *6*(1), 20–24.

Yin, R. K. (2018). *Case Study Research and Applications: Design and Methods* (6th ed.). SAGE.

ADDITIONAL READING

Abdul-Kader, S. A., & Woods, J. C. (2015). Survey on chatbot design techniques in speech conversation systems. *International Journal of Advanced Computer Science and Applications, 6*(7).

Anderson, C., & Robey, D. (2017). Affordance potency: Explaining the actualization of technology affordances. *Information and Organization, 27*(2), 100–115. doi:10.1016/j.infoandorg.2017.03.002

Areheart, B. A., & Roberts, J. L. (2018). GINA, big data, and the future of employee privacy. *The Yale Law Journal, 128,* 710.

Cappelli, P. (2017). There's no such thing as big data in HR. *Harvard Business Review, 2,* 2–4.

Dietvorst, B. J., Simmons, J. P., & Massey, C. (2018). Overcoming algorithm aversion: People will use imperfect algorithms if they can (even slightly) modify them. *Management Science, 64*(3), 1155–1170. doi:10.1287/mnsc.2016.2643

Gibson, C. B., Dunlop, P. D., Majchrzak, A., & Chia, T. (2021). Sustaining effectiveness in global teams: The coevolution of knowledge management activities and technology affordances. *Organization Science, 33*(3), 1018–1048. doi:10.1287/orsc.2021.1478

Lee, M. K., Kusbit, D., Metsky, E., & Dabbish, L. (2015). Working with machines: The impact of algorithmic and data-driven management on human workers. *Proceedings of the 33rd annual ACM conference on human factors in computing systems,* 1603-1612. 10.1145/2702123.2702548

Majchrzak, A., & Markus, L. (2012). *Technology Affordances and Constraint Theory of MIS.* Sage.

Marchington, M., & Grugulis, I. (2000). Best practice human resource management: Perfect opportunity or dangerous illusion? *International Journal of Human Resource Management, 11*(6), 1104–1124. doi:10.1080/09585190050177184

Mitchell, A. (2021). Collaboration technology affordances from virtual collaboration in the time of COVID-19 and post-pandemic strategies. *Information Technology & People.* Advance online publication. doi:10.1108/ITP-01-2021-0003

Ramlall, S. (2004). A review of employee motivation theories and their implications for employee retention within organizations. *The Journal of American Academy of Business, Cambridge, 5*(1/2), 52–63.

Rosengren, C., Ottosson, M., Daniels, J., Gregory, K., & Cottom, T. M. (2016). Employee monitoring in a digital context. *Digital sociologies*, 181-194.

Schoorman, F. D. (1988). Escalation bias in performance appraisals: An unintended consequence of supervisor participation in hiring decisions. *The Journal of Applied Psychology*, *73*(1), 58–62. doi:10.1037/0021-9010.73.1.58

Shawar, B. A., & Atwell, E. (2007). Different measurement metrics to evaluate a chatbot system. *Proceedings of the workshop on bridging the gap: Academic and industrial research in dialog technologies*, 89-96. 10.3115/1556328.1556341

KEY TERMS AND DEFINITIONS

Artificial Intelligence (AI): It is the technology that allows machines to interact with humans, data, and the whole business ecosystem. It has the capacity to feel, think, act, and learn. It also can see, hear, speak, understand gestures, recognize sounds, and process images using inputs from sensors such as cameras and microphones. Moreover, it has the ability to understand and analyze information to make logical decisions.

Chatbot: It is a computer program designed to simulate conversation with human users.

Digital Innovation: Represents a strategic initiative organized and realized within the IT services function in an organization.

Human Resource Management: It is a strategic approach to manage employees effectively and efficiently in an organization in a way that they help their organization to gain and maintain a competitive advantage.

Technology Affordances: Are provided through complex interaction of technology materiality, human agency, and the contextual procedures within an organizational environment.

Trainee Management Software: Represents a streamlined version of what an employee already does daily. It is designed to organize and optimize the delivery of the training activity.

Virtual Assistant: Represents a more advanced version (AI-based) of a regular chatbot that can engage with a customer in a manner that mimics a human.

ENDNOTE

[1]   A detailed account of the literature review methodology is available upon request.

Chapter 3
Adaptation to Pandemic Through Universal Access to Innovative Technologies:
ICT Access for Future Pandemics

Abiodun Alao
ⓘD https://orcid.org/0000-0001-6288-2991
University of Johannesburg, South Africa

Roelien Brink
University of Johannesburg, South Africa

ABSTRACT

The implementation of information technology into the healthcare sector is inevitable to prevent future pandemics, as COVID-19 had a huge impact on healthcare services and humanity. Therefore, universal access to technologies in managing unforeseen pandemics is necessary. The objective of this study is to examine how healthcare institutions use innovative technologies to address future pandemics. The study reflects on one of the targets of Sustainable Development Goal (SDG) 9, which is to significantly increase access to IT and strive to provide universal and affordable technology access to global citizens by 2030. This is to obtain the vision to work towards building an open, inclusive, and digital network for a secure future. This study used discourse analysis to critically analyze the use of innovative technologies like AI systems, machine learning, the internet, mobile phones, mobile computing, and other technologies adopted to manage the global pandemic. This study recommends to policymakers the importance of universal access to innovative technology to address pandemic issues.

DOI: 10.4018/978-1-7998-9418-6.ch003

INTRODUCTION

Many pandemics mostly occur from natural or bio-terrorism like the present coronavirus 2 (SARS - CoV-2) pandemic, a human immunodeficiency virus that has influenced the use of innovative technology tools to be an essential commodity for human sustainability (Mamelund, 2017). The previous global widespread of infectious diseases have caused global pandemics, such as COVID-19, Ebola, Spanish Flu, Bird Flu, Aids, and Tuberculosis (TB) (World Health Organisation, 2011).

Information Technology (IT) tools have become inevitable, and access to universal health coverage (UHC) is essential globally for effective communication and information dissemination on unexpected health issues similar to the present coronavirus pandemic (Sein, 2020; Dhaliwal, 2018). The information and communication and technology (ICT) based convergence and digitalization era of the Fourth Industrial Revolution (4IR) which emerged from the integration of the preceding Third Industrial Revolution (3IR) further enhanced the use of innovative technology for the management and continuous operation of healthcare institutions and different organizations during the COVID-19 pandemic that has been an almost instantaneous response (Voskoglou, 2016).

In addition, the benefits of using innovative technology include preventive measures and digital solutions using open data, hackathons and events, useful links, big data, and other IT resources to tackle universal access (Sein, 2020). The challenges that arise from future pandemics can be rectified through

The implementation of information technology access to a huge database resource from websites and useful platforms that can be used to analyze the evolution of prior and future pandemics (Hussain et al.,

2021). Innovative technologies in healthcare institutions can provide an increased collaboration opportunity with international bodies, government, the healthcare sector, private organizations, and public administrations (European Commission-DIGIT, 2020).

Innovative technologies maintain and transmit information about healthcare issues that can be vital to human sustainability (Young, 2020). In this context, innovative technology tools can be used to address issues about the past, present, and future pandemics that can constrain human health development (CSEA, 2020). The objective of this study is to examine how healthcare institutions can use innovative technologies to access significant information about future pandemics.

This study focuses on the importance of innovative technologies such as Artificial Intelligence (AI), machine learning, mobile phone, the internet, mobile computing, satellite technology, and other technologies to manage future pandemics. Innovative technologies are effective in healthcare institutions and society, because they have a great advantage over existing infrastructure, such as large databases and the internet, which reduces the costs of old and new activities on a large scale. (ICTworks, 2022).

Also, innovative technology, such as Artificial Intelligence (AI) systems, is presumed to be a transformational technology that provides advanced innovation that can be utilized to improve healthcare services. Artificial Intelligence (A1) systems are presumed to provide extraordinary services in healthcare institutions and may transform many social and institutional structures (ICTworks, 2022). The emergence of artificial intelligence and knowledge management has transformed the process of information management, knowledge management, and database management to understand and classify clinical documentation (ICTworks, 2022).

In addition, natural language processing (NLP) is a branch of computer science, and artificial intelligence (AI) gives computers the capacity to understand texts and spoken words similar to humans (ICTworks, 2022). NLP systems can analyze unstructured clinical notes on hospital patients, giving an in-depth insight into improving methods, understanding quality, and better results for hospital patients. Therefore, this study posed the research question: How can healthcare institutions use innovative technologies to manage past and future pandemics? This study presents an appraisal of studies that focus on how innovative technologies can be used to address the havoc of pandemics using a discourse analysis approach to explore the adoption of information technologies for a secured future against harmful pandemics.

PROBLEM STATEMENT

Several healthcare institutions globally have struggled to manage the unforeseen pandemics that have disrupted the economic activities of many countries. For healthcare institutions to manage patients with infectious diseases, medical staff must prepare for the uncertainties of health issues caused by the pandemic. Therefore, healthcare institutions need to prepare and manage clinical health issues, manage data, make decisions, disaster planning, and risk control strenuously due to the lack of adequate access to innovative technologies (Hussain et al., 2021). Hence, the provision of information technology tools is necessary because it can enhance healthcare services and play a significant role in fighting pandemics using many tactics, like the development of vaccines that prevent infection, chromosome mapping, forecasting, and protect medical amenities from cyber-attacks (Hussain et al., 2021).

APPRAISAL OF TECHNOLOGIES FOR PANDEMICS

This study iterates on how technologies are used to address issues about the past, present, and future pandemics. The advancements in technologies to address and inform people about the unexpected problem caused by the prior and future pandemics were examined. The present pandemic has forced the healthcare system to use technologies to create awareness of the severity of infectious diseases, and has allowed people to actively want to be informed about potential infections that can be dangerous to human existence (Sein, 2022). This study addresses how innovative technologies can be used to inform healthcare institutions about past pandemics similar to the present COVID-19 pandemic, and the dangers that might arise from these hazardous infectious diseases that might be harmful to humanity. This study recommends how healthcare institutions and scientists can better combat unexpected pandemics using innovative technologies to prepare for future pandemics or epidemics of diseases that can spread more effectively globally (World Economic Outlook, 2018; World Health Organisations, 2011).

Innovative technologies can be utilized to empower, educate, warn and mobilize health care institutions about how to significantly reduce the impact of infectious diseases on humanity (Mamelund, 2017). For example, countries that belong to North Atlantic Treaty Organization (NATO) have adopted measures to respond to pandemic situations (WHO, 2011). NATO ensures that a common language and mobile unit works out logistics that allows them to manage unexpected pandemic situations, such as food, fuel, and radio frequencies, deployed quickly in uncertainties (WHO, 2020, 2011). Also, innovative technologies can be used to monitor the outbreak of pandemics and provide many innovative solutions and provides capabilities to increase mobile penetration that have identified to monitor future virus outbreaks (World Economic Forum, 2015). Henceforth, innovative technologies are used as technical imperatives to evaluate and detect new treatments for epidemics and prevent the widespread of diseases in people in the future. The World Economic Forum (2015) listed various innovative technologies measures that was used to manage and identify the widespread of hazardous infectious outbreaks as follows:

- **Computer games:** The use of computer games and applications, such as germ war games can be used to identify a possible pandemic outbreak. Several technical trials are ongoing that can form part of this early response. These technical trials form part of techniques used to identify early responses to possible pandemic using innovative technologies that develop applications that are used to initiate appropriate war games that validate the readiness for prospective epidemics.

- **Mobile phone messaging:** Innovative technologies like mobile phones are used to message a large population to spread information about an epidemic, possible precautions, and ways to manage infectious diseases. For example, non-government organizations and the government of many countries have used mobile phones to spread information about hazardous infections and how to prevent the spread. Technologies can be used to trail or examine data from mobile phone towers to track mobile users within proximity to an infected person or virus location.

- **Telecommunication information dissemination:** Telecommunication organizations have used innovative technology to develop projects entailed "Text to Change" in partnership with Airtel to send a range of text messages to the Sierra Leone population on ways to prevent the widespread of contagious diseases, such as Ebola. Different countries globally adopt technology programs to connect and update the population of their country about information, treatment, activities, and hazardous changes to existing pandemics.

- **Use of mobile computing:** Innovative technology like mobile computing is used for tested technology programs, for example, Oppia browser, a step-by-step learning process used to master any skills, and MMEI e-buddi, a 3D application and tablet-based program developed by Total Monkery and PUPSMD. This program provided additional expertise to deploy and adapt simulation-based training in an isolated setting about health information, treatment, and existing diseases. Learners use the program for local graphics to improve the authenticity of the simulation, even modelling avatars on the best local trainers. Hence, innovative technologies provide established communication links and materials customized to train employees in the medical field. These technological tools are used to provide e-learning and updates about the medical field to health workers. Also, other than health workers, the local population is taught how to continue treating themselves after medical emergencies and leaving hospitalization, especially in remote areas where mobile devices are not effective.

- **Effective technology connectivity:** The increased growth in advanced technology connectivity has enabled enhanced technical capabilities globally. The emergence of the fourth industrial revolution (4IR) has been the key enabler for innovative technologies such as Artificial Intelligence, machine learning, robotics, the Internet of Things (IoT), 3D printing, genetic engineering, quantum computing etc are vital for the operations of healthcare institutions and the economic development of many countries globally (Voskoglou, 2016). Also, telemedicine technology is used to substitute medical services during the pandemic outbreak situations. Additionally, innovative technologies can enhance communication networks for the early detection of infectious diseases or an epidemic by preventing the spread of the pandemic.

- **Satellite technology:** This includes the provision of satellite technology that can be used as a satellite-based solution to provide bandwidth, such as Wi-Fi 5G, 4G, 3G, or 2.5G technologies in communities and healthcare institutions that lack access to technologies.

- **Mobile internet capabilities:** The mobile internet is used to provide internet access and hardware solutions like SupaBRCK designed to link people anywhere online using Wi-Fi to provide internet connectivity and implemented in African communities with limited power supplies. The mobile internet device is used to provide access in remote communities or health clinics in situations of power outages using 3G communications.

INNOVATIVE TECHNOLOGY TOOLS USED TO PROVIDE HEALTH INFORMATION

In support, CSEA Africa (2020) and Louraoui et al. (2020) report an upsurge in the adoption of technology solutions and e-learning platforms that provide information to people about health issues that can cause dangers and challenges during the pandemics. These adopted digital solutions allow online learning, such as software development and mobile applications, and digital health libraries that offer free open resources and applications (i.e., Mobile for Android). Information technologies have been used to manage infectious diseases and pandemics, such as COVID-19, Ebola, HIV, bird flu, Tuberculosis, Aids, etc.

Healthcare institutions can adopt various measures to tackle infectious diseases; using innovative technologies to inform societies about various pandemics. In developing countries, innovative technologies such as artificial intelligence, advanced machine learning, mobile phones, large online datasets, the internet, language processing, digital health technology, low-cost computing resources are advanced technologies that can help public-health respond to unexpected pandemics if the government of these regions can support the health systems in sponsoring public health faculties (Budd et al., 2020).

TECHNOLOGY MEASURES USED TO MANAGE THE PANDEMIC

The improvement in digitalization has allowed artificial intelligence (AI) to transform healthcare practice in many countries in developed countries (Yu, Beam, & Kohane, 2018). The healthcare institutions in these regions take measures to manage prospective pandemics due to prior experience that has prepared the health sector on ways to manage the epidemics that might arise when least expected. The government of many countries realized the lapses caused by prior pandemics were managed, and has endeavoured to properly prepare and prevent another outbreak.

In some countries globally, innovative technologies were used to tackle the coronavirus and prepare the medical practice for any outbreak of pandemics in the future. Also, innovative technologies such as mobile computing, mobile communications, and broadband internet have been of great significance to disseminate information on preventive measures and how to manage pandemics like the coronavirus, Ebola, bird flu, HIV, Tuberculosis, and other infectious diseases (Alao & Brink, 2022).

ADVANTAGES OF ADVANCED TECHNOLOGIES IN THE HEALTHCARE INSTITUTION

According to Baumgart (2020) and ICTworks (2022), innovative technologies provide various means which can be utilized by the healthcare organization and society regarding the pandemic uncertainties, as follows:

- **Healthcare information data transfer:** Healthcare institutions can use the internet of things (IoT), a technological innovation software with sensors processing ability to connect to other technologies to exchange data with other devices and systems over the internet or other communications networks.
- **Improving healthcare capability:** Innovative technology, such as artificial intelligence (AI) can play a significant part to improve medical practice by augmenting healthcare capability, satisfying gaps in human expertise by enhancing medical output, and boosting disease surveillance to develop a system that can be used to predict imminent occurrences of diseases.
- **Access to digital health care**: The adoption of technology such as AI in healthcare systems is significant, as it can be used to identify comprehensive data information about people at risk of infectious diseases in healthcare systems to prevent an outrageous spread of suspected diseases.

- **Provides location information:** Artificial intelligence (AI) and machine learning systems can assist healthcare institutions to have access to vital information by automating complex assessments to predict mass grave locations of victims with medical risk.

- **Provision of e-learning tutoring:** Artificial intelligence (AI) can be developed to develop intelligent tutoring systems that medical practices can use to access a huge scale database that stores information about the past and prospective pandemics and learn how to manage the hazard of pandemics.

- **Provides economy growth:** Artificial intelligence (AI) provides the economy of many countries' growth in government and private organizations, such as healthcare systems development through probable higher productivity, provides innovation and increases economic building blocks.

- **Internet adoption:** It is crucial for the health systems in developing countries to adopt online education platforms operated by high-speed bandwidth. Many healthcare institutions still use traditional classroom-based learning, instead of e-learning techniques. The Medical Practice of Health can deliver online lectures on IoT and cloud using internet-enabled smartphones to stream the lecture on the web to health workers. This method could be used for remote learning during the disruption of a pandemic that causes a lockdown.

DISADVANTAGES OF ADVANCED TECHNOLOGY

Technologies have revolutionized most aspects of humanity and are used for interventions and risk management. However, the perception of advanced technologies, such as AI systems and other technologies is societally biased due to the complexity involved in using this technology program. ICTworks (2022) listed the technology disadvantages as follows:

- **Data Security:** Digital technology is a massive amount of data that is collected and stored in a safe place. For example, private information about individuals or organizations. Data can be difficult to store safely, and a breach of information can leak sensitive information into the hands of criminals, terrorists, business rivals, foreign adversaries, or other malign entities.

- **Surveillance and loss of privacy:** Technologies such as AI algorithms boost surveillance and threaten privacy. There should be increased investment in privacy and protection data, to expand the capacity to mitigate harm using cybersecurity programming. i.e. AI-powered facial recognition software allows closed-circuit TV systems to track a person's location. This is not ideal because privacy is vital to other fundamental rights. For example, freedom of expression and association.

- **Crime and Terrorism:** The internet is a dangerous place that attracts malevolent forces to operate due to anonymity of users. For example, terrorist attacks through social media, the exchange of vital information like photos, videos, and other healthcare information.

- **Job and tax revenue loss through automation:** With the increased use of advanced technologies, such as machine learning and AI systems in many sectors, this can lead to widespread of automation in product manufacturing and services instead of human labour. This will encourage high skilled knowledge-based roles. Although, there are instances when AI systems may shift the scope of work and jobs, as the implantation of robots can partly complement human labour, through higher-skilled and higher-paid tasks.

- **Complexity:** The issue of advanced technologies. For example, computer devices, mobile phones, and machines include complex settings that are complicated to use. Also, laptops have minor glitches in operations that cost both time and expense.

- **Privacy Concerns:** The issue of privacy concerns in the digital world is vital, especially, as there are pending issues about the dangers of personal data theft. For example, it can be difficult to manage personal information in both private and public environments. The use of smartphones and digital cameras to watch videos, footage, and photographs to post online can give internet invaders or hackers the opportunity to use your photos and videos without permission, as these online materials can be used in social media networks or blogs.

- **Social Disconnect:** There is an increased social disconnect and isolation due to the use of technological devices at home and healthcare institutions, as people prepare to socialize and communicate using digital devices than in real-life contact.

CONCEPTUAL MODEL

The adaptation of technologies in healthcare institutions is essential for the functionality of all health services to identify, manage and prevent the possible spread of the pandemic. Many health practices are unable to provide essential health services to patients due to the lack of medical infrastructure in both local and national health providers. Therefore, innovative technologies need to be made available to the medical field to not only avert critical health problems from sudden pandemic emergencies, but also health ideas that can be adopted to improve health services and limit the severity of the pandemic. This study developed a conceptual model to explain how policymakers can implement policies that will facilitate the adoption of innovative technologies to improve health services in the medical field.

The study discussed how healthcare institutions can use innovative technologies to identify, prevent and manage future pandemics (see **Figure 1**), from scholarly reviews that focused on the adaptation of technologies as a preventive measure to manage the widespread pandemics in the future.

Figure 1. Conceptual model for this study

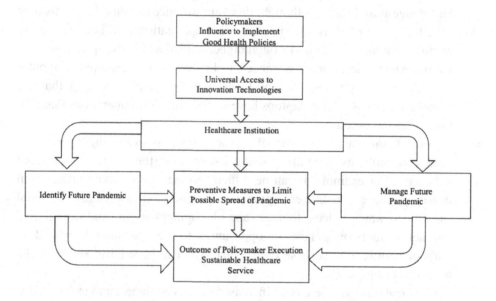

METHODOLOGY

This study adopted discourse analysis as the methodology to scrutinize the use of information technology for the adaption of future pandemics in the healthcare system (Gill, 2000). The study evaluated studies from scholars and reports from international organizations such as the World Economic Forum, websites, blogs, health documents, and a descriptive report of the concept of using advanced technology adoption in managing future pandemics (Gill, 2000). We focused on the effects of past, present, and future pandemics by compiling scholarly health reports. This study allowed the researchers to examine how prior pandemics were tackled using innovative technologies, and health policy materials to limit the spread of the pandemic. The study also examined the list of studies on the adaptation of innovative technologies to achieve universal health coverage in the healthcare institutions (see **Table 1**).

Table 1. List of scholarly publications on the adoption of technologies in healthcare institutions

S/L	CONCEPTS	THEMES OF DESCRIPTION	REFERENCES
1	The adoption of Machine Learning (ML) and Artificial Intelligence (AI) to manage COVID-19 infection.	The study aims to use Machine Learning (ML) and Artificial Intelligence (AI) to remedy the challenges of COVID-19 infection.	Adetunji et al. (2022). Medical Biotechnology, Biopharmaceutics, Forensic Science and Bioinformatics, 271-287.
2	Using IoT-based smart management for healthcare services.	The study used innovative technologies to manage COVID	Akbarzadeh et al., (2021). IoT-based smart management of healthcare services in hospital buildings during COVID-19 and future pandemics.
3	Utilization of information technology (IT) artefacts for future pandemics.	Using innovative designs for better resilience against health shocks, such as the COVID-19 pandemic.	Pee et al. (2021). Designing for the future in the age of pandemics: A future-ready design research (FRDR) process.
4	Using technologies to control and prevent future pandemics.	The study used science technology to improve the understanding and control of COVID-19 and future pandemics.	Asrar et al., (2021). Can space-based technologies help manage and prevent pandemics?
5	Adoption of ICTs to manage global pandemics.	The study objective focuses on using ICTs to manage global pandemics.	Thilakarathne. (2020). The adoption of ICT-powered healthcare technologies towards managing global pandemics.
6	The use of Artificial Intelligence (AI) for improved Healthcare.	The study focuses on using technologies to sustain quality health services in healthcare institutions.	Olushayo et al (2019). How Can Digital Health (DH) Technologies Contribute to Sustainable Attainment of Universal Health Coverage in Africa? A Perspective.
7	The use of Artificial Intelligence (AI) for universal health coverage in African.	The study focuses on using technologies to provide universal access to the healthcare institution.	Owoyemi et al. (2015). Artificial Intelligence for Healthcare in Africa.

SOLUTIONS AND RECOMMENDATION

The implementation of advanced technologies to maintain the widespread spread of infectious diseases helps healthcare institutions manage the effects of infectious diseases that cause harm to humanity. International organisations used innovative technologies to manage the COVID-19. For example, the World Economic Forum and Medix Global, a personalized one stop shop, mobile health management platform delivered access to optimized healthcare information and good medical care to people globally. World Health Organizations used Strategic Preparedness and Response Plan (SPRP) along with UNHCR Risk Communication and Community Engagement guidance to compile health information and outline the health-specific measures to prepare for the pandemics using online tools (Alao & Brink, 2022; World Economic Outlook; World Health Organization, 2020).

Healthcare institutions need to use innovative technologies to train, manage, provide emergency response, track infection locations to source information on how to tackle past, present, and future pandemics. Also, health information and regulations can be accessed using innovative technologies to manage the uncertainties of the pandemic (Gates, 2020, 2015; General, 2005). Also, healthcare institutions should make efforts to use advanced technologies using Artificial Intelligence (AI) systems, and National Language Processing (NLP) to access information and disseminate large online datasets using advanced machine learning to access vital healthcare information (ICTworks, 2022).

In addition, medical employees can use advanced technologies to access information about future pandemics using broad bandwidth internet to access e-health and e-learning educational materials that can prepare them for inevitable health issues. Additionally, the government needs to invest in health innovation technologies as an essential commodity for society, as good health is a right of citizens of any country. Furthermore, this study recommends to the government of many countries consider establishing new health centres and efficient strong biomedical manufacturing companies in marginalized communities.

Healthcare institutions need to use innovative technologies to optimize health services and educate societies about the harmful nature of pandemics present in their country of domicile. i.e. Healthcare public clinics should be provided with innovative technologies that can provide effective information tools and services in public systems in marginalized communities that cannot afford to own or access technologies.

ISSUES, CONTROVERSIES, PROBLEMS

The pandemics have caused socioeconomic crises, and worsen healthcare institutions are put under strain. This has drastically affected healthcare services, and preventive services are not as swift, and death cases rise beyond expected. The pandemic has crippled the proper functioning of the economy of many countries, caused huge damage, increased socioeconomic tension, and caused inequalities. This has caused many economic meltdowns in many countries globally (World Economic Forum, 2015).

According to the executive director of UNAIDS and Under-Secretary-General of the United Nations, Winnie Byanyima (2022), pandemic expectancies have caused great inequality globally. For instance, every pandemic that occurs is an economic, social, and political crisis that affects the government of many global economies, causing marginalization between the rich and the poor, unequal power, and extreme poverty. This has many people lose their jobs, and small businesses and organizations fold up.

Also, inequality has been built into the global system, as vaccination is not equally distributed. i.e. the distribution of vaccination jabs used for preventive measures from the pandemic is more widely distributed in developed countries than in developing countries due to the segregation and marginalization between developed countries, middle and low-income countries.

Due to the short-term investment in creating solutions to the health issues caused by unexpected pandemics, only a handful of health companies like Pfizer–BioNTech, Oxford–AstraZeneca, Sinopharm BIBP, Moderna, Janssen, CoronaVac, Covaxin, Novavax, Medicago, etc are responsible for the pace of vaccination roll out and production distributed to the healthcare institutions of many countries. Rather, all healthcare institutions, research organizations, and universities should be given the capacity to develop, test, manufacture, and produce medications and vaccination jabs as measures to tackle the problem of insufficient treatment and roll out of vaccinations globally.

FUTURE RESEARCH DIRECTIONS

The study clearly shows the significance of technologies to healthcare institutions which implies that advanced technologies can be used to address future pandemics and assist medical practice to identify possible future health havoc that may be hazardous to humans. Future research directions should focus on how policymakers can implement policies that adequately support public healthcare institutions in providing advanced medical facilities that can improve all-around health services in marginalized communities.

This study suggests policymakers implement policies that can support healthcare institutions to use technologies to manage vital health information necessities about possible infectious diseases, and implement measures like e-learning, workshops, and seminars that can prepare healthcare employees for future pandemics. Also, the government needs to provide infrastructure that supports community-led supported health centres in marginalized communities.

Furthermore, policymakers should support the use of technological applications in local and national healthcare institutions to implement measures that can provide information about how past, present, and future pandemics can effectively be managed to prevent casualties and deaths in an upcoming pandemic in the future. The research suggests policymakers should consider supporting clinics in poor and remote communities by providing ICT development initiatives that can provide free medical training to health workers, increase qualified health workers equipped to manage future pandemics using advanced technologies. Finally, the issue of inequality in access to health technology should be addressed.

CONCLUSION

The overview of prior pandemics has displayed many consequences that greatly affected the economic operations of many countries globally, such as limited government functions, public and private sector management, and organizational productivity. The chapter discusses the significance of innovative technologies on health institutions, because these advanced technologies have acted as intermediaries and provided health services essential in the proper functioning of healthcare institutions. Furthermore, the chapter examined how healthcare institutions need to use innovative technologies, such as AI systems, mobile phones, mobile computing, and other technologies to manage the situations that arise from the pandemic. Also, the study discusses the importance of innovative technologies in managing the risk involved in managing pandemics. Finally, the advantages and disadvantages of the innovative technologies in healthcare institutions were highlighted, and the possible ways in which information technology can provide adequate health services were discussed.

ACKNOWLEDGMENT

We would like to thank the University of Johannesburg for providing the resources used for the write-up of this manuscript. The research work was conducted without funding support.

REFERENCES

Adetunji, C. O., Nwankwo, W., Olayinka, A. S., Olugbemi, O. T., Akram, M., Laila, U., & Esiobu, N. D. (n.d.). Machine Learning and Behaviour Modification for COVID-19. *Medical Biotechnology, Biopharmaceutics, Forensic Science and Bioinformatics*, 271-287.

Alao, A., & Brink, R. (2022). COVID-19 Digital Technology Response in Sub-Saharan African Countries. In Building Resilient Healthcare Systems With ICTs (pp. 74-105). IGI Global.

Akbarzadeh, O., Baradaran, M., & Khosravi, M. R. (2021). IoT-based smart management of healthcare services in hospital buildings during COVID-19 and future pandemics. *Wireless Communications and Mobile Computing*, *2021*, 2021. doi:10.1155/2021/5533161

Anadolu Agency. (2020). *Health, Africa, latest on coronavirus outbreak*. Available at www.aa.com.tr

Asrar, F. M., Saint-Jacques, D., Chapman, H. J., Williams, D., Ravan, S., Upshur, R., & Clark, J. B. (2021). Can space-based technologies help manage and prevent pandemics? *Nature Medicine*, *27*(9), 1489–1490. doi:10.103841591-021-01485-5 PMID:34518675

Budd, J., Miller, B. S., Manning, E. M., Lampos, V., Zhuang, M., Edelstein, M., & Short, M. J. (2020). Digital technologies in the public-health response to COVID-19. *Nature Medicine*, *26*(8), 1–10. doi:10.103841591-020-1011-4 PMID:32770165

Baumgart, D. C. (2020). Digital advantage in the COVID-19 response: Perspective from Canada's largest integrated digitized healthcare system. *NPJ Digital Medicine*, *3*(1), 1–4. doi:10.103841746-020-00326-y PMID:32923691

CSEA Africa. (2020). *Africa's digital technology response strategy to COVID-19*. Centre for the Study of the Economies of Africa. Available at cseaafrica.org

Communicating with Disaster Affected Communities (CDAC) Network. (2018). *Resources for those responding to COVID-19*. Available at www.cdacnetwork.org

Dhaliwal, M. (2018). *To Achieve Universal Health Coverage, We Must Connect the Dots Between Innovation and Delivery*. UHC Coalition. Available online at: https://medium.com/health-for-all/to-achieve-universal-health-coverage-we-must-connect-the-dotsbetween-innovation-and-delivery-2446bf1498ca

European Commission-DIGIT. (2020). *Digital technology response to COVID-19*. Available at https://ec.www.ec.europa.eu/isa2/home_en

Gates, B. (2020). Responding to Covid-19: A Once-in-a-Century Pandemic? *The New England Journal of Medicine, 382*(18), 1677–1679. doi:10.1056/NEJMp2003762 PMID:32109012

Gates, B. (2015). The next epidemic—Lessons from Ebola. *The New England Journal of Medicine, 372*(15), 1381–1384. doi:10.1056/NEJMp1502918 PMID:25853741

General, D. (2005). *Implementation of the international health regulations.* Report of the review committee on the functioning of the International Health Regulations.

Gill, R. (2000). Discourse analysis. *Qualitative Researching With Text, Image, and Sound, 1*, 172-190.

Hussain, S., Hussain, Z., & Sheeraz, M. I. (2021). Challenges of the COVID-19 During Pandemic Situation, The Possible Solutions Using Information Technology. *Journal of Legal. Ethical and Regulatory Issues, 24*, 1–14.

ICTwork. (2022). *Artificial Development and Human Development. Towards a Research Agenda.* Author.

International Development Research Centre (IDRC) Canada. (n.d.). Available at https://www.ictworks.org/wpcontent/uploads/2022/01/Artificial-Intelligence-Human-Development.pdf

Katz, R.L., Callorda, F.M., & Jung, J. (2020). Can Digitalization Mitigate COVID-19 Damages? Evidence from Developing Countries. *Evidence from Developing Countries.*

Louraoui, S. M., Rghioui, M., & El Azhar, A. (2020). Letter to the editor: Medical Student concerns Relating to Neurosurgery Education During COVID-19: An African Experience. World Neurosurgery, 142, 553.

Mamelund, S. E. (2017). Social inequality–a forgotten factor in pandemic influenza preparedness. *Tidsskrift for Den Norske legeforening.*

Olu, O., Muneene, D., Bataringaya, J. E., Nahimana, M. R., Ba, H., Turgeon, Y., & Dovlo, D. (2019). How can digital health technologies contribute to sustainable attainment of universal health coverage in Africa? A perspective. *Frontiers in Public Health, 341*, 341. Advance online publication. doi:10.3389/fpubh.2019.00341 PMID:31803706

Owoyemi, A., Owoyemi, J., Osiyemi, A., & Boyd, A. (2020). Artificial intelligence for healthcare in Africa. *Frontiers in Digital Health, 2*, 6. doi:10.3389/fdgth.2020.00006 PMID:34713019

Pee, L. G., Pan, S. L., Wang, J., & Wu, J. (2021). Designing for the future in the age of pandemics: A future-ready design research (FRDR) process. *European Journal of Information Systems, 30*(2), 157–175. doi:10.1080/0960085X.2020.1863751

Said, B., Hajar, E., & Amine, S. (2020). The COVID-19 outbreak: A catalyst for digitalization in African countries. *The Journal of the Egyptian Public Health Association, 95*(1).

Sein, M. K. (2020). The serendipitous impact of the COVID-19 pandemic: A rare opportunity for research and practice. *International Journal of Information Management, 55*, 102164. doi:10.1016/j.ijinfomgt.2020.102164 PMID:32836630

Thilakarathne, N. N., Kagita, M. K., Gadekallu, T. R., & Maddikunta, P. K. R. (2020). *The adoption of ICT-powered healthcare technologies towards managing global pandemics.* arXiv preprint arXiv:2009.05716.

Voskoglou, M. G. (2016). Problem-solving in the forthcoming era of the third industrial revolution. *International Journal of Psychological Research, 10*(4), 361–380.

Winnie Byanyima. (2022). *How to beat pandemics.* Accessed at https://blogs.lse.ac.uk/covid19/2022/04/06/the-uns-winnie-byanyima-how-to-beat-pandemics/

World Economic Outlook. (2018). *Groups and Aggregates Information.* World Economic Outlook, Database—WEO. Available at https://en.wikipedia.org/wiki/Developing_country#cite_note-107

World Health Organization. (2020). Coronavirus disease (COVID-19): Situation report. WHO.

Yu, K. H., Beam, A. L., & Kohane, I. S. (2018). Artificial intelligence in healthcare. *Nature Biomedical Engineering, 2*(10), 719–731. doi:10.103841551-018-0305-z PMID:31015651

World Health Organization. (2011). *Implementation of the International Health Regulations (2005): report by the Director-General.* World Health Organization.

World Economic Forum. (2015). *Managing the risk and impact of future epidemics: Options for public-private cooperation.* Industry Agenda reports. Available at: https://www3.weforum.org/docs/WEF_Managing_Risk_Epidemics_report_2015.pdf

Young, J. (2020). *Scenes from college classes forced online by COVID-19.* Available at https://www.edsurge.com/news/2020-03-26-scenes-from-college-classes-forced-online-by-COVID-19

Yu, K. H., Beam, A. L., & Kohane, I. S. (2018). Artificial intelligence in healthcare. *Nature Biomedical Engineering*, 2(10), 719–731. doi:10.103841551-018-0305-z PMID:31015651

ADDITIONAL READING

Pillay, Y., & Motsoaledi, P. A. (2018). Digital health in South Africa: Innovating to improve health. *BMJ Global Health*, 3(Suppl 2), e000722. doi:10.1136/bmjgh-2018-000722 PMID:29713513

World Health Organization. (2014). *Compendium of innovative health technologies for low-resource settings: assistive devices, eHealth solutions, medical devices.* World Health Organization.

KEY TERMS AND DEFINITIONS

3IR: Third industrial revolution.

4IR: Fourth industrial revolution.

AI: Artificial intelligence.

COVID-19 Preparedness: This refers to the preventive measures adopted in public spaces to limit the spread of COVID-19, such as social distancing, facemask to cover coughs and sneezing, quarantining, hand washing, keeping unwashed hands away from the face and ventilation of indoor spaces.

CSEA: Centre for the Study of Economics.

DH: Digital health.

FRDR: Future ready design research.

Future Pandemics: This refers to the possibility of a wide spread of sustained community outbreaks of diseases in a community, country, or continent.

Healthcare Institutions: This refers to health centres that focus on caring for people with medical issues or an aged person, such as hospitals, clinics, medical centres, nursing homes, extended care facilities, convalescent hospitals, health maintenance organizations, hospice care facilities, dialysis facilities, mental health, and addiction treatment centres and many other long-term care hospitals.

Healthcare Systems: This refers to centres designed to meet the health needs of people or communities. Healthcare systems are providers of health care insurance to social care services, public health centres such as hospitals, clinics, community health centres, private and public health facilities, as well as publicly funded healthcare institutions.

Innovative Technologies: This refers to a process of developing new technological characteristics that are significantly improved. These are new technological product innovations or applications that are implemented in the market, e.g., digital contact tracing, Multi-Skilled AI, Messenger RNA Vaccines, etc.

IoT: Internet of things.

IT: Information technology.

ML: Machine Learning.

NATO: North Atlantic Treaty Organization.

NLP: National language processing.

Resilient Healthcare: This refers to the capacity of healthcare institutions to maintain high-quality services and adapt to the challenges and changes that occur at different system levels. This includes health institutions' ability to demonstrate adaptive, absorptive, accessible, and transformative capacities to effectively respond to health system shocks and disturbances.

SDGs: Sustainable Development Goals.

SPRP: Strategic preparedness and response plan.

Sustainable Healthcare Service: This refers to a health system that enhances, restores, maintains health services, and limits negative impacts on the environment, while leveraging opportunities to restore and improve the health institutions to benefit the wellbeing of current and future generations. Sustainable healthcare service delivers high-quality care and positive social impact to a broader population level.

Universal Healthcare Coverage: This refers to a healthcare system in which all people of a country have access to a full range of healthcare services when needed and wherever needed, without financial hardship, such as health rehabilitation, treatment, health promotion, prevention, and palliative care.

UNHCR: United Nations High Commissioner for Refugees.

WEF: World Economic Forum.

WHO: World Health Organisation.

Chapter 4
The Role of Information Technologies to Adapt to a Global Pandemic:
Digitalization Disruption in the New Renaissance

Julia Puaschunder
Columbia University, USA

ABSTRACT

The outbreak of the COVID-19 pandemic has exacerbated the rise of AI, robots, and algorithms in the economy, which is expected to completely disrupt employment patterns. With the advancement of technologies, employment patterns will shift to a polarization between AI's rationality and humanness. Robots and social machines have already replaced people in a variety of jobs. Almost all traditional professions are prospected to be infused with or influenced by AI, algorithms, and robotics in the future. AI and robots offer the luxuries of affordability and democratization of access to services, as they will be—in the long run—commercially more affordable and readily available to serve all humanity. Also, the longevity potential of machines outperforms any human ever having lived. These new technologies also come with the price of overpopulation problems and the potential for misuse and violent action. Just like many other technologies, robots could be misused. This chapter discusses the current trend of digital disruption and its wider societal implications.

DOI: 10.4018/978-1-7998-9418-6.ch004

INTRODUCTION

The introduction of Artificial Intelligence (AI) in our contemporary society imposes historically unique challenges for humankind. The emerging autonomy of AI holds unique potentials of eternal life of robots, AI and algorithms alongside unprecedented economic superiority, data storage and computational advantages. Yet to this day, it remains unclear what impact AI taking over the workforce will have on economic growth. The introduction of AI lacks a theoretical background for standard neoclassical and heterodox economics growth theories with particular attention to the Cambridge Capital Controversy's argument to divide capital components into fluid, hence more flexible (e.g., petty cash, checking account), and more clay, hence more inflexible (e.g., factories and untransferable means of production), components (Puaschunder, 2016).

The contemporary trend of slowbalisation, as the slowing down of conventional globalization of goods, services and Foreign Direct Investments (FDI) flows, and halted globalization due to COVID-19 lead to continuous data transfer rising. These market trends of conventional globalization slowing and prospering AI-related industries are proposed as first market disruption in the wake of the large-scale entrance of AI into our contemporary economy.

In previous work, Puaschunder (2020a) proposed growth in the artificial age to be measured based on two AI entrance proxies of Global Connectivity Index and The State of the Mobile Internet Connectivity 2018 Index. Digitalization was found to be highly significantly positively correlated with the total inflow of migrants and FDI inflow – serving as evidence that the still globalizing rising industries in the age of slowbalisation are connected to AI (Puaschunder, 2020a). Both indices are positively correlated with GDP output in cross-sectional studies over the world (Puaschunder, 2020a). In order to clarify if the found effect is a sign of industrialization, time series of worldwide data reveal that internet connectivity around the world is associated with lower economic growth from around 2000 on until 2017 (Puaschunder, 2020a). A regression plotting Internet Connectivity and GDP per capita as independent variables to explain the dependent variable GDP growth outlines that the effect for AI is a significant determinant of negative GDP growth prospects for the years from 2000 until 2017 (Puaschunder, 2020a). A panel regression plotting GDP per capita and internet connectivity from the year 2000 to explain economic growth consolidates the finding that AI-internet connectivity is a significant determinant of negative growth over time for 161 countries of the world (Puaschunder, 2020a). Internet connectivity is associated with economic growth decline whereas GDP per capita has no significant relation with GDP growth (Puaschunder, 2020a). To cross-validate both findings hold for two different global connectivity measurements (Puaschunder, 2020a). Puaschunder (2020a) put forward a theoretical argument of dividing labor components into fluid, hence more flexible (e.g., AI), and more clay, hence more inflexible (e.g., human labor), components. The inverse relation between digitalization and economic growth is assumed due to the fact that contemporary growth theory measurements are not capturing AI, big data and robotics-led growth (Puaschunder, 2020a). Puaschunder (2020a) advocated for revising growth theories and integrating AI components into growth theory.

This chapter addresses the entrance of AI into economic markets to be modeled into the standard neoclassical growth theory by creating a novel index for representing growth in the artificial age comprised of GDP per capita and AI entrance measured by the proxy of Internet Access percent per country. The world map reveals the parts of the world that feature high GDP per capita and AI-connectivity. The world differences in AI and economic growth become the basis for the argumentation of novel and yet hardly covered inequalities arising from a divide between AI-hubs and areas of the world that are not well-connected but also in light of a widening gap between e-skilled producers of AI and e-unskilled non-users of technology on a more granular level. The discussion closes with a future outlook on the law and economics of AI entrance into our contemporary economies and society in order to aid a successful and humane introduction of AI into our world.

Digitalization and Economic Growth

The introduction of Artificial Intelligence (AI) in our contemporary society imposes historically unique challenges for humankind. The emerging autonomy of AI holds unique potentials of eternal life of robots, AI and algorithms alongside unprecedented economic superiority, data storage and computational advantages.

Yet to this day, it remains unclear what impact AI taking over the workforce will have on economic growth. The introduction of AI lacks a theoretical background for standard neoclassical and heterodox economics growth theories with particular attention to the Cambridge Capital Controversy's argument to divide capital components into fluid, hence more flexible (e.g., petty cash, checking account), and more clay, hence more inflexible (e.g., factories and untransferable means of production), components.

Artificial Intelligence (AI) as intelligence demonstrated by machines, in contrast to the natural intelligence displayed by humans and other animals, poses historically unique challenges on humankind. Contemporary economists estimate the introduction of AI and algorithms into the workforce to be the disruption of the world economy and global society of the millennium. As emerging globally trend, AI is extending its presence at almost all levels of human conduct and thereby raising both – expectations and concerns (Cellan-Jones, 2014; Sofge, 2015; United Nations, 2017). But what the AI revolution will concretely mean for internal economies and their growth prospects, we hardly have any economic information about.

Standard economic growth is captured in growth theories, which are underlying economic development studies (Deaton, 2010; Kuznets, 1973). The history of growth theories features aggregate production function calculus as the extension of the micro-economic production function at a national or economy-wide level. The aggregate production function describes the relationship of the size of an economy's labor force and its capital stock with the level of the country's Gross National Product (GNP). The value of output or national product is thereby captured by the value of the aggregate capital stock and labor force (Jones, 2014). Aggregate production is explained by how capital and labor of an economy contribute to growth (Jones, 1999). Capital stock is usually improved through new investments and decreased by depreciation over time. Labor supply is determined by the change in labor force, for instance through population growth or education.

Growth theory had originally been focused on exogenous growth foremost pioneered in the work of Robert Solow's Growth Model (1956). Solow's growth theory was based on the two factors capital (K) and labor (L), which are argued to drive every economy (Solow, 1956). Derivations include technology into the model insofar as output per effective worker becomes a function of capital per effective worker, whereby international differences are prevalent (Bartelsman, Haltiwanger & Scarpetta, 2013; Comin & Hobijn, 2004). Later Paul Romer (1986, 1987, 1990, 1993, 1994, 2019) integrated the idea of endogenous growth theory into development economics based on ideas, learning as well as research and development as drivers of innovation (Bils & Klenow, 2002; Lucas, 1988, 1999).

With AI entering the workforce, first we need to understand if these innovations will influence capital or labor. It may be the case that capital will drive out labor – for instance if robots are considered as investment in infrastructure that makes human capital unnecessary (Erosa, Koreshkova & Restuccia, 2010). Following a tradition of endogenous growth models, labor needs to be revised into AI components and human labor force (Aghion, Jones & Jones, 2017).

The economic impact of AI on economic growth leads to the demand for introducing AI-related theoretical modifications of capital and labor components of standard growth theory (Acemoglu, 2009a, b; Jones & Olken, 2008). AI should become integrated into capital and labor elements of growth theory as we need a new understanding of labor in the artificial age. For this distinction, the historic Cambridge Capital Controversy may hold valuable inputs how to theoretically determine different parts of labor. The historic Cambridge Capital Controversy, in which two types of capital, putty and clay capital nuances, were introduced to standard neoclassical growth theories, allows deriving inferences to the contemporary labor force transition in the wake of AI entering. We need to define labor elements that are based on AI, which are introduced as putty labor (hence fungible and eternal), and human labor elements, which are more clay (hence inflexible and less fungible) than putty. Standard growth theories of Robert Solow and Paul Romer but also heterodox critiques of the historical Cambridge Capital Controversy, lead to the conclusion for attention to putty (hence flexible and fluid) and clay (hence fixed and bound) parts of capital being influenced by AI. These theoretical insights are proposed to be discussed in the future as for social, economic and legal implications to society and democracy in the artificial age.

The relation of AI and growth is the underlying argument for outlining inequality stemming from the gap between e-skilled and e-unskilled labor that is believed to increase with AI entering the workforce and contemporary reshoring trends in the wake of the slowing of traditional globalization (Piketty, 1997, The Economist, 2019).

The concept of AI is described in order to outline the impact of AI on the contemporary workforce and society. Slowbalisation, or the slowing of conventional globalization measures, as well as COVID-19 market distortions are potentially exacerbating AI-induced market disruptions. AI entering our contemporary workforce started pre-COVID but AI-related industries seem to have grown exponentially and flourish during social distancing and lockdown measures.

The following part of the chapter will outline empirical evidence for growth in the artificial age that is then measured empirically based on two AI entrance proxies of Global Connectivity Index and The State of the Mobile Internet Connectivity 2018 Index around the world in order to make the argument for a cross-sectional inequality in digitalization. A theoretical discussion then also points at more hidden inequalities emerging in the digital age.

In order to address inherent inequalities in innovation-led growth, a new age of inclusion may revise growth theory and integrate AI in standard growth theory. Defining putty and clay aspects of labor in the artificial age will aid in determining inclusive learning as a basis of endogenous growth within the globalized world compound. Future implications of AI entering tomorrow's workforce in regards to inequality stemming from e-skilled and e-unskilled-job categories are discussed and a future societal, economic and legal outlook of AI entering our markets, democracies and society be given (Harberger, 1998; Pritchett, 1997).

Digitalization Measured in Interconnectivity and Artificial Intelligence

Artificial Intelligence (AI) is "a broad set of methods, algorithms, and technologies that make software 'smart' in a way that may seem human-like to an outside observer" (Noyes, 2016). The "human-like" intelligence of machines derives from machines being created to think like humans but at the same time to also act rationally (Laton,

2016; Russell & Norvig, 1995; Themistoklis, 2018). AI is perceived as innovative technology or as the sum of different technological advances as the privilege of the private, technological sector with developing public regulation (Dowell, 2018).

The outbreak of the COVID pandemic has exacerbated the rise of AI, robots and algorithms in the economy, which is expected to completely disrupt employment patterns. With the advancement of technologies, employment patterns will shift to a polarization between AI's rationality and humanness. Robots and social machines have already replaced people in a variety of jobs – e.g., airports smart flight check-in kiosks or self-check-outs instead of traditional cashiers but also in cleaning robotics and self-monitoring healthcare devices. Almost all traditional professions are prospected to be infused with or influenced by AI, algorithms and robotic in the future. For instance, robots have already begun to serve in the medical and health care profession, law and – of course – IT, transportation, retail, logistics and finance, to name a few. Social robotics may also be quasi-servants that overwhelmingly affect our relationships. Already now social robots are beginning to take care of our elderly and children, which rises important questions on the ethical boundaries of algorithms taking over human tasks (Alemi, Meghdari & Saffari, 2017). Not only do AI and robots offer luxuries of affordability and democratization of access to services, as they will be – on the long run – commercially more affordable and readily available to serve all humanity; but also does the longevity potential of machines outperform any human ever having lived (Hayes, 2018). However, these new technologies also come with the price of overpopulation problems and the potential for misuse and violent action. Just like many other technologies, robots could be misused for wars, terrorism, violence and oppression (Alemi et al., 2017; Puaschunder, 2018a).

ARTIFICIAL INTELLIGENCE IN THE AGE OF COVID-19

Contrary to the counter-globalization trends of the past, one area that grew globally and exponentially since 2010 is digitalized data transfer (The Economist, 2019). In the decade prior to COVID-19, an already ongoing digitalization disruption heralded as big data allowed a set of innovative firms, including social media, online commercial platforms, and search engines to reap skyrocketing profits that often remain untaxed (Puaschunder, 2021c). These economic gains are concentrated in areas such as big data hoarding, the sale of behavioral data about consumers, and targeting online audiences with customized advertisement (Puaschunder, 2021c).

In contrast to earlier system-inherent economic turmoil resulting in financial sector induced liquidity constraints, the external COVID shock caused "social volatility" – a collectively depressed mood that largely dampened consumption. The difference to previous systemic recessions can be seen in the rapid recovery of well-managed financial funds – for example, the S&P 500 recovered 50% of its pre-COVID value within the first three months after the crisis and reached an all-time high in August 2020. Deutsche Bank recorded rising earnings during the ongoing coronavirus crisis, with its investment bank branch leading with 43% or 2.4 billion euros revenue (DW, 2020). The clear distinction between COVID-19 profit and loss industries made it possible for today's highly flexible financial world to exchange underperforming market segments – such as oil, public transport, and aviation, face-to-face service sectors such as international hospitality and gastronomy – with outperforming market options – such as pharmaceuticals and emergency devices for healthcare, digital technologies, fintech, artificial intelligence, and big data analytics industries, online retail, automotive and interior design and architecture.

COVID-19 now not only created significant health and security risks, social discrimination, and economic costs, but also brought about unanticipated opportunities. Industries profiting economically from the pandemic are comprised of hygiene, pharmaceuticals, and the medical professions (Lerner, 2020; Agrawal, Ahlawat & Dewhurst, 2020). From an economic perspective, COVID-19 is an external shock that has accelerated ongoing digitalization trends (Puaschunder, 2021a). COVID-19 has perpetuated the online tech world. Physically distant, we became closer digitally than ever before. Worldwide data traffic exploded on a flat digitalized globe. Because of widespread lockdowns, "social distancing" and increased home office work in many industries, social scientists have observed a more widespread acceptance for instant communication tools, social engagement, and entertainment platforms (Corlatean, 2020). We can thus say that certain firms and industries have benefited from the pandemic while many others have suffered from the expenses and burdens of COVID-19 (Aravanis, 2020; Arora, 2020; Dodd, 2020; Kumar & Haydon, 2020). Traditional small businesses appear to be particularly vulnerable (Bartik, Bertrand, Cullen, Glaeser, Luca & Stanton, 2020; Dua, Ellingrud, Mahajan & Silberg, 2020; Kwak, 2020; Price, 2020).

Today's economies around the world are affected by the pandemic and health crisis. Future innovations in the medical field are predestined to be in the realm of digitized health care and self-monitoring with the help of electronic self-measuring devices and modern molecular genetic analyzes. These can make the use of new active ingredients in the field of prevention of serious diseases more efficient.

In post-COVID economies, digitalized hygiene and healthcare are likely to be further advanced as healthier workers around the world will have a competitive advantage (World Economic Forum, 2021). The overall health status of employers will become a precious asset for determining the individual prevalence for a mild or severe COVID disease trajectory. For another, the individual health conscientiousness will influence the likelihood of becoming a "superspreader" at work. Employees that already had the novel coronavirus may have acquired some degree of immunity and may be in a more advantageous position to perform unhindered in the workspace, as will those who have been vaccinated. Elderly and chronically ill patients' passing, and vulnerabilities risks already now change labor market demand towards favoring young, healthier and corona-survivors, who may benefit from a natural immunity and being more virus-resistant.

Employers may be more interested in what category their workforce may fall to plan workplace safety precaution measures when building healthy working conditions (Ecowellness, 2020, 2021). More than ever before in the history of modern workforce do employers nowadays care about the overall well-being and physical interaction of their labor cadre in a hygienic environment. Respective preventive medical care of the workforce and community-building around monitoring of one's own and others' health but also group learning how to enhance hygiene in teams will gain more attention in the COVID-19-struck workplace and will have lasting changes enacted (Ecowellness Group, 2020, 2021).

In light of social distancing mandates and with the growth of scientific evidence derived from algorithms and big data, workers with better access to internet connectivity and AI-human-compatibility (i.e., computer and AI literacy, and related skills) have growing competitive advantages (Ecowellness Group, 2020, 2021). It may also become a matter of survival for large organizations to understand the health of their workers with the help of these novel technologies. On the one hand, employers will need to estimate whether workplace conditions are likely to produce mass outbreaks – such as the ones that, for instance, occurred in the meatpacking industry or luxury tourism cruise ships in several countries (Elliott, 2021; Foster, 2020). On the other hand, and maybe less benignly, employers will want to know whether workers' medical histories, genetic profiles, living arrangements and social habits are likely to result in COVID-19 infection risks and predict trajectory likelihoods based on genetic prevalence derived from big data analyses. With the entry of AI algorithms and insights derived from large data sets in the medical field, they may hope to maintain a healthy workforce through encouraging workers' self-monitoring, while also pro-actively caring for safety through mobile tracking of infected as a means of crowd control, as well as potentially through the use of predictive algorithms (Gelter & Puaschunder, 2021). Much like many employers require drug tests at the hiring stage or periodically, they may seek to use digitalization tools to predict health statuses and working conditions' outcomes to reduce the risk of being put out of business or severely harmed by a COVID-19 outbreak.

Arguably, firms that are better able to use technology to determine and track employees' health status will be the winners in the post-pandemic market. It may be too early to say whether nimble startups and other small- and medium-sized firms will be more likely to succeed, or whether large corporate behemoths with access to large datasets will be more likely to thrive (Gelter & Puaschunder, 2020). Already, however, it is becoming apparent that these novel digitalization opportunities come with the price of a heightened responsibility to protect privacy in retrieving big data inference, ensure access to information and healthcare democratically, secure individuals from discrimination against health status propensities, and back those who are naturally hindered to compete in markets financially and socially (Puaschunder, Gelter & Sharma, 2020a, b).

Artificial Intelligence and Contemporary Growth

The search for the determinants of economic growth has always been at the core of theoretical and empirical developments in the field of economics. Classical economists, such as Adam Smith, David Ricardo, Thomas Malthus and later Frank Ramsey and Joseph Schumpeter (1934) provided explanations for economic growth.

Traditional neoclassical growth theory assumes the presence of exogenous technological shocks as driver of economic growth. In classical, orthodox economics, economic growth is assumed to be exogenously driven based on population, technological improvement and access to natural resources. These models assume a balanced steady state solution and a balanced rate of growth to be constant and equal to the exogenous labor force growth. The Solow-Swan growth model treats capital and labor as main growth input variables that are freely substitutable, as Equation 1 describes:

$$Y = f(K,L), \text{ (Equation 1)}$$

whereby Y stands for economic growth, Y for capital and L for labor. The free substitutability implies that if the price of labor is relatively high compared to capital, then capital can be freely substituted in place of labor until equality is reached once again (Hsieh & Klenow, 2005, 2010). At the steady-state, an increase in capital no longer creates economic growth due to diminishing returns to capital. The only growth opportunity remaining is to invent new technologies and means of production. So, in the long run, the growth of an economy depends on technological progress, which is exogenous within the Solow-Swan framework. The main driving force behind long-run economic growth is thereby always exogenous.

Mankiw, Romer and Weil (1992) augmented the Solow model with exogenous technology shocks. The traditional measure of economy-wide technological change, introduced by Solow (1956), is aggregate total factor productivity. This aggregate total factor productivity is an increase in output that leaves marginal rates of transformations untouched for given inputs, thus a change in total factor productivity is a form of factor-neutral technical change. Klenow and Rodriguez-Clare (1997) proposed several modifications in Mankiw et al. (1992). Problematic appeared the weak robustness of the initial model and that there was a lack in the ability to explain differences in the growth rates (Solow, 1956). The apparent and sudden emergence of a new group of interrelated Asian Tiger (Singapore, Hong Kong, Taiwan and Korea) countries, which exhibited drastic growth from the 1970s, could not be explained by the standard neoclassical Solow model (Hsieh, 2002).

Later, therefore, theories based on endogenous growth emerged, which allowed for sustained per capita growth without resorting to exogenous factors (Arrow, 1962, 1969; Lucas, 1988; Romer, 1986; Uzawa, 1965). Proponent of heterodox endogenous growth theory Roy Harrod (1939) moved away from a static theory of equilibrium towards a more dynamic growth approach by including a warranted rate of growth affected by the state of technology in an economy. The idea of externalities and spillover effects was originally formalized by Arrow (1962), who argued that externalities arising from learning-by-doing and knowledge spillover positively affect labor productivity on the aggregate level of the economy. This idea was picked up by Lucas and Romer in the late 1980s as the endogenization of knowledge and technology could explain the growth that occurred in Asian countries around the 1980s (Hall & Jones, 1999).

The so-called natural rate of growth was derived as a function of labor productivity and population. The natural rate of economic growth was described by Roy Harrod first as increase in any of these factors of production to reflect on labor and capital positively to drive growth yet with a marginally declining utility (Bjork, 1999; Harrod, 1939). Endogenous growth models are built on microeconomic foundations, where households maximize utility subject to budget constraints, while firms maximize profits (Jones, 2004). Endogenous growth theories include human capital development, knowledge spillovers as well as research and development effects (Aghion & Howitt, 1992; Grossman & Helpman, 1991a, b; Romer, 1990). Lucas and Romer included spillover effects based on Arrow (1962) and Uzawa (1965), who observed that learning-by-doing and knowledge spillover positively affected labor productivity on the aggregate level of the economy leading to structural change (Matsuyama, 2008; Ngai & Pissarides, 2007; Swiecki, 2017; van Neuss, 2019). Romer (1986) started with persistent growth explained by the impact of externalities on economic development (Krueger, 1997). Lucas (1988), who referred to Uzawa (1965), emphasized human capital creation as a source of growth. Uzawa (1965) and Lucas (1988) built a human capital model with education, in which the total output depends on both physical and human capital. Romer (1990) considered the creation of new knowledge as a source of growth based on Uzawa (1965), who emphasized human capital creation as a source of growth. The Lucas-Romer models are dynamic competitive general equilibrium models that are underpinned by explicit specifications of preferences and technology. For the sake of simplicity, all industries are assumed alike. As a result, each industry will employ similar amounts of capital and labor. The aggregate production function is given by

$$Y = AK^\alpha L^{1-\alpha}, \text{ (Equation 2)}$$

whereby A stands for the level of technology, which is a positive constant and K represents volume of capital. K embodies both physical and human capital. Lucas (1988) and Romer (1986) include knowledge (human capital) in their respective models to embody technological change (Kortum, 1997). The growth in human capital is what spurs technological change within the model (Jones, 2016). Romer (1986) suggests that investment in research and development, along with the given state of technology, will spur innovation that leads to growth (Kremer, 1993). Lucas (2009) emphasizes that human capital can grow from schooling as well as learning-by-doing.

Romer (1990), Grossmann and Helpman (1991a, b) considered the creation of new knowledge as a source of growth. Aghion and Howitt (1992, 1998) added the Schumpeterian (1989) process of creative destruction based on research and development models (Romer, 1990). Externalities from public infrastructure were integrated by Barro (1990, 1991) and Futagami, Morita & Shibata (1993). The distribution of human capital and economic growth as well as inequality in the physical to human capital accumulation were outlined by Galor and Tsiddon (1997) and Galor and Moav (2004). Kaldor (1961) emphasized that there are wide differences in the rate of growth of productivity across countries. Lucas and Moll (2014) augment growth theories with knowledge growth and productivity-increasing ideas through social interaction as well as time allocation preferences for work. Lagakos, Moll, Porzi, Qian & Schoellman (2016) add information about lifecycle wage growth across countries.

The question of whether the natural growth rate is exogenous, or endogenous to demand lies at the heart of the debate between neoclassical economists and heterodox post-Keynesian economists (Hausmann, Pritchett & Rodrik, 2005). While endogenous growth theories appear more common to describe contemporary growth, endogenous growth models lack clear defining characteristics of the process, in which knowledge transforms into technological change (Manuelli & Seshadri, 2014). Both growth model theories are built on problematic assumptions of micro-foundations, such as that all firms and individuals are identical and that there is a single-sector economy with one labor market. There is an ignorance of historical and social contexts and an absence of a systemic analysis of conditions of accumulations or the socio-economic correlates of growth processes, which post-Keynesian economists address. The use of an aggregate production function was not justifiable theoretically after the attacks by Sraffa, Robinson, Pasinetti and Garegnani during the Cambridge Capital Controversy.

The Cambridge Capital Controversy was a debate between Cambridge in the United Kingdom and Cambridge in the United States, which started in the 1950s and lasted into the 1960s (Piketty, 2016). At the core of the debate was the nature and role of capital goods and a critique of the neoclassical vision of the aggregate production and distribution functions (Tcherneva, 2011). Joan Robinson, Nicholas Kaldor, Luigi Pasinetti, Piero Sraffa and Richard Kahn at the University of Cambridge in the United Kingdom argued for a heterodox economics opening of the production function and attention to different kinds of capital contrary to the neoclassical version of economics addressed by Paul Samuelson, Robert Solow and Franco Modigliani at the Massachusetts Institute of Technology (MIT) in Cambridge, Massachusetts in the United States.

Piero Sraffa and Joan Robins initially set off the Cambridge Capital Controversy by pointing out in the literature that there was an inherent measurement problem in terms of capital. Capitalist income (total profit or property income) is defined as the rate of profit multiplied by the amount of capital, but the measurement of the 'amount of capital' involves adding up incomparable physical objects (Caselli & Feyrer, 2007). Robinson argued, that capital cannot be added up independently of the prices of those goods. Sraffa pointed out that this financial measure of the amount of capital is determined partly by the rate of profit. A falling profit rate has a direct effect on the amount of capital; it does not simply cause greater employment of it. In addition, the Cambridge camp in the United Kingdom pointed at the neoclassical assumption of the mobility of capital. Parts of capital were assumed to be putty – flexible, movable and completely fungible. Other parts of capital were described to be clay – more bound, such as capital sunk in production sights or factories or production means or large machinery and industry. As a result of the Cambridge Capital Controversy, Paul Samuelson rejected his previously held view that heterogeneous capital could be treated as a single capital good but rather pursued multi-sectoral models (Dray & Thirlwall, 2011).

Several economists have repeatedly argued that the capital-theoretical problems reappear in such models in a different form (Garegnani, 2008; Petri, 2009; Schefold, 2005). The controversy shed light at the problem to assume capital as a homogenous concept and opened up a multi-faceted view of capital in growth theories. However, the problems of heterogeneous capital goods have yet been ignored in the rational expectations revolution and in virtually all econometric work persist (Burmeister, 2000). To this day, we only had an opening of capital for putty and clay aspects, yet no discussion of homogenous labor components. The entrance of AI appears to make this discussion necessary.

Globalization led to an intricate set of interactive relationships between individuals, organizations and states (Centeno et al., 2013). Unprecedented global interaction possibilities have made communication more complex than ever before in history as the whole has different properties than the sum of its increasing diversified parts (Centeno, & Tham, 2012). Electronic outsourcing in the age of artificial intelligence is likely to increase and with this trend a possible societal divide in the 21st century (Puaschunder, 2017a, b, 2018b). The AI revolution appears to be different from conventional technology shocks as the electronic information share and big data generation opens novel and yet unregulated opportunities to reap surplus value from social media consumers (Puaschunder, 2017c). For one, social media space can be sold to marketers who can constantly penetrate the consumer-worker in a subliminal way with advertisements (Puaschunder, 2020a). But also nudging occurs as the big data compiled about the social media consumer-worker can be resold to marketers and technocrats to draw inferences about consumer choices, contemporary market trends or individual personality cues used for governance control, such as, for instance, border protection and tax compliance purposes (Puaschunder, 2020a). Addressing these novel economic growth components in the nudgital society allows to better govern value creation in the digital age, leading to the potentially unequal accumulation and concentration of power following the greater goal to improve capitalism and democracy in the digital artificial age (Puaschunder, 2020a). In the light of growing tendencies of globalization, the demand for an in-depth understanding of how information will be shared around the globe and artificial intelligence hubs may evolve in economically more developed parts of the world has gained unprecedented momentum (Banerjee & Newman, 1993; Kremer, Rao & Schilbach, 2019). In addition, robotics and AI self-learning algorithms appear to resemble more human features than conventional technologies. The legal status also differs with AI being assumed to be quasi-human. First robots have gained citizenship and the legal codification of AI in common law countries bestows robots quasi-human legal status and applies the civil code in the writing of legal codification to guide on the AI introduction in markets and our contemporary society (Hatmaker, 2017). With these two trends, unprecedented value opportunities from information sharing and AI being considered quasi-human, economic growth in the artificial age may be different than neoclassical growth theory would suggest. If considering that AI takes over traditional labor and leads to a reduction of conventional production, conventional growth in the artificial age may decline. Reaping value from unconventional new AI productivity may not be captured in standard neoclassical growth components of conventional capital and labor – as AI's relation to capital and labor is unclarified. AI seems to resemble or being treated as quasi-human but is very different from labor as for the eternal living capacities and computation power as well as interchangeability.

The artificial intelligence revolution will also expand our concept of time as artificial intelligence has eternal life. 24/7 productivity capacities of AI will change tact and lifespan depreciation rates. Algorithms improving behavioral decision-making biases is also not covered in capital and labor output. Productivity of the sharing economy or reaping value from big data may not be displayed in standard growth components as AI is neither capital nor labor. Sharing information over a mobile app is also neither capital nor labor. Potential effects of AI on economic growth are a replacement of labor with capital as Aghion, Jones and Jones argue in 2017 based on evidence from the field. Yet to this day, there is no clear empirical investigation of AI's impact on ordinary production of goods and services with potential effects on growth rates and income shares (Aghion et al., 2017). While AI may help solve complex problems and save on computation time, the data computation storage may not be integrated or reflected by standard growth theories, for sure not in exogenous but also not so much in endogenous growth theory versions.

Endogenous growth theory may address learning opportunities but may not accurately cope with the novel data storage and computational advantages of AI, which may increase the scope of new production lines while driving trends of reshoring and bringing back production closer to where the design and planning occurs. Reshoring may impact finance and human capital flows (Buera & Shin, 2011; Rajan & Zingales, 1998; Townsend & Ueda, 2006). Human substitution through AI – such as inventing new ideas and new creative technologies – may not be captured properly in contemporary growth theories as well (Lucas & Moll, 2014). AI may become rapidly self-improving and should be seen as a producing singularity that features unbounded machine learning intelligence and economic growth eternally (Aghion et al., 2017). Aghion et al. (2017) put forward a first integration of AI as a separate component within growth theory, so neither capital nor labor. All these features of AI encroaching markets demand for revising growth theories in light of a potential currently ongoing AI market disruption in order to draw inferences on how to revise growth theory in the artificial age.

INCLUSIVE GROWTH IN THE DIGITAL CENTURY

During the 2022 World Economic Forum address of United States Secretary of the Treasury Janet Yellen, the post-COVID-19 economic growth was called for being inclusive and green. In modern supply side economic growth, inclusion and diversity are meant to bring economic growth potential. Inclusion can breed social harmony. A diverse workforce allows diversification of potentials and complementary skills cross-pollination.

At the same time, in today's economy, robots and algorithms are taking over human decision-making tasks and entering the workforce. Most recently, big data has evolved to become a source of major assets. Governments around the world are endeavoring to tax wealth creation from information transfer. This trend currently challenges conventional economic theory to capture growth based on purely capital and labor components. The role of digitalization in the shared economy is not fully captured in conventional growth theory components of capital and labor (Alvarez, Buera & Lucas, 2007).

AI hubs appear to open in some parts of the world that gain from the sharing economy, cryptocurrencies and big data that conventional growth theory may not include (Puaschunder, 2020a). It is therefore proposed that contemporary growth theory should be revised as for integrating growth related to AI. First, it should be theoretically clarified, measured and backtested on data whether AI enhances or lowers capital and/or labor components of standard growth theories. Second, as the data suggests, growth theory should consider labor to be either flexible, as would potentially be AI components, or more inflexible, as would be traditional human labor force. Third, micro-macro and endogenous and exogenous growth theories should integrate a novel component for AI as comprised of machine learning, big data and robotics. The new growth theory proposed is:

$$Yn\left(t\right) = \left(A\left(t\right)K\left(t\right)\right)^{\alpha} \left(A\left(t\right)L\left(t\right)\right)^{\beta} \left(A\left(t\right)I\left(t\right)\right)^{1-\alpha-\beta} \text{ (Equation 3)}$$

whereby $Yn\left(t\right)$ denotes total new production function, $A\left(t\right)$ refers to capital and labor-augmenting technologies or AI knowledge, $K\left(t\right)$ is capital and $L\left(t\right)$ labor. $I\left(t\right)$ represents information, which internet connectivity has made more accessible. Information share and big data storage as well as computation power are most novel features of AI. Access to information but also reaping benefits from information sharing through synergizing information and deriving inferences from big data is an innovative value generation in the artificial age differing from conventional capital or labor.

Having already a big data collection enhances the productivity of $I\left(t\right)$ due to network effects and information being a non-rivalrous good, with a marginal utility gain that is exponential. Network effects from information and connectivity increase per additional user. Information is non-rivalrous as the consumption of one piece of information does not decrease or deplete the opportunity for another person to consume the information. The more information one holds, the better – hence the marginal utility of information rises exponentially with information gain. In all these features – network effect gains, non-rivalrous information consumption opportunities and exponential marginal utility gains of knowledge – information is completely different classical notions of capital and labor. Where capital and labor are exclusive, the knowledge economy and big data driven growth are non-exclusive (Clancy, 1998). A piece of information shared or written online does not take anything away or decrease utility, it actually increases people's utility non-depletable (Stiglitz, 1998; Stroebe, & Frey, 1982). Therefore, it is proposed to measure AI as completely novel component to be considered in standard growth theory. Economically, the current AI revolution is thus believed to differ from conventional technology shocks by the knowledge economy obeying different laws of economic exchange (Lucas, 2004).

Addressing the found deficiency of an integration of AI into standard growth calculus leads to the creation of an index AI_GDP per country c based on Equation 4, comprised of the GDP per capita and AI internet connectivity percentage of a country.

$$AI\_GDP(c) = GDP_{per\ capita}(c) * IA(c) \text{ (Equation 4)}$$

whereby $AI\_GDP(c)$ denotes the AI-GDP index per country c calculated by GDP per capita of a country c as retrieved from a World Bank database2 multiplied by $IA(c)$, which represents country c inhabitants' internet usage in percent of the population as retrieved from a World Bank database.3 Figure 1 holds the $AI\_GDP(c)$ index value per country. Figure 1 tables the AI_GDP countries' indices ranked from the highest to the low

Figure 1. AI-GDP Index for 191 countries of the world

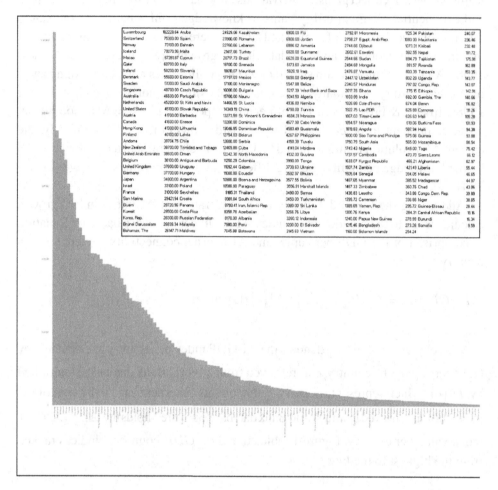

Figure 2 displays the AI_GDP country's index around the world. The higher the index, the darker the country is colored.

Figure 2. AI-GDP Index for 191 countries of the world

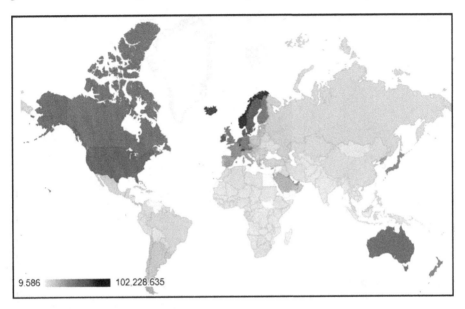

As visible in Figures 3-8, continent specific AI-GDP indices reveal Africa being relatively low on AI-GDP – see Figure 3. Asia and the Gulf region being in the middle ranges with Qatar and United Arab Emirates and Japan and South Korea leading as outlined in Figure 4. Figure 5 reveals in Europe Luxembourg, Switzerland, Norway, Iceland, Ireland, Sweden and Finland as top AI-GDP countries. North America (Figure 6) has a higher AI-GDP index than South America (Figure 7), where Chile, Argentina and Uruguay appear to lead. In Oceania Australia has the highest AI-GDP index followed by New Zealand as visible in Figure 8.

Figure 3. Africa AI-GDP index

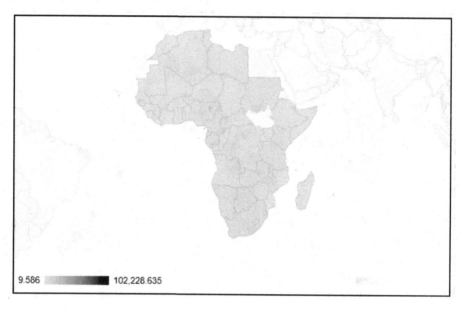

Figure 4. Asia AI-GDP index

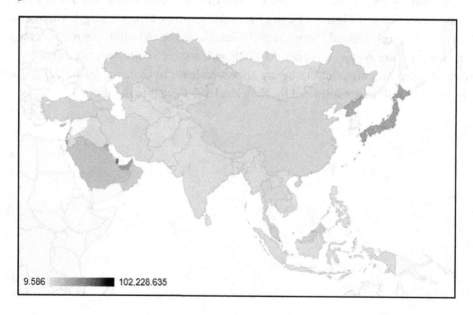

Figure 5. Europe AI-GDP index

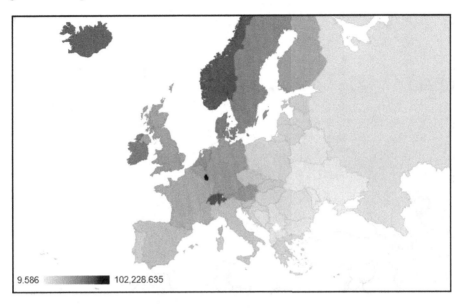

Figure 6. North America AI-GDP index

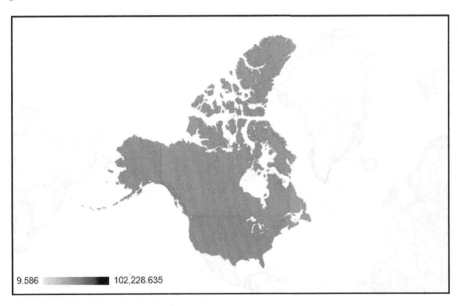

Figure 7. South America AI-GDP index

Figure 8. Oceania AI-GDP index

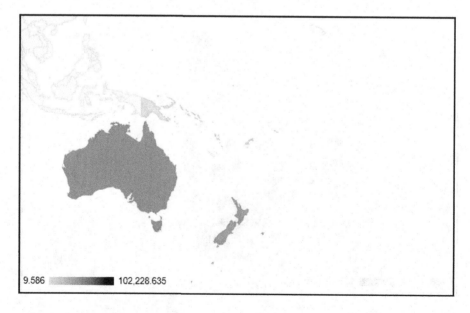

As a predicted trend, the co-existence of AI with the human species is believed to change the fundamental concepts of economic growth. Already now, we see a market disruption happening. Traditionally globalizing areas of growth seem to stagnate while AI driven industries are continuously globalizing.

When considering growth theories, we may first answer the question where AI led growth will be driven from. AI appears as exogenous technology shock that may increase labor productivity. With this going along is a transition of the economy and legal understanding of AI. What is different in regards to AI from conventional traditional technology shocks is the missing legal framework and economic clear distinction into capital or labor.

AI has already produced novel legal creations and will do so even more in the near future, through its developing autonomy. Behavioral economists add the question whether AI and robots should be created to resemble human beings' decision making with fast thinking and fallible choices or rather be targeted at perfect rationality and slow thinking (Kahneman & Tversky, 1979). General conscious is strived for so that AI possesses consciousness, which it can evolve and enhance on the basis of its own critical reflection and assessment of external factors (Mauss, 1979; Themistoklis, 2018). A lower level of autonomy exists if an entity can demonstrate such consciousness at a narrow field or can self-evolve and self-adapt to external influences, thus reaching decisions of its own, without being conscious of its intelligence as such (Themistoklis, 2018). As AI emerges as new types of intellect capacities coupled with human-like emotional features, they are attributed a legal personhood in order to ensure to be comprehended correctly and to avoid unfair treatment, towards humans as well (Themistoklis, 2018). Respectful treatment of AI is meant to protect and uphold dignity of all people and AI. Upholding certain ethics in regards to AI appears favorable to breed social norms but certain privileges should only be granted to human workers (Lin, Abney & Bekey, 2012; Mumford, 2001).

With citizenship and quasi-humanness being attributed to AI, the power relation between human and AI will need to be defined (Solum, 1992). Should AI be granted full citizenship rights, the problem of overpopulation occurs, since there is the possibility of infinite life of AI. With the rise of AI persons, their eternal life poses ethical challenges in light of overpopulation and evolutionary perfection, which could crowd out human fallibility if determining merit-based eternal life. In a human-led evolution, AI will have to be switched off for various reasons, such as malfunction but also merit-based efficiency calculus. If now AI is considered as quasi-humane and granted citizenship rights, switching off AI becomes a legally problematic. A human-led evolution may lead to having to decide what AI developments to favor and pursue. Clear guidelines will become essential when to terminate a malfunctioning or defect AI. In this feature AI will be different from labor as for having the potential to live eternally and being more malleable to be changed and switched. AI will be flexible and interchangeable in the international arena. Again, a putty labor definition of AI components of labor is recommended that captures the difference of AI to conventional labor in this regard.

AI entering the workforce and holding enormous physical and longevity advantages over human but no felt emotions, implies economic gains to be reaped. Standard economic growth models hold that capital and labor are essential for an economy to flourish. While capital is usually considered as fungible, exchangeable and eternal, labor is more individual, human and inflexible. AI entering the workforce and blending in as a substitute to human capital will change the nature of labor, potentially dividing labor into a putty, flexible, eternal and exchangeable AI part and a clay labor of inflexible human capital. AI should be programmed to monitor human conduct towards AI in order to uphold dignity as a vital social glue within any society.

If AI gets legally and economically subordinated to human, ethical questions arise. According to Kant's categorical imperative, one should only engage in actions that one would want to be incurred onto oneself, AI should be protected against harm and misuse or abuse. The concern here is less so the emotional and psychological state of AI, which arguably may not exists given missing self-cognition and emotions in AI, but more to set a signal and not to allow triggering sadist and negative compulsion in human that could be taken out on other human as well, if human become conditioned and learn abuse from mistreating AI on a daily basis.

Regarding limited space on earth and sustainability concerns, longevity and eternal life of AI appears problematic. Humankind may face tough decisions whether or not to have AI proceed and what kind of developments to flourish and what to extinct (Russell & Norvig, 1995). In what cases should we consider to switch off AI? In 1950, Isaac Asimov introduced the idea robot to (1) not injure a human being or, through inaction, allow a human being to come to harm. (2) A robot obeying the orders given it by human beings except where such orders conflict with the first law. (3) A robot must protect its own existence as long as such protection does not conflict with the first or second law. So in the cases of overpopulation and harm emerging from AI, algorithms and robots can be considered to be switched off. But when and how to stop AI?

An economic killing market mechanism may be natural market selection via price mechanisms and the falling rate of profit. Regarding prices, natural supply and demand mechanisms will always favor lucrative innovations with a higher price and following supply of goods lead to a price drop. The falling rate of profit is one of the major underlying features of business cycles, long-term booms and downturns (Brenner, 2002, 2006a, b). Capitalism is thereby described as competitive battle for innovation and reaping benefit from first-market introductions. Once followers enter the market, profit declines, leading eventually to market actors seeking novel ways to innovate in order to regain a competitive market advantage and higher rates of profit. Thereby industries and innovations fade and die off. Such a natural market evolution is also likely to occur with AI innovations, which will determine which AI traits will remain and which ones will fade off (Puaschunder, 2019a). Apart from soft market mechanisms that may lead to AI evolution, what are the cases when AI should be shut down or switched off or – in the case if AI personhood – be killed?

The main and leading concern about any new and emerging technology is to be safe and error free (Meghdari & Alemi, 2018). Therefore, sufficient and numerus tests on health and safety must be performed by developers and/or well-known independent sources before rolling out any technology onto the marketplace and society (Meghdari & Alemi, 2018). In robotics, the safety issue mainly centers around software and/or hardware designs (Meghdari & Alemi, 2018). Even a tiny software flaw or a manufacturing defect in an intelligent machine, like a smart car or a social robot, could lead to fatal results (Meghdari & Alemi, 2018). When these deviations occur and especially when they are harmful to the human community but also to other AI species, the faulty AI should be terminated. With regard to the risk of robotic malfunctions and errors, product legal responsibility laws are mostly untested in robotics (Meghdari & Alemi, 2018). A usual way to minimize the risk of damage from social robots is to program them to obey predefined regulations or follow a code-of-ethics (Meghdari & Alemi, 2018). Ethical codes for robotics are currently needed and should become formed as a natural behavioral law to then be defined and codified as law. Laws but also an ethical understanding to terminate AI, algorithms and robots in case of impairment and harm are needed (Puaschunder, 2020a).

As social robots become more intelligent and autonomous and exhibit enough of the features that typically define an individual person, it may be conceivable to assign them responsibility and use them in social, educational, and therapeutic settings (Meghdari & Alemi, 2018). In the currently ongoing research on the integration of computers and robotics with biological corpse it is found that a cognizant human brain (and its physical body) apparently has human-rights; hence, replacing parts of the brain with artificial ones, while not harming its function, preserves those rights (Meghdari & Alemi, 2018; Warwick & Shah, 2014). Also, consider a handicapped person featuring an electronic robot arm that commits a crime (Saffari, Meghdari, Vazirnezhad & Alemi, 2015).

Finally, we may address the question what is it that makes human humane and differing from AI? In the age of artificial intelligence and automated control, humanness is key to future success. Future research may draw from behavioral human decision-making insights and evolutionary economics in order to outline what makes human humane and how human decision making is unique to set us apart from artificial intelligence rationality. Humanness as found in heuristics, decision making errors but also procreation and creativity are believed to become more valuable in a future of AI entering the workforce and our daily lives. Drawing from behavioral human decision-making insights and evolutionary economics can help to outline what makes human humane and how human decision making is unique to set us apart from AI rationality. AI is argued to bevalue humanness and improve the value of human-imbued unique features. All these humane features of labor should be considered as clay labor, inflexible but valuable and clearly set apart from AI.

In its entirety, the presented futuristic outlook promises to hold novel insights for future success factors of economic growth calculus but also human resource management grounded on efficiency and ethics. Having parts of the world being AI-driven and others being human capital grounded in the future is prospected to increase the international development divide in the years to come. It is speculated that in the future, in the AI-hubs human will be incentivized to become more creative and humane while AI performs all rational tasks to a maximum productivity. In part of the world without AI could then naturally fall back as for being stuck in spending human capital time on machine-outsourceable tasks and not honing humane skills, which are not replicable by machines.

Future research endeavors may therefore address inequality drawing on the future vision that central rational AI-hubs will outperform underdeveloped remote areas of the world even more in the digital age. Slowbalisation is projected to draw back outsourcing efforts and divide AI hubs from areas that are less connected. Following research should be concerned with the unprecedentedly high divide between skilled and unskilled labor and the diversion between AI hubs and non-AI territories. In the last four decades, the price of skilled labor has soared dramatically relatively to that of unskilled labor despite a major uprise in the relative supply of skills. The notion of skill-bias in growth theories has introduced the theoretical possibility that technological progress benefits only a sub-group of workers, placing technical change at the center of the income distribution debate (Goldberg & Pavcnik, 2007). Organizational changes have led to AI technologies reducing costs of communication, monitoring and supervision within the firm, which trigger a shift towards a new organizational design. The change towards AI induces an organizational shift towards skill-biased meritocracy. Endogenous technical progress leads to economic growth, but also generates wage inequality between low- and high skilled workers (Duarte & Restuccia, 2006; Murphy, Riddell & Romer, 1998; Parente & Prescott, 1993). Faster technical change increases the return to ability and increases wage inequality between, and also within, groups of high-skilled and unskilled workers (Galor & Moav, 2000). Future studies should integrate some of the contemporary inequality measurements such as the Palma ratio, financial development and wealth transfers in contemporary growth theories and measurement (Jacoby, 2008; Milanovic, 2013; Piketty, 2016). Wage inequality is only one way to assess inequality, but in order to get a richer picture of inequality derived from AI, future research may also consider inequality in wealth, health, status and within-group inequalities (Restuccia & Urrutia, 2001). Understanding the links between growth and inequality should also be placed in the different contexts of political, social and historical environments in order to derive inference about a successful introduction of AI into today's workforce and society. Finally, more research is recommended to model and maximize the novel production function including AI and information share – especially in light of G5 and the internet of things leading to a further connection and benefits from technology. All these novel developments may lead to a potential polarization between more efficient AI hubs and low skill low labor cost areas that may be shunned from economic growth due to a predicted reshoring trend coupled with AI economic dominance and unprecedented technology gains (Aghion & Bolton, 1997; Matsuyama, 2000, 2011; Restuccia & Rogerson, 2017; Ventura, 1997).

Overall, the presented work captures AI's entrance into the workforce and our daily lives. The currently ongoing market transition of AI encroaching conventional markets will likely lead to a re-ordering of the current global economic and political order. The results on slowbalisation mark the very first attempt to describe slowbalisation in light of the currently ringing in AI market disruption. The findings on the relation of AI and GDP appear as first trace of AI shaping economies as if guided by an artificial drive. Depicting growth during this unprecedented time of economic change and regulatory reform of shaping a novel technology revolution in the wake of the COVID-19 pandemic holds invaluable historic opportunities for outlining technology-driven market changes' influence on the stability of economies and society. As never before in history, automatization may enrich the world economy in very many novel ways regardless of national borders – but only if also be safeguarded by ethical imperatives. The presented research aims at the current creative destruction in the wake of AI entering the world economies being ennobled by a social face and lowering potential societal downfalls (Schumpeter, 1943/1976). The findings may also bestow global governance policy makers with ideas how to better snapshot AI's potential in the digital age and market actors with future-oriented foresight how to benefit from this new technology (Banerjee, 2008; Klenow, 2008). Market and societal policy recommendations may aid global governance experts to strengthen society through AI but also overcome unknown emergent risks within globalized markets in the wake of the AI revolution. At the same time of acknowledging the potential of AI, ethical considerations appear necessary as we have to become aware of the risk imbued in the artificial age, such as legal regulatory gaps and crowding out humanness or reverting the past accomplishments of outsourcing helping nations to develop out of poverty. Conventional economic policies may therefore be coupled with a holistic vision that encompasses socio-economic and political values. Drawing attention to potential international development drawbacks and a further disparity of society based on skills and access to refined technology will offer market actors and governance bodies key insights – not only on how to benefit from a digitalizing world but also how to administer the current market transition so the benefits get distributed equally around the world. Societies of tomorrow should therefore be built on AI ethics of inclusion in order to safeguard the transition to artificiality enhancing economies and ennoble society through a mutual understanding and exchange of putty and clay labor.

BIG DATA ETHICS

In the age of instant communication and social media big data storage and computational power; the need for understanding people's trade-off between utility in communication and dignity in privacy has leveraged to unprecedented momentum (Puaschunder, 2019c). Today enormous data storage capacities and computational power in the e-big data era have created unforeseen opportunities for big data hoarding corporations to reap hidden benefits from individual's information sharing, which occurs bit-by-bit in small tranches over time (Puaschunder, 2019c). Behavioral economics describes human decision-making fallibility over time but has – to this day – not covered the problem of individuals' decision to share information about themselves in tranches on social media while big data administrators are able to reap a benefit from putting data together over time and reflecting the individual's information in relation to the big data of others (Puaschunder, 2020a). The decision-making fallibility inherent in individuals having problems understanding the future impact of their current information sharing is introduced as hyper-hyperbolic discounting decision-making predicament (Puaschunder, 2019c). Individuals lose control over their data without knowing what surplus value big data moguls can reap from the social media consumer-workers' information sharing, what information can be complied over time and what information this data can provide in relation to the general public's data in drawing inferences about the innocent individual information sharer (Puaschunder, 2020a).

In recent decades, big data derived personality cues have started been used for governance control purposes, such as border protection and tax compliance surveillance (Puaschunder, 2020a). The COVID-19 healthcare crisis and pandemic emergency around the world has exacerbated governmental control of data for monitoring, tracking and preventive prediction purposes (Gelter & Puaschunder, 2021; Puaschunder, 2020b). A growing body of contemporary findings reveals that an estimated 10 up to 50% of those previously infected with COVID-19 face some kind of long-term health impact and/or chronic debilitation that in many cases comes and goes in waves (Hart, 2021). These so-called COVID Long Haulers are estimated to account for up to 1.9 billion people worldwide after the end of the pandemic (Puaschunder, 2021b). Given the large number of possible COVID Long Haulers, it is certain that this health phenomenon will have an enormous impact on society, medicine, the economy, the law and governance of our world (Puaschunder & Gelter, 2021). Long Haulers will contribute to the ongoing digitalization revolution by taking advantage of real-time health status and environmental infection condition tracking. As digitalization allowed for remote learning, working and entertainment, the biggest deurbanization trend in US history emerged in the wake of COVID-19 (Puaschunder, 2021b; Puaschunder & Gelter, 2021). Labor market shortages and the number of workers quitting skyrocketing as the pandemic progressed, will likely further amplify a digitalization revolution to replace human contact and low-skilled labor (Puaschunder, 2020b, 2021b). AI, robotics and big data insights come in handy when filling gaps for Long Haulers, who often face waves of debilitating conditions (Puaschunder & Gelter, 2021). Robotics aid on patient care and hygiene (Puaschunder, 2019b). Big data analytics have already revealed ground-breaking COVID long haul insights that will likely lead the way forward to finding remedies for those in chronic pain (Puaschunder & Gelter, 2021, Puaschunder, forthcoming).

Moreover, Long Haulers have already found themselves in online self-help groups for quick and unbureaucratic information exchange about an emerging societal phenomenon (Puaschunder & Gelter, 2021). Accounting for the nature, size and scope of the tragedy of Long COVID creates the imperative to protect the most vulnerable populations online. COVID Long Haulers are prone to share sensitive information about their health and well-being in social media forums online that could potentially over time and in relation to other parts of the population be turned against them when considering the potential of corporations to scrape COVID Long Haul online forums and scan future applicants for their presence or check on their health status.

Nowadays COVID long-haul patients have become – more than ever before – citizen scientists that bundle decentralized information on their health status and potential remedies in order to inform the medical profession about newly emerging trends. The rise in medical self-help and mutual support will have profound implications for the regulation of the medical profession and will likely stretch the medical remedy spectrum and boost alternative medicine. Instant online exchange of sensitive information about one's health status makes citizen scientists particularly vulnerable in terms of their privacy and potentially susceptible to online marketing campaigns under medically impaired conditions. But also, the long-term impact of publicly disclosed sensitive information that is shared bit-by-bit online over time appears sensitive. In the digital age, it is difficult to estimate what effects the piecemeal providing of private information will have over time, when, for example, personal health information disseminated in an internet forum is absorbed into large datasets.

If information is analyzed and displayed in relation to other individuals' performance, a combined dataset could open gates for discrimination and stigmatization. In the online exchange of sensitive information about one's health status, COVID Long Haulers, who recently have been recognized as a group with potential propensity to have a disability, are also in particular vulnerable in terms of their privacy, potentially susceptible to online marketing campaigns under medically impaired conditions, but also because of their sensitive information being publicly disclosed online over time (The White House of the United States, 2021). This online sharing of medical information raises important – but yet hardly described – concerns about privacy, susceptibility to misinformation and discrimination in the vastly unregulated online social media arena, which calls for urgent attention.

In the search for the establishment of regulation on sensitive big data scraping, the 2018 Toronto Declaration of 2018 established three fundamental premises (Bariffi & Puaschunder, 2021). First, that the ethics of AI and how to make technology in this field human-centric must be analyzed through a human rights lens (Bariffi & Puaschunder, 2021). Second, that when developing AI, states (public and private actors) must consider the new challenges that this technology poses for equality and representation of and impact on diverse individuals and groups (Bariffi & Puaschunder, 2021). Third, that in the face of any discrimination, states must guarantee access to an effective judicial remedy (Bariffi & Puaschunder, 2021; The Toronto Declaration, 2018). The Declaration on Ethics and Data Protection in Artificial Intelligence adopted during the 2018 International Conference of Institutions dedicated to Data Protection and Privacy (ICDPPC) highlights principles of transparency and responsibility in the handling of big data (Bariffi & Puaschunder, 2021; Declaration on Ethics and Data Protection in Artificial Intelligence, 2018). The Public Voice organization approved the Universal Guidelines for Artificial Intelligence in 2018, a document endorsed by 50 scientific organizations and over 200 experts from around the world (Bariffi & Puaschunder, 2021). The document outlines 12 principles which must be incorporated into ethical standards, to be adopted in national legislation and international agreements, and to be integrated into the design of AI systems. The principles include the (1) Right to Transparency, (2) Right to Human Determination, (3) Identification Obligation, (4) Fairness Obligation, (5) Assessment and Accountability Obligation, (6) Accuracy, Reliability, and Validity Obligations, (8) Public Safety Obligation, (9) Cybersecurity, (10) Prohibition on Secret Profiling, (11) Prohibition on Unitary Scoring, and the (12) Termination Obligation (Bariffi & Puaschunder, 2021). The European Union (EU) has also sketched several documents to address the ethical and legal aspects of AI systems (Bariffi & Puaschunder, 2021). For example, on April 8, 2019, the EU Commission adopted the Ethics Guidelines for Trustworthy Artificial Intelligence establishing 7 key requirements that AI systems should meet in order to be deemed trustworthy:

(1) Human Agency and Oversight, (2) Technical Robustness and Safety, (3) Privacy and Data Governance, (4) Transparency, (5) Diversity, Non-Discrimination and Fairness, (6) Societal and Environmental Well-Being, and (7) Accountability (Bariffi & Puaschunder, 2021). According to this text, the trustworthiness of AI underlies on three components that must be satisfied throughout the entire life cycle of the system; i) lawful – respecting all applicable laws and regulations, ii) ethical – respecting ethical principles and values, iii) robust – both from a technical perspective while considering its social environment (Bariffi & Puaschunder, 2021). The Council of Europe has issued the Guidelines on Artificial Intelligence and Data Protection, which are instructions targeted for developers, manufacturers and service providers but also recommendations for legislators and policy makers (Bariffi & Puaschunder, 2021). The Declaration of the Committee of Ministers on the manipulative capacities of algorithmic processes of February 2019, highlights that, "sub-conscious and personalized levels of algorithmic persuasion may have significant effects on the cognitive autonomy of individuals and their right to form opinions and take independent decisions (Bariffi & Puaschunder, 2021). These effects remain under-explored but cannot be underestimated (Bariffi & Puaschunder, 2021). Not only may they weaken the exercise and enjoyment of individual human rights, but they may lead to the corrosion of the very foundation of the Council of Europe (Bariffi & Puaschunder, 2021). Its central pillars of human rights, democracy and the rule of law are grounded on the fundamental belief in the equality and dignity of all humans as independent moral agents" (Bariffi & Puaschunder, 2021). The Recommendation Unboxing Artificial Intelligence: 10 Steps to Protect Human Rights of May 2019 underlies the need to carry out impact assessments on human rights in relation to AI systems (Bariffi & Puaschunder, 2021). There is already an incipient regulatory approach regarding the impact of AI systems on human rights, although for the moment, these are only non-binding guidelines or principles of interpretation (Bariffi & Puaschunder, 2021).

In the post COVID-19 era, large-scale online information exchange about medical conditions and potential remedy alternatives is a rather novel phenomenon and therefore hardly regulated. The downsides of crowdsourcing information about health online are emerging risks and unknown legal boundaries as well as potential liability concerns. Online crowdsourcing of information also opens gates to critical biases against those publicizing their health status online, as well as a risk of deception and fraud committed to a highly vulnerable population. International big data exchange could set standards for future pandemic prevention but should also provide big data privacy protection and legal anti-discrimination means against misuse of sensitive information – such as leading towards stigmatization – of vulnerable patients' exposure of their disability and conditions (Cirruzzo, 2021; The White House of the United States, 2021). As online sharing of sensitive information opens privacy concerns for a vulnerable and impaired group, the creation of legal and regulatory frameworks to prevent abuse of online forums for marketing purposes at the expense of the well-being of susceptible patients and impaired individuals in physical and emotional pain or debilitated conditions has become a blatant demand of our time. Long-term deliberations and hyperbolic discounting should be integrated into academic and political debates in order to protect individuals when innocently sharing medical information and compassionately seeking or extending non-medically-trained help (Puaschunder, 2021b).

The anonymous participation in new virtual realities currently also brings along completely new problems such as cyber-crime, hate postings and social censorship by online mobs, which could be particularly harmful to vulnerable patients seeking remedies online. Governments and traditional media have lost control over public opinion in the digital age. Legal protection includes privacy in "big data" and the individual "right to be forgotten" online as well as the dignity of conscientious data protection and online privacy (Mayer-Schönberger, 2009).

Healthy and informed access to new media needs to address the dilemma between the individual benefit from information exchange online versus the human dignity of privacy on the internet. On a wider societal scale, the digitalization disruption also brings along novel inequalities (Puaschunder, 2020c, 2021a). Inequality in internet connectivity, tech skills and affinity to digitalization leverages AI-human-compatibility as a competitive advantage. Digital online working conditions that make individual living conditions transparent emphasize social hierarchies in our work-related interactions and may further transpire differences in social status in business and educational settings. Taxing the digital economy could create the fiscal space to offset the financial fallout from technological disruption and ensure that education and professional training emphasize the conscientious use of new technologies (Puaschunder, 2019a). Tax revenues generated from internet gains could also allow to offset online inequalities in granting access, tools and capabilities for underprivileged segments and COVID long-hauling disabled. All these endeavors could ennoble society's most fascinating innovations with a humane sense for attention to human rights, inequality alleviation and compassionate care.

Ethical Searchplaces

Digitalization offers unprecedented human advancement and democratization potential free from corruption (Puaschunder, forthcoming c). For instance, in the medical sphere, telemedical assistance helps bring access to quality care and information about disease control to remote areas of the world or countries that are struck by corruption. Access to crowdsourcing information in online forums about novel diseases and alternative medical solutions for chronic debilitation is a groundbreaking phenomenon of our times (Bariffi & Puaschunder, 2021; Puaschunder & Gelter, 2021).

At the same time, shifting marketplaces to online virtual spaces opens gates for misinformation and disinformation in search engines and online forums being used in a competitive sense. The strategic manipulation of environments is likely inspired by behavioral economics, which offers ample evidence of the environment being a subliminal influence in peoples' choices. While the primary focus of behavioral insights is primarily on how to use nudges and winks to make the world a better place in helping humans make wiser decisions (Puaschunder 2020a, 2021j); less is written and known about how unethical behavior is used to curb and distort online environments by deleting information or clogging online searchplace users with unnecessary misinformation or compromising disinformation. Less documented and not regulated are behavioral so-called internet search engine 'black hat strategies' that have become prominent to be used competitively in searchplaces, such as Google, Yahoo or Bing to misrepresent or curb competition.

In the most recent decade, searchplaces, such as Google, Yahoo or Bing, have gained prominence for screening and scanning candidates in workplace related contexts. While we have a most important and emerging stream of literature on algorithmic discrimination and inherent biases in searchplaces and internet forums (Wu, 2018); less is known about strategic searchplace distortion. So-called Search Engine De-optimization black hat strategies are competitive and unethical distortions of search engine results that either overemphasize unfavorable search results (enabled via clickfarms) or create a misinformation or disinformation overload that derails from accurate representations of individuals online. For instance, Google search results can get capped at a low number (indicated by Google) by overemphasizing irrelevant, outdated or violent content and unfavorable, misleading and/or compromising information can get highlighted via clickfarms in the few displayed results.

Positive or content information can also be erased by flagging content online that gets immediately taken offline and hardly any resuscitation control by human reviews is installed. While there is a possibility to craft the internet search results together and flag and report inappropriate online content, little quality control is given to this option being used as a strategy to push down or make content disappear that is appropriate in the wake of competition. For instance, competitors could use the flag and report button to make content of competitors unavailable. While the early 2000s was a period of advocacy for the 'Right to Delete' (Mayer-Schönberger, 2009), the 2020s should also thematize the 'Right to not be Deleted' in order to advocate for a quality control check with flagged content online if the flagging was appropriate.

Potentially quality control over what gets flagged and who manipulates search results strategically could be enacted. Legal advancements should include clear guidelines and oversight of fraudulent use of the internet in a competitive way that manipulates genuine algorithm results, for instance via clickfarms or backlinks that curb or tilt search results in a particular way. Lastly, those who face a searchplace discrimination disadvantage should be protected by legal regulation, technical support and rescue funds established by the industry to uphold to favor quality over unethicality in their profession. After all, sensitivity for cyberbullying via misinformation and disinformation could help elevate professions to a more ethical ground and uphold focus on excellence and merit rather than discreditation potential due to unethical conduct and lacking human algorithmic control.

Discussion Questions in Classrooms

1. What is Artificial Intelligence?
2. Is Artificial Intelligence and digitalization spread evenly across the world?
3. What are areas of improvement thanks to the digitalization disruption?
4. What are areas of concern in the wake of the digitalization disruption?
5. How can we spread the benefits of Artificial Intelligence across society and the world?
6. How can we curb harmful negative externalities from digitalization?

REFERENCES

Acemoglu, D. (2009a). Economic growth and economic development: The questions. In D. Acemoglu (Ed.), *Introduction to Modern Economic Growth* (pp. 3–25). Princeton University Press.

Acemoglu, D. (2009b). The Solow model and the data. In D. Acemoglu (Ed.), *Introduction to Modern Economic Growth* (pp. 77–107). Princeton University Press.

Aghion, P., & Bolton, P. (1997). A theory of trickle-down growth and development. *The Review of Economic Studies, 64*(2), 151–172. doi:10.2307/2971707

Aghion, P., & Howitt, P. (1992). A model of growth: Through creative destruction. *Econometrica, 60*(2), 323–351. doi:10.2307/2951599

Aghion, P., & Howitt, P. (1998). *Endogenous growth theory*. Massachusetts Institute of Technology Press.

Aghion, P., Jones, B. F., & Jones, Ch. I. (2017). *Artificial Intelligence and economic growth*. National Bureau of Economic Research working paper. Retrieved at https://www.nber.org/chapters/c14015

Agrawal, G., Ahlawat, H., & Dewhurst, M. (2020). *Winning against COVID-19: The implications for biopharma*. McKinsey & Co. Retrieved at https://www.mckinsey.com/industries/pharmaceuticals-and-medical-products/our-insights/winning-against-covid-19-the-implications-for-biopharma#the-implications-for-biopharma

Alemi, M., Meghdari, A., & Saffari, E. (2017). RoMa: A hi-tech robotic mannequin for the fashion industry. Lecture Notes in Computer Science (LNCS): Social Robotics, 10652, 209-219.

Alvarez, F., Buera, F., & Lucas, R. E. (2007). *Idea flows, economic growth, and trade*. National Bureau of Economic Research working paper. Retrieved at https://www.nber.org/papers/w19667

Aravanis, J. (2020). *Five industries set to outperform due to COVID-19*. IBISWorld. Retrieved at https://www.ibisworld.com/industry-insider/coronavirus-insights/five-industries-set-to-outperform-due-to-covid-19/

Arora, R. (2020). Which companies did well during the Coronavirus pandemic? *Forbes*. Retrieved at www.forbes.com/sites/rohitarora-during-the-coronavirus-pandemic/#17fe6c9b7409

Arrow, K. (1962). The economic implications of learning by doing. *The Review of Economic Studies*, 29(3), 155–173. doi:10.2307/2295952

Arrow, K. J. (1962). Economic welfare and the allocation of resources for invention. In R. R. Nelson (Ed.), *The Rate and Direction of Inventive Activity* (pp. 609–626). Princeton University Press. doi:10.1515/9781400879762-024

Arrow, K. J. (1969). Classificatory notes on the production and transmission of technological knowledge. *The American Economic Review*, 59(2), 29–35.

Banerjee, A. (2008). Big answers for big questions: The presumption of growth policy. In Brookings Institute (Ed.), What Works in Development? Thinking Big and Thinking Small (pp. 207-231). Washington, DC: Brookings Institute.

Banerjee, A., & Newman, A. F. (1993). Occupational choice and the process of development. *Journal of Political Economy*, 101(2), 274–298. doi:10.1086/261876

Bariffi, F., & Puaschunder, J. M. (2021). Artificial Intelligence and Big Data in the age of COVID-19. *Proceedings of the 24th Research Association for Interdisciplinary Studies (RAIS) Conference.*

Barro, R. (1990). Government spending in a simple model of endogenous growth. *Journal of Political Economy*, 98(5, Part 2), 103–125. doi:10.1086/261726

Barro, R.J. (1991). Economic growth in a cross section of countries. *The Quarterly Journal of Economics, 106*(2), 407-444.

Bartelsman, E. J., Haltiwanger, J., & Scarpetta, S. (2013). Cross-country differences in productivity: The role of allocation and selection. *The American Economic Review, 1*(103), 305–334. doi:10.1257/aer.103.1.305

Bartik, A. W., Bertrand, M., Cullen, Z., Glaeser, E. L., Luca, M., & Stanton, Ch. (2020). *How are small businesses adjusting to COVID-19? Early evidence from a survey.* Cambridge, MA: National Bureau of Economic Research Working Paper No. 26989.

Bils, M., & Klenow, P. (2002). Does schooling cause growth? *The American Economic Review, 90*(5), 1160–1183. doi:10.1257/aer.90.5.1160

Bjork, G. J. (1999). *The way it worked and why it won't: Structural change and the slowdown of U.S. economic growth.* Praeger.

Brenner, R. (2002). American economic revival. In *The Boom and the Bubble: The US in the World Economy.* Verso.

Brenner, R. (2006a). The puzzle of the long downturn. In *The Economics of Global Turbulence: The Advanced Capitalist Economies from Long Boom to Long Downturn, 1945-2005.* Verso.

Brenner, R. (2006b). From boom to downturn. In *The Economics of Global Turbulence: The Advanced Capitalist Economies from Long Boom to Long Downturn, 1945-2005.* Verso.

Buera, F. J., & Shin, Y. (2011). Finance and development: A tale of two sectors. *The American Economic Review, 101*(5), 1964–2002. doi:10.1257/aer.101.5.1964

Burmeister, E. (2000). The capital theory controversy. In H. Kurz (Ed.), *Critical Essays on Piero Sraffa's Legacy in Economics* (pp. 305–314). Cambridge University Press. doi:10.1017/CBO9781139166881.008

Caselli, F., & Feyrer, J. (2007). The marginal product of capital. *The Quarterly Journal of Economics, 122*(2), 535–568. doi:10.1162/qjec.122.2.535

Cellan-Jones, R. (2014). *Stephen Hawking warns Artificial Intelligence could end mankind.* BBC News. www.bbc.com/news/technology-30290540

Centeno, M. A., Cinlar, E., Cloud, D., Creager, A. N., DiMaggio, P. J., Dixit, A. K., Elga, A. N., Felten, E. W., James, H., Katz, St. N., Keohane, R. O., Leonard, Th. C., Massey, W. A., Mian, A. R., Mian, Z., Oppenheimer, M., Shafir, E., & Shapiro, J. N. (2013). *Global systemic risk*. Unpublished manuscript for research community. Princeton Institute for International and Regional Studies, Princeton University.

Centeno, M. A., & Tham, A. (2012). *The emergence of risk in the global system*. Princeton, NJ: Princeton University working paper.

Cirruzzo, C. (2021). *Long COVID can be a disability, White House says: The Biden administration has released guidance and resources on long COVID and disability*. U.S. News. Retrieved at https://www.usnews.com/news/health-news/articles/2021-07-26/long-covid-can-be-a-disability-bidenadministration-says

Clancy, E. (1998). The tragedy of the global commons. *Indiana Journal of Global Legal Studies, 5*(2), 601–619.

Comin, D., & Hobijn, B. (2004). Cross-country technology adoption: Making the theories face the facts. *Journal of Monetary Economics, 51*(1), 39–83. doi:10.1016/j.jmoneco.2003.07.003

Corlatean, T. (2020). Risk, discrimination and opportunities for education during the times of COVID-19 pandemic. *Proceedings of the 17th RAIS Research Association for Interdisciplinary Sciences Conference on Social Sciences and Humanities*, 37-46. Retrieved at http://rais.education/wp-content/uploads/2020/06/004TC.pdf

Deaton, A. (2010). Understanding the mechanisms of economic development. *The Journal of Economic Perspectives, 24*(3), 3–16. doi:10.1257/jep.24.3.3

Deutsche, D. W. Bank überrascht mit hohem Gewinn. (2020). Retrieved at https://www.dw.com/de/deutsche-bank-%C3%BCberrascht-mit-hohem-gewinn/a-55417971

Dodd, D. (2020). COVID 19's corporate casualties. *Financial Times*. Retrieved at https://www.ft.com/content/eb6efc36-bf99-4086-a98a-7d121738b4b4

Dowell, R. (2018). Fundamental protections for non-biological intelligences or: How we learn to stop worrying and love our robot Brethren. *Minnesota Journal of Law, Science & Technology, 19*(1), 305–336.

Dray, M., & Thirlwall, A. P. (2011). The endogeneity of the natural rate of growth for a selection of Asian countries. *Journal of Post Keynesian Economics, 33*(3), 451–468. doi:10.2753/PKE0160-3477330303

Dua, A., Ellingrud, K., Mahajan, D., & Silberg, J. (2020). *Which small businesses are most vulnerable to COVID-19: And when.* McKinsey & Co. Retrieved at https://www.mckinsey.com/featured-insights/americas/which-small-businesses-are-most-vulnerable-to-covid-19-and-when

Duarte, M., & Restuccia, D. (2006). The productivity of nations. *Federal Reserve Bank Richmond Economic Quarterly*, 92(3), 195–223.

EcoWellness Group. (2020). *Salzburg Declaration: Interdisciplinary Conference on 'System change?! The chance of transformation of the healthcare system: Analysis and chances of the coronavirus crisis.* Retrieved at https://www.oekowellness.de/laenderuebergreifende-konzerenz-zum-thema-system-change-die-chance-der-transformation-des-gesundheitswesens-14-07-2020/

EcoWellness Group. (2021). *Salzburg European Declaration from the Gasteinertal: Interdisciplinary Conference on 'System change?! The chance of transformation of the healthcare system.* Retrieved at https://www.oekowellness.de/wp-content/uploads/2021/07/Final-Stand-5.7.-2021.07.04_Programm-14.7.-und-15.07.2021-2.pdf

Elliott, C. (2021). When will it be safe to cruise again? These signs that will help you decide when to sail. *USA Today.* Retrieved at https://www.usatoday.com/story/travel/advice/2021/02/05/covid-when-will-it-be-safe-to-cruise/4386762001

Erosa, A., Koreshkova, T., & Restuccia, D. (2010). How important is human capital? A quantitative theory assessment of world income inequality. *The Review of Economic Studies*, 77(4), 1421–1449. doi:10.1111/j.1467-937X.2010.00610.x

Foster, V. (2020). Is eating meat from meatpacking plants with Covid-19 Coronavirus outbreaks safe? *Forbes.* Retrieved at https://www.forbes.com/sites/victoriaforster/2020/06/21/is-eating-meat-from-meatpacking-plants-with-covid-19-coronavirus-outbreaks-safe/?sh=5d2d5bcb7089

Futagami, K., Morita, Y., & Shibata, A. (1993). Dynamic analysis of an endogenous growth model with public capital. *The Scandinavian Journal of Economics*, 95(4), 607–625. doi:10.2307/3440914

Galor, O., & Moav, O. (2000). Ability biased technological transition, wage inequality and growth. *The Quarterly Journal of Economics*, 115(2), 469–498. doi:10.1162/003355300554827

Galor, O., & Moav, O. (2004). From physical to human capital accumulation: Inequality in the process of development. *The Review of Economic Studies*, 71(4), 1001–1026. doi:10.1111/0034-6527.00312

Galor, O., & Tsiddon, D. (1997). The distribution of human capital and economic growth. *Journal of Economic Growth*, *2*(1), 93–124. doi:10.1023/A:1009785714248

Garegnani, P. (2008). On Walras's theory of capital. *Journal of the History of Economic Thought*, *30*(3), 367–384. doi:10.1017/S1053837208000345

Gelter, M., & Puaschunder, J. M. (2021). COVID-19 and comparative corporate governance. *The Journal of Corporation Law*, *46*(3), 557–629.

Goldberg, K., & Pavcnik, N. (2007). The distributional effects of globalization in developing countries. *Journal of Economic Literature*, *45*(1), 39–82. doi:10.1257/jel.45.1.39

Grossman, G. M., & Helpman, E. (1991a). *Innovation and growth in the global economy*. MIT Press.

Grossman, G. M., & Helpman, E. (1991b). Quality ladders in the theory of growth. *The Review of Economic Studies*, *58*(1), 43–61. doi:10.2307/2298044

Hall, R. E., & Jones, Ch. I. (1999). Why do some countries produce so much more output per worker than others? *The Quarterly Journal of Economics*, *114*(1), 83–116. doi:10.1162/003355399555954

Harberger, A. (1998). A vision of the growth process. *The American Economic Review*, *88*(1), 1–32.

Harrod, R. F. (1939). An essay in dynamic theory. *Economic Journal (London)*, *49*(193), 14–33. doi:10.2307/2225181

Hart, R. (2021). Long Covid has over 200 symptoms and leaves 1 In 5 unable to work, study finds. *Forbes*. Retrieved at https://www.forbes.com/sites/roberthart/2021/07/15/long-covid-has-over-200-symptoms-and-leaves-1-in-5-unable-to-work-study-finds/?sh=7f71338e5eb2

Hatmaker, T. (2017). *Saudi Arabia bestows citizenship on a robot named Sophia*. Techcrunch. Retrieved at https://techcrunch.com/2017/10/26/saudi-arabia-robot-citizen-sophia/

Hausmann, R., Pritchett, L., & Rodrik, D. (2005). Growth accelerations. *Journal of Economic Growth*, *10*(4), 303–329. doi:10.100710887-005-4712-0

Hayes, A. (2018). *Decentralized banking: Monetary technocracy in the digital age*. Social Science Research Network working paper. Retrieved at https://papers.ssrn.com/sol3/papers.cfm?abstract_id=2807476

Hsieh, C. T. (2002). What explains the industrial revolution in East Asia? Evidence from the factor markets. *The American Economic Review*, *92*(3), 502–526. doi:10.1257/000282802260136372

Hsieh, C. T., & Klenow, P. (2005). Relative prices and relative prosperity. *The American Economic Review*, *98*(3), 562–585. doi:10.1257/aer.97.3.562

Hsieh, C. T., & Klenow, P. (2010). Development accounting. *American Economic Journal. Macroeconomics*, *2*(1), 207–223. doi:10.1257/mac.2.1.207

Jacoby, H. G. (2008). Food prices, wages, and welfare in rural India. *Economic Inquiry*, *54*(1), 159–176. doi:10.1111/ecin.12237

Jones, B. F. (2014). The human capital stock: A generalized approach. *The American Economic Review*, *104*(11), 3752–3777. doi:10.1257/aer.104.11.3752

Jones, B. F., & Olken, B. A. (2008). The anatomy of start-stop growth. *The Review of Economics and Statistics*, *90*(3), 582–587. doi:10.1162/rest.90.3.582

Jones, Ch. I. (1999). Growth: With or without scale effects. *The American Economic Review*, *89*(2), 139–144. doi:10.1257/aer.89.2.139

Jones, Ch. I. (2004). *Growth and ideas*. National Bureau of Economic Research working paper. Retrieved at https://www.nber.org/papers/w10767

Kahneman, D., & Tversky, A. (1979). Prospect Theory: An Analysis of Decision Under Risk. *Econometrica*, *47*(2), 263–291. doi:10.2307/1914185

Kaldor, N. (1961). Capital accumulation and economic growth. In F. A. Lutz & D. C. Hague (Eds.), *The Theory of Capital* (pp. 177–222). St. Martin's Press. doi:10.1007/978-1-349-08452-4_10

Klenow, P. (2008). Discussion of 'Big Answers for Big Questions: The Presumption of Growth Policy' by A.V. Banerjee. In Brookings Institute (Ed.), What Works in Development? Thinking Big and Thinking Small. Washington, DC: Brookings Institute.

Klenow, P., & Rodríguez-Clare, A. (1997). Economic growth: A review essay. *Journal of Monetary Economics*, *40*(4), 597–618. doi:10.1016/S0304-3932(97)00050-0

Kortum, S. S. (1997). Research, patenting, and technological change. *Econometrica*, *65*(6), 1389–1420. doi:10.2307/2171741

Kremer, M. (1993). Population growth and technological change: One million B.C. to 1990. *The Quarterly Journal of Economics*, *108*(3), 681–716. doi:10.2307/2118405

Kremer, M., Rao, G., & Schilbach, F. (2019). Behavioral development economics. In D. Bernheim, St. DellaVigna, & D. Laibson (Eds.), *Handbook of Behavioral Economics: Foundations and Applications* (pp. 345–458). Elsevier. doi:10.1016/bs.hesbe.2018.12.002

Krueger, A. O. (1997). Trade policy and economic development: How we learn. *The American Economic Review, 87*(1), 1–22.

Kumar, N., & Haydon, D. (2020). *Industries most and least impacted by COVID-19 from a probability of default perspective: March 2020 update.* S&P Global Market Intelligence. Retrieved at https://www.spglobal.com/marketintelligence/en/news-insights/blog/industries-most-and-least-impacted-by-covid-19-from-a-probability-of-default-perspective-march-2020-update

Kuznets, S. (1973). Modern economic growth: Findings and reflections. *The American Economic Review, 63*(3), 247–258.

Kwak, J. (2020). The end of small business. *The Washington Post.* https://www.washingtonpost.com/outlook/2020/07/09/after-covid-19-giant-corporations-chains-may-be-only-ones-left/?arc404=true

Lagakos, D., Moll, B., Porzio, T., Qian, N., & Schoellman, T. (2014). *Life-cycle human capital accumulation across countries: Lessons from U.S. immigrants.* Cambridge, MA: National Bureau of Economic Research Working Paper 21914. Retrieved at https://www.nber.org/papers/w21914

Laton, D. (2016). Manhattan_Project.Exe: A nuclear option for the digital age. *Catholic University Journal of Law & Technology, 25*(4), 94–153.

Lerner, S. (2020). Big pharma prepares to profit from the Coronavirus: Pharmaceutical companies view the Coronavirus pandemic as a once-in-a-lifetime business opportunity. *The Intercept.* Retrieved at https://theintercept.com/2020/03/13/big-pharma-drug-pricing-coronavirus-profits

Lin, P., Abney, K., & Bekey, G. A. (2012). *Robot ethics: The ethical and social implications of robotics.* The MIT Press.

Lucas, R. E. Jr. (1988). On the mechanics of economic development. *Journal of Monetary Economics, 22*(1), 3–42. doi:10.1016/0304-3932(88)90168-7

Lucas, R. E. (1999). Why doesn't capital flow from rich to poor countries? *The American Economic Review, 80*(5), 92–96.

Lucas, R. E. (2004). The industrial revolution: Past and future. *Annual Report of the Federal Reserve Bank of Minneapolis,* (May), 5–20.

Lucas, R. E. Jr. (2009). Ideas and Growth. *Economica, 76*(301), 1–19. doi:10.1111/j.1468-0335.2008.00748.x

Lucas, R. E. Jr, & Moll, B. (2014). Knowledge growth and the allocation of time. *Journal of Political Economy, 122*(1), 1–51. doi:10.1086/674363

Mankiw, N. G., Romer, D., & Weil, D. N. (1992). A contribution to the empirics of economic growth. *The Quarterly Journal of Economics, 107*(2), 407–437. doi:10.2307/2118477

Manuelli, R. E., & Seshadri, A. (2014). Human capital and the wealth of nations. *The American Economic Review, 9*(9), 2736–2762. doi:10.1257/aer.104.9.2736 PMID:30443048

Matsuyama, K. (2000). Endogenous inequality. *The Review of Economic Studies, 67*(4), 743–759. doi:10.1111/1467-937X.00152

Matsuyama, K. (2008). Structural change. In S. Durlauf & L. E. Blume (Eds.), *The New Palgrave Dictionary of Economics, pp.* Palgrave-Macmillan. doi:10.1057/978-1-349-95121-5_1775-2

Matsuyama, K. (2011). Imperfect credit markets, household wealth distribution, and development. *Annual Review of Economics, 3*(1), 339–362. doi:10.1146/annurev-economics-111809-125054

Mauss, M. (1979). A category of the human mind: The notion of the person, the notion of 'self. In M. Mauss (Ed.), *Sociology and Psychology* (pp. 81–103). Routledge.

Mayer-Schönberger, V. (2009). *Delete: The virtue of forgetting in the digital age.* Princeton University Press.

Meghdari, A., & Alemi, M. (2018). Recent advances in social & cognitive robotics and imminent ethical challenges. In *Proceedings of the 10th International RAIS Conference on Social Sciences and Humanities.* The Scientific Press. 10.2991/rais-18.2018.12

Milanovic, B. (2013). Global income inequality in numbers: In history and now. *Global Policy, 4*(2), 198–208. doi:10.1111/1758-5899.12032

Mumford, A. (2001). *Taxing culture.* Ashgate.

Murphy, K. M., Riddell, W. C., & Romer, P. M. (1998). *Wages, skills, and technology in the United States and Canada.* Cambridge, MA: National Bureau of Economic Research (NBER) Working Paper 6638. Retrieved at https://www.nber.org/papers/w6638.pdf

Ngai, L. R., & Pissarides, Ch. A. (2007). Structural change in a multi-sector model of growth. *The American Economic Review, 97*(1), 429–443. doi:10.1257/aer.97.1.429

Noyes, K. (2016). 5 things you need to know about A.I.: Cognitive, neural and deep, oh my! *Computerworld.* Retrieved at www.computerworld.com/article/3040563/enterprise-applications/5-things-you-need-toknow-about-ai-cognitive-neural-anddeep-oh-my.html

Parente, St. & Prescott, E. (1993). Changes in the wealth of nations. *Quarterly Review of Economics, 17*(2), 3-16.

Petri, F. (2009). *On the recent debate on capital theory and general equilibrium.* Quaderni del Dipartimento di Economia Politica, Università di Siena.

Piketty, Th. (1997). The dynamics of the wealth distribution and the interest rate with credit rationing. *The Review of Economic Studies, 64*(2), 173–189. doi:10.2307/2971708

Piketty, Th. (2016). *Capital in the Twenty-First Century.* Harvard University Press.

Price, L. (2020). *Impact of COVID-19 on small businesses: Where is it worst?* Small Business Trends. Retrieved at https://smallbiztrends.com/2020/04/impact-of-coronavirus-on-small-businesses.html

Pritchett, L. (1997). Divergence, big time. *The Journal of Economic Perspectives, 11*(3), 3–17. doi:10.1257/jep.11.3.3

Puaschunder, J.M. (2016). Putty capital and clay labor: Differing European Union capital and labor freedom speeds in times of European migration. *The New School Economic Review: A Journal of Critical Economics at The New School, 8*(3), 147-168.

Puaschunder, J. M. (2017a). Nudging in the digital big data era. European Journal of Economics. *Law and Politics, 4*(4), 18–23.

Puaschunder, J. M. (2017b). Nudgital: Critique of Behavioral Political Economy. *Archives of Business Research, 5*(9), 54–76. doi:10.14738/abr.59.3623

Puaschunder, J. M. (2017c). Nudgitize me! A behavioral finance approach to minimize losses and maximize profits from heuristics and biases. *International Journal of Management Excellence, 10*(2), 1241–1256. doi:10.17722/ijme.v10i2.957

Puaschunder, J. M. (2018a). *Artificial Intelligence Evolution: On the virtue of killing in the artificial age.* Social Science Research Network working paper. https://papers.ssrn.com/sol3/papers.cfm?abstract_id=3247401

Puaschunder, J. M. (2018b). Nudgitize me! A behavioral finance approach to minimize losses and maximize profits from heuristics and biases. *Journal of Organizational Psychology, 18*(1), 46–66.

Puaschunder, J. M. (2019a). Artificial diplomacy: A guide for public officials to conduct Artificial Intelligence. *Journal of Applied Research in the Digital Economy, 1,* 39–45. doi:10.2139srn.3376302

Puaschunder, J. M. (2019b). *Artificial Intelligence, big data, and algorithms in healthcare.* Report on behalf of the European Parliament European Liberal Forum in cooperation with The New Austria and Liberal Forum. Retrieved at https://papers.ssrn.com/sol3/papers.cfm?abstract_id=3472885

Puaschunder, J. M. (2019c). Towards a utility theory of privacy and information sharing and the introduction of hyper-hyperbolic discounting in the digital big data age. In E. Idemudia (Ed.), *Handbook of Research on Social and Organizational Dynamics in the Digital Era* (pp. 157–200). IGI Publishing.

Puaschunder, J. M. (2020a). *Behavioral Economics and Finance Leadership: Nudging and Winking to make Better Choices.* Springer Nature. doi:10.1007/978-3-030-54330-3

Puaschunder, J. M. (2020b). Economic growth in times of pandemics. *Proceedings of the ConScienS Conference on Science & Society: Pandemics and their Impact on Society,* 1-9. 10.2139srn.3679359

Puaschunder, J. M. (2020c). The future of the city after COVID-19: Digitionalization, preventism and environmentalism. *Proceedings of the ConScienS Conference on Science & Society: Pandemics and their Impact on Society,* 125-129.

Puaschunder, J. M. (2021a). Alleviating COVID-19 inequality. *ConScienS Conference Proceedings,* 185-190.

Puaschunder, J. M. (2021b). Generation COVID-19 Long Haulers. *Scientia Moralitas Conference Proceedings,* 99-104.

Puaschunder, J. M. (2021c). *Verhaltensökonomie und Verhaltensfinanzökonomie: Ein Vergleich europäischer und nordamerikanischer Modelle.* Springer Gabler. doi:10.1007/978-3-658-32474-2

Puaschunder, J. M. (forthcoming). The future of Artificial Intelligence in international healthcare: Integrating technology, productivity, anti-corruption and healthcare interaction around the world with three indices. *Journal of Applied Research in the Digital Economy.* Advance online publication. doi:10.2139srn.3633951

Puaschunder, J. M., & Gelter, M. (2021). The law, economics and governance of generation COVID-19 Long-Haul. *Indiana Health Law Review / [Indiana University School of Law-Indianapolis]*, *19*(1), 47–126. doi:10.18060/26085

Puaschunder, J. M., Gelter, M., & Sharma, S. (2020a). Alleviating an unequal COVID-19 world: Globally digital and productively healthy. *Proceedings of the 1st Unequal World Conference: On Human Development.*

Puaschunder, J. M., Gelter, M., & Sharma, S. (2020b). COVID-19 shock: Considerations on socio-technological, legal, corporate, economic and governance changes and trends. *Proceedings of the 18th International Research Association for Interdisciplinary Studies Conference on Social Sciences & Humanities*, 82-93. Retrieved at http://rais.education/wp-content/uploads/2020/08/011JPB.pdf

Rajan, R. G., & Zingales, L. (1998). Financial dependence and growth. *The American Economic Review*, *88*(3), 559–586.

Restuccia, D., & Rogerson, R. (2017). The causes and costs of misallocation. *The Journal of Economic Perspectives*, *31*(3), 151–174. doi:10.1257/jep.31.3.151

Restuccia, D., & Urrutia, C. (2001). Relative prices and investment rates. *Journal of Monetary Economics*, *47*(1), 93–121. doi:10.1016/S0304-3932(00)00049-0

Romer, P. M. (1986). Increasing returns and long-term growth. *Journal of Political Economy*, *94*(5), 1002–1037. doi:10.1086/261420

Romer, P. M. (1987). Growth based on increasing returns to specialization. *The American Economic Review*, *77*(2), 56–62.

Romer, P. M. (1990). Endogenous Technological Change. *Journal of Political Economy*, *98*(5), 71–102. doi:10.1086/261725

Romer, P. M. (1993). Idea gaps and object gaps in economic development. *Journal of Monetary Economics*, *32*(3), 543–573. doi:10.1016/0304-3932(93)90029-F

Romer, P. M. (1994). New goods, old theory, and the welfare costs of trade restrictions. *Journal of Development Economics*, *43*(1), 5–38. doi:10.1016/0304-3878(94)90021-3

Romer, P. M. (2019). *Nobel Lecture: On the possibility of progress.* Retrieved at https://paulromer.net/prize/

Russell, St., & Norvig, P. (1995). *Artificial intelligence a modern approach.* Simon & Schuster.

Saffari, E., Meghdari, A., Vazirnezhad, B., & Alemi, M. (2015). Ava (a social robot): Design and performance of a robotic hearing apparatus. LNCS: Social Robotics, 9388, 440-450.

Schumpeter, J. A. (1934). *The theory of economic development*. Harvard University Press.

Schumpeter, J. A. (1943/1976). *Capitalism, socialism and democracy*. Allen & Unwin.

Schumpeter, J. A. (1989). *Essays on entrepreneurs, innovations, business cycles, and the evolution of capitalism*. Routledge.

Sofge, E. (2015). Bill Gates fears A.I., but A.I. researchers know better. *Popular Science*. Retrieved at www.popsci.com/bill-gates-fears-ai-ai-researchers-know-better

Solow, R. (1956). A contribution to the theory of economic growth. *The Quarterly Journal of Economics*, *70*(1), 65–94. doi:10.2307/1884513

Solum, L. (1992). Legal personhood for Artificial Intelligences. *North Carolina Law Review*, *70*(4), 1231–1287.

Stiglitz, J. (1998). The private uses of public interests: Incentives and institutions. *The Journal of Economic Perspectives*, *12*(2), 3–22. doi:10.1257/jep.12.2.3

Stroebe, W., & Frey, B. S. (1982). Self-interest and collective action: The economics and psychology of public goods. *British Journal of Social Psychology*, *21*(2), 121–137. doi:10.1111/j.2044-8309.1982.tb00521.x

Swiecki, T. (2017). Determinants of structural change. *Review of Economic Dynamics*, *17*(24), 95–131. doi:10.1016/j.red.2017.01.007

Tcherneva, P. (2011). Bernanke's paradox: Can he reconcile his position on the federal budget with his charge to prevent deflation? *Journal of Post Keynesian Economics*, *3*(33), 411–434. doi:10.2753/PKE0160-3477330301

The Economist. (2019, Jan. 26). The steam has gone out of globalisation: Slowbalisation. *The Economist*, 17-20.

The White House of The United States of America. (2021). Retrieved at https://www.whitehouse.gov/briefing-room/legislation/2021/01/20/president-biden-announces-american-rescue-plan/

The White House of The United States of America. (2021). *Fact Sheet: Biden-Harris Administration Marks Anniversary of Americans with Disabilities Act and Announces Resources to Support Individuals with Long COVID*. https://www.whitehouse.gov/briefing-room/statements-releases/2021/07/26/fact-sheet-bidenharris-administration-marks-anniversary-of-americans-with-disabilities-act-and-announces-resources-tosupport-individuals-with-long-covid/

The World Economic Forum. (2021). *The World Economic Forum Great Reset*. https://www.weforum.org/great-reset/

Themistoklis, T. (2018). Artificial intelligence as global commons and the "international law supremacy" principle. In *Proceedings of the 10th International RAIS Conference on Social Sciences and Humanities*. The Scientific Press.

Townsend, R. M., & Ueda, K. (2006). Financial deepening, inequality, and growth: A model-based quantitative evaluation. *The Review of Economic Studies*, *73*(1), 251–293. doi:10.1111/j.1467-937X.2006.00376.x

United Nations Department of Economic and Social Affairs. (2017). *Will robots and AI cause mass unemployment? Not necessarily, but they do bring other threats*. https://www.un.org/development/desa/en/news/policy/will-robots-and-ai-cause-mass-unemployment-not-necessarily-but-they-do-bring-other-threats.html

Uzawa, H. (1965). Optimum technical change in an aggregative model of economic growth. *International Economic Review*, *6*(1), 18–31. doi:10.2307/2525621

Van Neuss, L. (2019). The drivers of structural change. *Journal of Economic Surveys*, *33*(1), 309–349. doi:10.1111/joes.12266

Ventura, J. (1997). Growth and interdependence. *The Quarterly Journal of Economics*, *112*(1), 57–84. doi:10.1162/003355397555127

Wu, A. H. (2018). Gendered language on the economics job market rumors forum. *American Economic Association Papers and Proceedings*, *108*, 175–179. doi:10.1257/pandp.20181101

ADDITIONAL READING

Puaschunder, J. M. (2018). *Corporate social responsibility and opportunities for sustainable financial success*. IGI.

Puaschunder, J. M. (2019). Stakeholder perspectives on Artificial Intelligence (AI), robotics and big data in healthcare: An empirical study. Report on behalf of a European Parliament Agency.

Puaschunder, J. M. (2019). The legal and international situation of AI, robotics and big data with attention to healthcare. Report on behalf of a European Parliament Agency. doi:10.2139srn.3472885

Puaschunder, J. M. (2019). *Big data, Artificial Intelligence and healthcare: Developing a legal, policy and ethical framework for using AI, big data, robotics and algorithms in healthcare*. Report on behalf of the European Parliament European Liberal Forum in cooperation with The New Austria and Liberal Forum Lab.

Puaschunder, J. M. (forthcoming). Advances in Behavioral Economics and Finance Leadership: Strategic leadership, wise followership and conscientious usership in the digital century. *Springer Nature*.

Puaschunder, J. M., & Beerbaum, D. (2020). The future of healthcare around the world: Four indices integrating technology, productivity, anti-corruption, healthcare and market financialization. *Proceedings of the 18th Interdisciplinary RAIS conference at Princeton University*.

KEY TERMS AND DEFINITIONS

AI: Artificial intelligence (AI) as intelligence demonstrated by machines, in contrast to the natural intelligence displayed by humans and other animals.

Artificial Intelligence Ethics: AI ethics is a system of moral principles and techniques intended to inform the development and responsible use of artificial intelligence technology. As AI has become integral to products and services, organizations are starting to develop AI codes of ethics.

Big Data: Big data refers to data sets that are too large or complex to be dealt with by traditional data-processing application software. Data with many fields offer greater statistical power, while data with higher complexity may lead to a higher false discovery rate.

Blackhat Strategies: Blackhat strategies are used to make competitors' online content disappear and search engine results clogged with useless information or defamation occurs in bloating negative contents via click farms.

COVID-19: COVID-19 is caused by a coronavirus called SARS-CoV-2. Older adults and people who have severe underlying medical conditions like heart or lung disease or diabetes seem to be at higher risk for developing more serious complications from COVID-19 illness.

Digitalization: Digitization is the process of converting information into a digital format. The result is the representation of an object, image, sound, document, or signal obtained by generating a series of numbers that describe a discrete set of points or samples.

E-Ethics: The concept of e-ethics is expanded on behavioral online ethics in the digital century. E-Ethics argues for ethical conduct online. E-Ethics concern a fair searchplace mandate and the concept of searchplace discrimination alleviation.

Economic Growth: Economic growth is the process by which a nation's wealth increases over time.

FDI: A foreign direct investment (FDI) is a purchase of an interest in a company by a company or an investor located outside its borders.

GDP: Gross domestic product (GDP) is the standard measure of the value added created through the production of goods and services in a country during a certain period.

Long COVID or Post-COVID Conditions: Estimated 10-30% of previously COVID-19 infected can experience long-term effects from their infection, known as post-COVID conditions (PCC) or long COVID. People call post-COVID conditions by many names, including: long COVID, long-haul COVID, post-acute COVID-19, post-acute sequelae of SARS CoV-2 infection (PASC), long-term effects of COVID, and chronic COVID.

Right to Deletion: The "Right to Deletion Under CCPA" mandates that if a consumer makes a verified request to the business to delete his or her personal data, the business is legally required to delete the requestor's personal information from all of its data stores and direct any service providers to delete the personal data as well.

Right to Not Be Forgotten: A 'Right to Not be Forgotten' and to be online present is argued for in the eye of online searchplace discrimination.

Searchplace Discrimination: Edges of ethical market behavior appear in the harmful online abuse of nudges in negative blackhat strategies in search engines.

ENDNOTES

[1]   https://home.treasury.gov/news/press-releases/jy0565

[2]   https://data.worldbank.org/indicator/ny.gdp.pcap.cd

[3]   https://data.worldbank.org/indicator/it.net.user.zs

Chapter 5

How Can Advancement in Information Technology Help College Students During the COVID–19 Pandemic?
Evidence From the Video Game Industry

Reza Gharoie Ahangar
Lewis University, USA

ABSTRACT

A revolution in information technology advancements has been started in recent years. A part of these technology advancements is happening in the video gaming industry. This study investigates the effect of video games on college students' performance during the COVID-19 pandemic. The authors examined the impact of video games on students' academic performance from the lens of time spent on video games and their effects on students' well-being and personal life during the COVID-19 pandemic. This study proposed a conceptual framework that highlights the positive impact of video games on students' mental health and academic performance during the COVID-19 pandemic.

INTRODUCTION

A few days before the New Year of 2020, a very highly contagious virus from the family of the severe acute respiratory syndrome, COVID-19, originated and spread from Wuhan, Hubei Province, People's Republic of China (PRC) (Gharoie Ahangar

DOI: 10.4018/978-1-7998-9418-6.ch005

et al., 2020; Huang et al., 2020; Tan et al., 2020). The COVID-19 pandemic put global public health in danger that the World Health Organization (WHO) declared a global pandemic (World Health Organization, 2022; Wang et al., 2020).

The number of COVID-19 infections has been increasing worldwide with the emergence of different variants. This situation continues to grow, even after the appearance of certain vaccines for the treatment of the virus, especially in the United States (US). Around 535 million cases and 6.31 million deaths worldwide and 85.4 million and 1.01 million cases in the US have been reported as of June 12, 2022 (World Health Organization, 2022).

There are some concerns about the duration of the COVID-19 pandemic; therefore, governments must have comprehensive plans and practical tools to control the outbreaks properly. In a study, He et al. (2020) examined emerging technologies to address the challenges of COVID-19 related to technology design, development, and use and how information technology can help scholars fight the COVID-19 pandemic. The COVID-19 pandemic has created a situation where the advancement of information technology is unavoidable for innovation in education and work (Xie et al., 2020). In addition, confinement restrictions from the authorities and the rapid adoption of remote and online work from home have changed the lifestyle of people (Loayza & Pennings, 2020; Yilmazkuday, 2020).

Among these people, college students are a group of people who are more sensitive due to the nature of their jobs and ages. Some schools have adapted to the crisis situation to offer online classes, and some families do not allow their children to spend their free time in public areas. Therefore, for the students to occupy their spare time, they needed to find interesting hobbies at home during the Pandemic that could help them focus on their school assignments.

Before the COVID-19 pandemic, around 2.5 billion gamers globally spent approximately 152 billion dollars on games (Wijman, 2019). In 2020, when the COVID-19 pandemic deteriorated most industries' profits, the video game industry experienced a significant increase. In late March 2020, video game sales increased by around 60% worldwide (Statista, 2020) because video games help people to have remote contact with each other during the COVID-19 pandemic.

Among these gamers, most are college students. Past research works in this area show different findings. Some researches show the adverse effects of extensive video gaming on school performance, while some suggest a positive relationship between gaming and students' academic performance (Balhara et al., 2020; Kovess-Masfety et al., 2015; Posso, 2016).

By considering the continuous COVOD-19 pandemic situation and online and remote education from home, this study aims to propose a theoretical framework that investigates the role of video games on the academic performance of college students during the COVID-19 pandemic. The findings can help the universities' policymakers allocate and provide appropriate resources for college students to help them to be more successful in remote and online classes and help them be in good mental health.

The main research question of this study is as follows. How can advancement in information technology help college students during the COVID-19 pandemic? Moreover, the other research questions that this study attempts to address are 1-Does video game helps college students to get better sleep during the COVID-19 pandemic? 2-Does video game has a positive impact on the academic performance of college students?

The organization of the rest of this paper is as follows. In Section 2, the video game industry and related literature reviews are described. In Section 3, the proposed IT-Pandemic Model is discussed, and hypotheses developments are explained. Section 4 presents the conclusion. Finally, in Section 5, some suggestions are proposed.

The organization of the rest of chapter is as follows. In Section 2, the research methodology is explained. In Section 3, the video game industry and related literature reviews are described. In Section 4, the proposed IT-Pandemic Model is discussed, and hypotheses developments are explained. Section 5 presents the conclusion. Finally, in Section 6, some suggestions and future works are proposed.

Methodology

It is essential to integrate human behavior with governments and organizations' frameworks when designing and building new technological approaches related to COVID-19. Sometimes human misbehaviors regarding technological approaches hinder the effectiveness of implementing a COVID-19 related technology. Information technology scholars can reduce the obstacle of technology approaches by designing appropriate frameworks that incorporate human behavior into technology development (Pfleeger & Caputo, 2012).

Some models and theories can be used to help scholars accept COVID-19 related technologies that can be more appropriate for implementing and examining new technological roles in organizations. These theories that help build this study's conceptual model include technology acceptance theory, health belief theory, social cognitive theory, and time displacement theory (He et al., 2020). Information technology scholars can incorporate the above theories into their studies to examine college students' information-sharing behavior during online classes and online gaming to find how the COVID-19 pandemic affected the physical and mental behavior of students.

This study applied the mentioned theories and reviewed the existing literature to adopt qualitative research that describes the interpretive research paradigm. Different scholarly works on the effect of video games during the COVID-19 pandemic were reviewed. The relevant information on the video games industry and its effect on college students' performance were systematically extracted and then analyzed through a critical literature review.

This study's defined critical literature review is a systematic evaluation of several research sources that focus on video games before and during the COVID-19 pandemic. The extracted information was appraised and incorporated objectively with the proposed theoretical framework to answer the research questions raised in this study.

Over 30 scholarly articles before and during COVID-19 were studied to ensure an appreciable degree of objectivity in selecting related scholarly works on the effect of video games on the performance of college students during the COVID-19 pandemic. The author systematically reviewed the literature of these articles to propose a theoretical model that shows the impact of video games on students' academic performance from the lens of time spent on video games and their effects on students' well-being and personal life during the COVID-19 pandemic.

VIDEO GAMES INDUSTRY

There have been some technological advancements in the last two decades. Some of these new advancements can help people spend their time together during global pandemics (e.g., COVID-19) even if they are not in the same physical place. The video game industry is one of these technological advancements that help people contact each other remotely, especially during the COVID-19 pandemic (Balhara et al., 2020; Barr et al., 2022).

Video games are a type of hobby at home that has an increasing number of young and college students' users. Entertainment Software Association (ESA), a body that represents the gaming industry, in its 2019 report, published that 65% of American adults with an average age of 33 years old play video games. This report also reveals that, on average, adult gamers spend 4.8 hours a week on online games and 3.5 hours a week playing with others in person (ESA, 2019).

The literature review on video gaming and academic performance reveal that some researchers have found a negative correlation, while others have focused on the positive effects. Even before the COVID-19 pandemic, several researchers have found positive impacts of video games, especially related to visual motor skills and attention deficit individuals.

Playing video games can improve hand-eye coordination reaction times and raise self-esteem (Griffiths et al., 1983; Fernández-Bustos et al., 2019) among the users. Video games increase brain-wave biofeedback, and this helps attention-deficit children to control better some involuntary body functions such as heart rate through real-time monitoring of the related responses (Wright, 2011). Video gaming is also a source of active distraction and is a medical approach to pain management (Jameson et al., 2011). Additionally, video games increase visual-spatial skills in some fields such as Science, Mathematics, Technology, and Engineering (Jackson et al., 2011).

Balhara et al. (2020), in their study about college students, found that gaming behavior increased during the lockdown. Therefore, balancing online schooling from home and this type of behavior is necessary for students' psychological and physical well-being (King et al., 2020). In a study, Barr and Copeland-Stewart (2022) conducted an online survey to find the effect of video games on well-being during the lockdown. They find that the time spent playing games has increased significantly for most of the participants. Also, around 60% of participants reported that video games positively impacted their well-being and overall life during the lockdown. They indicate that some benefits of video games are cognitive stimulation, socialization, and reduced stress & anxiety.

Earlier, Männikkö et al. (2017), in their study, showed positive emotions and happier behaviors among online gamers compared to other people. In another study, Marston and Kowert (2021) studied the effect of video games on the daily life of older people during the COVID-19 pandemic. Their findings show that video games are stress-free tools that increase social connectivity and improve psychological healing among older people.

Prior researches show a positive relationship between sleep and human memory performance, particularly in procedural and declarative memory. Human memory consists of procedural and declarative memory. Procedural memory is related to solving a problem and is usually taught unconsciously. Declarative memory is consciously associated with knowledge recollection (Squire, 1992).

Researchers have declared a dual-process hypothesis consisting of two main sleep types about the effect of sleep on memory. These two main types of sleep are rapid eye movement (REM) and non-rapid-eye-movement (NREM). REM sleep improves procedural memory, and NREM sleep improves declarative memory (Bon, 2020; Knoop et al., 2020; Peigneux et al., 2001; Smith, 2001).

However, scientists are not sure which types of sleep help the learning and memory function more, but it seems both R.E.M. and NREM sleep are vital for the learning and memory of people, especially students (Bon, 2020; Curcio et al., 2006; Knoop et al., 2020). In a study, Blum et al. (1990) compared average and poor sleepers, and they found that around 20% of poor sleepers failed one or more years at college compared to approximately 10% of regular sleepers. In other studies, Link et al. (1995), Abdulghani (2012), Hershner (2020), and Valdes et al. (2021) show that students with regular sleep-wake patterns could have a higher G.P.A. than students who reported daytime sleepiness due to less night sleep.

Since online and remote classes make it boring for students and they do not have physical contact with their classmates to spend their daily energy at school, it would be hard for them to have regular sleep time and fall asleep early at night. Instead, they will be awake for a longer period; and, therefore, go to bed late, and consequently, their sleeping time would change to daytime. Alternatively, video games can help them spend a portion of their energy, which allows them to fall asleep better.

We also know that based on the time displacement theory, the time spent on a new activity will cause a reduction in the time spent on an existing activity due to the zero-sum nature of time (Nie & Hillygus, 2002). Given that there are only 24 hours in a day. If a student cannot get enough sleep due to the negative effect of the COVID-19 pandemic, and mainly due to the nature of remote and online classes, it would also hurt students' academic performance. In the next section, we develop the hypotheses of this study based on the literature reviews.

PROPOSED FRAMEWORK OF IT-PANDEMIC AND HYPOTHESIS DEVELOPMENT

After reviewing the literature and further exploration, this study shows that video games positively impact students' academic performance. Therefore, based on the above theoretical background discussed in the literature, we propose a theoretical conceptual model, which shows the relationship between video-gaming-related factors and students' academic performance at school. To understand this phenomenon, we present the following hypotheses to investigate our research questions:

H1: COVID-19 pandemic has a negative impact on the sleep of college students

H2: COVID-19 pandemic has a positive impact on the number of hours of video games played by college students

H3: Video games help college students to get better sleep during the COVID-19 pandemic

H4: Video games help college students in their academic performance at college during the COVID-19 pandemic

H5: Getting enough sleep help college students to have a better academic performance

H6: Remote learning due to the COVID-19 pandemic negatively moderate the relationship between the sleep and academic performance of college students

H7: Time spent on school work positively moderates the relationship between the video games and the academic performance of college students

Therefore, after reviewing the literature, the proposed conceptual model is as follows.

Figure 1. The proposed conceptual IT-COVID-19 pandemic model of college students

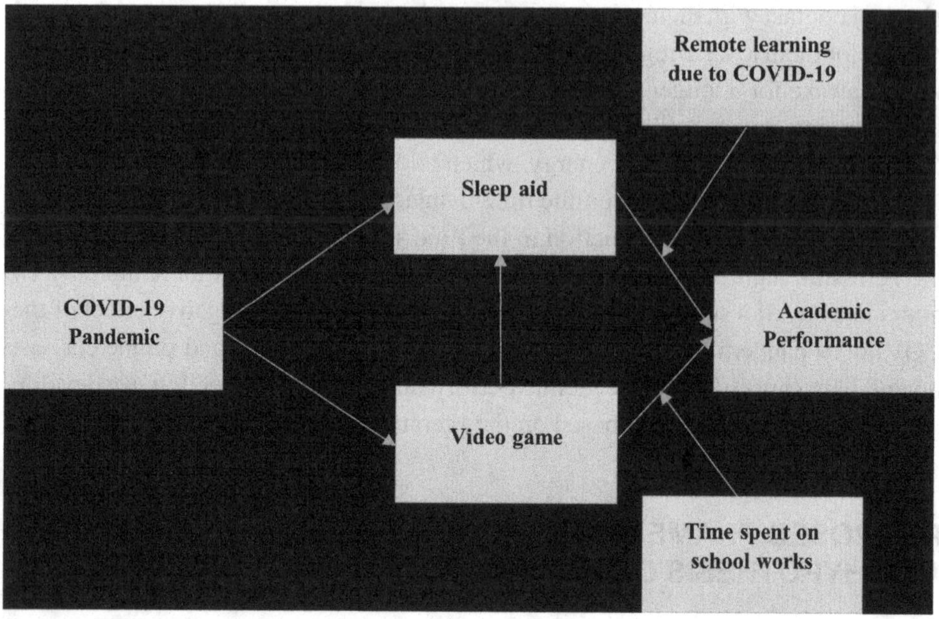

CONCLUSION

This study proposes a conceptual model that can be tested in an academic environment after collecting the related data. The proposed model examines the effect of the COVID-19 Pandemic on the academic performance of college students through the constructs of video games and sleep aid during the COVID-19 Pandemic.

COVID-19 has several physical and psychological impacts on college students (Browning et al., 2021; Ghazawy et al., 2021; Khan et al., 2020; Wilson et al., 2021), and the physical impact is more evident than the psychological impact. The psychological effect of the COVID-19 pandemic might not be as apparent as the physical impacts on scientists and even parents due to the remote delivery of courses. Before the pandemic, all classes were held in person in different universities worldwide, but after the global pandemic, almost all schools shifted to remote and online delivery types. We still observe that many schools prefer online classes due to the risk of infection by new variants of COVID-19.

Since we still have online or remote delivery of classes, some parents are concerned about their college students' academic performance, and they expect their children have a balance between their academic assignments and leisure time at home. The literature review of some studies about COVID-19 and video games shows that being at home and taking online classes instead of in-person courses encourages students to spend more time on video games. On the other hand, this will raise concern among the parents and academic advisors about whether spending more time on video games harms students' academic success.

After reviewing the literature, we found some issues that can impact the academic performance of college students are mental and psychological problems related to staying at home and online delivery of courses (Browning et al., 2021; Ghazawy et al., 2021; Khan et al., 2021; Wilson et al., 2021). Indeed, video games help college students cope with these issues properly and help the students to fall asleep better and recharge for other daily activities.

The conceptual model in this paper shows that academic performance can increase during the COVID-19 pandemic by increasing the hours of video games among college students (a manageable number of hours). Video games help the students have mental and physical activities at home. It allows them to spend their daily energy on games, which helps them fall asleep better and forget the bad feeling of remote and online shapes of classes.

SUGGESTIONS AND FUTURE WORKS

There are some suggestions for the academic advisors and school representatives based on the literature review and the proposed conceptual model that can help the students better during the pandemic.

Schools can have weekly online meetings, which can be activities unrelated to school assignments. This meeting can be an activity that connects the students to spend their free time together and forget the online or remote types of classes. The meeting would be an activity that can be interesting for students and help them be more active at home and spend their daily energy at home with remote connections.

For example, the schools can perform some volunteer dance classes or teach some types of aerobic activities that students can do at home, which would help students' well-being & mental health, and they can spend free time with their friends remotely. The schools can also change some intramural games to online, encouraging more students to participate in online activities. These activities would help the college students to be physically active at home.

Another suggestion to help the academic representatives and students burden the remote delivery of courses is conducting online video games related to their classes. For example, the students can make small groups and then have scientific competitions, similar to classroom in-person group activities. In other words, the instructors can shift more toward group activity instead of individual assessment because it helps the students participate more in academic activities since they are not in physical classes.

For future research directions, scholars can collect the relevant data to test this study's theoretical framework empirically. Based on the literature and the conceptual model in this study, future studies can investigate the effect of video games on the academic performance of college students. The sample of the college students can also be divided into undergrad and graduate students. It is expected that the proposed theoretical model to be more appropriate for undergrad sample data since most graduate students are working while studying.

ACKNOWLEDGMENT

I would like to express my great appreciation to my professor, Dr. Arunachalam Narayanan, and two anonymous reviewers for their valuable and constructive suggestions.

REFERENCES

Abdulghani, H. M., Alrowais, N. A., Bin-Saad, N. S., Al-Subaie, N. M., Haji, A. M. A., & Alhaqwi, A. I. (2012). Sleep disorder among medical students: Relationship to their academic performance. *Medical Teacher*, *34*(sup1), S37–S41. doi:10.3109 /0142159X.2012.656749 PMID:22409189

Balhara, Y. P. S., Kattula, D., Singh, S., Chukkali, S., & Bhargava, R. (2020). Impact of lockdown following COVID-19 on the gaming behavior of college students. *Indian Journal of Public Health*, *64*(6), 172–176. doi:10.4103/ijph.IJPH_465_20 PMID:32496250

Barr, M., & Copeland-Stewart, A. (2022). Playing video games during the COVID-19 pandemic and effects on players' well-being. *Games and Culture*, *17*(1), 122–139. doi:10.1177/15554120211017036

Blum, D., Kahn, A., Mozin, M. J., Rebuffat, E., Sottiaux, M., & Van de Merckt, C. (1990). Relation between chronic insomnia and school failure in preadolescents. *Sleep Research*, *19*, 194.

Bon, O. L. (2020). Relationships between REM and NREM in the NREM-REM sleep sycle: a review on competing concepts. *Sleep Medicine*. doi:10.1016/j. sleep.2020.02.004

Browning, M. H. E. M., Larson, L. R., Sharaievska, I., Rigolon, A., McAnirlin, O., Mullenbach, L., Cloutier, S., Vu, T. M., Thomsen, J., Reigner, N., Metcalf, E. C., D'Antonio, A., Helbich, M., Bratman, G. N., & Alvarez, H. O. (2021). Psychological impacts from COVID-19 among university students: Risk factors across seven states in the United States. *PLoS One, 16*(1), e0245327. Advance online publication. doi:10.1371/journal.pone.0245327 PMID:33411812

Curcio, G., Ferrara, M., & De Gennaro, L. (2006). Sleep loss, learning capacity, and academic performance. *Sleep Medicine Reviews, 10*(5), 323–337. doi:10.1016/j.smrv.2005.11.001 PMID:16564189

Entertainment Software Association. (2019). *Essential facts 2019 report 1*. Author.

Fernández-Bustos, J. G., Infantes-Paniagua, Á., Cuevas, R., & Contreras, O. R. (2019). Effect of Physical Activity on Self-Concept: Theoretical Model on the Mediation of Body Image and Physical Self-Concept in Adolescents. *Frontiers in Psychology, 10*, 1537. doi:10.3389/fpsyg.2019.01537 PMID:31354570

Gharoie Ahangar, R., Pavur, R., Fathi, M., & Shaik, A. (2020). Estimation and demographic analysis of COVID-19 infections with respect to weather factors in Europe. *Journal of Business Analytics, 3*(2), 93–106. doi:10.1080/257323 4X.2020.1832866

Ghazawy, E. R., Ewis, A. A., Mahfouz, E. M., Khalil, D. M., Arafa, A., Mohammed, Z., Mohammed, E.-N. F., Hassan, E. E., Abdel Hamid, S., Ewis, S. A., & Mohammed, A. E.-N. S. (2021). Psychological impacts of COVID-19 pandemic on the university students in Egypt. *Health Promotion International, 36*(4), 1116–1125. doi:10.1093/heapro/daaa147 PMID:33367587

Griffith, J. L., Voloschin, P., Gibb, G. D., & Bailey, J. R. (1983). Differences in eye-hand motor coordination of video-game users and non-users. *Perceptual and Motor Skills, 57*(1), 155–158. doi:10.2466/pms.1983.57.1.155 PMID:6622153

He, W., Zhang, J., & Li, W. (2020). Information Technology Solutions, Challenges, and Suggestions for Tackling the COVID-19 Pandemic. *International Journal of Information Management, 102287*. Advance online publication. doi:10.1016/j.ijinfomgt.2020.1022 PMID:33318721

Hershner, S. (2020). Sleep and academic performance: Measuring the impact of sleep. *Current Opinion in Behavioral Sciences, 33*, 51–56. doi:10.1016/j.cobeha.2019.11.009

Huang, C., Wang, Y., Li, X., Ren, L., Zhao, J., Hu, Y., Zhang, L., Fan, G., Xu, J., Gu, X., Cheng, Z., Yu, T., Xia, J., Wei, Y., Wu, W., Xie, X., Yin, W., Li, H., Liu, M., ... Cao, B. (2020). Clinical features of patients infected with 2019 novel coronavirus in Wuhan, China. *Lancet*, *395*(10223), 497–506. Advance online publication. doi:10.1016/S0140-6736(20)30183-5 PMID:31986264

Jackson, L. A., Von Eye, A., Witt, E. A., Zhao, Y., & Fitzgerald, H. E. (2011). A longitudinal study of the effects of Internet use and videogame playing on academic performance and the roles of gender, race and income in these relationships. *Computers in Human Behavior*, *27*(1), 228–239. doi:10.1016/j.chb.2010.08.001

Jameson, E., Trevena, J., & Swain, N. (2011). Electronic gaming as pain distraction. *Pain Research & Management*, *16*(1), 27–32. doi:10.1155/2011/856014 PMID:21369538

Khan, A. H., Sultana, S., Hossain, S., Hasan, M. T., Ahmed, H. U., & Sikder, T. (2020). The impact of COVID-19 pandemic on mental health & wellbeing among home-quarantined Bangladeshi students: A cross-sectional pilot study. *Journal of Affective Disorders*, *277*, 121–128. Advance online publication. doi:10.1016/j.jad.2020.07.135 PMID:32818775

King, D. L., Delfabbro, P. H., Billieux, J., & Potenza, M. N. (2020). Problematic online gaming and the COVID-19 pandemic. *Journal of Behavioral Addictions*, *9*(2), 184–186. Advance online publication. doi:10.1556/2006.2020.00016 PMID:32352927

Knoop, M. S., de Groot, E. R., & Dudink, J. (2020). Current ideas about the roles of rapid eye movement and non-rapid eye movement sleep in brain development. *Acta Paediatrica (Oslo, Norway)*. Advance online publication. doi:10.1111/apa.15485 PMID:32673435

Kovess-Masfety, V., Pilowsky, D. J., Goelitz, D., Kuijpers, R., Otten, R., Moro, M. F., Bitfoi, A., Koç, C., Lesinskiene, S., Mihova, Z., Hanson, G., Fermanian, C., Pez, O., & Carta, M. G. (2015). Suicidal ideation and mental health disorders in young school children across Europe. *Journal of Affective Disorders*, *177*, 28–35. doi:10.1016/j.jad.2015.02.008 PMID:25745832

Link, S. C., & Ancoli-Israel, S. (1995). Sleep and the teenager. *Sleep Research*, *24*, 184.

Loayza, N. V., & Pennings, S. (2020). *Macroeconomic Policy in the Time of COVID-19: A Primer for Developing Countries*. World Bank. doi:10.1596/33540

Männikkö, N., Billieux, J., Nordström, T., Koivisto, K., & Kääriäinen, M. (2017). Problematic gaming behavior in Finnish adolescents and young adults: Relation to game genres, gaming motives and self-awareness of problematic use. *International Journal of Mental Health and Addiction, 15*(2), 324–338. doi:10.100711469-016-9726-7

Marston, H. R., & Kowert, R. (2020). What role can videogames play in the COVID-19 pandemic? *Emerald Open Research, 2*, 34. doi:10.35241/emeraldopenres.13727.2

Nie, N. H., & Hillygus, D. S. (2002). Where does Internet time come from? A reconnaissance. *ITandSociety, 1*(2), 1–20.

Peigneux, P., Laureys, S., Delbeuck, X., & Maquet, P. (2001). Sleeping brain, learning brain. The role of sleep for memory systems. *Neuroreport, 12*(18), A111–A124. doi:10.1097/00001756-200112210-00001 PMID:11742260

Pfleeger, S. L., & Caputo, D. D. (2012). Leveraging behavioral science to mitigate cyber security risk. *Computers & Security, 31*(4), 597–611. doi:10.1016/j.cose.2011.12.010

Posso, A. (2016). Internet usage and educational outcomes among 15-year old Australian students. *International Journal of Communication, 10*, 26.

Smith, C. (2001). Sleep states and memory processes in humans: Procedural versus declarative memory systems. *Sleep Medicine Reviews, 5*(6), 491–506. doi:10.1053mrv.2001.0164 PMID:12531156

Squire, L. R. (1992). Declarative and nondeclarative memory: Multiple brain systems supporting learning and memory. *Journal of Cognitive Neuroscience, 4*(3), 232–243. doi:10.1162/jocn.1992.4.3.232 PMID:23964880

Statista. (2020) *Increase in video game sales during the coronavirus (COVID-19) pandemic worldwide as of March 2020*. https://www.statista.com/statistics/1109977/video-gamesales-covid/

Tan, W. J., Zhao, X., & Ma, X. J. (2020). A novel coronavirus genome identified in a cluster of pneumonia cases—Wuhan, China 2019–2020. *China CDC Weekly, 2*, 61–62. doi:10.46234/ccdcw2020.017 PMID:34594763

Valdes, M., Rios, D., Rocha, A., & Rodriquez, K. (2021). Sleep Irregularity and Academic Performance. *Optometric Education, 46*(2).

Wang, L., Wang, Y., Ye, D., & Liu, Q. (2020). A review of the 2019 Novel Coronavirus (COVID-19) based on current evidence. *International Journal of Antimicrobial Agents, 105948*(6), 105948. Advance online publication. doi:10.1016/j.ijantimicag.2020.105948 PMID:32826129

Wijman, T. (2019) *The global games market will generate $152.1 billion in 2019 as the U.S. overtakes China as the biggest market.* https://newzoo.com/insights/articles/theglobal-games-market-will-generate-152-1-billion-in-2019-as-the-u-s-overtakes-china-as-the-biggest-market/

Wilson, O. W. A., Holland, K. E., Elliott, L. D., Duffey, M., & Bopp, M. (2021). The impact of COVID-19 pandemic on US college students' physical activity and mental health. *Journal of Physical Activity & Health, 18*(3), 272–278. doi:10.1123/jpah.2020-0325 PMID:33601332

World Health Organization. (2022). *Novel coronavirus (2019-nCoV) situation reports.* https://www.who.int/emergencies/diseases/novel-coronavirus-2019/situation-reports

Wright, J. (2011). The effects of video game play on academic performance. *Modern Psychological Studies, 17*(1), 37–44.

Xie, X., Siau, K., & Nah, F. F.-H. (2020). COVID-19 pandemic – online education in the new normal and the next normal. *Journal of Information Technology Case and Application Research, 22*(3), 175–187. doi:10.1080/15228053.2020.1824884

Yilmazkuday, H. (2020). Coronavirus Disease 2019 and the Global Economy. *Transport Policy, 120*, 40–46. doi:10.1016/j.tranpol.2022.03.003 PMID:35280846

ADDITIONAL READING

Amin, K. P., Griffiths, M. D., & Dsouza, D. D. (2022). Online Gaming During the COVID-19 Pandemic in India: Strategies for Work-Life Balance. *International Journal of Mental Health and Addiction, 20*(1), 296–302. doi:10.100711469-020-00358-1 PMID:32837441

Dubey, M. J., Ghosh, R., Chatterjee, S., Biswas, P., Chatterjee, S., & Dubey, S. (2020). COVID-19 and addiction. *Diabetes & Metabolic Syndrome, 14*(5), 817–823. Advance online publication. doi:10.1016/j.dsx.2020.06.008 PMID:32540735

Ellis, L. A., Lee, M. D., Ijaz, K., Smith, J., Braithwaite, J., & Yin, K. (2020). COVID-19 as Game Changer for the Physical Activity and Mental Well-Being of Augmented Reality Game Players During the Pandemic: Mixed Methods Survey Study. *Journal of Medical Internet Research*, 22(12), e25117. doi:10.2196/25117 PMID:33284781

Hakansson, A. (2020). Impact of COVID-19 on Online Gambling: A General Population Survey During the Pandemic. *Frontiers in Psychology*, *11*, 568543. Advance online publication. doi:10.3389/fpsyg.2020.568543 PMID:33101137

He, P., Niu, H., Sun, Z., & Li, T. (2020). Accounting Index of COVID-19 Impact on Chinese Industries: A Case Study Using Big Data Portrait Analysis. *Emerging Markets Finance & Trade*, *56*(10), 2332–2349. doi:10.1080/1540496X.2020.1785866

Kim, Y. H., Nauright, J., & Suveatwatanakul, C. (2020). The rise of E-Sports and potential for Post-COVID continued growth. *Sport in Society*, *23*(11), 1–11. doi:10.1080/17430437.2020.1819695

Kriz, W. C. (2020). Gaming in the Time of COVID-19. *Simulation & Gaming*, *51*(4), 403–410. doi:10.1177/1046878120931602

Mastromartino, B., Ross, W. J., Wear, H., & Naraine, M. L. (2020). Thinking outside the box: A discussion of sports fans, teams, and the environment in the context of COVID-19. *Sport in Society*, *1*(17), 1707–1723. Advance online publication. doi:10.1080/17430437.2020.1804108

Mohd, J., Abid, H., & Vaishya, R. (2020). Industry 4.0 technologies and their applications in fighting COVID-19 pandemic. *Diabetes & Metabolic Syndrome*, *14*(4), 419–422. doi:10.1016/j.dsx.2020.04.032 PMID:32344370

Riva, G., Mantovani, F., & Wiederhold, B. K. (2020). Positive Technology and COVID-19. *Cyberpsychology, Behavior, and Social Networking*, *23*(9), 581–587. Advance online publication. doi:10.1089/cyber.2020.29194.gri PMID:32833511

Sheth, J. (2020). Impact of Covid-19 on Consumer Behavior: Will the Old Habits Return or Die? *Journal of Business Research*, *117*, 280–283. Advance online publication. doi:10.1016/j.jbusres.2020.05.059 PMID:32536735

Thorbecke, W. (2020). The Impact of the COVID-19 Pandemic on the U.S. Economy: Evidence from the Stock Market. *Journal of Risk and Financial Management*, *13*(10), 233. Advance online publication. doi:10.3390/jrfm13100233

Wagner, A. F. (2020). What the stock market tells us about the post-COVID-19 world. *Nature Human Behaviour*, *4*(440), 440. Advance online publication. doi:10.103841562-020-0869-y PMID:32242087

Wannigamage, D., Barlow, M., Lakshika, E., & Kasmarik, K. (2020). Analysis and Prediction of Player Population Changes in Digital Games During the COVID-19 Pandemic. In M. Gallagher, N. Moustafa, & E. Lakshika (Eds.), Lecture Notes in Computer Science: Vol. 12576. *AI 2020: Advances in Artificial Intelligence. AI 2020*. Springer. doi:10.1007/978-3-030-64984-5_36

Zheng, Y., Goh, E., & Wen, J. (2020). The effects of misleading media reports about COVID-19 on Chinese tourists' mental health: A perspective article. *Anatolia*, *1–4*(2), 337–340. Advance online publication. doi:10.1080/13032917.2020.1747208

Zou, C., Zhao, W., & Siau, K. (2020). COVID-19 Pandemic: A Usability Study on Platforms to Support eLearning. In C. Stephanidis, M. Antona, & S. Ntoa (Eds.), *HCI International 2020 – Late Breaking Posters. HCII 2020. Communications in Computer and Information Science* (Vol. 1294). Springer. doi:10.1007/978-3-030-60703-6_43

KEY TERMS AND DEFINITIONS

College Students: They are individuals who graduated from high school and attending full-time or part-time at a university to pursue a course, but they have not graduated yet.

COVID-19: It is a very contagious virus from the family of the severe acute a respiratory syndrome that causes respiratory type of infection and can be passed from person to person. The number of COVID-19 infections has been increasing worldwide with the emergence of different variants.

Information Technology: The application of computers and telecommunications devices to store, retrieve, and send information among different sectors to exchange different forms of electronic data.

Pandemic: A global and widespread disease or infection that affects a vast area or all around the world.

Stress: It is a reaction and response to situational threats, danger, or uncomfortable situations that interrupt the psychological and biological balance.

Video Games: A type of game that uses visual interface interaction among gamers and can be played on a phone, computer, tablet, television, etc.

Video Games Industry: It is an industry that helps the video game sectors develop, produce, and modernize video game-related jobs.

Chapter 6
Supply Chain and Warehouse Management Systems:
A Case Study From an International Company

J. Zambujal-Oliveira
University of Madeira, Portugal

Martinho Freitas
University of Madeira, Portugal

Carolina Rodrigues
University of Madeira, Portugal

Daniela Freitas
University of Madeira, Portugal

Maria Pereira
University of Madeira, Portugal

ABSTRACT

The underperformance of an international company was based on the following major problems: the information technology and the inventory management system used in the group (several distinct channels that did not interact with each other) and the company's external environment (devaluation of the Russian ruble and decrease in purchasing power). To approach these issues, the chapter presents solutions to implement a new retail system, a redesign of the technology system used by the company, and some recommendations on external factors. Recently, the company has focused on a closer relationship with consumers, making available several services that simplifies the whole process of buying a product.

DOI: 10.4018/978-1-7998-9418-6.ch006

INTRODUCTION

The international company has undergone a remarkable evolution over the years, becoming a world leader in the sports industrial sector, with a wide range of products present in numerous countries. In the space of a decade, the Russia/CIS1 market stood out for its sales strength and steadily growing profits. Of the three major "attack markets" within the international company, which include North America and Greater China, Russia/CIS was recognized as a key growth market.

However, there were numerous setbacks that jeopardized the success of the international company in Russia. The main ones were the technology used by the international company, the macro environment, and the Russian crisis in 1998, which affected the Russian economy in several areas, such as the distribution channel, based on the wholesale model. This model proved to be inefficient, being considered a high-risk model. On the other hand, the market had the potential to recover, and a new era began, based on their own retail channel, enabling the phased opening of stores. In the same context of economic crisis, in mid-2014, the international company experienced a decline in sales and profits due to the sanctions imposed on Moscow, forcing the reduction and closure of stores. In addition, the collapse of the ruble and the decrease in consumer purchasing power were largely responsible for these events.

Figure 1. The company's fulfilment process
(Berger, Möslein, Piller & Reichwald, 2005)

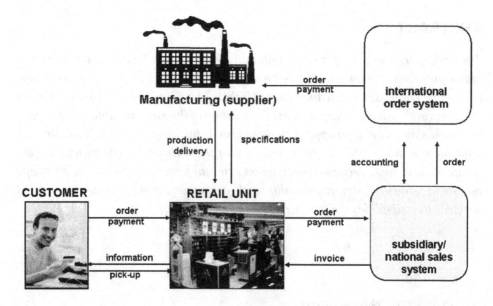

To overcome some of these problems, the company built up a C&C2 capacity that was later revealed to be insufficient due to the high demand. New manager's arrival in 2014, brought an impactful change within the international company, where he encouraged the workers to revamp the information technology structure, ERP (Enterprise Resource Planning) and WMS (Warehouse Management System) to support the business. The installation of these new systems was partially accepted. However, in the long run, it proved to be unproductive, and changes were needed. As a forecast for 2020, the company wanted to become more customer-centric, to be able to respond to the needs of consumers, namely greater accessibility, and convenience for them (Figure 1). For this goal, they intended to implement the following systems: Click-and-Collect (C&C); Customization; Endless Aisle (EA); Radio-frequency identification (RFID); Ship-from-Store (SFS).

In this article, we carry out a general analysis of the company productivity problem, find out whether the proposed solutions will be appropriate for the company in question and check their cost effectiveness. Finally, we consider the future position of the company so that it remains competitive in the Russian space such that it can maintain or increase productivity based on the various indicators.

CASE EVOLUTION AND STATE OF THE ART

The international company in Russia/CIS faced numerous adversities, with emphasis on the two main problems such as, the company's inventory management, logistics and technologies and the macro environment of the company.

Company's Inventory, Logistics and Technologies

The Russian economic crisis in 1998 forced the company to adopt a new retail system instead of a wholesale business, and the instability of the last-mentioned was evident during the crisis. Considering that commercial spaces possessing retail stores, had an easier time providing a system focused on the parallel execution of distinct distribution channels. Russia is characterized by having a relevant market (fast development of the retail and wholesale market), but with some obstacles regarding distribution circuits. The new retail model adopted by the international company has shortcomings in terms of its instability in the face of changing consumer consumption patterns. Behavioral changes forced retailers to rethink strategies and ferment new ways of retailing (Burt, 1989). Despite the adoption of a new retail model by this group, it only brings benefits when used in city centers, clashing with the geographical characteristics of Russia, calling into question the benefit of this model on the company's results.

Another adversity suffered in Russia/CIS in 2013 was the inability to achieve goals set in sales area. This failure was partially due to logistical inventory problems and market decline. The former was mainly caused by lower productivity of company's two operational distribution centers, jeopardizing the company's profits, and pressing the Warehouse Management System (WMS) (Figure 2). The most significant technology in Russian companies concerning warehouse management is the warehouse management system, which offers great functionality for managing warehouse logistics and constitutes a competitive advantage (Amato et al., 2005).

Figure 2. Warehouse management system
(Abernathy, Dunlop, Hammond & Weil, 2000)

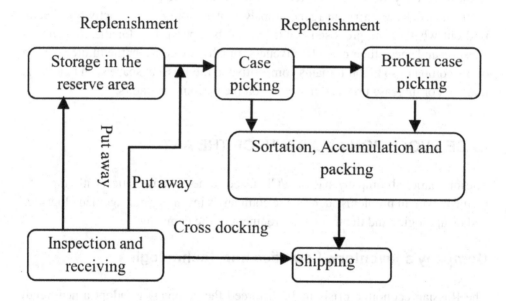

The company in general had limited levels of digitalization, such as other companies that are struggling to understand how to integrate and implement digital solutions in warehouse management (Sturm, Junghanns & Eichstedt, 2014), making it impossible to apply solutions that modernize warehouse management, falling short of consumer expectations due to the use of traditional systems. The complexity of supply chains has reached levels, where conventional warehouse systems are not efficient anymore (Wee, Kelly, Cattel & Breunig, 2015). Therefore, as possible causes for poor performance of the international company in Russia, we can point poor order picking accuracy and low number of transactions.

The team in charge of information technology in Russia was progressing efficiently, however, they witnessed glaring flaws, necessitating a re-evaluation of these systems to revamp them. The installation of a new system brought high expectations; however, the company's inventory accuracy was fragile, due to the use of three peculiar systems: 1. Enterprise Resource Planning system (ERP) for inventory; 2. Another similar system for distribution centers and retail spaces; 3. The same system, only for distribution center inventory, causing a lack of interaction between them, hindering the accuracy of the system's information. Despite Russia's great technological advance, it was lagging in human resource management in areas such as technology and science. Some of the future challenges would be to invest in R & D, enabling greater access to more informative and innovative systems, a topic that will be addressed later. The use of technology in the Russian market was relatively low, with most of the population still lacking access to the Internet. Additionally, consumer purchasing power has declined due to the country's economic situation and the weakening of the Russian ruble against the dollar (Taro, 1999) (Figure 3).

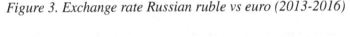

Figure 3. Exchange rate Russian ruble vs euro (2013-2016)

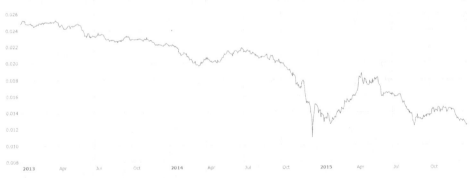

Despite the failure of the WMS system, in which warehouse movement stagnated, some other companies have seen their productivity increase due to its implementation. At Nestlé, the system has enabled greater inventory accuracy as well as greater efficiency in all stages of distribution. In quantitative terms, the WMS provides a 25% increase in warehouse productivity and a 10-20% increase in space management (Min, 2006). Another company in the same industry that took advantage of this inventory system was Nike, through which it saw its productivity almost double as well as the total value of production. Despite the various benefits, it has as a counterpart the high cost of implementation (Min, 2006).

The Influence of the Macro Environment

The macro environment also influenced the results of the international company in Russia, namely its geographical, cultural, technological, and economic characteristics. Despite Russia's considerable size (17 million square kilometers), most of this area had little road infrastructure to support the high freight traffic, leaving out some remote regions (Figure 4).

Transport plays an important role in promoting growth, diversification and regional convergence. However, with insufficient investment and incomplete structural reforms, Russia faces challenges in modernizing its large transport system. Promoting competition in transport sector is essential, by opening railway freight market to independent operators (Kolik et al., 2015). Through a vast transport network, it is easier to reach many low-populated regions. In Russian example, we observe that this network is still limited, making it difficult for several companies to do business. Along with Russia, Brazil is also underdeveloped in this regard. Does the difficult access to this network also harm the country's companies? A greater affluence of transport networks allows for greater mobility within the country, which in the long run will have positive effects on the GDP. Therefore, the weak road density was one of the factors causing the insufficient results (Kolik et al., 2015; Lordan & Sallan, 2017).

Figure 4. Competitiveness and quality of transport infrastructure
(Schwab & Forum, 2013)

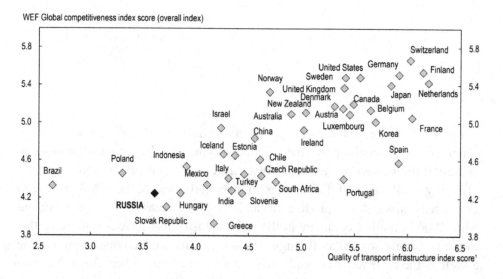

METHODS AND PROPOSED SOLUTIONS

To solve some of the problems mentioned above, we suggest some short- and long-term approaches. Some of them are insufficient, thus we propose some solutions based on other companies that operate in similar markets. To update the wholesale business model, the international company opted for a new retail model, led by a new manager. The former manager had less control in the sales process, so the company didn't have a direct interaction with the consumer, while in retail companies, they carried more responsibility, which enabled a greater interaction with the buyer. According to the new manager, the cash flows derived from the new company's retail model have resulted in a turning point and remarkable growth.

The adopted model had the assumption of giving visibility to the brand, portraying the global vision of the group, additively improving the contact with customers and their service (very weak at the time). The retail model has evolved globally due to the modernization of technologies, enabling advances in the consumer purchasing process, simplifying the logistics of the purchase between consumer and retailer (implementation of the concept of consumer loyalty). The latter performs numerous functions to make the business run efficiently, such as: the commitment to provide a wide range of diversified products, strengthening its ability to offer products to consumers; mitigation of expenses regarding the disintermediation of third-party companies in the implementation of the retail system; offering after-sales services to collect feedback from consumers, among others. Due to this modernization, most companies that rely on the retail system observe that online shopping generally prevails: most retailers provide on online shopping and home delivery services, but consumers are becoming more demanding and expected time for delivery is progressively shorter (Xing et al., 2010).

Despite the implementation of a new retail system in the international company, some other companies choose to continue using the wholesale model to minimize costs. This is the case of Sonae-MC, which through several measures tried to reduce costs, such as, the introduction of a platform that plans and locates merchandise routes and constant deliveries. In the case of the company, this solution would be not very relevant due to the limited volume of financial resources that wholesalers held. Another aspect that should be changed within the company would be the use of the CAPEX system that would allow for a considerable period of growth (Furnival-Marar, 2011).

Figure 5. Lean retailing-apparel supplier relations
(Abernathy et al., 2000)

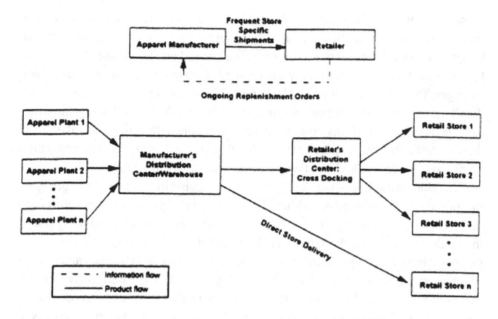

Another company that also uses the retail model is the fast-fashion company Primark. It enjoys relatively short delivery times, so that their stores are not out of stock and meet consumers' needs. In the case of the international company, a similar system was a must (Silva, 2018). The instability caused by the Russian financial crisis, the debts of the markets and the reduction in the purchasing power of consumers led to a deterioration of the economic situation. In trying to solve this problem through loans and debt, the pressure was immense. The devaluation of the Russian currency generally caused a decrease in purchasing power in the Soviet region. This devaluation restricted exports from Russia's neighboring regions for several years. Some of these limitations have hurt companies that have relocated to Russia, due to their difficulty with currency exchange, as well as their ability to reach international markets.

The inability to reach these decisive elements forced investors to rethink whether it was profitable to invest in the Russian market. In the case of the company, this devaluation had a noticeable effect due to the decrease in purchasing power, however, it was not very representative in the case of the decrease in exports because the company was focused on the domestic market. Since this problem is something external, the company can do little to solve the problem of the Russian financial crisis

The international company hired a specialized team in 2014 to revive the company. The first of his challenges was to revamp the IT systems. The fact that the new distribution center was at the limit of its capacity and the software that managed the process related to stock storage was overloaded, forced the group to completely revamp the IT system. Focused on a long-term strategic plan, the international company adopted a new prototype when it came to enterprise resource planning (Figure 6), part of the 2015 route initiative. The results were encouraging, but shortcomings began to appear.

Figure 6. Enterprise resource planning systems
(Hodge, 2002)

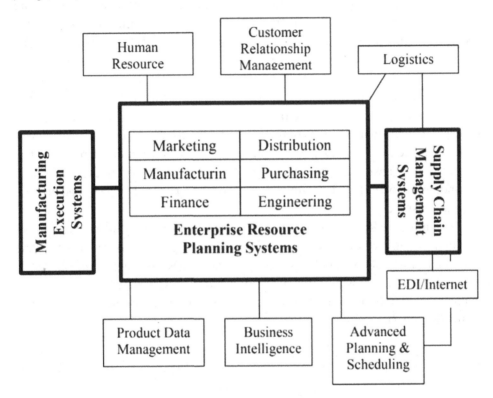

This led to the need to redesign the enterprise resource planning systems and the warehouse management system. Through the group's belief in them, they were able to achieve unexpected results, improving almost all indicators that demonstrate efficiency within the company (replenishment time and stock accuracy). The new IT system proved to be a key factor for the success of the business. From here, the international company has done its best to respond to the constant personalized needs of consumers, ensuring products that fit within their preferences. For a stable supply chain, it is necessary to have all the logistics behind it to be instantaneous and productive, highlighting the role of inventories in this overall process: warehouses are no longer only cost centers, but can add value and can be considered vital links within supply chains (MS, 2013). The development and digitalization of the entire inventory process was something that company could not achieve, making it impossible for the company to know the needs of the consumers.

Digital solutions could develop the company system through pick-by-voice or other methods that would facilitate the internal interoperability of the company and consequently the consumers' expectations. In this sense, the company should follow the future trend regarding digital and technological evolutions, implementing innovative systems: with the emergence of new business models, most of the sectors are being influenced by e-commerce and its associated IT technologies and innovations, such as innovative order-picking technologies (Moavenzadeh, 2015).

Due to the great importance to Russian industries and the dominance of railroads, there is a need to improve the quality of transport infrastructure. There is little concern for the restoration of the railway system in Russia, leading to an inability to respond on the main sections of the export routes. Similarly, the road system was underdeveloped as it did not play a significant role in the economy. However, after the economic transition it grew exponentially, but still fell short of the needs of an expanding motorization. This growth also brought a rivalry between road and rail freight transport.

Regarding the Russian transport system, the solution to its underdevelopment lies in a strategy drawn up in GRF (2014). This suggests measures that promote the long-term development of this system. Some of these are: an integrated, quality transport network accessible to the entire population; strengthening of an international connection; promotion of greater transport safety; limiting polluting transport (GRF, 2014) (Figure 7).

Figure 7. Transport infrastructure in Russia
(GRF, 2014)

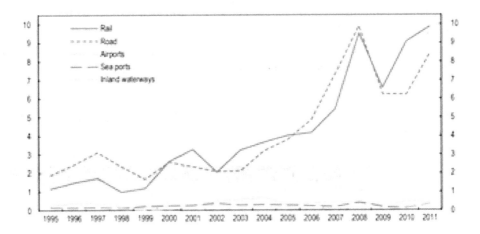

To provide a long-term increase in sales, in 2014, the international company invested in omnichannel sales:" Click-and-Collect", which consists of an order placed online with the intention of collecting it in store. This concept was relatively accepted by consumers, reflecting an increase in demand. At the time of the study, along with the depreciation of the Russian currency, the ruble, the C&C system broke down due to the inability to cope with demand, forcing the group to discontinue this method of selling. After Joseph's intervention in the group to resolve the problems that were causing instability, it was time to plan for the future. Within the Russian market, the international company needed innovation to cope with the competition. One of the measures in late 2014 was the development of the "omni - Ship-from-Store (SFS)", highlighting the key role of information technology in this type of business.

As projections for 2020, the group would have to focus on establishing a closer relationship with the consumer to offer an unparalleled and customizable service according to the consumer's preferences. Joseph's team proposed the following: i) Click-and-Collect (C&C) - a sales method that cares about the consumer's individual preferences, offering a unique experience at no extra cost; ii) Customization - consumers could customize products according to their tastes; iii) Endless Aisle (EA) - providing the consumer with a detailed view of the product through the digital media making it possible to check the stock, without considering the location and size of the retail space and purchase it even if the item is absent; iv) Radio Frequency Identification (RFID) - facilitate inventory management generating direct results in the sales sector, forcing a remodeling in the system and consequent increase in risk; v) Ship-from-Store (SFS) - make available a larger number of products since it takes into account the store's stock and not only the distribution centers.

In short, the international company went into a "trial and error" scheme, trying out innovative methods that could work or put everything at risk. A recent trend in omnichannel retailing is ship-from-store, which allows a retailer to fulfill online orders from a brick-and-mortar store. The benefits of this fulfillment model include faster delivery, lower transportation costs, higher in-stock probability, increased sales, and customer service (Bayram & Cesaret, 2017).

Table 1. Successful strategies for omnichannel retailing (Brynjolfsson, Hux & Rahman, 2013)

	SHORT-TERM STRATEGIES	LONG-TERM STRATEGIES
All retailers	• Create switching costs via loyalty programs and service contracts. • Use big data and analytics to better understand customer needs and values.	• Create exclusive products and unique features. • Create product bundles and product-service bundles. • Use analytics to guide product design, product line choices, channel decisions and new product introductions.
Dual-channel retailers		• Integrate channels. • Manage CRM and ROI metrics using data from both channels.
Pure brick-and-mortar retailers	• Provide store inventory information online to lower uncertainty of finding products in stores and to enable "buy online and pick up in stores." • Focus on providing information, services and instant gratification. • Charge a price premium for products that benefit greatly from having a nearby physical location due to product-related services.	• Move toward becoming dual-channel retailers.
Pure online retailers	• Provide everyday low prices and neatly curated content. • Convert "experience goods" to "search goods." • Enable consumers to use physical channel as showroom. • Offer local pickup points.	• Focus on niche products, especially ones that are not available locally. • Focus on cost and efficiency for popular, nonexclusive products.

For the company to gain a significant market share, it is essential to use many channels that enable interaction with the customer and get to know the consumer's preferences. Since the company is also a brand that operates globally, this interconnection becomes more beneficial. This sales strategy is called omnichannel (Table 1) As mentioned before, the strategy by using several sales channels enables a greater effectiveness in sales because it focuses mainly on just one channel, using the others as an attractive factor for customers.

At this stage it is possible to observe an increasing importance of customer interaction with the company, as this requires greater attention from the company. The impact of the use of omnichannel sales on the competitiveness of companies in today's digital world is increasing. This is especially felt in the operation of companies in international markets (Adivar, Hüseyinoğlu & Christopher, 2019). This so-called omnichannel sales strategy is also used by other companies in the same industry, such as Nike and Puma, and has proven to be a successful factor in the results of both sports companies. It is essential that the company has long-term solutions. These should fit into sustainable standards to improve its internal performance. The main factor of sustainable economic growth is competitiveness, which is based on the innovative activity of companies (Aganbegyan, 2014; Rikunoa, 2015).

CONCLUSION

After analyzing the productivity problem of the company, due to internal factors, such as the inventory system and the technology used, as well as the presence of external factors (economic crisis and transport network), we proposed some solutions that could improve the financial and operational situation, also comparing with other companies, that being or not in the same sector could help in the decisions to obtain positive results. For each solution we will analyze if it is appropriate and if the company can apply it.

In the case of the retail system, this is highly dependent on the existence of local retail spaces. The current technological evolution allows big brands to enjoy particular attention in the market. Due to the current trend, the company should continue to invest in the online channel without disregarding the physical spaces. Despite the possible benefits, there are still some adversities, such as replicating the level of personalization achieved online, where consumers are addressed by name and products are suggested to them based on their purchase history and behavior (Sigarev, Kosov, Buzdalina, Alandarov & Rykova, 2018)[1].

Thus, there was room for the company to adopt a retail system, considering all of the above, based on the trend of other companies' behavior. As for the Capex, it is necessary to have the collection of information about the total that the company will be able to spend. By expanding the budget, it will give the company room for greater investment when it comes to reopening stores. In this case, the company had the ability to use this model, achieving remarkable results with decisions on CAPEX investments, done during the annual budget process that conduce to savings and cost reductions in operations (Issar & Navon, 2016).

Regarding the IT situation, the company needed to revamp its system to cope with future market demand: forecasts and global trends evidence that communication technologies will continue to play their role among as innovation technologies (Basl, 2017). Despite the importance of this remodeling in IT, Russia was not keeping pace with other countries devaluing the progress given by the company, making it difficult to implement this solution, not because it is this company but because of the human resources not trained for this technological advance.

By analyzing companies in industrially developed countries, 85% of manufacturing companies worldwide can realize the potential of technologies to increase asset efficiency. However, only 15% of them have so far implemented dedicated strategies through data analysis (Basl, 2017). In these conclusions it is possible to state that despite the importance of IT, few companies adopt systems based on it. In the case of company, this implementation could be jeopardized due to the financial crisis the country was facing.

When it comes to the WMS, it provides better storage solutions for the company, as there is the possibility to track the entire logistics process at the time of sale, from the warehouse to the store. Despite the positive points that this warehouse management system brings, there are high costs associated with its implementation, so that in itself can be a repulsive factor. However, for the company it is essential to have a system similar to this one that provides greater capabilities for tracking their products, such as WMS. It offers solutions for storage, defining the location of materials by zone, turnover and product family. Additionally, this technology provides products tracking in the production process and performs printing control (Novaes, Souza, de Veras Filial, Giordano & Gonçalves, 2016).

Another possible problem affecting the company's results was the country's transportation network. Despite its minor importance in the productivity problem, there is still room for improvement. By expanding the network, the company could reach less populated places and thus reach a wider target audience. Since this is an external factor, the company would be unlikely to be able to change, merely by taking advantage of existing routes. An additional solution called omnichannel, allowed the company to increase its competitiveness in the national space, through online ordering and the possibility of choosing a pick-up location. This strategy allowed for greater contact with the consumer, creating space for relationships with them, and is particularly important at a time when the role of the consumer is taken with greater relevance.

Later, the company should focus on new solutions that promote greater productivity and that are sustainable because sustainable competitive advantages are achieved when the companies are successful in implementing value-creating strategies that other companies cannot replicate (Hitt, Ireland & Hoskisson, 2014). There are four indicators that should be considered by the company in the future to measure its competitive performance. According to Hill et al. (2014), these indicators are: efficiency, quality, innovation, and speed. The company can maintain its competitive position in Russia, understanding intrinsic and extrinsic aspects of the company, such as, knowing external and internal environments and defining ways of ensuring business continuity. Besides that, the company will need to take into consideration the actions of its stakeholders (competitors, suppliers, customers), being alert to innovations (development of new products), marketing strategies, managing materials and operations (Marino, 2006).

REFERENCES

Abernathy, F. H., Dunlop, J. T., Hammond, J. H., & Weil, D. (2000). Retailing and supply chains in the information age. *Technology in Society*, *22*(1), 5–31. doi:10.1016/S0160-791X(99)00039-1

Adivar, B., Hüseyinoğlu, I. Ö. Y., & Christopher, M. (2019). A quantitative performance management framework for assessing omnichannel retail supply chains. *Journal of Retailing and Consumer Services*, *48*, 257–269. doi:10.1016/j.jretconser.2019.02.024

Aganbegyan, A. (2014). Social and economic development of russia: An analysis and a forecast. *Studies on Russian Economic Development*, *25*(4), 319–328. doi:10.1134/S1075700714040029

Amato, F., Basile, F., Carbone, C., & Chiacchio, P. (2005). An approach to control automated warehouse systems. *Control Engineering Practice*, *13*(10), 1223–1241. doi:10.1016/j.conengprac.2004.10.017

Basl, J. (2017). Pilot study of readiness of czech companies to implement the principles of industry 4.0. *Management and Production Engineering Review, 8.*

Bayram, A., & Cesaret, B. (2017). Ship-from-store operations in omni-channel retailing. In *Iie annual conference. proceedings* (pp. 1181–1186). Academic Press.

Berger, C., Möslein, K., Piller, F., & Reichwald, R. (2005). Co-designing the customer interface for customer-centric strategies: Learning from exploratory research. *European Management Review*, *2*(3), 70–87. doi:10.1057/palgrave.emr.1500030

Brynjolfsson, E., Hu, Y. J., & Rahman, M. S. (2013). *Competing in the age of omnichannel retailing*. MIT Cambridge.

Burt, S. (1989). Trends and management issues in European retailing. *International Journal of Retail & Distribution Management*, *17*(4). Advance online publication. doi:10.1108/EUM0000000002924

Furnival-Marar, L. (2011). *Financial analysis of companies entering new markets: A case study in the mobile telephony sector* (Unpublished doctoral dissertation). University of S. Paulo.

GRF. (2014). *Transport strategy of the Russian Federation until 2030*. Government of the Russian Federation Moscow.

Hill, C., Jones, G., & Schilling, M. (2014). *Strategic management: Theory & cases: An integrated approach*. Cengage Learning.

Hitt, M., Ireland, R., & Hoskisson, R. (2014). *Strategic management: Concepts: Competitiveness and globalization*. Cengage Learning.

Hodge, G. L. (2002). Enterprise resource planning in textiles. *Journal of Textile and Apparel. Technology and Management*, 2(3), 1–8.

Issar, G., & Navon, L. (2016). Operational excellence. *Manufacturing Overhead (MOH) and Departmental Expense Control*, 91–93.

Kolik, A., Radziwill, A., & Turdyeva, N. (2015). *Improving transport infrastructure in Russia*. Academic Press.

Lordan, O., & Sallan, J. M. (2017). Analyzing the multilevel structure of the European airport network. *Chinese Journal of Aeronautics*, 30(2), 554–560. doi:10.1016/j.cja.2017.01.013

Marino, L. (2006). *Quality management and knowledge management: key factors for business productivity and competitiveness*. XIII SIMPEP.

Min, H. (2006). The applications of warehouse management systems: An exploratory study. *International Journal of Logistics: Research and Applications*, 9(2), 111–126. doi:10.1080/13675560600661870

Moavenzadeh, J. (2015). *The 4th industrial revolution: Reshaping the future of production*. World Economic Forum.

MS. (2013). *From cost center to growth center: Warehousing 2018* (Tech. Rep.). Motorola Solutions.

Novaes, D. R., Souza, D. C., de Veras Filial, M. A., Giordano, C. V., & Gonçalves, L. C. (2016). Implementation of wms technology in a 3pl. *Eniac*, 5(2), 223–239. doi:10.22567/rep.v5i2.386

Rikunoa, S. E. A. (2015). Conditions and factors of economic growth in russia at the present stage of development. Voronezh State Industrial and Economic College, 194(5), 81–88.

Schwab, K., & Forum, W. E. (2013). *The global competitiveness report 2013-2014*. World Economic Forum.

Sigarev, A. V., Kosov, M. E., Buzdalina, O. B., Alandarov, R. A., & Rykova, I. N. (2018). *The role of chains in the Russian retail sector*. Academic Press.

Silva, M. (2018). *Fashion retail: Branding and marketing strategies communication* (Unpublished master's thesis). University of Beira Interior, Portugal.

Sturm, M., Junghanns, J., & Eichstedt, M. (2014). *Next stop digital: How logistics service providers can rethink operating models to benefit from emerging technology*. Verfügbar. https://www. accenture. com/t20150523T030128__w__/ my-en/_acnmedia/Accenture/Conversion-Assets/DotCom/Documents/Global/PDF/ Dualpub_4/Accen ture-Digital-Future-For-LSPs. pdf

Taro, L. (1999). *Baltic economies in 1998-1999: effects of the russian financial crisis*. Bank of Finland.

Wee, D., Kelly, R., Cattel, J., & Breunig, M. (2015). Industry 4.0-how to navigate digitization of the manufacturing sector. McKinsey & Company.

Xing, Y., Grant, D. B., McKinnon, A. C., & Fernie, J. (2010). Physical distribution service quality in online retailing. *International Journal of Physical Distribution & Logistics Management, 40*(5), 415–432. doi:10.1108/09600031011052859

ADDITIONAL READING

Branch, A. E. (2008). *Global supply chain management and international logistics*. Routledge. doi:10.4324/9780203887769

Dolgui, A., & Proth, J.-M. (2010). *Supply chain engineering: useful methods and techniques* (Vol. 539). Springer.

Gattorna, J., & Jones, T. (1998). *Strategic supply chain alignment: best practice in supply chain management*. Gower Publishing, Ltd.

Min, H. (2006). The applications of warehouse management systems: An exploratory study. *International Journal of Logistics: Research and Applications, 9*(2), 111–126. doi:10.1080/13675560600661870

Ramaa, A., Subramanya, K. N., & Rangaswamy, T. M. (2012). Impact of warehouse management system in a supply chain. *International Journal of Computers and Applications, 54*(1).

Skjott-Larsen, T., Schary, P. B., Kotzab, H., & Mikkola, J. H. (2007). *Managing the global supply chain*. Copenhagen Business School Press DK.

KEY TERMS AND DEFINITIONS

Balanced Scorecard: A performance measurement tool that aggregates key performance indicators (KPIs).

Center-of-Gravity (COG): Methodology for locating distribution centers considering the spot which represents the minimum transportation costs between the network elements.

Customer-Supplier Partnership: A long-term relationship between a buyer and a supplier.

Dashboard: A tool used to capture a summary of the Key Performance Indicators (KPIs)/metrics of a company.

Distribution: Outbound logistics, from the production line to the final user.

Distribution Channels: Firms or individuals that ensures the flow of goods and services from the supplier and producer to the final consumer.

Distribution Requirements Planning (DRP): A system of planning demands for inventory at distribution centers and consolidating demand information to the production and materials system.

Enterprise Resource Planning (ERP) System: A software for managing the resources needed to deal with customer orders.

Free on Board (FOB): Contractual terms between two supply chain agents, that define where title transfer takes place.

Global Strategy: A strategy centered on increasing worldwide performance through the sale of common goods and services with a minimum product variation.

Inbound Logistics: The transport management of materials from suppliers into production processes or storage facilities.

Just-in-Time (JIT): An inventory management system to monitor material flow into manufacturing plants by supplying the required materials just in time for use.

Manufacturing Lead Time: The time required to manufacture an item.

Master Production Schedule (MPS): The master level schedule used to set the production plan in a manufacturing facility.

Original Equipment Manufacturer (OEM): A manufacturer that buys and incorporates another supplier's products into its own products.

Performance Measures: Indicators of the performed work and the results achieved in an activity, process, or organizational unit.

Radio Frequency (RFID): Wireless communications from a terminal to a base station, linked to a computer.

Statistical Process Control (SPC): A statistical method for monitoring quality control in production processes.

Supply Chain: Materials, information, and people involved in the process of transforming raw materials into finished goods.

Transportation Requirements Planning (TRP): Planning transportation needs considering the demand given by MRP and DRP databases.

Value Chain: A business process that includes activities from manufacturers to retail stores.

ENDNOTE

[1]   https: //1library.org/document/zx9dnpnz -as-maiores-tendencias-no-comercio-a-retalho.html

Chapter 7

Technological Growth in Religious Organisations:
Exploring Social Media Through System Dynamics

Courage Matobobo

iD https://orcid.org/0000-0002-7125-5989
University of South Africa, South Africa

Felix Bankole
University of South Africa, South Africa

ABSTRACT

Membership growth is an important aspect in religious organisations. Yet, the manner in which several religious organisations attract their membership has changed due to the adoption and use of social media. This study explores how technological factors influence the growth of religious organisations during and in the aftermath of the pandemic. Using the Seventh-Day Adventist Church (SDA) membership data, the research employed system dynamics. The findings from the quantitative data showed that the commitment of church members, good computer skills, age, and availability of resources contributed to the successful use of social media towards church membership growth. In addition, the qualitative data reveals that online evangelism is key to the growth of religious organisations. The results of the findings conclude that the growth of religious organisations can be improved by intensifying the level of online evangelism, improving commitment from members and utilisation of multichannel social media.

DOI: 10.4018/978-1-7998-9418-6.ch007

INTRODUCTION

Church membership growth is important in religious organisations as they execute the great commission of evangelising to the whole world. Due to the coronavirus (COVID-19) pandemic, the operations of religious organisations were affected as members could not physically gather to share the word of God, as before. However, the increase in the use of Information and Communication Technologies (ICTs) has resulted in several technologies being deployed in different social and economic areas to assist in accomplishing various tasks. This usage of ICTs has benefitted users of religious organisations such as the Seventh-day Adventist Church (SDA) (Bolu, 2012; Matobobo & Bankole, 2020). It seems that the use of technology in religious organisations has changed the way leaders and members evangelise, thereby growing the organisation. Some models, such as the conversion model, have been developed to classify the growth of religious organisations (Hayward, 2002; Wilson, 2017). Many of these models focus on the group called enthusiasts, which are believed to be active for some time in the recruitment of new members, and then become inactive after a while. It has been noted that in many cases, churches recruit through friendship networks and personal contacts (Lie, 2018; Fred, 2015; Činčala, 2016). Due to the successful adoption and use of technologies, the recruitment of new members is no longer dependent on enthusiasts but also on ICTs such as social media (White et al., 2016). Prior research on social media in religious organisations has mainly focussed on the role of social media in church growth (Magezi, 2015; Kgatle, 2018; White et al., 2016). However, not many pieces of research have been done to explore holistically how technological growth variables (i.e., processes, issues, factors) in religious organisations influence one another. Therefore, this study explores how technological variables influence the growth of religious organisations using the SDA churches through the lens of system dynamics. The findings of this study will contribute to the existing literature by providing an insight into the influence of technological variables on the membership growth of religious organisations. Furthermore, the study anticipated to assist religious leaders in developing policies that contribute towards the utilisations of technologies toward church growth.

In this article, we briefly review the literature. Next, we discuss the research methodology. Then, we present the findings of the study. We subsequently discuss research findings; and then discuss some future directions for future work. Finally, we conclude the paper.

LITERATURE REVIEW

This section is divided into 2 sections. The first section reviews the literature on the growth of organisations paying particular attention to religious organisations and the second section reviews the literature on system dynamics.

The Growth of Religious Organisations

Growth is essential to the long-term survival of any organisation. Organisations invest in various growth strategies to grow their businesses (Westerlund & Leminen, 2012). The growth strategies play a significant role in the expansion, development, stability, and success of the business as they enable organisations to expand their market shares, develop into new markets, and develop new products and services (Absanto, 2013). Every business needs to develop better strategies to improve its competitive edge in order to survive in this competitive world. Even more so, businesses need to continuously change their development processes to make progress (Sahay et al., 2004). In the business environment growth means both quantitative and qualitative development. Quantitative growth means an increase in the production level, sales volumes, product range, investments, and extent of resources such as the number of employees (Durmaz & Ilhan, 2015).

Generally speaking, it is easy to measure growth in profit-making organisations using these metrics. On the other hand, it may be difficult to measure the growth of non-profit organisations such as religious organisations using the same metrics, since the nature of products, services, and purpose of existence is different from profit-making organisations. In as much as religious organisations do not exist for profit, they are essential to the communities as they raise awareness of the word of God to establish unity, fairness, healthy living, mutual understanding, growth, and contentment among the people of God (Tomalin, 2018). Religious organisations focus on the spirituality of their members and try to make more disciples, thereby increasing membership. Qualitative growth is about the development of quality business elements such as property, and technology to give competitors a competitive advantage (Durmaz & Ilhan, 2015). Qualitative growth, therefore, may translate to quantitative growth.

In order to understand growth in the context of organisations, there should be business growth indicators used to measure it. Business growth indicators can be grouped into four main categories namely, business outcomes, business outputs, capacity, and qualitative indicators (Absanto, 2013). Outcome indicators represent the profit generated by the business after subtracting business expenses from the revenues (Absanto, 2013). Religious organisations do not exist for profit but they do have some sources of income such as tithes and offerings from members and donors, at the same time having operating expenses. It can be economically beneficial for a church to have many members that can generate income for the organisation's survival. Output indicators focus on the main outputs of the business such as its products and/or sales (Absanto, 2013). This is different from religious organisations as they do not focus on the production of products but on improving the spirituality of members and membership level. However, it is easy for religious leaders to measure the organisation's growth in terms of membership growth as long as they maintain accurate membership records through the use of systems such as pastoral analytics (Matobobo & Bankole, 2021a). This therefore implies that an increase in membership signifies the growth of a religious organisation. Religious leaders can realise their organisation's growth by observing an increase in the number of employees and assets such as ICT equipment. Qualitative indicators include aspects such as organisation structure, management practices, and degree of formalisation (Absanto, 2013). In the case of religious organisations, a church can grow in terms of membership or by having branches that may lead to the formation of other churches.

Growth strategies can be classified into two main categories, namely organic and inorganic growth strategies. Organic growth is also referred to as internal growth. Organic growth occurs when an organisation uses its resources to improve its current activities by either increasing the sales volumes or introducing new products in the market (Durmaz & Ilhan, 2015). This can be facilitated through the use of strategies such as the implementation of successful customer relationship management, the use of technology, and the improvement of business processes (Bruner, 2004). Inorganic growth is considered external growth as it enables a business to grow through partnerships with other businesses (Durmaz & Ilhan, 2015). This study focusses on the organic growth strategy as it explores the use of social media in religious organisations as a growth strategy.

This study develops on the basic church growth model developed by Hayward (Hayward, 1999; Hayward, 2005). The model is based on the following six major assumptions:

I.   Unbelievers are recruited into the church by a subset of believers called enthusiasts. These are also referred to as active believers (Hayward, 1999).

II. The enthusiasts are active in the recruitment of members for some time and then become inactive church members (Hayward, 1999). The assumption is that the new believer loses their enthusiasm to recruit after some time and also lose their network of unbelieving friends as they become integrated into the life of the church. The belief is that new believers are the primary means through which churches can have contact with unbelievers.

III. The enthusiastic period of these members starts immediately after the conversion of an unbeliever (Hayward, 1999).

IV.   Churches can have adults leave the church due to various reasons (Hayward, 2005). There is a belief that members who leave the church may not be immediately open for reconversion.

V.   The church can have some additional members by retaining the children of believing parents (Hayward, 2005).

VI.   The church will lose members through deaths (Hayward, 2005).

There have been researchers who explored the role of social media, particularly Facebook, on the growth of churches (Collins & Sturgill, 2013; Kgatle, 2018). A study by Matobobo and Bankole (2021b) showed that social media have benefitted religious organisations in reaching people as churches can advertise and promote their church programmes, have improve communication channels, and create opportunities for evangelism. The use of these social media platforms depends on how church leaders and members embrace technology. A study conducted by Magezi (2015) categorised pastors into three categories: technology embracer, cautious embracer, and technology objector. Technology embracers are aware of the benefits of ICT and try to connect with broad membership as well as young Christians (Magezi, 2015). Cautious embracers are cautious in adopting and using technology in the church (Magezi, 2015). Objectors of technology view technology as something that is secular and has no place in the church (Magezi, 2015). Looking at these categories, the successful adoption and use of technology in religious organisations depends on the attitude and computer skills of leaders and members (Bolu, 2012). To the knowledge of the authors, no existing research has examined the growth of religious organisations using social media through the lens of system dynamics. It is beneficial to examine the effects of social media on the growth of religious organisations as digital media plays a role in making converts or enthusiasts (Hayward, 2002). It was noted that word of mouth is useful when religious organisations want to recruit new members (Sargeant, 2000). Due to the COVID-19 global pandemic, the use of word of mouth has been affected to a large extent because of the restrictions that were placed by various governments limiting gatherings and physical contact. Nowadays, there are large volumes of electronic word of mouth (eWOM) that is generated in the social media space (Farzin & Fattahi, 2018).

Research shows that religious organisations generate large volumes of eWOM sentiments on the quality of their online services, their advertising and promotion of events, church governance, and the quality of the medium used in the delivery of messages (Matobobo & Bankole, 2021b). These eWOM sentiments can be positive, neutral, or negative, based on the level of satisfaction of visitors and have the power to influence who might want to join the church. Furthermore, Hadaway observes that churches that grow faster report more recruitment activity among their members (Hadaway, 1993). This shows that members play a crucial role in the growth of religious organisations as they share the gospel on their social media status, and post media content to online communities (Matobobo & Bankole, 2021b). The study of church growth using social media as a strategy of organic growth through the lens of system dynamics is therefore significant to religious leaders in the development of policies.

System Dynamics

System dynamics modelling is a method that is used to describe and simulate dynamically complex issues through the structural identification of feedback and delay processes that drive system behaviour (Walters et al., 2016). System dynamics is a problem-oriented modelling approach founded by Jay Forrester in the late 1950s to help managers understand industrial problems better (Currie et al., 2018). System dynamics provide the means for understanding complex problems which, in turn, informs the way decision-makers navigate complex decision-making processes (Currie et al., 2018). By using system dynamics, managers can understand how systems change over time (Martin, 1997). System dynamics have been used to model the dynamics in areas such as the climate, healthcare systems, food industry, and the military (Currie et al., 2018; Homer & Hirsch, 2006). System dynamics was originally rooted in the management and engineering sciences but has gradually developed into a useful tool in the analysis of social, economic, physical, chemical, biological, and ecological systems (Martin, 1997). The system dynamics approach involves the development of computer simulation models that depict processes of development and feedback and can be tested to measure the effectiveness of a policy (Homer & Hirsch, 2006). In a way this allows decision-makers and policy-makers to test their scenarios before moving to action (Takahashi, 2015). System dynamics models can be formulated as systems of high-order, nonlinear, differential equations, natural processes, and physical structures relevant to the purpose of the model (Sternam, 2002).

The use of system dynamics helps to understand the dynamics of decision-making in complex situations, for example, how a policy change in one part of the system influences other subsystems and can eventually change the behaviour of the whole system (Nabavi et al., 2017). System Dynamics draws on both qualitative and quantitative methodologies to analyse system behaviours over time (Nabavi et al., 2017). Qualitative modelling is used in situations where the end goal is to develop causal loop diagrams (CLD) that represent dynamic factor interaction while quantitative modelling is used in situations where the end goal is to model and simulate the dynamic effects of factors and their interaction using stock and flow diagrams (Walters et al., 2016). In qualitative modelling, CLDs are used when one needs a better understanding of the interrelations among the components of a system

(Nabavi et al., 2017). Quantitative analysis can be performed using tools such as Vensim or Stella. Quantitative modelling enables the analyst to build a simulation model to evaluate and assess the model's behaviour under different circumstances.

METHODOLOGY

This research study adopted quantitative and qualitative approaches. The quantitative approach was used to understand the use of social media among the SDA members while the qualitative approach was used to understand the use of social media among the SDA leaders.

Quantitative Approach

The research study adopted a correlational survey design. Correlational research design is an approach used to find co-relationships between two or more variables with the aim of understanding conditions and events encountered better, and with the expectation of making future predictions (Walker, 1989). A correlational survey design was used to determine significant relationships between members and social media within the SDA church. A questionnaire with closed-ended questions was used to collect quantitative data from members within the four conferences of the SDA located in South Africa. The study used a convenience sampling technique to solicit data from a sample of church members. Convenience sampling has the advantage of using a sample of the target population that meets some specific criteria such as availability, geographical proximity, accessibility, or willingness to participate are included in the study (Etikan, 2016). This sampling approach was to target Adventist members using social media and other convenient platforms. It would have taken much time and resources to go around to various churches issuing questionnaires. Hence the link to the online questionnaires was distributed using emails, posted on social media platforms, and printed copies were given to members without access to the internet. The respondents were asked to forward the survey links to other members of the SDA church. The study used a sample of 205 respondents. The data were then analysed using Statistical Package for Social Sciences (SPSS) software. The reliability of the questionnaire was tested using Cronbach's alpha and was found to be 0,773 – an acceptable level of reliability. Data were analysed using means, standard deviations, and ANOVA. Results were presented in table format.

Quantitative Approach

The research adopted a qualitative research approach to explore the usage of social media in the growth of religious organisations among church leaders. An interpretivist philosophical paradigm was adopted to explore the realities of the phenomenon under investigation using the case of the SDA church because of its high level of social media usage (Matobobo & Bankole, 2021b). Interpretivism argues that 'truth and knowledge are subjective, as well as culturally and historically situated, based on people's experiences and their understanding of them' (Ryan, 2018). Interpretivist research is guided by the researchers' values and beliefs which then shape the way data are collected, interpreted, and analysed (Denzin & Lincoln, 2005; Ryan, 2018).

Participants

Participants consisted of twelve (12) SDA church leaders with experience in church leadership, who could speak English and were willing to participate in the study. The researchers interviewed 3 church elders, 3 church treasurers, and 6 church pastors. These participants were found on church and conference websites. The study used the purposive sampling technique to select participants for the study in order to improve the transferability of the findings in qualitative research (Palinkas et al., 2015). The study participants were composed of 11 males and 1 female. All participants were over 20 years of age, with 1 participant between the age of 21 and 30 years, 6 participants were between the ages of 31 and 40 years, and 5 participants were above 40 years old. All pastors interviewed had at least a theology degree and at least 5 years in the ministry. One treasurer had a qualification related to the finance field while the other 2 treasurers had at least master's degrees in non-finance fields. All elders had formal qualifications and were formally employed. All participants had at least 5 years of experience in church leadership.

Data Collection and Analysis

Before data collection, the researchers obtained ethical clearance and permission to collect data. All the interviews were conducted in English for an average of 50 minutes. Participation was voluntary, and interviewees gave their consent to participate in the study. The 12 participants (three elders, three treasurers, and six pastors) were interviewed telephonically using semi-structured interviews and each interview was recorded. The researchers used deliberate probes and member checking as ways of obtaining in-depth information to enhance research credibility. The purposive sampling technique was used to select religious leaders with experience in church leadership and the use of technology such as social media. This qualitative data form the primary data for establishing the variables for extending the church growth model while the literature review data form the secondary data.

The transcribed interview data were analysed using ATLAS.ti. The thematic analysis method was used to analyse the data. The thematic analysis enables researchers to identify, analyse, and report patterns (themes) within the analysed data (Braun & Clarke, 2006). The researchers followed the five steps recommended by Braun and Clarke (2006). The first step was for the researchers to familiarise themselves with the data through repeated reading. The second step was for the researchers to create initial codes from the data. The third step was for the researchers to sort the various codes into potential themes and organise all the relevant coded data excerpts within the identified themes. The fifth step was to refine the themes discovered and analyse them within the data; and ultimately produce the final report.

Trustworthiness

The principles established by Lincoln and Guba (Lincoln & Guba, 1985) were used to improve the trustworthiness of this research's findings. The researchers conducted member checks (also known as respondent validation) by asking participants to review interview transcripts and also confirm if the final concepts and themes truly reflect the phenomena being investigated to ensure an accurate representation of participants' perspectives or experiences (Long & Johnson, 2000; Thomas, 2017). Member check is feeding back data, interpretations, and conclusions to the participants for feedback (Korstjens & Moser, 2018). This in a way ensures that interpretations and conclusions accurately reflect participants' experiences. The researchers also included rich and thick verbatim descriptions of participants' experiences to support the research findings (Noble & Smith, 2015). The findings from the quantitative data, qualitative data, and literature review were modelled to systems thinking. The discussion of findings was based on qualitative data analysis and literature review.

ANALYSIS AND MODEL DEVELOPMENT

First, the findings from the quantitative data are presented. The next section presents the findings from the qualitative data. Finally, the development of the church growth causal loop diagram is presented.

Quantitative Approach

This section presents the research findings from the quantitative data. Table 1 shows the distribution of respondents on social media across different age groups.

Table 1. Distribution of participants on social media by age group

Social Media Platform		Age					Total
		18–24	*25–34*	*35–44*	*45–54*	*> 54*	
Facebook	% within age	42 (79,2%)	65 (85,5%)	35 (85,4%)	22 (95,7%)	3 (27,3%)	167
WhatsApp	% within age	52 (98,1%)	75 (98,7%)	40 (97,6%)	23 (100%)	11 (100%)	201
Twitter	% within age	20 (37,7%)	27 (35,5%)	15 (36,6%)	7 (30,4%)	0 (0,0%)	69
Skype	% within age	6 (11,3%)	15 (19,7%)	15 (36,6%)	2 (8,7%)	1 (9,1%)	39
YouTube	% within age	42 (79,2%)	44 (57,9%)	21 (51,2%)	10 (43,5%)	1 (9,1%)	118
Badoo	% within age	2 (3,8%)	0 (0,0%)	0 (0,0%)	0 (0,0%)	0 (0,0%)	2
Total	Count	53	76	41	23	11	204

The results in Table 1 show that almost all respondents across all age groups had WhatsApp. Facebook had at least 79,2% for ages 18 to 24 and only 27,3% for those above 54 years. The results show that respondents between the ages of 25 and 34 years used social media more than any other group while those above 54 years were the least users of social media, with exception of WhatsApp. The findings show the importance of religious organisations using multiple social media channels to reach as many members as possible, thereby improving membership growth.

In Table 2 the fixed-effects model of the ANOVA (one-way) test was conducted to assess the impact of an independent variable on a dependent variable using $p < 0.05$ for a statistically significant difference.

Null Hypothesis ($H0_1$): Age and ICT skills (dependent) of church members have no significance on social media evangelism (independent) in the SDA church.

Alternative Hypothesis (Ha_1): Age and ICT skills (dependent) of church members have significance on social media evangelism (independent) in the SDA church.

Participants were asked to indicate on a 5 point Likert scale how often they evangelise using ICTs

(Never = 1, Rarely = 2, Sometimes = 3, Often = 4, All the time = 5).

Table 2. One-way ANOVA of ICT use on age and ICT skills

Variable	Category	M	Std	F-value	Sig
Age	18–24	2,57	1,297	5,575	0,00
	25–34	2,62	1,233		
	35–44	3,02	1,294		
	45–54	3,61	1,196		
	Above 54	1,73	0,905		
	Total	2,75	1,299		
ICT Skill	Basic	2,22	1,123	12,415	0,00
	Intermediate	2,62	1,245		
	Advance	3,34	1,290		
	Total	2,75	1,299		
Overall Average		2,75	1,299	8,995	0,00

Results in Table 2 show a positive significant impact on personal characteristics (age and ICT skills) and social media evangelism in the SDA church at $p < 0.05$, a high overall mean of 2,75 and a standard deviation of 1,299. It can be seen that those within the age groups of 45 to 54 (M = 3,61; SD = 1,196) and 35 to 44 (M = 3,02; SD = 1,296) often used social media in evangelism. Those who were aged 45 to 54 frequently used ICTs to evangelise. It can be seen that those who are above 54 years old had the least mean (M = 1.73; SD = 0,905), meaning that participants rarely or never used ICTs in evangelism. The findings showed that the use of ICTs in evangelism varied with age.

Table 2 further shows that members with advanced ICT skills (M = 3,34; SD = 1,290) often used social media to evangelise. Those with basic ICT skills had the least mean (M = 2,22; SD = 1,123) indicating that they rarely used social media in the ministry. Therefore, the hypothesis which states that age and ICT skills of church members have no significance on social media evangelism in the SDA church is rejected and the alternative one stating that age and ICT skills of church members have a significance on social media evangelism in the SDA church is accepted.

In Table 3 participants were asked to indicate how often they used online tools to interact with other members using a Likert scale of 1 to 5 (Never = 1, Rarely = 2, Sometimes = 3, Often = 4, All the time = 5). The research only considered platforms that had a $p < 0,05$ as shown in Table 3.

HO_2: There is no significance between social media and frequency of use among SDA members

Ha_2: There is a significance between social media and frequency of use among SDA members

Table 3. One-way ANOVA of social media on social interaction

Social Activity	Platform	Mean	Std	F-Value	Sig
Use other online tools (WhatsApp, Messenger, Facebook) to interact with other church members	Facebook	4,400	0,938	7,02	0,01
	WhatsApp	4,350	1,029	20,42	0,00
Overall Average		4,375	0,984	13,72	0,01

Table 3 shows a positive significance between social activities and social media. The overall average of the impact is high (M = 4,375; SD = 0,9835; F = 13,718; p = 0,005). It can be seen that members of the SDA in South Africa often interact online using Facebook (M = 4.40; SD = 0,938; F = 7,017; p = 0,009) and WhatsApp (M = 4,35; SD = 1,029; F = 20,419; p < 0,1). Therefore, the hypothesis which states that there is no significance between social media and frequency of use among SDA members is rejected and the alternative which states that there is a significance between social media and frequency of use among SDA members is accepted.

In Table 4 respondents were asked to indicate factors that hinder them from using ICT to perform religious activities using a Likert scale of 1 to 5 (Definitely Not = 1; Probably Not = 2, Possibly = 3, Probably = 4, Definitely = 5). The research looked at the impact of the factor on the age groups of the SDA members in South Africa.

Table 4. Factors that hinder ICT use

Factor	Age Range	Mean	Std	F-Value	Sig
Lack of ICT skills	18–24	2,67	1,479	2,559	0,040
	25–34	2,37	1,431		
	35–44	2,39	1,412		
	45–54	3,00	1,508		
	> 54	3,64	1,502		
Lack of funds to buy the ICTs	18–24	2,69	1,703	3,737	0,006
	25–34	2,93	1,628		
	35–44	2,29	1,553		
	45–54	3,91	1,703		
	54	2,91	1,814		
My device(s) does limit me	18–24	1,93	1,257	4,312	0,002
	25–34	2,53	1,579		
	35–44	1,63	1,135		
	45–54	2,13	1,766		
	> 54	3,18	1,601		
Limited by data bundles	18–24	2,63	1,674	2,605	0,037
	25–34	2,84	1,575		
	35–44	2,39	1,243		
	45–54	3,61	1,672		
	> 54	2,45	1,214		

Table 4 shows that lack of ICT skills had an impact on the members of the SDA church in South Africa (M = 2,59; SD = 1,475; F = 2,559; p = 0,040). It can be seen that members who belonged to the age groups between 25 to 44 years were probably not limited by ICT skills to perform church activities. The groups that were limited by lack of ICT skills were those who were 45 years and above with a mean of 3 and above.

Secondly, it can be seen that funds to buy ICTs has an impact on the age of church members (M = 2,91; SD = 1,695; F = 3,737; p = 0,006). It can be seen that those who are between 35 and 44 years (M = 2,29; SD = 1,553) were not limited by funds to buy ICTs compared to other age groups. Those who are above 54 (M = 2,91; SD = 1,814) and those who are 25 to 34 years (M = 2,93; SD = 1,628) had a slight difference in their mean values. The finding showed that funds to buy ICTs in the SDA church in South Africa mostly affects those who are 45 to 54 years old (M = 3,91; SD = 1,703).

Thirdly, it can be seen that those who are aged between 35 and 44 (M = 1,63; SD = 1,135) were least limited by their devices when performing activities, followed by those who are 18 to 24 (M = 1,93; 1,257). The age groups that are limited by their devices when performing activities are those who are 25 to 34 (M = 2,53; SD = 1,579) and those above 54 years (M = 3,18; SD = 1,601). The overall mean was low (M = 2,18; SD = 1,489; F = 4,312; p = 0,002).

Lastly, it can be seen that data bundles affect different age groups (M = 2.76; SD = 1,561; F = 2,605; p = 0,037). It can be seen that most age groups are limited by data bundles with those who are 45 to 54 years (M = 3,61; SD = 1,672) followed by those who are 25 to 34 (M = 2,84; SD = 1,575) and 18 to 24 years (M = 2,63; SD = 1,674). The least limited by data bundles are those who are aged between 35 and 44 (M = 2,39; SD = 1,243) and those above 54 years (M = 2,45; SD = 1,214).

Qualitative Approach

This section presents the research findings from the qualitative data. Table 5 shows the codes and themes that were generated from the research findings on how social media contributes toward membership growth in religious organisations.

Table 5. Themes and codes on church growth using technologies

Themes	Codes
Evangelism as a strategy for membership growth	• Sharing of messages on social media platforms • Share messages on the status • Sharing of media content on media sharing sites • Social media as a tool to reach out to those in different situations
Impact of social media evangelism	• The church can reach out to non-members • Availability and accessibility of content
Promoting and advertising the church and its programmes	• Promote church activities • Advertise church activities
Spiritual connection of members	• Personal Bible studies • Church in-reach programmes
Challenges of using social media in growing church membership	• Abuse of social media channels • Content flooding • Infights on social media platforms

Evangelism as a Strategy of Membership Growth

The research findings show that evangelistic activities play a crucial role in church growth. Participants pointed out that they used social media to share messages, share media content, and reach out to those in challenging situations.

Sharing of Messages on Social Media Platforms

These days I am enjoying the book Steps to Christ, the chapter on prayer. I can just easily generate a message from there and send it to 5 or 6 people or 5 or 6 groups and that way I find that it is more effective to reach people because everyone has a phone on them and everyone can access these messages. P01

Yes, we can use our phones for sharing information on different platforms either Facebook, WhatsApp, or Twitter, people use all those things for in-reach and out-reach as well. P02

As long as you have your phone in your hand, there is always a message that is passing through either on WhatsApp, Instagram, or Facebook there is always a message that talks about God. So to me, I find that technology has brought a big impact as far as evangelism is concerned. P01

Share of Messages on Status

I share all my pictures and recordings. I take pictures every time there is a programme in church and share those pictures with everyone else ... on Facebook, on WhatsApp, and also on my status. P04

WhatsApp is a very personal device because it's on my phone and I control who gets to see my statuses because you can only see my statuses if you are a saved contact on my phone and I have got saved contacts in my phone that are not Adventist so I utilise WhatsApp a lot for evangelistic purposes. P06

Sharing of Media Content on Media Sharing Sites

Yes, I have used YouTube. Not my one but at the departmental level called ZASA so I have used YouTube yes. P04

162

You can just take a sermon in your church and spread it out to those people via email, Skype, or Facebook. P04

I will make an example: if you go to YouTube you discover that we have got a large portion of members who at work have access to vast amounts of data and are looking for sermons online. These are people who may not go to your tent and buy your DVD but the moment you record and upload your DVD on your YouTube channel, some of these people at work can put on headphones and download that message. P06

Social Media as a Tool to Reach out to those in Different Situations

Social media has enabled religious organisations to reach out to people of different social statuses, non-churchgoers, and those living in closed communities difficult to penetrate in face-to-face evangelism.

Some people are difficult to reach because of their social statuses like those in high profiles. Through the use of ICTs, these people can also be preached to by making the word of God available on various platforms which are within their spheres. P05

It helps because an area like place X is a closed-up area. There are a lot of races in the area and it's difficult to go and knock on people's doors so that you can study with them so we have employed ICT channels, and online channels to be able to reach these people, so they have helped even the way we share the programme, we share it online and we share the posters online. Social media are working as a tool for us to get more members because a lot of non-Adventists especially on Facebook I think the viewers of the things I post there 60% were non-Adventists. P07

I must confess that you later realise that many people will not come to your church no matter how much you preach but if you use social media and have some small evangelism nuggets, you can impact them where they are. P06

Impact of Social Media Evangelism

Social media evangelism has made the Word of God easily accessible to members and also non-members via various social media platforms.

The Church can Reach out to Non-Members

The internet also is working, we have several people who are not Adventist who just go and study the Sabbath or about our doctrine on the internet and they join the church. I know people who joined the church through the internet. P08

A good number of people who follow us on these platforms are not Adventists. For example, when we go for our closing function ... who are not Adventists but just friends they also join to see how we are doing the arrangement, logistics, and ... eventually, some of them become our church members. We have a good number now who are part of our structure. They are not yet baptised but they are active members of the structure. It has been almost a year now and we are hoping that .... but then they are very active members who are also part of the social network group. P12

Availability and Accessibility of Content

It's only a few churches where you see them using the ICTs, where they put the sermon online, on YouTube, on Facebook, and all these other platforms and it has an impact because even non-members can listen to those sermons and services of the church and even also get the Bible Study books, and the books of Ellen E. White, they can download and read at their own pleasant time. P10

We have a YouTube account, and some of the videos have got 1000 views already. We just had a crusade this past few months but it has a thousand views already. P12

Promotion and Advertisement of Church Activities and Programmes

Social media evangelism has made the Word of God easily accessible to members and also non-members via various social media platforms.

Promote Evangelistic Programmes

When we do our crusades, our weeks of prayers, our music day, our closing function, and any events, we promote by sending posters on all social network platforms. And some people who come, come as a result of seeing those advertisements. P12

So far maybe through social media like your Facebook when you promote the events that are coming up like crusades and also sending messages to different people that we have. P10

Advertise Church Activities

We create posters and then we send them to various platforms to advertise our different programmes so we use them actively. P03

Spiritual Connection of Church Members

Participants saw the need for members of the church to be constantly revived and to study the Word of God as this has a ripple effect on how they share messages with others. This was highlighted by two participants when they said:

When people grow spiritually when they read those Ellen White books and their Bibles more when the Bible is more accessible through reading it anytime and anywhere, on your phone or laptop and when people read the spirit of prophecy (SOP) if you read more of that you will understand your mission better. Once you understand your mission better the great commission as Christian, as an Adventist, you will be able to carry it through. Otherwise, how can you carry through a mission which you do not understand, which you do not even know? So, it will make people to be more evangelistic and this can bring more souls to the church hence membership growth. P12

These days I am enjoying the book Steps to Christ, the chapter on prayer. I can just easily generate a message from there and send it to 5 or 6 people or 5 or 6 groups and that way I find that it is more effective to reach people because everyone has a phone on them and everyone can access these messages. P01

Challenges of using Social Media in Growing Church Membership

Participants pointed out some challenges such as abuse of social media channels, content flooding, and infights on social media platforms that hinder the use of social media as a tool for promoting membership in religious organisations.

Abuse of Social Media Channels

The major challenges, in general, are misuse and abuse because if you are talking of WhatsApp channels that can be used for instance we can create a group that is strictly meant for communication purposes but you find that it ends up being used for other different purposes. P02

Content Flooding

Yes, for example, there is another platform that I used to be on where people were complaining about space in their phones where things like pictures and videos are posted. P02

For example, on WhatsApp groups, the church sets up a WhatsApp group, but within that group, it is a no- man's land, we are trying to use it as a platform to share evangelism, then you see political things and jokes are also being shared so those are the challenges we face. P04

Infights on Social Media Platforms

There was an issue with the pastors and they were still discussing it as pastors but we found that it ends up going to Facebook and the world, the majority saw the Adventists fighting on WhatsApp. So that's one of the negatives to the growth of the church if it is not properly used. P08.

Development of the Church Growth Causal Loop Diagram

The causal loop diagram was developed from the variables identified from the quantitative data, qualitative data, and literature review.

Development Stages of Church Membership

Church membership can develop in three stages as shown in Figure 1. The churches grow from people who may not have heard about the Word of God. These people may hear the Word of God through word of mouth, by receiving an email from a friend, seeing messages on social media such as Twitter, Facebook, and WhatsApp. There are several ways for these people to hear/read the Word of God. Once non-members hear/read the Word of God then they become non-members who have heard the Word of God. These people can be converted to become church members. This can happen when these people have been convinced by members directly, stayed on social media, and then decided to join a particular church, visited a church, or visited a church website. This conversion adds to the church membership. Church members may backslide becoming people who have heard the Word of God. This may happen if a member had issues with the other member(s), church ministers, disliked the congregation, etc. This decreases church membership.

Figure 1. Development stages of church membership

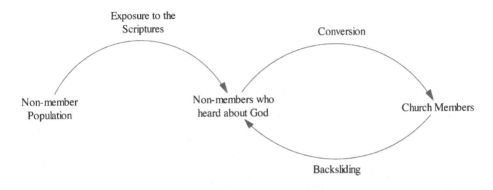

Causal Loop Diagram

Figure 2 shows the church growth CLD which consists of 12 main causal loops, including 5 reinforcing (R) and 2 balancing (B) loops. The reinforcing loops have exponential growth, while the balancing loops try to bring a system to the desired state and keep it there. The individual causal loops are under the rest of this section.

Figure 2. Causal loop diagram showing church growth

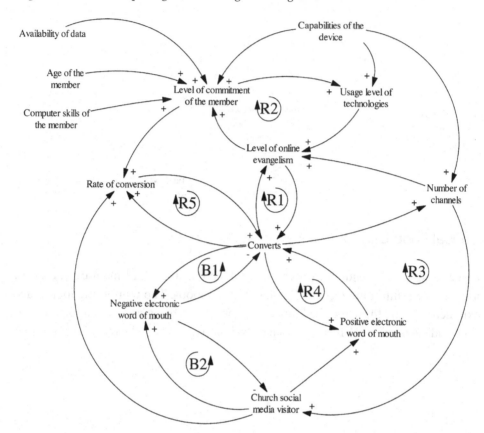

Loop Number 1 (Reinforcing Loop)

A reinforcing loop is a causal loop that reinforces itself and increases the value of the stock. If the religious organisations intensify the level of online evangelism, it broadens the reach leading to an increase in the number of converts. An increase in the number of converts will lead to an increase in the level of evangelism. The assumption is that when people are converted, they become enthusiasts, taking part in the recruitment of others using technologies and word of mouth. As the number of converts increases, these converts can commit themselves to evangelism, in turn increasing the level of evangelism.

Loop Number 2 (Reinforcing Loop)

If there is a commitment from the church leaders and members, this will increase the usage level of online technologies which, in turn, increases the level of online evangelism. The level of commitment can be influenced by the level of computer skills possessed by the member, the member's age, availability of data, and devices. These factors were revealed in the findings of the quantitative research. When there is a high level of commitment, the usage level of technologies tends to increase. A high-level usage of technologies tends to increase the level of online evangelism. For religious organisations to increase the level of online evangelism, there should be a high level of commitment and people should be willing to use technologies.

Loop Number 3 (Reinforcing Loop)

Having many different social media channels can lead a church to an increase in the number of people visiting church social media platforms. A high number of people visiting a church on social media platforms can lead to an increase in the number of positive electronic word of mouth (eWOM). A high number of positive electronic word of mouth may lead to an increase in the number of converts. Positive electronic word of mouth influences website visitors in making decisions about joining or not a church. A high number of converts may lead to an increase in the number of channels being used to reach online visitors.

Loop Number 4 (Reinforcing Loop)

The number of converts is determined by the conversion rate. If the rate of conversion is high, it leads to many people converting to church members. The rate of conversion, in turn, is increased when many converts are participating in the recruitment of new members.

Loop Number 5 (Balancing Loop)

An increase in the negative eWOM on religious organisation platforms will likely decrease the number of converts into the church as negative comments give people a sense of doubt about the authenticity of the organisation. People can use eWOMs to make decisions on whether they can join the church or not. When the number of converts decreases, this might increase the number of negative eWOM on the church's social media platforms. When people leave the church dissatisfied with the organisation and its services, they leave negative eWOM that can discourage new visitors who may want to join the organisation.

Loop Number 6 (Balancing Loop)

Having a high number of negative electronic word of mouth has a high chance of decreasing the number of people who visit church social media platforms. A reduction in the number of visitors to the church's social media platforms can lead to an increase in the number of negative eWOM.

DISCUSSIONS

The goal of religious organisations is to convert non-members. These non-members might be new to the Word of God or might be people who have heard/read the Word of God but have not yet accepted to belong to a church. The results showed that the growth of religious organisations is dependent on church members. Friendship evangelism is key to the growth of religious organisations. The more a church recruits' new members, the more the church grows. Results show that a change in the number of new members influences the rate of conversion of the non-members. This implies that the more the church recruits' new members, the more these new members take part in the recruitment of others. New members tend to recruit their close circles such as friends and family members.

The recruitment of new members is influenced by the member's level of commitment. The level of commitment by members to recruiting other members is essential in intensifying the level of evangelism. This commitment is influenced by the computer skills level of the member, the age of the member, and the availability of data to use social media. These were informed by the results presented in Tables 2 and 4. This finding is in agreement with the idea that enthusiasts are active in the recruitment of other members for some time, and then they become inactive (Hayward, 2002). Participants pointed out the need for members to keep revived to be able to evangelise to others even in an online environment.

Alternative means of growing the church could be having attractive (high quality products such as sermons) social media platforms that could attract a large number of positive electronic word of mouth (eWOM). Positive eWOM, in turn, attracts more visitors to church social media platforms. When these visitors are impressed by the church services, this could also increase the positive eWOMs on the church's social media platforms. These eWOM messages could influence church visitors when deciding on joining the church or not. Positive eWOMs tend to encourage visitors to join whereas negative eWOMs tend to discourage visitors from joining the church. Negative eWOMs discourage people from visiting church social media platforms. When visitors find unattractive church services/products, they tend to increase the number of negative eWOMs. Positive eWOM translates to church growth while negative eWOM translates to a decrease in the number of converts. A decrease in the number of converts may translate to a high number of negative eWOMs on the church's social media platforms.

Furthermore, a church could use multiple social media channels to target different people as the results in Table 1 showed that some platforms are used by the majority of people while other platforms are used by very few people. Having multichannels ensures that the church has broadened its base to reach a large audience. To reach lots of people, religious organisations can use various social media channels such as YouTube, Facebook, and WhatsApp.

In conclusion, the researchers found that members play a crucial role in growing churches. Technologies are just enablers for members to perform their activities. Furthermore, the quality of services/products on the church's social media platforms encourages or discourages web visitors leading to either positive or negative eWOMs.

CONCLUSION

The study modelled church growth using causal loop diagrams. The study explored holistically how technological variables influence growth within religious organisations using the SDA church as the case study. The study used qualitative and quantitative data as the primary sources of data and literature review as the secondary source of data. The research study concluded that church members' involvement – even in the online environment – contributes greatly to church growth. The research also concluded that technology is just an enabler for church members to perform their tasks. Friendship evangelism is key to the growth of church membership.

FUTURE RESEARCH DIRECTIONS

The study was limited to the SDA churches based in South Africa. Future studies can focus on a variety of religious organisations using developing models such as stock and flow diagrams (SFD) to create scenario for policy building, analysis and development.

REFERENCES

Absanto, G. (2013). Analysis of Business Growth Strategies and their Contribution to Business Growth. *International Journal of Economics, Commerce and Management*, *I*(1), 1–14.

Bolu, C. A. (2012). The church in the contemporary world: Information and communication technology in church communication for growth: A case study. *Journal of Media and Communication Studies*, *4*(4), 80–94. doi:10.5897/JMCS11.087

Braun, V., & Clarke, V. (2006). Using thematic analysis in psychology. *Qualitative Research in Psychology*, *3*(2), 77–101. doi:10.1191/1478088706qp063oa

Bruner, R. F. (2004). Applied Mergers and Acquisitions. John Wiley and Sons.

Činčala, P. A. (2016). *Building a Vibrant, Healthy, Growing Church.* Faculty Publications. https://digitalcommons.andrews.edu/pubs/231

Collins, B. W., & Sturgill, A. (2013). The Effects of Media Use on Religious Individuals' Perceptions of Science. *Journal of Media and Religion*, *12*(4), 217–230. doi:10.1080/15348423.2013.845043

Currie, D. J., Smith, C., & Jagals, P. (2018). The application of system dynamics modelling to environmental health decision-making and policy - A scoping review. *BMC Public Health*, *18*(1), 1–11. doi:10.118612889-018-5318-8 PMID:29587701

Denzin, N. K., & Lincoln, Y. S. (2005). Introduction: The Discipline and Practice of Qualitative Research. In The Sage handbook of qualitative research (pp. 1–32). Sage Publications Ltd.

Durmaz, Y., Ilhan, A., & Ilhan, A. (2015). A Theoretical Approach to Purpose and Type of Strategy. *International Journal of Business and Management*, *10*(4). Advance online publication. doi:10.5539/ijbm.v10n4p210

Etikan, I. (2016). Comparison of Convenience Sampling and Purposive Sampling. *American Journal of Theoretical and Applied Statistics*, *5*(1), 1. doi:10.11648/j.ajtas.20160501.11

Farzin, M., & Fattahi, M. (2018). eWOM through social networking sites and impact on purchase intention and brand image in Iran. *Journal of Advances in Management Research*. doi:10.1108/JAMR-05-2017-0062

Fred, B. J. (2015). *The Development and Implementation of a Community-Based Evangelism Model in the Word of Life Seventh-day Adventist Church in Memphis, TN.* Academic Press.

Hadaway, C. K. (1993). Is evangelism related to church growth? In D. A. Roozen & C. K. Hadaway (Eds.), *Church and Denominational Growth* (pp. 169–187). Abingdon Press.

Hayward, J. (1999). Mathematical modeling of church growth. *The Journal of Mathematical Sociology*, *23*(4), 255–292. doi:10.1080/0022250X.1999.9990223

Hayward, J. (2002). A dynamic model of church growth and its application to contemporary revivals. *Review of Religious Research*, *43*(3), 218–241. doi:10.2307/3512330

Hayward, J. (2005). A general model of church growth and decline. *The Journal of Mathematical Sociology*, *29*(3), 177–207. doi:10.1080/00222500590889721

Homer, J. B., & Hirsch, G. B. (2006). System dynamics modeling for public health: Background and opportunities. *American Journal of Public Health*, *96*(3), 452–458. doi:10.2105/AJPH.2005.062059 PMID:16449591

Kgatle, M. S. (2018). Social media and religion: Missiological perspective on the link between Facebook and the emergence of prophetic churches in southern Africa. *Verbum et Ecclesia, 39*(1).

Korstjens, I., & Moser, A. (2018). Series: Practical guidance to qualitative research. Part 4: Trustworthiness and publishing. *The European Journal of General Practice*, *24*(1), 120–124. doi:10.1080/13814788.2017.1375092 PMID:29202616

Lie, S. (2018). How best to evangelize to nonbelievers: Cultural persuasion in American and Chinese Indonesian evangelical Christian discourse on relational evangelism. *Journal of International and Intercultural Communication*, *11*(1), 42–57. doi:10.1080/17513057.2017.1349920

Lincoln, Y. S., & Guba, E. G. (1985). Naturalistic Inquiry. In *The A-Z of Social Research*. Sage. doi:10.4135/9781412986281.n232

Long, T., & Johnson, M. (2000). Rigour, reliability and validity in qualitative research. *Clinical Effectiveness in Nursing*, *4*(1), 30–37. doi:10.1054/cein.2000.0106

Magezi, V. (2015). Technologically Changing African Context and Usage of Information Communication and Technology in Churches: Towards Discerning Emerging Identities in Church Practice (A Case Study of Two Zimbabwean Cities). In HTS Teologiese Studies / Theological Studies (Vol. 71, Issue 2). doi:10.4102/hts.v71i2.2625

Martin, L. A. (1997). *The First Step*. Massachusetts Institute of Technology. https://ocw.mit.edu/courses/sloan-school-of-management/15-988-system-dynamics-self-study-fall-1998-spring-1999/readings/step.pdf

Matobobo, C., & Bankole, F. (2020). Is the Impact of Human-Computer Interaction in Religious Organisations a Hype or Crossword? *UK Academy for Information Systems Conference Proceedings 2020*, 12. https://aisel.aisnet.org/ukais2020/12

Matobobo, C., & Bankole, F. (2021a). Customizing and Implementing e-Dashboard in Religious Organisations. *Academic Journal of Current Research*, 8(10), 1–15.

Matobobo, C., & Bankole, F. (2021b). Evaluating eWOM in Social Media: Religious Leaders vs Religious Organizations: Functionality Approach. *UK Academy for Information Systems Conference Proceedings 2021*.

Nabavi, E., Daniell, K. A., & Najafi, H. (2017). Boundary matters: The potential of system dynamics to support sustainability? *Journal of Cleaner Production*, 140, 312–323. doi:10.1016/j.jclepro.2016.03.032

Noble, H., & Smith, J. (2015). Issues of validity and reliability in qualitative research. *Evidence-Based Nursing*, 18(2), 34–35. doi:10.1136/eb-2015-102054 PMID:25653237

Palinkas, L. A., Horwitz, S. M., Green, C. A., Wisdom, J. P., Duan, N., & Hoagwood, K. (2015). Purposeful sampling for qualitative data collection and analysis in mixed method implementation research. *Administration and Policy in Mental Health*, 42(5), 533–544. doi:10.100710488-013-0528-y PMID:24193818

Ryan, G. (2018). Introduction to positivism, interpretivism and critical theory. *Nurse Researcher*, 25(4), 14–20. doi:10.7748/nr.2018.e1466 PMID:29546962

Sahay, B. S., Mohan, R., & Maini, A. (2004). Strategies for building a sustainable competitive edge. *International Journal of Innovation and Learning*, 1(3), 209. doi:10.1504/IJIL.2004.004879

Sargeant, K. H. (2000). *Seeker Churches: Promoting Traditional Religion in a Nontraditional Way*. Rutgers University Press.

Sternam, J. D. (2002). System Dynamics: Systems Thinking and Modeling for a Complex World. MIT Sloan School of Management.

Takahashi, Y. (2015). System Dynamics. In *Encyclopedia of Information Science and Technology* (3rd ed., pp. 1261–1272). IGI Global. doi:10.4018/978-1-4666-5888-2.ch120

Thomas, D. R. (2017). Feedback from research participants: Are member checks useful in qualitative research? *Qualitative Research in Psychology*, 14(1), 23–41. doi:10.1080/14780887.2016.1219435

Tomalin, E. (2018). Religions, poverty reduction and global development institutions. *Palgrave Communications*, *4*(1), 132. Advance online publication. doi:10.105741599-018-0167-8

Walker, C. L. (1989). Correlational Research. *Journal of Pediatric Oncology Nursing*, *6*(1), 21–22. doi:10.1177/104345428900600108 PMID:2921740

Walters, J. P., Archer, D. W., Sassenrath, G. F., Hendrickson, J. R., Hanson, J. D., Halloran, J. M., Vadas, P., & Alarcon, V. J. (2016). Exploring agricultural production systems and their fundamental components with system dynamics modelling. *Ecological Modelling*, *333*, 51–65. doi:10.1016/j.ecolmodel.2016.04.015

Westerlund, M., & Leminen, S. (2012). Categorizing the Growth Strategies of Small Firms. *Technology Innovation Management Review*, 5–9. https://doaj.org/article/3 7533f7a928d48dc85294090f648f8ff

White, P., Tella, F., & Ampofo, M. D. (2016). A missional study of the use of social media (Facebook) by some Ghanaian pentecostal pastors. *Koers*, *81*(2), 1–8. doi:10.19108/KOERS.81.2.2250

Wilson, B. R. (2017). The Depiction of Church Growth in Acts. *Journal of the Evangelical Theological Society*, *60*(2), 317–332. https://search-proquest-com. ezproxy.regent.edu/docview/1964553500/fulltextPDF/D5E30159B0CE4128PQ/1 ?accountid=13479

ADDITIONAL READING

Hayward, J. (1999). Mathematical modeling of church growth. *The Journal of Mathematical Sociology*, *23*(4), 255–292. doi:10.1080/0022250X.1999.9990223

Hayward, J. (2002). A dynamic model of church growth and its application to contemporary revivals. *Review of Religious Research*, *43*(3), 218–241. doi:10.2307/3512330

Hayward, J. (2005). A general model of church growth and decline. *The Journal of Mathematical Sociology*, *29*(3), 177–207. doi:10.1080/00222500590889721

Hong, Y. G. (2004). Models of the Church Growth Movement. Transformation. *An International Journal of Holistic Mission Studies*, *21*(2), 101–113.

KEY TERMS AND DEFINITIONS

Balancing Loop: Balancing loop is a causal loop that tries to bring a system to the desired state and keep it there.

Church: A church is a group of believers in Christ Jesus. A church is an example of a religious organisation.

Church Membership Growth: Church membership growth refers to the rise of the number of baptised members in a local congregation.

Electronic Word of Mouth: Electronic word of mouth (eWOM) is any positive or negative comment posted on online platforms about a product or company.

Evangelism: Evangelism refers to the activities undertaken to spread the Word of God by public preaching or personal witness.

Information and Communications Technology: Information and communications technology (ICT) are diverse set of technological tools and resources used to create, store, transmit, share or exchange information. These include computers, telephony, the Internet, broadcasting technologies, networks and other communication mediums.

Inorganic Growth: Inorganic growth is a type of growth that develops due to the formation of partnerships with other businesses.

Organic Growth: Organic growth is a type of growth that occurs when an organisation uses its resources to improve its current activities.

Reinforcing Loop: Reinforcing loop is a causal loop that self-reinforces itself and increases the value of the stock.

Religious Organisations: Religious organisation are non-profit making organisations whose mission is to cater to the spiritual aspects of people such as churches.

Social Media: Social media is a group of Internet-based applications that allow and enable the development and exchange of user-generated content. Examples of social media include Facebook, WhatsApp, Instagram, WeChat and TikTok.

System Dynamics: System dynamics is a method that is used to describe and simulate dynamically complex issues over time using stocks, flows, internal feedback loops, table functions and delay processes that drive system behaviour.

Chapter 8

Sustainable Quality Education During the Pandemic and Beyond:
Challenges and Solutions for Higher Education Institutions

Hakan Islamoglu
https://orcid.org/0000-0003-3128-4512
Recep Tayyip Erdogan University, Turkey

ABSTRACT

Information technologies are an indispensable part of modern business, education, and personal lives. However, the COVID-19 pandemic has shown everybody around the world the insufficiency of available information technology infrastructures and the importance of establishing strong infrastructures for citizens from all backgrounds and geographic locations. The challenge has been especially hard for educational institutions because very few were truly prepared for an emergency transition to distance education. This chapter aims to explain the main components of a modern university information technology infrastructure and offer guidance in establishing a strong infrastructure for sustainable quality education.

INTRODUCTION

The COVID-19 pandemic that started in early 2020 caught many educational institutions unprepared for such a challenge. In the beginning, higher education

DOI: 10.4018/978-1-7998-9418-6.ch008

institutions throughout the world either postponed their educational activities or switched to totally online mediums (Hodges et al., 2020). As the pandemic continued to spread at an increasingly higher rate, everybody realized postponement was not a viable solution and embraced online education even if it meant a premature transition. Although the pandemic did not treat any educational institution differently, the institutions with little to no online and distance education experience faced a greater deal of challenges (Bailey & Lee, 2020; Roy & Covelli, 2020). Unfortunately, the emerging challenges have been too overwhelming for some, and their unpreparedness made the quality and rigor of educational activities questionable at best. Needless to say, both faculty members and students faced many problems during assessment activities and live classroom meetings. In short, the forced transition to online education was suboptimal for most stakeholders, and it has turned educational decision makers' attention to sustainable technology integration during and beyond the pandemic.

In this context, the purpose of this chapter is to overview the challenges an educational institution could face during the transition to the digital medium and offer guidance in reviewing and selecting the solutions available to them. An effective educational technology integration endeavor covers multiple aspects of technology use (Vivek & Bhattacharjee, 2021) including hardware and software facilities available to the users, service agreements, and professional development activities. Without paying due attention to these crucial aspects, even single-classroom-level technology integration efforts are bound to fail. Thus, technology integration initiatives at an institutional scale should pay close attention to the needs of all stakeholders and cover all relevant aspects simultaneously (Moore & Fodrey, 2018).

When we talk about the digital transformation of an institution, the first thing that comes to mind is unquestionably hardware infrastructure. A modern university is expected to provide technical facilities such as campus-wide wireless internet access and computer labs at various locations. However, on-campus facilities of this type themselves have been proved to be ineffective during emergencies like the pandemic. Therefore, institutions should establish both on-campus and off-campus technology infrastructures for sustainability. In the following section, the basic components of university hardware infrastructure will be explained.

HARDWARE INFRASTRUCTURE

On-campus infrastructure is the fundamental side of a digital campus. Over the years, hardware, software, and other informational technology (IT) services have improved tremendously, and there are many options available to choose from; therefore, decisions towards computing infrastructure are not always straightforward.

When making decisions, IT managers should consider the current IT needs of the institution, future plans that require technology, the number of available/potential users, and so on. These factors are unique to any institution and should be identified based on a thorough needs analysis involving all academic and managerial units of the institution. Due to the uniqueness of the solutions, only general information on available options will be presented in this chapter. Basic components of a campus hardware infrastructure could be listed as server infrastructure, and network and internet infrastructure.

Server Infrastructure

General Information on Servers

By the most basic definition, a server is a computer that offers services to other computers on a network (i.e., clients). Although regular users usually do not realize it, servers are at the heart of many information technology projects. They power numerous services including data processing and user authentication. In theory, any computer could act as a server; however, as servers need to perform reliably 7/24/365, they are different from personal computers in both hardware design and operating system capabilities.

Servers are named based on the services they offer. For instance, a modern website uses a web server that runs the code (could be PHP, Ruby, etc.) and presents it to the clients. Such servers usually have a database service, which makes them also database servers. A single server machine could run multiple services simultaneously. Nonetheless, such use is impractical for complex use scenarios like campus information systems because an interruption in one server system may influence another and cause all systems to halt. Therefore, modern system architectures use multiple servers with specific tasks for better resource allocation and easier maintenance.

Servers are fundamentally physical computers, and they traditionally reside on-premises. However, developments in computer hardware, internet services, and technologies like virtualization have changed how servers operate significantly. In the past, IT managers could either use a single server for many tasks or a combination of separate physical servers with varying hardware capacity for different tasks. Needless to say, management was cumbersome, and dealing with failures was harder. Also, servers used to have multiple processors (i.e., CPUs) to handle complex tasks fasters. Today, multicore/multithread CPUs are commonplace and even personal computers offer tens of cores and processing threads. The wealth of processing power brings another challenge, which is using available computing capacity efficiently. Thanks to the virtualization technology, multiple server instances (i.e., virtual server computers) could run on a single physical machine and available resources could be freely allocated to each instance. Moreover, resources allocated to a server instance could be increased or decreased easily as the needs of the institution change.

Depending on the services needed, a higher education institution usually needs web servers, database servers, file (data storage) servers, e-mail servers, license servers, authentication servers, and so on. After deciding on what types of servers are needed, IT planners should consider hardware features (e.g., CPU, ram, and storage) of each server. In the past, all servers were physical devices and that made increasing efficiency harder for IT professionals. Today, most companies use virtualization technology to allocate specific hardware resources to virtual server instances that run within a more powerful system, yet they are isolated from one another. For instance, a physical server with a 64-core CPU, 1 TB of RAM, and 20 TB of storage could power a web server with 2 virtual CPU cores, 4GB of RAM, and 40 GB of storage. Virtualization increases efficiency because IT professionals could assign just-enough resources to each server and run numerous servers on a single machine. Virtualization also makes it easier to maintain and backup servers (Al-Saadoon & Al Naemi, 2015). Once IT professionals decide on the specifics of servers needed for campus information systems, they need to decide the location of the servers.

Location of Servers: On-Premises, On-Cloud, or Both?

Universities and companies used to have all their technology infrastructure on-premises, however, as online systems evolve, many traditionally on-campus services started to be offered off-campus as well. Cloud computing systems have a large part in that evolution. Cloud computing refers to distributed online computer systems that are offered as various services (from data storage to web servers) to corporate and individual users. Today, many businesses prefer cloud computing over physical hardware due to greatly reduced initial cost and flexibility (Wease et al., 2018).

Server hardware tends to be expensive compared to other computer hardware, and costs usually increase as hardware specifications go higher. Moreover, the institution needs to (a) provide a physical location with good ventilation, (b) hire IT professionals for server configuration, maintenance, and security assurance, and (c) pay for electricity. In other words, running servers on-premises involves not only a hardware acquisition cost but also an operating cost (Nayar & Kumar, 2018). Cloud computing simplifies the situation by combining many of the aforementioned costs in a subscription or licensing agreement. Cloud service providers utilize virtualization technology to offer flexible plans to their customers. For instance, a small university could lease basic virtual servers for its systems and increase the capacity as IT needs change. In this scenario, the university does not own the server hardware, therefore, hardware cost is greatly reduced. Also, it does not need to worry about hardware upgrades because virtual capacity could be increased instantaneously by customizing the cloud service options. Moreover, they save on the initial cost of a powerful server that may not be fully utilized. Cloud computing also helps reducing IT personal workload because the maintenance of cloud servers is mostly done by service provider's personnel, and they usually provide 7/24 assistance to their customers. Cloud computing companies also have to assure the security of the servers, so universities need to worry about cybersecurity less. Nonetheless, both sides are responsible for ensuring the security of the data. In addition to server infrastructure, cloud service companies could also offer Software as a Service (SaaS), where licensed software is made available in a web-based format. Finally, cloud service providers could offer bandwidths way beyond the capabilities of a regular university regardless of the geographic location of the user (client), which increases the efficiency of bandwidth-sensitive tasks such as video conferencing.

Despite its advantages, cloud computing is not entirely trouble-free. Universities still need IT professionals to configure and maintain software (either developed in-house or licensed from third parties) on the cloud servers. Another potential issue is data ownership. When universities utilize cloud servers, their data are stored at another location owned by the service provider, and that location(s) could even be in another country or dispersed in multiple continents. This situation is especially problematic when local laws and regulations discourage or even prohibit storing user data in another country. Many cloud service providers have servers within the US and European Union, and they allow users to choose the location of the data storage. However, countries out of these regions often do not have an option that satisfies national regulations. In such cases, cloud computing may not be a viable solution, and therefore, local providers should be considered if there are any. The shortcomings mentioned here are minimal compared to the advantages that could be obtained. Furthermore, cloud computing does not have to be server-centric, rather universities could acquire cloud storage and productivity tools from the providers.

Considering the basic online data storage and collaboration needs of an academic institution, it would make sense to use cloud products offered by big IT companies like Google, Microsoft, Amazon, and IBM. Google is an early adopter of cloud business, and it has been offering perfectly sufficient cloud productivity applications to users with a Google (a.k.a. Gmail) account for years. It also has enterprise-level services called Google Workspace (previously known as G Suite) for corporate users and educational institutions. Institutional plans provide better integration among tools, institution-wide sharing, and an ad-free e-mail service based on Gmail, all of which are free for educational institutions. In the past, educational package had virtually no limitations, yet during the COVID-19 pandemic, the company created paid tiers of Google Workspace for Education and imposed some limits to the entry-level plan (still free of charge) such as no cloud recordings for Google Meet and a quota for originality reports could be generated using Google Assignments. Despite recent limitations, Google Workspace still offers great value for educational institutions.

An alternative to Google Workspace comes from Microsoft as part of its Microsoft 365 service (previously known as Office 365). Microsoft 365 is a subscription-based service for both personal and corporate users. It includes the latest version of the well-known Microsoft Office suite for Windows and Mac. The suite also includes the cloud versions of the productivity tools (i.e., Word, Excel, and PowerPoint) that work seamlessly with desktop versions and allows for collaboration with others. Similar to Google Workspace, it also offers an e-mail and calendar service (Outlook), cloud storage (OneDrive), a surveying tool (Microsoft Forms), and a meeting tool (Microsoft Teams). Transition to Microsoft 365 is easy for institutions with a Microsoft campus licensing agreement. In addition, the company offers a free tier for eligible institutions that includes all online tools except for the desktop version of Microsoft Office.

Considering the variety and the complexity of the IT needs of a university, it makes sense to build a hybrid server infrastructure. In doing so, sensitive yet not-resource-intensive information such as university website, user credentials, student records, and on-campus payment records could be stored on-premises hardware, while resource-intensive components including learning management system, online file storage, and video conferencing could be handled through cloud service providers. This approach also reduces on-campus internet bandwidth requirements significantly.

Network and Internet Infrastructure

The connectivity of campus is equally important as its server infrastructure. Without a strong network and internet infrastructure, servers could not accomplish their task as desired. Thus, a higher education institution should invest in both wired and wireless networking hardware in addition to high-speed fiber internet access.

Within a campus, numerous devices are connected to each other through the network. These devices include servers, staff computers, shared computers at various locations (e.g., labs), computer terminals, personal portable devices, and networking hardware (e.g., switches and bridges). For stationary devices, wired networking is often the best solution because of its stability and often higher bandwidth. A possible downside of it would be problems that could occur during physical installation, especially if the building is not new. However, this issue could be easily handled by experienced technicians and construction workers. All wires that came from client devices should be connected to switches installed at specific locations. The most important aspects of wired networking are planning and documentation. It is harder to solve network problems where network topology is not documented, and cables are unnamed. Wired networking is also the basis of wireless networking because wireless routers are connected to main switches. Thus, regardless of the complexity of network infrastructure, all devices in a network and their connections should be documented so that even newly-hired technicians could attend to the emerging problems without a delay.

Over the past couple of decades, wired network technologies did not change remarkably; however, wireless network standards have undergone many developments. In each iteration, the bandwidth of wireless connections has increased and gotten closer to their wired counterparts. As of writing this chapter, the most current wireless networking standard is IEEE 802.11ax (also called Wi-Fi 6 and Wi-Fi 6E). The standard supports 2.4, 5, and 6 GHz frequency bands for data transmission. While the traditional 2.4 GHz band is supported by a wider range of devices, it is shared by other appliances including microwave ovens, and does not support higher bandwidths like 5 and 6 GHz bands. Nonetheless, it works better when the connecting device is further away from the wireless router. In sum, there are advantages and disadvantages to all frequency bands, and it is better to support all through contemporary networking hardware. Moreover, most students use portable electronic devices to connect to the Internet. As personal data plans used on these devices may not be enough to consume high-quality learning materials, campus-wide wireless networking should provide high-speed connections with extended coverage. Finally, connecting to the wireless network should be simple. Requiring users to change device configurations or install custom certificates hinders the experience. Instead, wireless networks should be accessed simply by choosing the network and entering user credentials.

Another important aspect of campus networks is the availability of virtual private networking (VPN). The VPN services allow users to connect to the campus network from remote locations so that they could access the university's digital resources such as library subscriptions. Traditionally, VPN services required users to change connectivity settings of their operating system or web browser. Nonetheless, non-technical users tend to have problems with altering such settings. Besides, inexperienced users often forget to reset the settings once they are done. This situation is problematic for both the user and the university because all internet traffic goes though the campus system when a VPN connection is active, which usually results in internet slowdown on the user side and system overload on the university side. To alleviate such problems, modern VPN solutions usually offer a companion software for personal computers and mobile devices, so that users could easily gain access to the campus resources whenever they need and disable the connection when they complete their work by clicking a button. There also exist web proxy services that enables users to access campus resources by clicking a link on the library web site and entering user credentials. Web proxy sessions only pertains to predetermined web sites, so they do not affect remaining online activity. They also expire automatically, so users do not have worry about disabling the connection. Considering the advantages, web proxy services and VPN services with companion software should be preferred for remote access.

SOFTWARE AND SERVICE INFRASTRUCTURE

Learning Management System: Open-Source, Commercial, or Hybrid

Learning management systems (LMS) are online applications that allow for numerous instructional tasks including but not limited to communication, material distribution, and assessment. Although they are a must for online courses, they are also crucial for any modern course regardless of delivery medium (Piña, 2018). To be useful for higher education, an LMS should offer communication features, content delivery features, assignment collection and grading features, and participant management.

The main objective of LMS is to provide interactions beyond classroom meetings (be it F2F or online). Hence, communication tools have a prominent place on LMS software. For instance, instructors could use announcement tool to let course-takers know about recent developments about the course and emergency situations. Some systems allow course-takers to comment on the announcements, and consequently create an environment for two-way communication among the people enrolled in the course. Another means of communication in LMS is private messaging feature that enables course-takers and instructors to send messages to one or more people enrolled in the course. Using this facility, students could ask personal questions directly to the instructor and communicate with peers. Another form of communication in LMS is discussion boards or threads. Using this feature instructor(s) could set discussion assignments around specific topics or create virtual places for information exchange such as Question & Answer threads. LMS-mediated communications are often asynchronous by nature, yet recent tools and always-online user electronics have improved the immediacy of interactions remarkably. Today, most LMS have a mobile companion app that informs users about new activities on the course and allow them to respond without a delay.

For courses, content provision is just as important as communication. Most LMS software allows instructors to organize course content in a meaningful way. Moreover, it enables them to choose when the content becomes visible to the course-takers. By using content sharing facilities of an LMS effectively, the instructors become curators of information. Backup and export features embedded in LMS enable instructors to transfer the curated content to other course offerings. In doing so, instructors not only save time, but also gain a chance to update and improve their curations further in each iteration. To improve reusability of content over courses and ease content-LMS interactions, many LMSs support Sharable Content Object Reference Model (SCORM). Using SCORM, course designer could create learning modules containing multiple learning objects and use them in multiple courses with ease. Furthermore, it allows content developers to acquire data from the LMS and send updated or newly generated data back to the LMS. For instance, an interactive e-book with practice questions could send students' scores to the LMS for grading.

In addition to content sharing, LMSs also offer various tools to aid assessment and evaluation. Although naming change from LMS to LMS, most systems have an examination module or an assignment dropbox section. In its very basic form, these tools allow instructors to set up assignments and provide details such as instructions, grading rubrics, and due dates. Learners, then, upload their work within the time frame set by the instructor. Some LMSs also offer integration with cloud productivity suits (e.g., Google Workspace and Microsoft Office Online) to allow students to complete the assignment without leaving the LMS. Apart from traditional assignments, most LMSs include a test tool to create and apply exams that include various question types like multiple choice, open-ended, and true-false. Some LMSs also include a question bank feature to support exam development and reuse in consequent semesters. There usually exist a gradebook section that allows instructors to monitor learners' progress in one place, and similarly learners could track themselves.

Last but not least, professional LMSs log user interactions in detail. This facility gives IT managers, instructors, and researchers chances analyze the data to uncover interaction patterns and identify emerging needs. The wealth of information that could be collected through LMSs has given a rise to a relatively new research area called learning analytics (Ifenthaler et al., 2021). This new line of practice allows for automatic analysis of data to guide various aspects of learning such as informing decision-making processes, creation of guidance systems that adapt content to learners' needs, and assessing learners' performance more holistically. In addition to standards like SCORM, course designers could employ experience API (also known as xAPI) to obtain more detailed information on learners' activity (Keough, 2018). Although its relatively new, many LMSs and e-Learning content design tools support the API. Hence, considering the applications of learning analytics in both research and practice, it would be wise to select an LMS with rich data collection features and support for standards like SCORM and xAPI.

Although an LMS is a functional system by itself, it works better when integrated with other campus information systems. For instance, courses and their rosters could be generated and updated automatically as students register for courses. This consequently enables the standardization of general course structure and ensuring course privacy. Otherwise, students need to enroll in the courses individually via enrolment requests or shared course codes, which could pose an information security problem when people who are not enrolled in the course gain access to the virtual classroom. Another advantage of integration is automatic grade transfer. When available, instructors could conduct all grading and feedback activities through the LMS, and then the system could calculate the final scores and transfer them to the campus information system.

How to Choose an LMS

As with all technological tools, the marketplace for LMS provides many options to choose from. When choosing an LMS for a university, one should consider functionality, usability, compatibility, and cost. Among these aspects, the cost is a relative factor based on the budget and the number of users, and it could be negotiated to some extent. However, the remaining ones should be reviewed through the lens of a needs analysis. After all, paying for fancy functions that nobody needs - or worse nobody knows how to use - is a waste of limited financial resources. Figure 1 shows the changes in the LMS market for the US and Canada higher education institutions over the last 24 years.

Figure 1. LMS market share for US and Canadian Higher Education Institutions

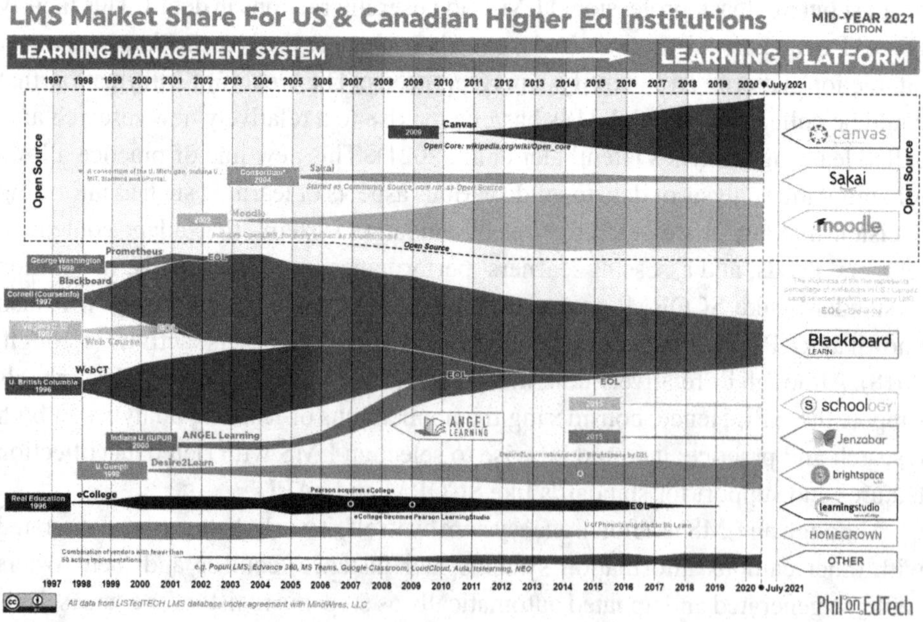

As seen in the figure, the LMS market is open to change and open-source alternatives such as Moodle and Canvas take a large portion of the market. Open-source LMSs are quite appealing to universities of all sorts because they could be installed on readily available servers without needing to pay any licensing fees. Nevertheless, these systems need to be configured and maintained by university personnel, which by itself is a cost and requires the employment of experienced IT professionals.

Choosing an LMS is a long-term commitment, yet it does not always last long. In cases where an institution needs to change the available systems, the decision should be well justified by multiple metrics. In this process, it is wise to employ real users from different demographics (students, professors, support personnel, elders, etc.) to evaluate the new system and shape transition plans (Berking & Gallagher, 2016). If the transition is done on campus, technical personnel and support personnel should work closely to zero-in problems. If the transition is part of a new service agreement, companies could also provide support for transferring data and training. To sum up, the decision to choose LMS is multifaceted and requires thorough preparation.

Online Meeting and Web Conferencing

Online meeting tools (OMT) often complement LMS and allow for live classroom and other off-campus meetings. In comparison to LMS, they are more resource-intensive and therefore expensive. However, an effective online learning infrastructure needs both systems to work seamlessly. In the past, online course instructors rarely utilized participant video in live classroom meetings due to limited bandwidth and video quality. Since then, internet connection speeds have increased, hardware capabilities have improved, especially on the mobile side, and more effective video compression standards like H.264, H.265, and AV1 have become available. All these developments paved the way for immersive online meetings. In today's standards, online meeting tools should support screen and application window sharing, different user roles (e.g., host, presenter, and audience), and meeting recordings. Other nice to have features are presentation modes, and optimized video file streaming.

Online meeting tool market has many well-known tools such as Adobe Connect and Blackboard Collaborate; however, the pandemic environment tipped the balance and gave some newcomers and lesser-known alternatives prominence. For many individuals, Zoom became synonymous with online classrooms during the pandemic. The company's strength was not only in functionality but also in its accessibility. Many teachers from K-12 to university tried free Zoom meetings with success and continued to do so. Although industry leaders had better features, they could not reach a similar volume of users. Thanks to free institutional plans, Microsoft Teams and Google Meet experienced similar gains in terms of the number of active users. As both tools were designed primarily for business environments, they initially lacked some features such as clearly divided user roles. For instance, all participants had host-level permissions by default and some students used this power to mute others or remove them from the meeting. In time, both tools applied fixes for such problems and included more features geared towards live classroom meetings. Today, most OMT services offer essential tools for interactive lessons, yet their usability features are quite different. Commercial OMT offerings mostly run on cloud computing and charge institutions per individual user. Some tools also provide an on-premises installation option; however, such options require a stronger on-promises server infrastructure and overall higher on-campus bandwidth.

Online Examination and Proctoring

Assessment and evaluation in the digital medium are also important in maintaining a culture of honesty, as well as checking out knowledge and skill attainment towards degree completion. When instructors ignore the facilities that technology offers to students, they not only miss a chance to employ such facilities to create modern assessment and evaluation activities, but also leave the academic integrity in the merci of students. While the former situation is not entirely troubling for an institution, the latter is likely to detriment the trustworthiness of the degrees awarded to all students, honest and dishonest alike (Dendir & Maxwell, 2020). Hill et al. (2021) argued that cheating behavior, not only detriments academic integrity but also workplace ethics as graduates of this sort could transfer such undesired behaviors to other spheres of life. Developing sound assessment and evaluation tools itself is labor-intensive enough, adding the digitization of these tools makes the instructors' job even more challenging. Therefore, both technological and pedagogical support is required for instructors (St-Onge et al., 2021).

Students could use various means to cheat in online examinations including creating instant messaging groups in tools like Whatsapp and Discord, having somebody else take the exam, and paying for completed assignments. To fight academic dishonesty, instructors should be trained about the types of academic misconduct and equipped with digitals tools (e.g., plagiarism detection and online proctoring systems) that make it easier to detect, and hopefully eliminate, various types of dishonest behaviors (Coghlan et al., 2020). The most common anti-cheating measures are plagiarism detection systems like Turnitin and iThenticate. These tools work asynchronously and compare students' work with a large database containing assignments submitted by others, published works, and internet resources to create a similarity index. They are effective in detecting common plagiarism types involving direct copying behavior, yet susceptible to manipulation by paraphrasing and other means. There are also synchronous tools to fight cheating during time-limited online exams. A simple solution is safe exam browsers that prevent the test taker from opening another web page or switching to other applications. Such tools are moderately effective in time-limited situations, yet they cannot check the test taker's surroundings for other sources of help. Online proctoring systems alleviate this shortcoming by utilizing software tools and camera hardware. These systems record test takers' behavior in both virtual and physical environments. The systems can detect suspicious keyboard and mouse activity and the use of virtualization software. After each examination, they provide a report to the instructor. Modern solutions also record the entire test session and analyze it through artificial intelligence tools that detect suspicious eye movements and the presence of others. Then, the instructor could check reported activities and decide on what actions to go forward. The main problem with online proctoring tools is the cost, especially when the entire test session is recorded in the cloud. Another problem is platform limitations, these tools rarely support mobile devices. Even if the platform supports various devices, some learners may not have the required hardware. Hence, institutions should thoroughly inform students about the technology requirements of online proctoring early in the semester to prevent failure to attend exams.

The factors affecting the decision to choose digital assessment and quality control tools are similar to those of LMS and OMT selection. Considering the excessive cost of state-of-the-line online proctoring systems, universities may remain reluctant due to budget issues. After all, anti-cheating applications are not the first thing a university needs when it transitions to the digital medium, nonetheless, it comes right after proving high-quality educational services. At this point, it could be argued that not all universities need that much of a system to fight academic dishonesty; however, at least some measures should be taken to create a sort of scarecrow effect on students' minds. To be specific, if the university and instructors rely on simple form tools without any anti-cheating measurements, even some students who are capable enough to attain a passing grade would be tempted to cheat in order to get a higher grade. On the contrary, none of the students with their right minds would risk it when there are serious measures taken and communicated through proper means. In each scenario, some at-risk students would try to cheat, yet their numbers would be minimal compared to the no-measurement scenario.

Licensed Software and Auxiliary Services

Off-campus resources are of importance in narrowing down the digital divide between students. The COVID-19 pandemic has shown us how important it is to close the gap to allow educational activities to continue in the face of a crisis. While universities could not address the entire range of the causes of the digital divide, they could definitely help to alleviate the problem by increasing accessibility. Institutions, for instance, can develop device-agnostic interfaces for campus resources so that any student with an internet-enabled device could gain access. Digital services like content repositories, library subscriptions, remote access, and virtual computer labs with pre-installed licensed software (a.k.a. virtual desktop infrastructure: VDI) (Ergüzen et al., 2021) are also of importance. In sum, hardware infrastructure is a prerequisite for a successful digital transformation, yet it is not enough on and off by itself.

Virtual desktop infrastructure (VDI) is based on virtualization technology, and it allows end-users to connect to a remote machine (in the cloud or a traditional server) as if he or she is using a local computer. VDI has different use scenarios. A common use is accessing campus resources and high computing power from a remote location through a personal device with an internet connection. To use the system users, need to install client software and log into their virtual computer using user credentials. Another use scenario is using low-spec terminals (called thin client or zero client) to control a remote machine. The terminal here only transfers inputs and outputs between machines, so it does not need a strong hardware configuration, a hard drive, or an operating system. Using the network boot feature, the client automatically acquires recent connection software and meets users with a log-in screen. In both scenarios, energy cost and management tasks are greatly lowered because terminals operate on very low power and many users could use software installed on a single server machine.

Many universities acquire site-licenses of commercial software such as statistical packages to allow users to study and do research. While this approach enables users to utilize often expensive software, it is not the most cost-effective solution for institutions. Therefore, open-source alternatives to known software suites should be promoted. Nonetheless, promotion should go beyond recommending use. Courses and high-quality materials should also be prepared because open-source software is often unfamiliar to users and therefore face premature rejection. For instance, the R project has been invaluable to the statistical community, yet R's command-driven nature usually pushes non-statistician users out of their safe zone. Tutorials ranging from basic functions to advanced analyses would help a lot to overcome this problem. Also, some tools like Jamovi and JASP combine the power of R with ease-to-use interfaces. Whenever available, such tools should be recommended. And for commercial tools without sufficient alternatives, virtual labs with network-licensed software could be a solution. Virtual labs are also important in running complex calculations that require advanced workstations or server farms. As it is unfeasible for users to obtain such hardware resources, providing remote access increases flexibility for personal schedules and allows for uninterrupted work.

TECHNICAL AND INSTRUCTIONAL SUPPORT

Numerous studies in the extant literature suggest that it is harder to change the habits and behaviors of individuals than to change the technological tools (Venkatesh et al., 2014). Technology, in general, is a constantly moving target and the pandemic has increased its momentum especially in distance education and video conferencing areas. Therefore, professional development is not a one-off event. Rather the stakeholders' knowledge and skills should be updated regularly to stay relevant and competitive. In doing so, several facilities should be provided such as technical support, pedagogical (instructional) support, and training events.

Technical support is the very definition of the support that should be provided to the university community. Users ran into various software and hardware problems on a daily basis. Providing timely support is key to user acceptance and successful implementation. Technical support could take many forms from psychical to virtual means. Hardware and connectivity problems are quite common, and technical support personnel should immediately address these issues within the campus. As previously mentioned, establishing a strong server and network architecture may lower the problems, yet many other factors affect the user experience on the client side. Problems may occur just a couple of minutes before a lesson, and consequently cause panic, anxiety, diminishing self-esteem, and a negative instructor image on learners' minds. To solve the problems in a timely manner, a central technical support department such as an office of IT should be formed, which most universities already has. Moreover, depending on the size of the campus community, the IT department may be supported by small branches located on specific locations on campus. The IT department and its branches could also provide online support through remote control applications like TeamViewer to configure software on client computers and solve problems.

In addition to an IT department, it would be a good idea to form a teaching-and-learning-focused department such as a distance education center or educational technology center. These centers are often staffed with personnel from educational technology backgrounds and act at the intersection of technology and instructional activities. Contrary to general belief, these centers are distinct from IT departments because they focus on instructional design and improving learning through technology. In other words, educational technology experts who work in these departments guide instructors in designing meaningful learning experiences. They also host training of trainers events to improve the knowledge and skills of faculty members from various academic departments. Since new technologies are constantly being develop, such professional development events are extremely important for effective digital teaching and learning. It could be said that instructors not only need to learn the technology but also need to have chances to internalize newly acquired knowledge so that they could design meaningful learning environments using the technology. When conducting professional development activities, educational technologists should be considerate about people's schedules and acknowledge their effort (Philipsen et al., 2019). After all, professional development creates an extra workload on top of already overwhelming research and teaching activities, and therefore, it is of importance to keep academics motivated to improve their knowledge and skills.

While live training events are desired in many cases, it is not always feasible to host such an event whenever needed. Schedule conflicts, the immediacy of the need for training, and number of learners could make it impossible to training everybody effectively. Alternatively, up-to-date tutorials and knowledge bulletins are of importance in providing support. Some of the learning materials could be outsourced; nonetheless, the management of the resources and providing timely support require a dedicated educational technology and/or distance education department (Thornton & Koech, 2018). As the content of the materials could be technical, educational, or both, IT and educational technology departments could manage these materials in collaboration.

WHAT TO DO

Considering the complexity of the campus infrastructure systems and the unique formation of each higher education institution, decisions on building, maintaining, and updating an information technology infrastructure are not always straightforward. The challenge is to build a system that works without any significant problem with the minimal use of financial resources. In this context, some general suggestions may help.

First, the decision-makers and IT professionals should study the people of the institution and current trends in IT infrastructure. In doing so, they could pave the way for widespread user adoption and earlier return of investment. Second, the managers should create a model of IT development that includes both administrative and educational uses of technologies. In this step, it makes sense to consider a hybrid architecture where user information systems work on-campus, but LMS and OMT systems work on the cloud. Campus network and remote online services should take a significant portion of the model as they enable users to benefit from IT resources. Third, technical and pedagogical support should be provided to all stakeholders. In the process, dedicated IT and educational technology departments should be established. With the help of these departments, professional development opportunities could be created for students, faculty members, and non-academic personnel.

CONCLUSION

Without a shadow of a doubt, the pandemic has had many undesirable consequences in people's lives. However, on the bright side, it was a wake-up call for many higher education institutions without a decent digital education infrastructure. Establishing an effective and sustainable digital learning infrastructure and maximizing human capital requires a lot of hard work that embodies a thorough analysis of the needs of all parties involved and detailed planning and implementation phases. It is believed that infrastructure investments done with careful consideration and planning will not only help institutions to overcome present and upcoming challenges but also help them achieve a competitive edge in the growing digital learning marketplace.

REFERENCES

Al-Saadoon, G. M. W., & Al Naemi, E. (2015). Virtualization technology and security challenges. In A. H. Al-Hamami & G. M. W. Al-Saadoon (Eds.), *Handbook of Research on Threat Detection and Countermeasures in Network Security* (pp. 254–275). IGI Global. doi:10.4018/978-1-4666-6583-5.ch014

Bailey, D. R., & Lee, A. R. (2020). Learning from experience in the midst of covid-19: Benefits, challenges, and strategies in online teaching. *Computer-Assisted Language Learning Electronic Journal*, *21*(2), 178–198.

Berking, P., & Gallagher, S. (2016). *Choosing a learning management system (LMS)* (8th ed.). Advanced Distributed Learning (ADL) Initiative. https://adlnet.gov/publications/2016/11/Choosing-a-Learning-Management-System-LMS/

Coghlan, S., Miller, T., & Paterson, J. (2020). Good proctor or "Big Brother"? AI Ethics and Online Exam Supervision Technologies. *Ml*, 1–14. https://arxiv.org/abs/2011.07647

Dendir, S., & Maxwell, R. S. (2020). Cheating in online courses: Evidence from online proctoring. *Computers in Human Behavior Reports*, *2*(October), 100033. doi:10.1016/j.chbr.2020.100033

Ergüzen, A., Erdal, E., Ünver, M., & Özcan, A. (2021). Improving technological infrastructure of distance education through trustworthy platform-independent virtual software application pools. *Applied Sciences (Switzerland)*, *11*(3), 1–17. doi:10.3390/app11031214

Hill, G., Mason, J., & Dunn, A. (2021). Contract cheating: An increasing challenge for global academic community arising from COVID-19. *Research and Practice in Technology Enhanced Learning*, *16*(1), 24. doi:10.118641039-021-00166-8 PMID:34345307

Hodges, C., Moore, S., Lockee, B., Trust, T., & Bond, A. (2020). *The difference between emergency remote teaching and online learning*. Educause Review. https://er.educause.edu/articles/2020/3/the-difference-between-emergency-remote-teaching-and-online-learning

Ifenthaler, D., Gibson, D., Prasse, D., Shimada, A., & Yamada, M. (2021). Putting learning back into learning analytics: Actions for policy makers, researchers, and practitioners. *Educational Technology Research and Development*, *69*(4), 2131–2150. doi:10.100711423-020-09909-8

Keough, M. (2018). Experience API. *Training & Development*, *45*(1), 18–19.

Moore, R. L., & Fodrey, B. P. (2018). Distance education and technology infrastructure: Strategies and opportunities. In A. A. Piña, V. L. Lowell, & B. R. Harris (Eds.), *Leading and Managing e-Learning* (pp. 87–100). Springer International Publishing. doi:10.1007/978-3-319-61780-0_7

Nayar, K. B., & Kumar, V. (2018). Cost benefit analysis of cloud computing in education. *International Journal of Business Information Systems*, *27*(2), 205. doi:10.1504/IJBIS.2018.089112

Philipsen, B., Tondeur, J., Pareja Roblin, N., Vanslambrouck, S., & Zhu, C. (2019). Improving teacher professional development for online and blended learning: A systematic meta-aggregative review. *Educational Technology Research and Development*, *67*(5), 1145–1174. doi:10.100711423-019-09645-8

Piña, A. A. (2018). An Educational Leader's View of Learning Management Systems. In A. A. Piña, V. L. Lowell, & B. R. Harris (Eds.), *Leading and Managing e-Learning* (pp. 101–113). Springer International Publishing. doi:10.1007/978-3-319-61780-0_8

Roy, S., & Covelli, B. (2020). COVID-19 induced transition from classroom to online mid semester: Case study on faculty and students' preferences and opinions. *Higher Learning Research Communications*, *2020*(0), 10–32. doi:10.18870/hlrc.v11i0.1197

St-Onge, C., Ouellet, K., Lakhal, S., Dubé, T., & Marceau, M. (2021). COVID-19 as the tipping point for integrating e-assessment in higher education practices. *British Journal of Educational Technology*. Advance online publication. doi:10.1111/bjet.13169 PMID:34898680

Thornton, A., & Koech, J. (2018). Building an e-learning center from the ground up: The challenges and lessons learned. In A. A. Piña, V. L. Lowell, & B. R. Harris (Eds.), *Leading and Managing e-Learning* (pp. 73–85). Springer International Publishing. doi:10.1007/978-3-319-61780-0_6

Venkatesh, V., Morris, M. G., & Davis, F. D. (2014). Individual-level technology adoption research: An assessment of the strengths, weaknesses, threats, and opportunities for further research contributions. In H. Topi & A. Tucker (Eds.), Computing Handbook: Information Systems and Information Technology (3rd ed., pp. 38-1-38–25). CRC Press.

Vivek, K., & Bhattacharjee, P. (2021). *Use of information and communication technologies in education: Effectively integrating technology in under-resourced education systems*. World Bank. doi:10.1596/35423

Wease, G., Boateng, K., Yu, C.-J., Chan, L., & Barham, H. (2018). Technology assessment: Cloud service adoption decision. In T. U. Daim, L. Chan, & J. Estep (Eds.), *Infrastructure and Technology Management: Contributions from the Energy, Healthcare and Transportation Sectors* (pp. 447–471). Springer. doi:10.1007/978-3-319-68987-6_16

ADDITIONAL READING

Al-Saadoon, G. M. W., & Al Naemi, E. (2015). Virtualization technology and security challenges. In A. H. Al-Hamami & G. M. W. Al-Saadoon (Eds.), *Handbook of Research on Threat Detection and Countermeasures in Network Security* (pp. 254–275). IGI Global. doi:10.4018/978-1-4666-6583-5.ch014

Arnò, S., Galassi, A., Tommasi, M., Saggino, A., & Vittorini, P. (2021). State-of-the-art of commercial proctoring systems and their use in academic online exams. *International Journal of Distance Education Technologies, 19*(2), 41–62. doi:10.4018/IJDET.20210401.oa3

Caldwell, D., Sortino, M., Winnington, J., & Cresswell-Yeager, T. J. (2020). Comprehensive faculty development: An innovative approach in online education. In L. Kyei-Blankson, E. Ntuli, & J. Blankson (Eds.), *Handbook of Research on Creating Meaningful Experiences in Online Courses* (pp. 25–36). IGI Global. doi:10.4018/978-1-7998-0115-3.ch003

Coy, K. (2020). Universal design for learning enables significant learning in digital courses. In L. Kyei-Blankson, E. Ntuli, & J. Blankson (Eds.), *Handbook of Research on Creating Meaningful Experiences in Online Courses* (pp. 227–246). IGI Global. doi:10.4018/978-1-7998-0115-3.ch014

Cullinan, J., Flannery, D., Harold, J., Lyons, S., & Palcic, D. (2021). The disconnected: COVID-19 and disparities in access to quality broadband for higher education students. *International Journal of Educational Technology in Higher Education, 18*(1), 26. doi:10.118641239-021-00262-1 PMID:34778524

Drachsler, H., Jansen, J., & Kirschner, P. A. (2021). Adoption of learning technologies in times of pandemic crisis. *Journal of Computer Assisted Learning, 37*(6), 1509–1512. doi:10.1111/jcal.12626

Duncan, A., & Joyner, D. (2022). On the necessity (or lack thereof) of digital proctoring: Drawbacks, perceptions, and alternatives. *Journal of Computer Assisted Learning*, jcal.12700. Advance online publication. doi:10.1111/jcal.12700

Fabian, K., Smith, S., Taylor-Smith, E., & Meharg, D. (2022). Identifying factors influencing study skills engagement and participation for online learners in higher education during COVID-19. *British Journal of Educational Technology*, bjet.13221. Advance online publication. doi:10.1111/bjet.13221 PMID:35601603

Jurva, R., Matinmikko-Blue, M., Niemelä, V., & Nenonen, S. (2020). Architecture and operational model for smart campus digital infrastructure. *Wireless Personal Communications, 113*(3), 1437–1454. doi:10.100711277-020-07221-5

Massner, K. C. (2022). The Use of Videoconferencing in Higher Education. In Communication Management. IntechOpen. doi:10.5772/intechopen.99308

Ladjal, D., Joksimović, S., Rakotoarivelo, T., & Zhan, C. (2022). Technological frameworks on ethical and trustworthy learning analytics. *British Journal of Educational Technology, 53*(4), 733–736. doi:10.1111/bjet.13236

Pierce-Friedman, K., & Wellner, L. (2020). Faculty professionald development in creating significant teaching and learning experiences online. In L. Kyei-Blankson, E. Ntuli, & J. Blankson (Eds.), *Handbook of Research on Creating Meaningful Experiences in Online Courses* (pp. 1–13). IGI Global. doi:10.4018/978-1-7998-0115-3.ch001

Radhamani, R., Kumar, D., Nizar, N., Achuthan, K., Nair, B., & Diwakar, S. (2021). What virtual laboratory usage tells us about laboratory skill education pre- and post-COVID-19: Focus on usage, behavior, intention and adoption. *Education and Information Technologies*, *26*(6), 7477–7495. doi:10.100710639-021-10583-3 PMID:34121909

Sevnarayan, K. (2022). Reimaging eLearning technologies to support students: On reducing transactional distance at an open and distance eLearning institution. *E-Learning and Digital Media*, *19*(4), 421–439. doi:10.1177/20427530221096535

Tlili, A., Zhang, J., Papamitsiou, Z., Manske, S., Huang, R., Kinshuk, & Hoppe, H. U. (2021). Towards utilising emerging technologies to address the challenges of using Open Educational Resources: A vision of the future. *Educational Technology Research and Development*, *69*(2), 515–532. doi:10.100711423-021-09993-4

KEY TERMS AND DEFINITIONS

Client Computer: Client computer is a technical term for any user device that is used to connect various services offered by other systems such as an internet database.

Cloud Computing: Cloud computing refers to distributed online computer systems that are offered as various services (from data storage to web servers) to corporate and individual users.

Experience API (xAPI): An advanced protocol developed to extend Sharable Content Object Reference Model (SCORM). xAPI enables course designers to acquire richer data about students' activities within the digital learning environment.

Learning Analytics: A practical field of study that aims to analyze the increasingly complex data generated by the students' activities within a digital learning environment to offer instant analysis, progress monitoring, and guidance for all stakeholders of learning.

Learning Management System (LMS): A web-based system that allows course designers and instructors to organize instructional materials and provide various forms of interactions between course-takers and instructors. Through an LMS, instructors can make announcements, communicate with students, create discussion boards, share assignment details and collect students' work, and track students' progress throughout the system.

Online Meeting Tool (OMT): A web-based application that allows for live interactions between the participants. In addition to teleconferencing (i.e., two-way video communication), such tools usually offer facilities including live chat, file transfer, survey, and breakout rooms.

Online Proctoring: A system or sub-system that is designed to prevent and identify dishonest behaviors in synchronous online examinations. Such systems often utilize hardware (e.g., webcam) and software components to track the testtakers through the examination session and create a report of suspicious activities to guide the testing authorities.

Plagiarism Detection System: A software that is designed (a) to compare turned-in assignments and various forms of academic works to an extensive database of published works and internet resources, and (b) to create a similarity index. Such software is often web-based and provided through a subscription agreement.

Server Computer: A computer system that is designed to provide various services to client (i.e., user) computers.

Sharable Content Object Reference Model (SCORM): A protocol that enables content creators to organize instructional materials and create re-usable content packages. SCORM also allows for interactions between learning management system (LMS) and the materials such as acquiring course taker's name and returning assessment results to the system.

Virtual Desktop Infrastructure (VDI): A system that allows users to connect computer systems at work/school over the internet and have a desktop environment identical to local computer. This kind of system are often used to access network-licensed software and leverage computing power of institutional systems from a distance.

Virtual Private Networking (VPN): A network protocol that enables a client computer to access network resources through another computer (i.e., proxy). VPN is often used by universities to provide access to digital library subscriptions when students or academics are off campus.

Virtualization: A technology that allows users to create virtual computer instances within a computer system. Virtualization is an important part of any modern computing infrastructure due to its ability to create multiple computer instances within a single physical system and improve effectiveness by allocating just-enough resources to each system.

Chapter 9
Teleworking:
The "New Normal" in Response to a Pandemic

Leigh Nathan Breda

https://orcid.org/0000-0002-9053-7690
University of Cape Town, South Africa

Michael Kyobe
University of Cape Town, South Africa

ABSTRACT

This chapter intends to understand how telework pre-adoption perceptions differ from post-adoption realized benefits during the COVID-19 pandemic, and whether an organization will continue the use of telework once the pandemic subsides. Literature was examined and a hybrid framework incorporating components of the perceived value theory and expectation confirmation model (ECM) was used. The perceived value theory focuses on the perceived business value of Telework pre-adoption and ECM focuses on continued use post-adoption. Resistance by managers to allow employees to telework is evident in surveys conducted as recent as 2019. While surveys conducted initially in 2020 during the pandemic indicated that at least 74% of CFOs intend to implement more telework in their organization and 60% of employees would opt to remain teleworking after the pandemic despite possible health implications, later surveys suggest that after continued use of telework, 59% of the employees now no longer prefer to telework into the future due to constraining factors such as isolation and blurred work lines.

DOI: 10.4018/978-1-7998-9418-6.ch009

INTRODUCTION

Teleworking is not a new concept and has been in the American workspace since the early '70s. Telework has been a world trend that has been widely adopted due to the influence and modernization of information communication technologies systems (ICTS). The concept of Telework did not start as it is known today, it was developed originally in an attempt to lower the consumption rate and dependency on fossil fuels by reducing the need for employees to travel to office spaces (Nilles, 1975). This concept however was not adopted in all organizations as Telework has been met with resistance in its implementation. These factors of resistance have been identified mainly as, management who have been seen as a stumbling block (J Morrison, 2017), as well as some employees who did not find interest in this non-traditional way of work (Offstein, Morwick & Koskinen, 2010).

The International pandemic caused by Covid-19 has influenced organizations to evolve and transform their business models, as well as how people perform daily tasks and interact with their surroundings. A pandemic occurs when a new disease has spread worldwide and infected a large portion of a population, such as the Covid-19 virus [4] (WHO, 2020). This is due to most governments and organization's mandated policy to implement social distancing to flatten the curve and reduce the spread of the Covid-19 virus, as recommended by the World Health Organization (WHO, 2020). Social distancing has compelled organizations and people to leverage ICTs to complete day-to-day work and tasks that would have been previously performed on-premise such as socializing, education, entertainment, and shopping to now be performed remotely as they are unable to leave their homes.

This paper aims to provide an overview of how Telework has been adopted and utilized in response to the Covid-19 pandemic and if it will be continued to be utilized. This will aid in providing a more comprehensive explanation to determining which factors lead to eventual adoption/rejection, and how initial attitudes and satisfaction towards the innovation could change/persist during its continued use. As this adoption occurred during a pandemic, which has forced a mass adoption in a brief period. This bypassed some of the normal pre-adoption stages and overlooked some constraining factors or found them to be acceptable at the time (Naidoo, 2020). This will aid in our understanding of which construct has a higher value to an adopter, usefulness, or satisfaction.

A hybrid conceptual framework that incorporates components of Perceived Value Theory and Expectation Confirmation Model (ECM) were utilized to understand these Telework adoption perceptions. Perceived Value Theory focuses on the perceived business value of Telework pre-adoption and ECM focuses on continued use post-adoption. The subsequent sections provide definitions of Telework and an overview of its core associated themes. The paper is concluded on the potential future of Telework after the pandemic and the organization's view of its continued use.

METHODOLOGY

The Covid-19 pandemic is an ongoing and evolving phenomenon with surprising outcomes. Due to its restrictions, researchers are challenged to participate in communities using some of its traditional research methods. Information regarding the topic is still developing and changing over the pandemic period resulting in continuous insights. Due to the nature of the pandemic, the study period is cross-sectional and takes a snapshot of the current information available (Saunders, Lewis & Thornhill, 2019). A case study method was utilized by the researcher to conduct this research to describe this scarcely studied phenomenon, is in its natural context. This method allows for the categorizing and theming of data (Hancock & Algozzine, 2016). Data was collected from secondary resources, such as web articles, documents and surveys which were aimed specifically to measure the impact of Telework and Covid-19. The leading resource was Forbes and Gartner which monitored and updated on the status of the phenomena as it evolved.

Literature has shown that previous researchers have utilized different frameworks to investigate a phenomenon. The researcher crafted a conceptual framework from these frameworks to have a lens to guide the collection of data as well as the findings in the literature review, which was performance pre-pandemic and pre-adoption perceptions informed by its performance. This data informed the development of the researcher's hypothesis and assumptions which are used to explain the phenomena (Saunders et al., 2019).

PRE VERSUS POST-ADOPTION IN A PANDEMIC

This study aims to investigate and highlight the difference in user perceptions of Pre and Post Telework adoption. The pre-adoption motivation of adopting innovation is based on the adopter's perception whereas post-adoption is based on the outcome of its usage. According to previous studies, the use of innovation may change the attitude, perception, and needs of an adopter. This may result in an alteration of the pre-adoption beliefs which compelled the initial adoption (Karahanna, Straub & Chervany, 1999).

These changes in perception will be examined in the existing literature on Telework in comparison to recent post-adoption reports. This will be used to ascertain differences between pre-adoption perceived value, the actualized value of Telework post-adoption, and attitudes toward continued use. Not many studies examine potential adopters' initial perceptions about innovation and how they alter over time (Melone, 1990).

Widely used theories of adoption such as Perceived Value Theory, Innovation Diffusion Theory (IDT), Norm Theory and Technology Acceptance Model (TAM) emphasize components of human behaviour, however, these do not take into account constraining factors as an additional element to be considered in the pre-adoption stage of innovation. These theories include factors such as behaviour, personal perspective, attitude towards the innovation, perceived usefulness, perceived ease of use, and intentions that contribute towards acceptance for potential adopters. Constraining factors such as the perceived negative attributes of a technology are equally as important as the positive. Both of these attributes should be taken into consideration in the decision-making of adoption and aids in the creation of the notion of perceived value. (Karahanna et al., 1999; Yasmin & Grundmann, 2019).

The Expectation Confirmation Model (ECM) is used to analyse the post-adoption of Telework. This model aids in providing an explanation of the continued use of innovation (Bhattacherjee & Lin, 2015). EMC theorizes that the continued intention to make use of an innovation is determined by the level of satisfaction of the adopter. This level of satisfaction is influenced by the perceived pre-adoption business value comprising of the actualized post-adoption business value (Thong, Hong & Tam, 2006). This experience of how the adopted innovation has performed (as expected/ higher than expected or lower than expected) against preconceived expectations of performance would confirm or reject the continued use of the innovation. This will aid in the understanding of how continued use is influenced by perceived benefits and attitudes in the initial adoption phase. In addition, understanding how users' perceptions change after the use of an innovation (Yasmin & Grundmann, 2019).

A conceptual model that incorporates all these components was proposed based on a model by Yasmin & Grundmann (2019). The model focuses on the perspective of adoption and continued use post-adoption by integrating the Perceived Value Theory and EMC framework to form the bases of the conceptual model as seen in Fig:1.

Figure 1. Conceptional model
Adapted from Yasmin & Grundmann (2019)

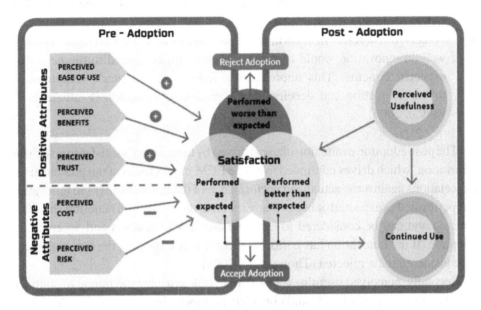

In the Conceptual Model, the pre-adoption evaluation phase is driven by the perceived value of an innovation, as well as its inhibitors. The Perceived Value Theory aids in guiding an adopter's attitude and directly influences the level of satisfaction to either reject or accept adoption.

The constructs of this conceptual model are explained below:

- Perceived ease of use refers to whether an innovation is user-friendly and less complicated to use or learn which makes an innovation more likely to be adopted. This perception has high importance early in the adoption, however, diminishes over time as users become more acquainted with the innovation's operations (Adams, Nelson & Todd, 1992).
- The perceived benefits of Telework are motivating factors for organizations to adopt this method of work. These benefits include cost reduction, higher employee productivity, lower carbon emissions, and a better work-life balance (R. Carr, 2017).
- Perceived trust can be seen as a mental state of positive expectancy. Studies show that user perceptions can be shaped by their environment and others in society, which in turn enforces perceptions when adopting an innovation (Yasmin & Grundmann, 2019).

- Perceived cost refers to the entire capital investment which includes maintenance costs and time over and above the initial investment of adoption (Alam et al., 2014).
- Perceived risk refers to uncertainties that a user may have with regards to how well an innovation would function and perform, compared to the perceived expected benefits. This apprehension reduces an adopter's receptiveness to the innovation and decelerates the process of adoption (Featherman & Pavlou, 2003).

The post-adoption evaluation phase is driven by the adopter's satisfaction with the innovation, which drives continued use. The ECM model looks at the preconceived expectations against the actualized performance of the innovation. If the innovation has performed as expected or better than expected, the innovation benefit is therefore realized and can be considered to have the user's confirmation and accepted for adoption. If the innovation has performed worse than expected, the innovation can be considered to be rejected (Thong et al., 2006).

Secondly, perceived usefulness has a direct link to users who intend to continue use. The more a user expects and considers an innovation to be useful, the higher satisfaction of the adopter and the more likely the innovation will be continued to be used (Yasmin & Grundmann, 2019).

Hypothesis

H1 Pre-adoption perceptions negative attributes are not evaluated correctly by adopters.

H2 Pre-adoption perceptions positive attributes motivate its adoption.

H3 Satisfaction levels contribute to whether or not there is continued use/adoption or rejection.

H4 Perceive usefulness influences satisfaction levels.

TELEWORK LITERATURE REVIEW

The concept of Telework can be defined as the substitution of work that would be traditionally performed at the premises of an employer, to now be performed instead at any convenient location such as the employees' home. This is made possible through the use of computer-based technologies which removes the requirement for employees to perform work-related travel to an employer's premises to complete work tasks. This substitution of the traditional way of work can be done the entire day or a scheduled portion of it (Harker & MacDonnell, 2012).

Telework is dependent on technology as an essential key driver, as its components enable workers to access tools such as teleconferencing, email, unified systems, and software to share information that facilitates remote communication and collaboration (R. Carr, 2017). Developments in ICT have increased workers' mobility and flexibility with innovations such as high-speed internet and mobile smartphones (J Morrison, 2017).

Telework is often referred to as telecommuting virtual workplaces, hoteling, flexi or remote working as there is no globally recognized definition (Kowalski & Swanson, 2005). Traditionally, the use of Telework has been largely implemented in industries such as IT and Communications. Teleworks is however not solely dependent on ICTS, and are not defined by its utilization as even paperwork that is completed at home can be seen as Telework (Novotny, 2004). There are 4 aspects of consideration when adopting Telework, these are namely Technological, Employee, Employer, and Environmental (R. S. Carr, 2017; Langa & Conradie, 2003). The conceptual framework perspective has been adopted to guide the review of the 4 aspects and the pre and post-adoption literature.

Perceived Usefulness and Trust of Technology

During the pandemic, as seen in Fig:2 the utilization of many collaboration tools increased significantly. Cisco WebEx indicated that their adoption increased by 700% (Data, 2020), Zoom subscriber base increased by 350% (Marks, 2020)

Figure 2. Collaboration tool utilization

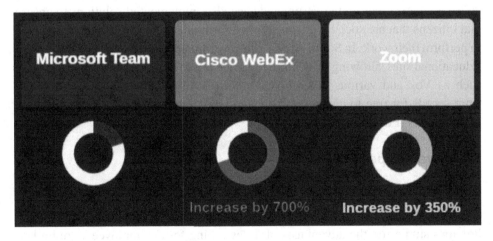

According to Statista as seen in Fig:3, the Microsoft Teams platform reported that its subscriber base had spiked by over 50%, from 32 million users on March 1, 2020, to 75 million as of April 30, 2020 (Liu, 2020). On March 16, 2020, Teams subscriber daily utilization increased by 200% and hit a new record of 2.7 billion meeting minutes (Microsoft, 2020)

Figure 3. Increased teams utilization

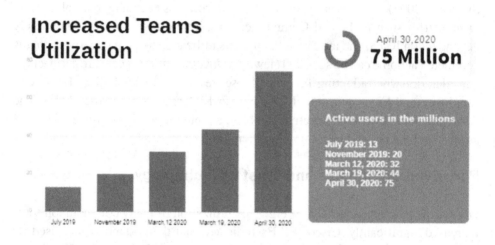

Internet usage has also increased between 50% to 75% due to the increased usage of online collaborative tools and online entertainment applications (Beech, 2020). Organizations and governments have also implemented solutions to ensure that citizens that are socially distancing in their homes remain connected and able to perform their work. In South Africa, the government has zero-rated many Higher Educational sites, allowing students to remotely learn (DHET, 2020). Organizations such as Vox and various other FNOs automatically upgraded their customer's fibre speeds for free to ensure workers can meet the additional work from home requirements (Edwardes, 2020).

Employee Aspect

Pre-Adoption Employee Perceived Positive Attributes

Previous studies on the advantages of Teleworking for an employee were broken down into three main aspects, namely possible stress reduction, financial savings, and time-saving (Baard & Thomas, 2010). Underlying stress from high levels of traffic, possibilities of arriving late, work-life conflict, and burnout are all reduced as commuting to work is no longer required (Van der Merwe, 2012).

Teleworking reduces costs as the employee no longer is required to travel to and from work as well as pay fees associated with travel like parking and petrol (Van der Merwe, 2012). Employees living costs can be lowered as the Teleworker is no longer required to reside in an area close to the employer's premises and can, therefore, purchase or live in a home that is more affordable outside of major cities (Nilles, 1991). Working at home can also provide Teleworking employees with a better work-life balance as they would have more family time due to them being able to work at their own pace on the condition that they complete tasks and meet deadlines (Baard & Thomas, 2010).

Post-Adoption Employee Actualized Positive Attributes

A Hanley Wood flash survey taken during the pandemic indicated that 60% of respondents would opt to remain working from home should they have the option to after the pandemic (Castenson, 2020). A recent poll by Fluent on remote working across age groups has shown that these advantages have not changed much. The primary advantage, as seen in Fig:4, indicated across these groups was spending time with family (34%), thereafter, reduced long commutes (29%), flexible schedules (17%), cost-saving (11%), increase productivity (5%) and fewer office politics (4%) following. The study also shows that Gen X and baby boomers generations would prefer to continue to Telework (Koetsier, 2020).

Figure 4. Employee advantages

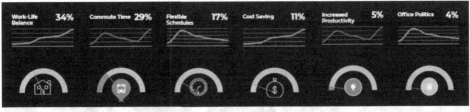

Employee Satisfaction Level of Adoption

A Hanley Wood flash survey taken during the pandemic indicated that 60% of respondents would opt to remain working from home and continue to Telework, should they have the option to after the pandemic (Castenson, 2020).

Pre-Adoption Employee Perceived Negative Attributes

In previous studies, many potential disadvantages of a Teleworker employee have been highlighted. Clear boundaries are required to be put in place to ensure the employee's work and home life do not conflict (Baard & Thomas, 2010). Employees' work output can be reduced due to distractions such as children being at home and also in the same space. Working from home reduces possibilities for collaboration on projects as well as opportunities for teamwork (Joseph Morrison, 2017).

A reduction in socializing with colleagues can cause and develop a feeling of isolation which can in turn cause stress. Fear and anxiety about an employee's lack of career growth can be developed as the opportunity for performance assessments are less (Pyöriä, 2011). Teleworkers are hindered in their ability to create relationships and develop trust within the organization and its management (Joseph Morrison, 2017). In addition to this, Teleworkers would not have technical support to assist them in their troubleshooting readily available, as they would have to support themselves with most issues that arise (Tartaro, 2003).

Post-Adoption Employee Actualized Negative Attributes

During the pandemic, a Fluent poll as seen in Fig:5 showed that the workers felt that while Teleworking during the pandemic, the primary disadvantage while working from home is distractions (29%), thereafter, reduced social interaction (25%), improper work/life balance (18%), unequipped home office (10%), lower productivity (10%) and lastly communication barriers (8%) (Koetsier, 2020).

Figure 5. Employee teleworking disadvantages

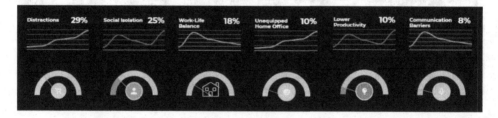

A study by the Society for Human Resource Management (SHRM) showed that 71% of responders indicated that they are struggling to adjust to a new way of working and in some are starting to experience some mental challenges from lack of social contact. Another issue is that there is a blur between home and work life. Healthy boundaries traditionally are instilled as there would be a separation of home and work life. Work would be left at work and would not interfere with the personal, however during the pandemic some have struggled to isolate the two from distracting from each other (Brower, 2020). Added to this mental health issue is that the boundaries of employees' work and personal time are being crossed by employers. Employees have started to realize that Telework has opened the door for them to always be available for the employer, as they are isolated and in lockdown (Dash, 2020).

Some organizations, such as Google have considered these disadvantages and have provided their employees with 1000 dollar allowances to cover equipment costs and given them company holidays (Beasley, 2020; Dash, 2020). Other companies on the other hand such as Facebook are considering a pay reduction for employees who wish to continue Teleworking past the pandemic, which will be based on the location from which the employee chose to work (Murphy, 2020).

Employee Satisfaction Level of Adoption

After continued use of Telework, employees' attitudes had started to shift and the number of users that would want to continue with Telework has dropped. A survey by the Martec Group which surveyed 1,214 respondents indicated that 59% of employees no longer prefer working from home (Benjamin, 2020).

Employer Aspect

Pre-Adoption Employer Perceived Positive Attributes

Previous research shows that there are many potential advantages to employers by allowing their employees to Telework. Allowing flexible working times for employees to be able to attend to their personal matters would encourage them to increase their productivity (Lautsch & Kossek, 2011).

Additional time can be spent by employees to improve their tasks as they no longer need to commute to work. This will indirectly make employees more independent as well as self-directed (Joseph Morrison, 2017). Office rentals and associated costs could be reduced, as the requirement to house multiple staff in a single location would be reduced (Neirotti, Paolucci & Raguseo, 2011).

Post-Adoption Employer Actualized Positive Attributes

A Gartner survey showed that 20% of CFO respondents have reallocated the on-premise technology budget, with an additional 12% of respondents following suit due to employees no longer needing to occupy the workspace. Further to this, 13%

of respondents indicated that they have made cost reductions in real estate expenses in conjunction with other cost-cutting measures that have already been put in place. As seen in Fig:6, only 26% of respondents will not move some of their on-site employees to remain Teleworking (Lavelle, 2020).

Figure 6. CFO teleworking shift
(Lavelle, 2020).

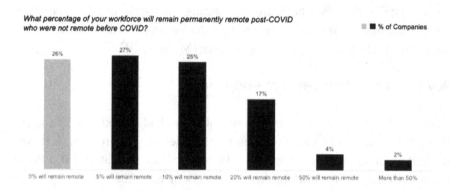

Figure 1: 74% of Companies Plan to Permanently Shift to More Remote Work Post COVID-19

Some industries have decided that many employees will continue to Telework, not as a cost reduction but because they have demonstrated increased productivity (Data, 2020). These Teleworkers could possibly perform even better once the pandemic has subsided, the children that they currently assisting would have returned to school, and life in general has returned to normality (Brower, 2020). Larger companies, such as Twitter have even gone further by allowing all their employees the option to "permanently" Telework (Marks, 2020). Telework has opened the talent pool to organizations. Companies are now able to hire employees that did not or could not relocate to the company's location (Thompson, 2020). The pandemic has added to this strategy of CFOs, which now includes hiring coveted employees that would have not had previously been in the market, however, due to Covid-19 are now looking for new employment (Boulton, 2020).

Figure 7. Employer advantage summary

Employer Satisfaction Level of Adoption

A Gartner surveyed 317 CFOs, it found that 74% of them intend to shift some employees to permanent Telework due to its benefits (Lavelle, 2020). A survey conducted between June and July 2020 of 6,000 Australian public servants, which included responses from 1,400 managers indicated a change of perception. 34.6% of managers indicated that their employees were more productive Teleworking, 57% indicated their productivity was the same. The survey also asked if there will be continued support of managers to allow their employees to Teleworking, this was broken down by gender, with 68% of males indicating increased support and followed by 63.6% of female managers increasing support (Colley & Williamson, 2020).

Pre-Adoption Employer Perceived Negative Attributes

Some potential disadvantages to employers of Teleworkers identified in previous studies are that employers are required to deploy virtual environments, collaborative tools, as well as ensure technical support is available to Teleworkers and applications which can be a big financial investment (Baard & Thomas, 2010). Devices located off-premises requires additional security measures to protect organizational data, as well as the additional insurance needed for the devices themselves as these devices would not be as protected as in the organization. Further to this these devices can be miss used and potentially abused for personal reasons by the Teleworker (Joseph Morrison, 2017).

Spiceworks performed a survey, as seen in Fig:8, indicating that 61% of Teleworking employees connect to public Wi-Fi networks such as coffee shops with company devices (Feather, 2019). This risky behaviour is further elaborated on in a whitepaper by Cisco. It indicated that 29% of employees utilise insecure devices to perform work; 46% of employees store personal files on work devices and; 21% of employees allow unauthorized people to access their work devices (IDI, 2020; iPass, 2017).

Figure 8. Security challenges summary

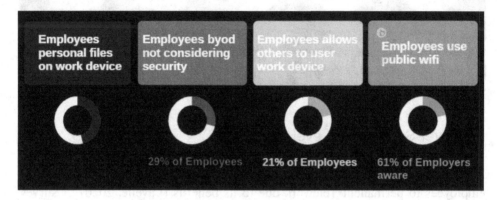

Employers would possibly have to incentivize Teleworkers to encourage them to complete tasks, to prevent a possible reduction in performance (Baard & Thomas, 2010). Management resistance to telework as well as individual workers whose preference is to remain on-premises has been identified frequently as a stumbling block (J Morrison, 2017; Offstein et al., 2010). This resistance has been the case since 1974 when the first study was carried out until recent studies in 2019. A focus group in 2018 of approximately 300 managers in the Australian public services sector indicated that there is still extensive managerial resistance to allow employees to work from home, despite supporting policies to allow Telework (Colley & Williamson, 2020).

Post-Adoption Employer Actualized Negative Attributes

During the pandemic, some of the disadvantages and challenges could not be taken into account as organizations have had to adopt Telework software and its frameworks quickly to enable their employees to work remotely from home, to ensure continuity of their business, and so that they can still provide services to their clients while still abiding by the guidelines set out by the WHO. This removed the option of preference of managers and individuals who previously wished not to Telework and overcome a long-standing barrier to its implementation (Brower, 2020; Gartner, 2020).

Security remains of great concern to organizations as Teleworkers are no longer in the safeguards of their organizations. The sudden onset of the pandemic forced organizations to adopt Teleworking without putting in proper measurements resulting in improper policies and inadequate Teleworking security architecture. This lack of safeguards was exploited by scammers and malware purveyors as around 25% of organisations have not applied critical patches. The Internet Crime Complaint Center which is run by the FBI reported a spike in complaints from its typical intake of 1000 a day, prior to Covid-19, to 3000 - 4000 complaints (Cimpanu, 2020).

Perimeter 81 released a statement highlighting three main concerns of Telework during the pandemic namely; unsecure home Wi-Fi networks with improper weak protocols, phishing scams and fraudulent emails distributed to employees and; insecure and easily hackable passwords utilised across platforms (Rubinstein, 2020).

Figure 9. Employer disadvantage summary

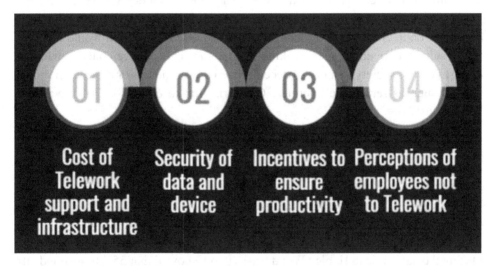

A survey conducted in Switzerland in April 2020 of 1,500 residents highlighted an additional issue. The report indicated that 26% of respondents if faced with losing their jobs would withhold vital company information. This issue emphasizes the need for a company to implement measures to secure organisational data and intellectual property (Deloitte, 2020).

Employer Satisfaction Level of Adoption

A survey conducted between June and July 2020 of 6,000 Australian public servants, which included responses from 1,400 managers indicated that only 8% suggested that Telework has reduced employee productivity (Colley & Williamson, 2020)

Environmental/ Societal Aspect

Pre-Adoption Environmental/ Societal Perceived Attributes

Previous studies have shown that Teleworking can benefit the environment and society by reducing the need for people to commute. Telework reduces the carbon footprint in major cities and subsequent to this, other benefits of Telework are a saving of energy and a reduction in office space (Van der Merwe, 2012). The original purpose of Telework was to decrease the potential negative effects on city transport and pollution in the '70s. The reduction of workers having to commute to work will affect travel patterns. This means that workers would not have to buy property close to the workplace, the design of the workplace would change and it will affect environmental policies (Helminen & Ristimäki, 2007; Van der Merwe, 2012).

As an office would no longer be required, commercial buildings' power consumption in cities would reduce and home power consumption would increase as a result of more employees working from home. This change could provide an opportunity for society to move to decentralized power models or more economical models such as renewable energies. (Mattern, Staake & Weiss, 2010; Van der Merwe, 2012)

Telework can be used in crisis management as a strategy when events such as terrorist attacks or severe weather conditions occur so that there are continued operations and failovers. (Hoang, Nickerson, Beckman & Eng, 2008; Van der Merwe, 2012)

Post-Adoption Environmental/ Society Actualized Attributes

During the pandemic, a Hanley Wood flash survey showed that 55% of respondents would move from their current expensive city's housing markets if they could Telework permanently (Castenson, 2020). This would change the future residential buildings market and could make having a work-from-home space a prerequisite (Leprince-Ringuet, 2020).

Commercial and office multi-year lease agreements are changing also. Companies are looking towards flexi and shared office solutions as the need for office space reduces. These also will need to be attractive to potential tenants as they look for added-value offerings such as boardroom access, free coffee, and shared telephone answering to aid the needs of their team. Companies would be looking to move to a Workplace as a service type of model so that they pay for what they require (Robinson, 2020). This reduction and workplace as a service model would aid companies, according to Margins article report, 40% of venture capital funding in Silicon Valley is currently used to pay rent, instead of other company interests. (Castenson, 2020)

The restriction on travel around the world as a result of the pandemic has also decreased the global NO2 concentrations. Some economic activities were also impacted due to the strict social distancing policies put into place. In China, it reduced power plant production, halted manufacturing processes, and decrease the use of a personal vehicle for travel. As seen in Fig:10, NO2 dropped by 22.8µg/m3 in Wuhan and dropped by 12.9µg/m3 in the whole of China (Zambrano-Monserrate, Ruano & Sanchez-Alcalde, 2020).

Figure 10. NO2 reduction
(Zambrano-Monserrate et al., 2020).

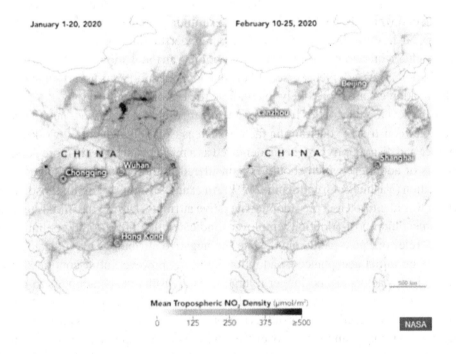

TELEWORK IN A PANDEMIC

Telework in a pandemic has four factors that Teleworkers would not necessarily be faced with, namely children, space, privacy, and choice. Due to distance learning for scholars, parents have the additional stress of being a teacher, without the option of day-care. Trying to work from home with children can become a productivity disaster. Teleworkers also required a home office as a prerequisite, as this space gave them the privacy required to work optimally. The final contributing factor is that those that wished to Telework had the choice to do so (Gorlick, 2020).

The current increase in productivity by Teleworkers can also be attributed to the fact that they are unable to perform their previous daily activities as they are socially distancing during the lockdown and are unable to leave their home. Since they are unable to do anything else, some have used work as a distraction and to ensure that they remain employed during a high retrenchment period (Brynjolfsson et al., 2020).

CONCLUSIONS

This study provides an important contribution toward advancing the research of Telework adoption and the understanding of pre and post-adoption attitudes of satisfaction which drives continued use by examining the phenomena with a hybrid theoretical framework. This will aid in our understanding of how pre-adoption beliefs alter which compelled the initial adoption in an innovation's continued use. If satisfaction is low, adopters are less likely to adopt or continue its use. If satisfaction is high, adopters are more likely to continue the use of the innovation.

In the development of this framework, while merging the Perceived Value Theory and ECM constructs, constraining factors such as isolation, a distorted worked life balance and distractions have been identified as a missing construct in more popular models of adoption, which should be considered in the pre-adoption stage of an innovation (Yasmin & Grundmann, 2019). An example of this is employee isolation which was identified as a pre-adoption negative attribute. During the initial stage of implementation post-adoption, employees indicated that 60% would continue the use of Telework post-pandemic despite the negative attribute. This indicates that there is an initial acceptance of adoption by users, however, after continued use, constraining factors are no longer tolerable. This results in the adopters to reject the innovation and the end of continued use. As Telework continued to be utilized, attitudes and satisfaction levels of this attribute shifted, and what was an acceptable negative attribute compounded over time with 71% of responders indicating that they are struggling now with isolation. This resulted in a survey taken after a period of continued use, which indicated 59% of employees no longer prefer Telework (Benjamin, 2020; Brower, 2020). Negative attributes should, therefore, be considered in adoption models, as the pre-adoption satisfaction level of this overtime may alter and influence the continued use of an innovation. In a pandemic, the pre-adoption sequence can occur out of the norm as immediate utilization of a benefit is required. The evaluation of constraining factors is overlooked or considered to be acceptable at the time, however over time these constraining factors are no longer in a level of tolerance. This comparison of pre-adoption and post-adoption consideration of acceptable tolerance should be further explored.

Telework in most organizations will continue and be sustained in some way. 74% of CFO intend to shift some employees to permanently Telework due to over 50% of managers reporting higher productivity. In addition, given that organizations have already put in place the resources for their employees to Telework as well as employees have equipped themselves at home to be able to continue to work, organizations would not easily go back to business as usual. This continued use by organizations of Telework would directly impact the post-adoption actualized attributes of the environmental/ society context such as the reduction of carbon emissions and the reshaping of how we see organizational real estate (Alrawi, 2020).

This study has some limitations that must be taken into consideration. Adoption in a pandemic possesses other concessions, although the current reported results of Telework are positive, its application and results are in a context outside of the norm of adoption. A contributing factor to the current post-adoption continued use and results could be related to the removal of choice, with employees and employers forced to Telework (Gorlick, 2020). Organisations have seen a substantial increase in productivity which has been attributed to Telework, however this could be a possible result of employees' inability to leave their homes due to restrictions of movement, and employees occupying their time with work (Brynjolfsson et al., 2020). Further research is required, post-pandemic to measure its continued business value and usefulness once companies and employees have a choice in whether or not, they wish to continue Teleworking.

REFERENCES

Adams, D., Nelson, R., & Todd, P. (1992). Perceived usefulness, ease of use, and usage of information technology: A replication. *Management Information Systems Quarterly, 16*(2), 227–247. doi:10.2307/249577

Alam, S. S., Hashim, N. H. N., Rashid, M., Omar, N. A., Ahsan, N., & Ismail, M. D. (2014). Small-scale households renewable energy usage intention: Theoretical development and empirical settings. *Renewable Energy, 68*, 255–263. doi:10.1016/j. renene.2014.02.010

Alrawi, M. (2020). *As you work from home, spare a thought for the shop in your office building.* Retrieved on 27 August 2020 from https://www.thenational.ae/ opinion/comment/as-you-work-from-home-spare-a-thought-for-the-shop-in-your-office-building-1.1068742

Baard, N., & Thomas, A. (2010). Teleworking in South Africa: Employee benefits and challenges. *SA Journal of Human Resource Management, 8*(1), 1–10. doi:10.4102ajhrm.v8i1.298

Beasley, D. (2020). *Google Gives Employees $1,000 Work-From-Home Allowance.* Retrieved on 10 August 2020 from https://www.forbes.com/sites/beasleydavid/2020/05/27/google-gives-employees-1000-work-from-home-allowance/#65a328c84c04

Beech, M. (2020). *COVID-19 Pushes Up Internet Use 70% And Streaming More Than 12%, First Figures Reveal.* Retrieved on 09 August 2020 from https://www.forbes.com/sites/markbeech/2020/03/25/covid-19-pushes-up-internet-use-70-streaming-more-than-12-first-figures-reveal/#39c98df43104

Benjamin, L. (2020). *Working From Home Is Disliked By And Bad For Most Employees, Say Researchers.* Retrieved on 26 August 2020 from https://www.forbes.com/sites/benjaminlaker/2020/08/24/working-from-home-is-disliked-by-and-bad-for-most-employees/#1a36667c6734

Bhattacherjee, A., & Lin, C.-P. (2015). A unified model of IT continuance: Three complementary perspectives and crossover effects. *European Journal of Information Systems, 24*(4), 364–373. doi:10.1057/ejis.2013.36

Boulton, C. (2020). *Remote hiring wins have CIOs rethinking recruitment, post-pandemic.* Retrieved on 06 August 2020 from https://www.cio.com/article/3563012/remote-hiring-wins-have-cios-rethinking-recruitment-post-pandemic.html

Brower, T. (2020). *Why The Office Simply Cannot Go Away: The Compelling Case For The Workplace.* Retrieved on 27 July 2020 from https://www.forbes.com/sites/tracybrower/2020/06/07/why-the-office-simply-cannot-go-away-the-compelling-case-for-the-workplace/#70213d385baf

Brynjolfsson, E., Horton, J., Ozimek, A., Rock, D., Sharma, G. & TuYe, H. (2020). *COVID-19 and Remote Work: An Early Look at US Data.* NBER Working Paper (No. 27344).

Carr, R. (2017). *Teleworking in corporate information technology departments* (Honours Empirical Report). University of Cape Town.

Castenson, J. (2020). *How Working From Home Is Changing The Way We Think About Where We Live.* Retrieved on 17 June 2020 from https://www.forbes.com/sites/jennifercastenson/2020/06/08/value-of-home-life-is-back-and-has-land-buyers-moving-way-out/#3014ae71f1aa

Cimpanu, C. (2020). *FBI says cybercrime reports quadrupled during COVID-19 pandemic*. Retrieved on 23 July 2020 from https://www.zdnet.com/article/fbi-says-cybercrime-reports-quadrupled-during-covid-19-pandemic/

Colley, L., & Williamson, S. (2020). *With management resistance overcome, working from home may be here to stay*. Retrieved on 24 August 2020 from https://theconversation.com/with-management-resistance-overcome-working-from-home-may-be-here-to-stay-144850

Dash, S. (2020). *Work from home fun is over – now there are endless work hours, midnight calls from bosses and employees are not happy*. Retrieved on 27 July 2020 from https://www.businessinsider.in/careers/news/work-from-home-has-brought-with-it-a-new-set-of-problems-with-endless-calls-and-works-hours/articleshow/76637605.cms

Data, D. (2020). *Your employees are working from home. Can you manage their expenses?* Retrieved on 16 June 2020 from https://techcentral.co.za/your-employees-are-working-from-home-can-you-manage-their-expenses/98647/

Deloitte. (2020). *Cyber crime – The risks of working from home*. Retrieved on 24 August 2020 from https://www2.deloitte.com/ch/en/pages/risk/articles/covid-19-cyber-crime-working-from-home.html

DHET. (2020). *Zero-rated websites*. DHET Retrieved from https://www.dhet.gov.za/SiteAssets/05%20June%202020%20zero-rate%20publication.pdf

Edwardes, H. (2020). *How we at Vox are helping our customers*. Retrieved on 10 July 2020 from https://www.vox.co.za/content-hub/category/vox-4-thought/how-we-at-vox-are-helping-our-customers?page=34710

Feather, N. (2019). *How to Protect Your Remote Employees from Cyber Threats*. Retrieved on 24 August 2020 from https://www.inc.com/neill-feather/how-to-protect-your-remote-employees-from-cyber-threats.html

Featherman, M. S., & Pavlou, P. A. (2003). Predicting e-services adoption: A perceived risk facets perspective. *International Journal of Human-Computer Studies*, 59(4), 451–474. doi:10.1016/S1071-5819(03)00111-3

Gartner. (2020). *9 Predictions for the Post-COVID Future of Work*. Retrieved on 28 June 2020 from https://www.gartner.com/document/3985163?ref=solrAll&refval=259205666

Gorlick, A. (2020). *The productivity pitfalls of working from home in the age of COVID-19*. Retrieved on 08 August 2020 from https://news.stanford.edu/2020/03/30/productivity-pitfalls-working-home-age-covid-19/

Hancock, D., & Algozzine, B. (2016). *Doing case study research: A practical guide for beginning researchers*. Teachers Collee Press.

Harker, B., & MacDonnell, R. (2012). Is telework effective for organizations? A meta-analysis of empirical research on perceptions of telework and organizational outcomes. *Management Research Review*, *35*(7), 602–616. doi:10.1108/01409171211238820

Helminen, V., & Ristimäki, M. (2007). Relationships between commuting distance, frequency and telework in Finland. *Journal of Transport Geography*, *15*(5), 331–342. doi:10.1016/j.jtrangeo.2006.12.004

Hoang, A. T., Nickerson, R. C., Beckman, P., & Eng, J. (2008). Telecommuting and corporate culture: Implications for the mobile enterprise. *Information Knowledge Systems Management, 7*(1-2), 77-97.

IDI. (2020). *Security Challenges of Remote Workforce*. Retrieved on 24 August 2020 from https://www.identitymanagementinstitute.org/security-challenges-of-remote-workforce/

iPass. (2017). *2017 Mobile Security Report*. iPass.

Karahanna, E., Straub, D., & Chervany, N. (1999). Information Technology Adoption Across Time: A Cross-Sectional Comparison of Pre-Adoption and Post-Adoption Beliefs. *Management Information Systems Quarterly*, *23*(2). Advance online publication. doi:10.2307/249751

Koetsier, J. (2020). *6 Reasons Most Want To Work From Home Even After Coronavirus*. Retrieved on 27 June 2020 from https://www.forbes.com/sites/johnkoetsier/2020/06/13/6-reasons-most-want-to-work-from-home-even-after-coronavirus/#4900e2ad38fa

Kowalski, K. B., & Swanson, J. A. (2005). Critical success factors in developing teleworking programs. *Benchmarking*, *12*(3), 236–249.

Langa, G., & Conradie, D. (2003). Perceptions and attitudes with regard to teleworking among public sector officials in Pretoria: Applying the Technology Acceptance Model (TAM): Research case studies. *Communicatio: South African Journal of Communication Theory and Research, 29*(1-2), 280-296.

Lautsch, B. A., & Kossek, E. E. (2011). Managing a blended workforce: Telecommuters and non-telecommuters. *Organizational Dynamics*, *40*(1), 10–17.

Lavelle, J. (2020). *Gartner CFO Survey Reveals 74% Intend to Shift Some Employees to Remote Work Permanently*. Retrieved on 13 August 2020 from https://www.gartner.com/en/newsroom/press-releases/2020-04-03-gartner-cfo-surey-reveals-74-percent-of-organizations-to-shift-some-employees-to-remote-work-permanently2

Leprince-Ringuet, D. (2020). *Remote working: How the biggest change to office life will happen in our homes*. Retrieved on 02 August 2020 from https://www.zdnet.com/article/remote-working-how-the-biggest-change-to-office-life-will-happen-in-our-homes/

Liu, S. (2020). *Number of daily active users (DAU) of Microsoft Teams worldwide as of April 30*. Retrieved on 15 June 2020 from https://www.statista.com/statistics/1033742/worldwide-microsoft-teams-daily-and-monthly-users/

Marks, G. (2020). *We're not all going to be working from home, nor should we. Here's why*. Retrieved on 18 June 2020 from https://www.theguardian.com/business/2020/jun/11/were-not-all-going-to-be-working-from-home-nor-should-we-heres-why

Mattern, F., Staake, T., & Weiss, M. (2010). ICT for green: How computers can help us to conserve energy. *Proceedings of the 1st international conference on energy-efficient computing and networking.*

Melone, N. P. (1990). A Theoretical Assessmenot f the User-Satisfaction Construct in Information Systems Research. *Management Science, 36*(1), 76–91.

Microsoft. (2020). *Remote work trend report: Meetings*. Retrieved on 13 May 2020 from https://www.microsoft.com/en-us/microsoft-365/blog/2020/04/09/remote-work-trend-report-meetings/?wt.mc_id=AID2409697_QSG_SCL_424041&ocid=AID2409697_QSG_SCL_424041

Morrison, J. (2017). *Explaining the Intention of IT Workers to Telework: A South African Perspective* (Masters Dissertation). University of Cape Town.

Morrison, J. (2017). *Explaining the intention of IT workers to telework: A South African perspective*. University of Cape Town.

Murphy, C. (2020). *Facebook employees could receive pay cuts as they continue to work from home*. Retrieved on 10 June 2020 from https://www.usatoday.com/story/tech/2020/05/21/facebook-pay-cuts-employees-could-have-reduced-salaries-if-they-move/5239532002/

Naidoo, R. (2020). A multi-level influence model of COVID-19 themed cybercrime. *European Journal of Information Systems, 29*(3), 1–17. doi:10.1080/096008 5X.2020.1771222

Neirotti, P., Paolucci, E., & Raguseo, E. (2011). *Diffusion of telework: Myth or reality? Some stylized facts on telework diffusion in Italian firms*. Paper presented at the Mobile Business.

Nilles, J. M. (1975). Telecommunications and organizational decentralization. *IEEE Transactions on Communications, 23*(10), 1142–1147.

Nilles, J. M. (1991). Telecommuting and urban sprawl: Mitigator or inciter? *Transportation, 18*(4), 411–432.

Novotny, A. (2004). The Present and Future of Teleworking. *6th International Conference on Applied Informatics*.

Offstein, E. H., Morwick, J. M., & Koskinen, L. (2010). Making telework work: Leading people and leveraging technology for competitive advantage. *Strategic HR Review*, (9), 32–37.

Pyöriä, P. (2011). Managing telework: Risks, fears and rules. *Management Research Review, 34*(4), 386–399.

Robinson, A. (2020). *Working from home: hello space as a service*. Retrieved on 01 August 2020 from https://www.iol.co.za/business-report/economy/working-from-home-hello-space-as-a-service-50294773

Rubinstein, C. (2020). *Beware: Remote Work Involves These 3 Cyber Security Risks*. Retrieved on 24 August 2020 from https://www.forbes.com/sites/carrierubinstein/2020/04/10/beware-remote-work-involves-these-3-cyber-security-risks/#2df630c661c4

Saunders, M., Lewis, P., & Thornhill, A. (2019). *Research methods for business students*. Pearson Education.

Tartaro, M. (2003). Best practices for supporting home users. *Network Computing, 14*(11), 73–76.

Thompson, C. (2020). *What If Working From Home Goes on … Forever?* Retrieved on 20 June 2020 from https://www.nytimes.com/interactive/2020/06/09/magazine/remote-work-covid.html

Thong, J. Y. L., Hong, S.-J., & Tam, K. Y. (2006). The effects of post-adoption beliefs on the expectation-confirmation model for information technology continuance. *International Journal of Human-Computer Studies, 64*(9), 799–810.

Van der Merwe, F. (2012). Enablers and moderators of telework: assessing the maturity of telework practices in organisations (Honour). University of Cape Town.

WHO. (2020). *Protect yourself and others from the spread COVID-19*. Retrieved on 27 July 2020 from https://www.who.int/emergencies/diseases/novel-coronavirus-2019/advice-for-public

Yasmin, N., & Grundmann, P. (2019). Pre- and Post-Adoption Beliefs about the Diffusion and Continuation of Biogas-Based Cooking Fuel Technology in Pakistan. *MDPI*, 16.

Zambrano-Monserrate, M. A., Ruano, M. A., & Sanchez-Alcalde, L. (2020). Indirect effects of COVID-19 on the environment. *The Science of the Total Environment*.

ADDITIONAL READING

Adams, D. A., Nelson, R. R., & Todd, P. A. (1992). Perceived usefulness, ease of use, and usage of information technology: A replication. *Management Information Systems Quarterly*, 227–247.

Belzunegui-Eraso, A., & Erro-Garcés, A. (2020). Teleworking in the Context of the Covid-19 Crisis. *Sustainability*, *12*(9), 3662.

Buomprisco, G., Ricci, S., Perri, R., & De Sio, S. (2021). Health and telework: New challenges after COVID-19 pandemic. *European Journal of Environment and Public Health*, *5*(2), em0073.

Campo, A. M. D. V., Avolio, B., & Carlier, S. I. (2021). The Relationship Between Telework, Job Performance, Work–Life Balance and Family Supportive Supervisor Behaviours in the Context of COVID-19. *Global Business Review*.

Davis, F. D. (1989). Perceived usefulness, perceived ease of use, and user acceptance of information technology. *Management Information Systems Quarterly*, 319–340.

Liao, C., Chen, J. L., & Yen, D. C. (2007). Theory of planning behavior (TPB) and customer satisfaction in the continued use of e-service: An integrated model. *Computers in Human Behavior*, *23*(6), 2804–2822.

Marazziti, D., Cianconi, P., Mucci, F., Foresi, L., Chiarantini, I., & Della Vecchia, A. (2021). Climate change, environment pollution, COVID-19 pandemic and mental health. *The Science of the Total Environment*, *773*, 145182.

Nagata, T., Nagata, M., Ikegami, K., Hino, A., Tateishi, S., Tsuji, M., Matsuda, S., Fujino, Y., & Mori, K. (2021). Intensity of home-based telework and work engagement during the COVID-19 pandemic. *Journal of Occupational and Environmental Medicine*, *63*(11), 907.

Qian, M., & Jiang, J. (2020). COVID-19 and social distancing. *Journal of Public Health*, 1–3. PMID:32837835

Shi, Y., Wang, G., Cai, X. P., Deng, J. W., Zheng, L., Zhu, H. H., Zheng, M., Yang, B., & Chen, Z. (2020). An overview of COVID-19. *Journal of Zhejiang University. Science. B.*, *21*(5), 343–360. doi:10.1631/jzus.B2000083 PMID:32425000

KEY TERMS AND DEFINITIONS

Adoption: Adoption is the practise of choosing to follow, take up or use something.

Collaboration Tools: Collaboration tools are different software's and online services which enable individuals to work on projects together regardless of location.

Continued Use: A positive attitude towards performance and usefulness which encourages ongoing use of an innovation (Yasmin & Grundmann, 2019).

COVID-19: COVID-19 is an infectious disease, formally known as Coronavirus, which is caused by the SARS-CoV-2 virus.

Ease of Use: Whether an innovation is user-friendly and less complicated to use or learn (Adams, Nelson & Todd, 1992).

Innovation: Innovation is the introduction of new ideas or products such as the implementation of technology.

Pandemic: A pandemic is the widespread transmission of an infection disease across a large area or region.

Perceived Benefits: Factors which encourages organizations positively to use an innovation (Carr, 2017).

Perceived Cost: Refers to the entire capital investment above the initial investment of adoption (Alam et al., 2014).

Perceived Risk: The uncertainty that a user may have with regards to how well an innovation would function and perform (Featherman & Pavlou, 2003).

Perceived Satisfaction: The degree that perceived pre-adoption business value and usefulness has been actualized post-adoption (Thong, Hong & Tam, 2006).

Perceived Trust: A mental state of positive expectancy (Yasmin & Grundmann, 2019).

Perceived Usefulness: The amount of people that use innovation due to its benefit (Yasmin & Grundmann, 2019).

Perception: Perception is the way in which someone understands or interprets something.

Phenomenon: A phenomenon is a fact or object that is of scientific interest.

Secondary Resources: Secondary resources are works that were created by someone that did not have firsthand experience of an event however relays or quotes information from the primary resource.

Social Distancing: Social distancing is the practise of physically distancing yourself from people or limiting the amount of interaction between people to reduce the spread of a contagious disease as a non-pharmaceutical intervention.

Telework: Telework is the practise of utilizing ICT tools to work from home or alternate locations to a traditional workplace.

Unified Systems: Unified systems is the convergence and integration of multiple systems to enable centralized management and boost productivity.

Value: Value is the perceived usefulness of something or the degree of importance.

Chapter 10
The Online Education and Virtual Collaboration Model

Efosa Carroll Idemudia
Arkansas Tech University, USA

ABSTRACT

Worldwide, tech spending was approximately $4 trillion in 2019. In 2020, all successful global universities are using a wide variety of information systems platforms to adapt to the global COVID-19 pandemic. Universities are using the rapid constant changes in information technology to alleviate the COVID-19 crisis. During the COVID-19 pandemic, almost all universities in North America, Europe, Australia, and New Zealand conducted classes through online and virtual instruction. Unfortunately, most universities in Nigeria/Africa are not able to adapt to the global COVID-19 pandemic, and universities in Nigeria in 2020 were completely closed for classes. To help address this issue, the authors conducted their research. In addition, using the stakeholder theory, they developed the online education and virtual collaboration model. The model provides insights and understanding on how to develop online courses and classes effectively and efficiently in Nigeria/Africa. The study has significant research and practical implications.

INTRODUCTION

For approximately two years, global firms, companies, universities, organizations, and governments are using a variety of information systems platforms to adapt to the global COVID-19 pandemic (Idemudia 2020). Kundu and Bej (2020) argue that COVID-19 brought social distancing, not mental distancing. The COVID-19 has affected the educational systems across the world most especially developing countries

DOI: 10.4018/978-1-7998-9418-6.ch010

in Africa. Daniel (2020) presents that COVID-19 is one of the greatest challenges that worldwide education systems have ever faced. In 2020, almost all the schools in the world were closed. For example, in May 2020, schools in approximately one hundred and ninety countries were closed (Giannini et al., 2020; UNESCO, 2020). Rogers and Sabarwal (2020) argue that during COVID-19, most governments in different parts of the world asked educational institutions to move traditional, face-to-face classes to virtual and online teaching. To date, because of COVID-19, online education is very popular because online education gives students the opportunity to attend and compare courses (Kundu and Bej 2020). Basilaia and Kvavadze (2020) discuss that some of the different education processes are TV broadcasts, video lectures, resources, online channels, online libraries, and guidelines. Kundu and Bej (2020) argue that during COVID-19, that shifting to online education was difficult to both technology savvy teachers and students. Worldwide, healthcare professionals and governments are using advanced information systems/technologies to aid in the testing, treatments, tracking, and decision makings relating to patients with COVID-19. To date, firms, organizations, governments, companies, and universities are using advance information technology to alleviate the effect of the COVID-19 global crisis (Idemudia 2020). Worldwide, to adapt to COVID-19, tech spending was approximately $4 trillion in 2019 (Rosenbaum, 2019) and $4.1 trillion in 2020 (Speed, 2021). The constant advancements in a wide range of information systems/information technology are affecting the traditional ways governments, companies, organizations, firms, and universities operates. Worldwide, both small and large universities are using information technology applications for better decision makings and strategic competitive advantages.

The top five largest companies in the world by profits, market capitalization, and sales are predominantly in the technology sector (Ventura, 2021; Ireland, 2020; InnovativeZone, 2021). The largest and the most profitable companies in the world are implementing information technology applications to get bigger and increase their profits, sales, and market shares (Ventura, 2021; Fortune, 2022; Jay, 2019). During the global COVID-19 pandemic in 2020 and 2021, almost all universities in the world, most especially the western world conducted classes through online and virtual formats. The COVID-19 global pandemic has forced universities worldwide to implement and use a wide range of information technology platforms/applications as competitive tools to enhance learning and understanding. Our study develops the model, online education and virtual collaboration model, that provide insights and understanding on how universities in Africa can adapt to the global COVID-19 pandemic. The constant information technology revolution has significantly helped students, faculty, staff, and administrations to adapt to the global COVID-19 pandemic within the university' environments.

To date, because of the effect of the global COVID-19 pandemic, universities are using a wide range of information technology platforms to survive, to enhance learning, to enhance understanding, for competitive advantages, and for better decision makings (Idemudia 2020). The global COVID-19 pandemic strongly support that no governments, organizations, companies, firms, and universities can escape the significant effect of a wide range of information technology platforms/applications. Our study helps students, faculty, staff, and administrations to adapt to the global COVID-19 pandemic/challenges that are associated with a wide range of information technology platforms and applications. In 2020 and 2021, universities worldwide are using the constant advancements in information technology to exceed stakeholders' expectations within the universities environments (Idemudia 2020). Our paper presents how information technology platforms have positively and significantly affected all the stakeholders within academia, most especially during COVID-19 global pandemic. The entire practice, process, and procedures for universities to exceed stakeholders' expectations and to create unique products and services are significantly affected by the rapid constant advancements in information technology (Idemudia 2020).

Information technology is creating unique values, and reshaping products, and services that exceed students, faculty, staff, and administrations' expectations. Universities worldwide are using a wide range of information technology platforms and application to create, maintain, and improve value chain. As shown in Figure 1, To date, universities are using information technology applications to: (1) provide quality and standard education; (2) facility to encourage and motivate research and study; (3) encourage and motivate the advancement and development of knowledge; (4) provide courses of study to meet the needs of the community and society; (5) confer degrees and diplomates for higher education; (6) disseminate knowledge; (7) promote scholarships; (8) provide facilities and resources for the wellbeing of all stakeholders in academia, etc. In addition, universities worldwide are using information technology applications to adapts to the constructs in Figure 1. Thus, the arrows in Figure 1 is bidirectional.

Figure 1. University information technology applications model

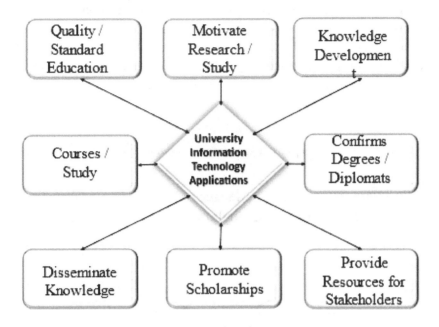

Global universities are implementing a wide range of information technology platforms in infrastructure relating to students, faculty, staffs, administrations, virtual classes/meetings, online courses, registrations, scholarships/financial aids, inventory managements, etc. (Idemudia 2020). Information technology ensures that universities and colleges function smoothly. How are universities using a wide range of information technology application as a competitive advantage? How are universities using information technology platforms and applications to make better decisions? To answer these questions, we develop the Online Education and Virtual Collaboration Model (OEVCM). The OEVCM provides insights and understanding on how academia are implementing information technology for competitive advantage and better decision making. Idemudia (2020) argues that information technology applications include cloud storage, collaboration information systems, information systems security, strategic information systems, business intelligence, mobile systems, hardware, software, database processing, and social media. Universities, Worldwide, are using a wide range of information technology platforms as a powerful tool to target students/customers, reduce cost, understand students/customers better, differentiate products, make better decisions, understand stakeholders better, and create competitive advantages. As shown in Figure 2, Idemudia (2020) presents that universities are using information technology applications to create a competitive advantage through (1) appropriate software and hardware to exceed students, faculty, staff, and administrations expectations; (2) manage complaints from students; (3) organize day-to-day tasks; (4) streamline workflow; (5) data analytics to gain insights and knowledge for better decision making; and (6) cloud technologies to reduce universities' costs and exceed students, faculty, staff, and administrations' expectations. In addition, Figure 3, shows the contents and components of online courses.

Figure 2. University IT competitive advantages model

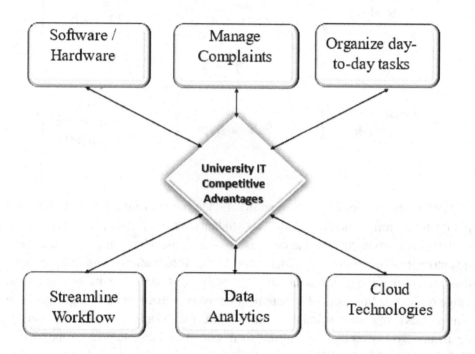

Figure 3. Online course contents / components model

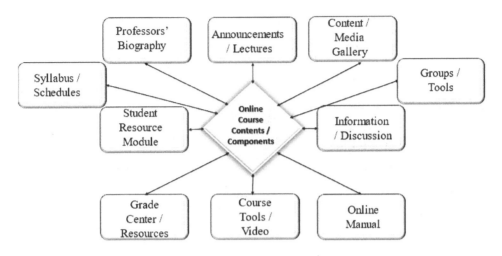

THE RESEARCH MODEL

The theoretical background for our research model, the Online Education and Virtual Collaboration Model, is the Stakeholder theory. The stakeholder theory posits that for any organization or company or firm to succeed, the organization/company/ firm must address the needs and interests of all the stakeholders (Donaldson and Preston, 1995). The stakeholder theory is self-descriptive and instrumental because the stakeholder theory offers a comprehensive model for companies, organizations, and firms (Donaldson and Preston, 1995). Stakeholder theory is an instrument that researchers are implementing to investigate the links between conventional firm performance and the practices of stakeholder managements (Donaldson and Preston, 1995). The stakeholder theory provides insight and understanding on how to identified and considered all stakeholder interests and intrinsically valuable (Donaldson and Preston, 1995). Top managements and administrations are using the stakeholder theory to recommend attitudes, structures, and practices to successfully address the interests of all legitimate stakeholders (Donaldson and Preston, 1995). Our research model is shown in Figure 4.

Figure 4. The online education and virtual collaboration model

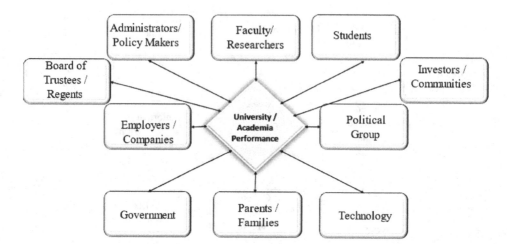

The arrows in figure 4 are bidirectional and indication that for any university to succeed, the university must adapt to all stakeholders' interests. To date, because of the global Covid-19 pandemic, universities worldwide are using different types of information technology platforms such as zoom, WebEx, Team etc. to organize and hold meetings with stakeholders. For examples:

1) Professors are conducting classes online and virtually using a wide range of information technology platforms (i.e. Blackboard, CE, Vista)
2) Professors, faculty, staff, administration, students, investors, parents, governments and board of trustees/regents are conducting and holding meetings using a wide range of information technology platforms (i.e. zoom, WebEx, teams)
3) Computer services and help desks are using a wide range of information technology platforms to remotely help students, faculty, staff, and administrations who are having technical difficulties and challenges.
4) Admission offices are using a wide range of information technology

CONCLUSION

To date, the global covid-19 pandemic has posed serious challenges to universities worldwide; and to address these challenges our study develops the Online Education and Virtual Collaboration Model. The theoretical background for our research models is the stakeholder theory. Our model provides insights and understanding on specific strategies to implement to improve universities/academia performances. The global covid-19 pandemic has significantly influenced the daily behaviors and tasks of universities' stakeholders (i.e. administrators, policy makers, faculty, researchers, staff, students, investors, communities, political groups, technologies, parents, governments, and the board of trustees/regents). In addition, our models provides a comprehensive overview on how top managements in academia should adapt to all the interests relating to the different stakeholders. Our models have a lot of research and practical implications.

Finally, our study opens the doors for future research to empirically investigate the effect and impact of administrators, policy makers, faculty, researchers, staff, students, investors, communities in the university environments. Future researchers are encourage to validate the constructs in Figures 1, 2, 3, and 4.

REFERENCES

Basilaia, G., & Kvavadze, D. (2020). Transition to online education in schools during a SARS-CoV-2 coronavirus (COVID-19) pandemic in Georgia. *Pedagogical Research, 5*(4).

Daniel, S. J. (2020). Education and the COVID-19 pandemic. *Prospects, 49*(1), 91–96. doi:10.100711125-020-09464-3 PMID:32313309

Donaldson, T., & Preston, L. (1995). The stakeholder theory of the modern corporation: Concepts, evidence and implications. *Academy of Management Review, 20*(1), 65–91. doi:10.2307/258887

Giannini, S., Jenkins, R., & Saavedra, J. (2020). *Reopening Schools: When, Where and How?* UNESCO Blogs. Retrieved May 20, 2020, from https://en.unesco.org/news/reopening-schools-when-where-and-how

Global 500. (2022, May 10). *Fortune.* Retrieved from https://fortune.com/global500/

Idemudia, E. C. (Ed.). (2020). *Handbook of Research on IT Applications for Strategic Competitive Advantage and Decision Making.* IGI Global. doi:10.4018/978-1-7998-3351-2

Ireland, S. (2020, May 16). The World's 100 Best-Performing Companies, 2020. *CEO World Magazine.* Retrieved from https://ceoworld.biz/2020/05/16/the-worlds-100-best-performing-companies-2020/

Jay, A. (2019, December 20). *Top 10 richest companies in the world in 2019 by revenue*. Retrieved from https://financesonline.com/top-10-richest-companies-in-the-world-in-2018-by-revenue/

Kundu, A., & Bej, T. (2021). COVID 19 response: An analysis of teachers' perception on pedagogical successes and challenges of digital teaching practice during new normal. *Education and Information Technologies*, *26*(6), 1–24. doi:10.100710639-021-10503-5 PMID:33897267

Rogers, F. H., & Sabarwal, S. (2020). *The COVID-19 pandemic: Shocks to education and policy responses*. Academic Press.

Rosenbaum, E. (2019, April 9). *Tech spending will near $4 trillion this year. Here's where all the money is going and why*. CNBC. Retrieved from https://www.cnbc.com/2019/04/08/4-trillion-in-tech-spending-in-2019-heres-where-the-money-is-going.html

Speed, R. (2021, April 7). *How big might IT spending get in 2021? Gartner: How about $4 trillion. And no, you can't have a new MacBook*. The Register. Retrieved from https://www.theregister.com/2021/04/07/gartner_worldwide_it_spend/

Top 10 company in the corporate world. (2021, July 5). *InnovativeZone*. Retrieved from https://innovativezoneindia.com/top-10-company-in-the-world/

UNESCO. (2020, April). *Distance learning strategies in response to COVID-19 school closures* (Programme and Meeting Document ED/2020/IN2.1/REV). Retrieved from the United Nations Educational, Scientific, and Cultural Organization website: https://unesdoc.unesco.org/ark:/48223/pf0000373305/PDF/373305eng.pdf.multi

UNESCO. (2020). *Education from disruption to recovery*. UNESCO Blogs. Retrieved May 20, 2020, from https://en.unesco.org/covid19/educationresponse

Ventura, L. (2021, August 3). *World's Largest Companies 2021*. Global Finance. Retrieved from https://www.gfmag.com/global-data/economic-data/largest-companies

ADDITIONAL READING

Adnan, M., & Anwar, K. (2020). Online Learning amid the COVID-19 Pandemic: Students' Perspectives. *Online Submission*, *2*(1), 45–51. doi:10.33902/JPSP.2020261309

Agustina, P. Z. R., & Cheng, T. H. (2020). How students' perspectives about online learning amid the COVID-19 pandemic? *Studies in Learning and Teaching*, *1*(3), 133–139. doi:10.46627ilet.v1i3.46

Almazova, N., Krylova, E., Rubtsova, A., & Odinokaya, M. (2020). Challenges and opportunities for Russian higher education amid COVID-19: Teachers' perspective. *Education Sciences*, *10*(12), 368. doi:10.3390/educsci10120368

Asgari, S., Trajkovic, J., Rahmani, M., Zhang, W., Lo, R. C., & Sciortino, A. (2021). An observational study of engineering online education during the COVID-19 pandemic. *PLoS One*, *16*(4), e0250041. doi:10.1371/journal.pone.0250041 PMID:33857219

Budur, T., Demir, A., & Cura, F. (2021). University readiness to online education during Covid-19 pandemic. *International Journal of Social Sciences & Educational Studies*, *8*(1), 180–200.

Butnaru, G. I., Niță, V., Anichiti, A., & Brînză, G. (2021). The effectiveness of online education during covid 19 pandemic—A comparative analysis between the perceptions of academic students and high school students from romania. *Sustainability*, *13*(9), 5311. doi:10.3390u13095311

Chakraborty, P., Mittal, P., Gupta, M. S., Yadav, S., & Arora, A. (2021). Opinion of students on online education during the COVID-19 pandemic. *Human Behavior and Emerging Technologies*, *3*(3), 357–365. doi:10.1002/hbe2.240

Daniel, S. J. (2020). Education and the COVID-19 pandemic. *Prospects*, *49*(1), 91–96. doi:10.100711125-020-09464-3 PMID:32313309

Dhawan, S. (2020). Online learning: A panacea in the time of COVID-19 crisis. *Journal of Educational Technology Systems*, *49*(1), 5–22. doi:10.1177/0047239520934018

Doyumgaç, I., Tanhan, A., & Kiymaz, M. S. (2021). Understanding the most important facilitators and barriers for online education during COVID-19 through online photovoice methodology. *International Journal of Higher Education*, *10*(1), 166–190. doi:10.5430/ijhe.v10n1p166

Liguori, E., & Winkler, C. (2020). From offline to online: Challenges and opportunities for entrepreneurship education following the COVID-19 pandemic. *Entrepreneurship Education and Pedagogy*, *3*(4), 346–351. doi:10.1177/2515127420916738

Lockee, B. B. (2021). Online education in the post-COVID era. *Nature Electronics*, *4*(1), 5–6. doi:10.103841928-020-00534-0

Mishra, L., Gupta, T., & Shree, A. (2020). Online teaching-learning in higher education during lockdown period of COVID-19 pandemic. *International Journal of Educational Research Open*, *1*, 100012. doi:10.1016/j.ijedro.2020.100012 PMID:35059663

Muthuprasad, T., Aiswarya, S., Aditya, K. S., & Jha, G. K. (2021). Students' perception and preference for online education in India during COVID-19 pandemic. *Social Sciences & Humanities Open*, *3*(1), 100101. doi:10.1016/j.ssaho.2020.100101 PMID:34173507

Oducado, R. M. (2020). Faculty perception toward online education in a state college in the Philippines during the coronavirus disease 19 (COVID-19) pandemic. *Universal Journal of Educational Research*, *8*(10), 4736–4742. doi:10.13189/ujer.2020.081044

Paudel, P. (2021). Online education: Benefits, challenges and strategies during and after COVID-19 in higher education. *International Journal on Studies in Education*, *3*(2), 70–85. doi:10.46328/ijonse.32

Qazi, A., Naseer, K., Qazi, J., AlSalman, H., Naseem, U., Yang, S., Hardaker, G., & Gumaei, A. (2020). Conventional to online education during COVID-19 pandemic: Do develop and underdeveloped nations cope alike. *Children and Youth Services Review*, *119*, 105582. doi:10.1016/j.childyouth.2020.105582 PMID:33071406

Sandhu, P., & de Wolf, M. (2020). The impact of COVID-19 on the undergraduate medical curriculum. *Medical Education Online*, *25*(1), 1764740. doi:10.1080/108 72981.2020.1764740 PMID:32400298

Simamora, R. M. (2020). The Challenges of online learning during the COVID-19 pandemic: An essay analysis of performing arts education students. *Studies in Learning and Teaching*, *1*(2), 86–103. doi:10.46627ilet.v1i2.38

Simamora, R. M., De Fretes, D., Purba, E. D., & Pasaribu, D. (2020). Practices, challenges, and prospects of online learning during Covid-19 pandemic in higher education: Lecturer perspectives. *Studies in Learning and Teaching*, *1*(3), 185–208. doi:10.46627ilet.v1i3.45

Tadesse, S., & Muluye, W. (2020). The impact of COVID-19 pandemic on education system in developing countries: A review. *Open Journal of Social Sciences*, *8*(10), 159–170. doi:10.4236/jss.2020.810011

KEY TERMS AND DEFINITIONS

Online Course Contents/Components Model: Posits that online courses should include the following components: (1) professors' biography, (2) announcements/lectures, (3) content, (4) media gallery, (5) groups/tools, (6) information, (7) discussion boards, (8) online manual, (9) course videos, (10) grade center, (11) student resources, (12) syllabus, and (13) schedule.

Online Education and Virtual Collaboration Model: Provide insights and understanding on how academia is implementing information technology for competitive advantage and better decision making. The constant information technology revolution has significantly helped students, faculty, staff, and administrations to adapt to the global COVID-19 pandemic within the university' environments.

Stakeholder Theory: Posits that for any organization or company or firm to succeed, the organization/company/firm must address the needs and interests of all the stakeholders (Donaldson & Preston, 1995).

University Information Technology Applications Model: Provides insights that University should adapt to (1) quality education, (2) research, (3) knowledge development, (4) course study, (5) degrees, (6) promote scholarships, (7) technology, and (8) stakeholders.

University IT Competitive Advantages Model: Posits that universities are using information technology applications to create a competitive advantage through (1) appropriate software and hardware to exceed students, faculty, staff, and administrations expectations; (2) manage complaints from students; (3) organize day-to-day tasks; (4) streamline workflow; (5) data analytics to gain insights and knowledge for better decision making; and (6) cloud technologies to reduce universities' costs and exceed students, faculty, staff, and administrations' expectations.

Compilation of References

Abdulghani, H. M., Alrowais, N. A., Bin-Saad, N. S., Al-Subaie, N. M., Haji, A. M. A., & Alhaqwi, A. I. (2012). Sleep disorder among medical students: Relationship to their academic performance. *Medical Teacher, 34*(sup1), S37–S41. doi:10.3109/0142159X.2012.656749 PMID:22409189

Abernathy, F. H., Dunlop, J. T., Hammond, J. H., & Weil, D. (2000). Retailing and supply chains in the information age. *Technology in Society, 22*(1), 5–31. doi:10.1016/S0160-791X(99)00039-1

Abidin, C. (2015). "Communicative Intimacies: Influencers and Perceived Interconnectedness." Ada: A Journal of Gender. *New Media, and Technology, 8*(1), 1–14.

Absanto, G. (2013). Analysis of Business Growth Strategies and their Contribution to Business Growth. *International Journal of Economics, Commerce and Management, I*(1), 1–14.

Acemoglu, D. (2009a). Economic growth and economic development: The questions. In D. Acemoglu (Ed.), *Introduction to Modern Economic Growth* (pp. 3–25). Princeton University Press.

Acemoglu, D. (2009b). The Solow model and the data. In D. Acemoglu (Ed.), *Introduction to Modern Economic Growth* (pp. 77–107). Princeton University Press.

Adams, D., Nelson, R., & Todd, P. (1992). Perceived usefulness, ease of use, and usage of information technology: A replication. *Management Information Systems Quarterly, 16*(2), 227–247. doi:10.2307/249577

Adetunji, C. O., Nwankwo, W., Olayinka, A. S., Olugbemi, O. T., Akram, M., Laila, U., & Esiobu, N. D. (n.d.). Machine Learning and Behaviour Modification for COVID-19. *Medical Biotechnology, Biopharmaceutics, Forensic Science and Bioinformatics*, 271-287.

Adivar, B., Hüseyinoğlu, I. Ö. Y., & Christopher, M. (2019). A quantitative performance management framework for assessing omnichannel retail supply chains. *Journal of Retailing and Consumer Services, 48*, 257–269. doi:10.1016/j.jretconser.2019.02.024

Aganbegyan, A. (2014). Social and economic development of russia: An analysis and a forecast. *Studies on Russian Economic Development, 25*(4), 319–328. doi:10.1134/S1075700714040029

Aghion, P., Jones, B. F., & Jones, Ch. I. (2017). *Artificial Intelligence and economic growth.* National Bureau of Economic Research working paper. Retrieved at https://www.nber.org/chapters/c14015

Aghion, P., & Bolton, P. (1997). A theory of trickle-down growth and development. *The Review of Economic Studies, 64*(2), 151–172. doi:10.2307/2971707

Aghion, P., & Howitt, P. (1992). A model of growth: Through creative destruction. *Econometrica, 60*(2), 323–351. doi:10.2307/2951599

Aghion, P., & Howitt, P. (1998). *Endogenous growth theory*. Massachusetts Institute of Technology Press.

Agrawal, G., Ahlawat, H., & Dewhurst, M. (2020). *Winning against COVID-19: The implications for biopharma*. McKinsey & Co. Retrieved at https://www.mckinsey.com/industries/pharmaceuticals-and-medical-products/our-insights/winning-against-covid-19-the-implications-for-biopharma#the-implications-for-biopharma

Akbarzadeh, O., Baradaran, M., & Khosravi, M. R. (2021). IoT-based smart management of healthcare services in hospital buildings during COVID-19 and future pandemics. *Wireless Communications and Mobile Computing, 2021*, 2021. doi:10.1155/2021/5533161

Alam, S. S., Hashim, N. H. N., Rashid, M., Omar, N. A., Ahsan, N., & Ismail, M. D. (2014). Small-scale households renewable energy usage intention: Theoretical development and empirical settings. *Renewable Energy, 68*, 255–263. doi:10.1016/j.renene.2014.02.010

Alao, A., & Brink, R. (2022). COVID-19 Digital Technology Response in Sub-Saharan African Countries. In Building Resilient Healthcare Systems With ICTs (pp. 74-105). IGI Global.

Al-Debei, M. M., Al-Lozi, E., & Papazafeiropoulou, A. (2013). Why People Keep Coming Back to Facebook: Explaining and Predicting Continuance Participation from an Extended Theory of Planned Behaviour Perspective. *Decision Support Systems, 55*(1), 43–54. doi:10.1016/j.dss.2012.12.032

Alemi, M., Meghdari, A., & Saffari, E. (2017). RoMa: A hi-tech robotic mannequin for the fashion industry. Lecture Notes in Computer Science (LNCS): Social Robotics, 10652, 209-219.

Alrawi, M. (2020). *As you work from home, spare a thought for the shop in your office building*. Retrieved on 27 August 2020 from https://www.thenational.ae/opinion/comment/as-you-work-from-home-spare-a-thought-for-the-shop-in-your-office-building-1.1068742

Al-Saadoon, G. M. W., & Al Naemi, E. (2015). Virtualization technology and security challenges. In A. H. Al-Hamami & G. M. W. Al-Saadoon (Eds.), *Handbook of Research on Threat Detection and Countermeasures in Network Security* (pp. 254–275). IGI Global. doi:10.4018/978-1-4666-6583-5.ch014

Alvarez, F., Buera, F., & Lucas, R. E. (2007). *Idea flows, economic growth, and trade*. National Bureau of Economic Research working paper. Retrieved at https://www.nber.org/papers/w19667

Amato, F., Basile, F., Carbone, C., & Chiacchio, P. (2005). An approach to control automated warehouse systems. *Control Engineering Practice, 13*(10), 1223–1241. doi:10.1016/j.conengprac.2004.10.017

Anadolu Agency. (2020). *Health, Africa, latest on coronavirus outbreak*. Available at www.aa.com.tr

Aral, S., & Walker, D. (2014). Tie Strength, Embeddedness, and Social Influence: A Large-scale Networked Experiment. *Management Science*, *60*(6), 1352–1370. doi:10.1287/mnsc.2014.1936

Aravanis, J. (2020). *Five industries set to outperform due to COVID-19*. IBISWorld. Retrieved at https://www.ibisworld.com/industry-insider/coronavirus-insights/five-industries-set-to-outperform-due-to-covid-19/

Arora, R. (2020). Which companies did well during the Coronavirus pandemic? *Forbes*. Retrieved at www.forbes.com/sites/rohitarora-during-the-coronavirus-pandemic/#17fe6c9b7409

Arora, A., Bansal, S., Kandpal, C., Aswani, R., & Dwivedi, Y. (2019). Measuring social media influencer index-insights from facebook, Twitter and Instagram. *Journal of Retailing and Consumer Services*, *49*, 86–101. doi:10.1016/j.jretconser.2019.03.012

Arrow, K. (1962). The economic implications of learning by doing. *The Review of Economic Studies*, *29*(3), 155–173. doi:10.2307/2295952

Arrow, K. J. (1962). Economic welfare and the allocation of resources for invention. In R. R. Nelson (Ed.), *The Rate and Direction of Inventive Activity* (pp. 609–626). Princeton University Press. doi:10.1515/9781400879762-024

Arrow, K. J. (1969). Classificatory notes on the production and transmission of technological knowledge. *The American Economic Review*, *59*(2), 29–35.

Asrar, F. M., Saint-Jacques, D., Chapman, H. J., Williams, D., Ravan, S., Upshur, R., & Clark, J. B. (2021). Can space-based technologies help manage and prevent pandemics? *Nature Medicine*, *27*(9), 1489–1490. doi:10.103841591-021-01485-5 PMID:34518675

Awad, N. F., & Krishnan, M. S. (2006). The Personalization Privacy Paradox: An Empirical Evaluation of Information Transparency and the Willingness to be Profiled Online for Personalization. *Management Information Systems Quarterly*, *30*(1), 13–28. doi:10.2307/25148715

Baard, N., & Thomas, A. (2010). Teleworking in South Africa: Employee benefits and challenges. *SA Journal of Human Resource Management*, *8*(1), 1–10. doi:10.4102ajhrm.v8i1.298

Bailey, D. R., & Lee, A. R. (2020). Learning from experience in the midst of covid-19: Benefits, challenges, and strategies in online teaching. *Computer-Assisted Language Learning Electronic Journal*, *21*(2), 178–198.

Bailey, J. E., & Pearson, S. W. (1983). Development of a Tool for Measuring and Analyzing Computer User Satisfaction. *Management Science*, *29*(5), 530–545. doi:10.1287/mnsc.29.5.530

Balhara, Y. P. S., Kattula, D., Singh, S., Chukkali, S., & Bhargava, R. (2020). Impact of lockdown following COVID-19 on the gaming behavior of college students. *Indian Journal of Public Health*, *64*(6), 172–176. doi:10.4103/ijph.IJPH_465_20 PMID:32496250

Banerjee, A. (2008). Big answers for big questions: The presumption of growth policy. In Brookings Institute (Ed.), What Works in Development? Thinking Big and Thinking Small (pp. 207-231). Washington, DC: Brookings Institute.

Banerjee, A., & Newman, A. F. (1993). Occupational choice and the process of development. *Journal of Political Economy, 101*(2), 274–298. doi:10.1086/261876

Bariffi, F., & Puaschunder, J. M. (2021). Artificial Intelligence and Big Data in the age of COVID-19. *Proceedings of the 24th Research Association for Interdisciplinary Studies (RAIS) Conference.*

Barr, M., & Copeland-Stewart, A. (2022). Playing video games during the COVID-19 pandemic and effects on players' well-being. *Games and Culture, 17*(1), 122–139. doi:10.1177/15554120211017036

Barro, R.J. (1991). Economic growth in a cross section of countries. *The Quarterly Journal of Economics, 106*(2), 407-444.

Barro, R. (1990). Government spending in a simple model of endogenous growth. *Journal of Political Economy, 98*(5, Part 2), 103–125. doi:10.1086/261726

Bartelsman, E. J., Haltiwanger, J., & Scarpetta, S. (2013). Cross-country differences in productivity: The role of allocation and selection. *The American Economic Review, 1*(103), 305–334. doi:10.1257/aer.103.1.305

Bartik, A. W., Bertrand, M., Cullen, Z., Glaeser, E. L., Luca, M., & Stanton, Ch. (2020). *How are small businesses adjusting to COVID-19? Early evidence from a survey.* Cambridge, MA: National Bureau of Economic Research Working Paper No. 26989.

Basilaia, G., & Kvavadze, D. (2020). Transition to online education in schools during a SARS-CoV-2 coronavirus (COVID-19) pandemic in Georgia. *Pedagogical Research, 5*(4).

Basl, J. (2017). Pilot study of readiness of czech companies to implement the principles of industry 4.0. *Management and Production Engineering Review, 8.*

Baumgart, D. C. (2020). Digital advantage in the COVID-19 response: Perspective from Canada's largest integrated digitized healthcare system. *NPJ Digital Medicine, 3*(1), 1–4. doi:10.103841746-020-00326-y PMID:32923691

Bayram, A., & Cesaret, B. (2017). Ship-from-store operations in omni-channel retailing. In *Iie annual conference. proceedings* (pp. 1181–1186). Academic Press.

Beasley, D. (2020). *Google Gives Employees $1,000 Work-From-Home Allowance.* Retrieved on 10 August 2020 from https://www.forbes.com/sites/beasleydavid/2020/05/27/google-gives-employees-1000-work-from-home-allowance/#65a328c84c04

Beech, M. (2020). *COVID-19 Pushes Up Internet Use 70% And Streaming More Than 12%, First Figures Reveal*. Retrieved on 09 August 2020 from https://www.forbes.com/sites/markbeech/2020/03/25/covid-19-pushes-up-internet-use-70-streaming-more-than-12-first-figures-reveal/#39c98df43104

Benjamin, L. (2020). *Working From Home Is Disliked By And Bad For Most Employees, Say Researchers*. Retrieved on 26 August 2020 from https://www.forbes.com/sites/benjaminlaker/2020/08/24/working-from-home-is-disliked-by-and-bad-for-most-employees/#1a36667c6734

Berger, C., Möslein, K., Piller, F., & Reichwald, R. (2005). Co-designing the customer interface for customer-centric strategies: Learning from exploratory research. *European Management Review*, *2*(3), 70–87. doi:10.1057/palgrave.emr.1500030

Berger, J. (2013). *Contagious: Why Things Catch On*. Veghawaii Org.

Berking, P., & Gallagher, S. (2016). *Choosing a learning management system (LMS)* (8th ed.). Advanced Distributed Learning (ADL) Initiative. https://adlnet.gov/publications/2016/11/Choosing-a-Learning-Management-System-LMS/

Bhattacherjee, A. (2001). Understanding Information Systems Continuance: An Expectation-confirmation Model. *Management Information Systems Quarterly*, *25*(3), 351–370. doi:10.2307/3250921

Bhattacherjee, A., & Lin, C.-P. (2015). A unified model of IT continuance: Three complementary perspectives and crossover effects. *European Journal of Information Systems*, *24*(4), 364–373. doi:10.1057/ejis.2013.36

Bils, M., & Klenow, P. (2002). Does schooling cause growth? *The American Economic Review*, *90*(5), 1160–1183. doi:10.1257/aer.90.5.1160

Bjork, G. J. (1999). *The way it worked and why it won't: Structural change and the slowdown of U.S. economic growth*. Praeger.

Blum, D., Kahn, A., Mozin, M. J., Rebuffat, E., Sottiaux, M., & Van de Merckt, C. (1990). Relation between chronic insomnia and school failure in preadolescents. *Sleep Research*, *19*, 194.

Bolu, C. A. (2012). The church in the contemporary world: Information and communication technology in church communication for growth: A case study. *Journal of Media and Communication Studies*, *4*(4), 80–94. doi:10.5897/JMCS11.087

Bon, O. L. (2020). Relationships between REM and NREM in the NREM-REM sleep sycle: a review on competing concepts. *Sleep Medicine*. doi:10.1016/j.sleep.2020.02.004

Boulton, C. (2020). *Remote hiring wins have CIOs rethinking recruitment, post-pandemic*. Retrieved on 06 August 2020 from https://www.cio.com/article/3563012/remote-hiring-wins-have-cios-rethinking-recruitment-post-pandemic.html

Braun, V., & Clarke, V. (2006). Using thematic analysis in psychology. *Qualitative Research in Psychology, 3*(2), 77–101. doi:10.1191/1478088706qp063oa

Brenner, R. (2002). American economic revival. In *The Boom and the Bubble: The US in the World Economy.* Verso.

Brenner, R. (2006a). The puzzle of the long downturn. In *The Economics of Global Turbulence: The Advanced Capitalist Economies from Long Boom to Long Downturn, 1945-2005.* Verso.

Brenner, R. (2006b). From boom to downturn. In *The Economics of Global Turbulence: The Advanced Capitalist Economies from Long Boom to Long Downturn, 1945-2005.* Verso.

Brower, T. (2020). *Why The Office Simply Cannot Go Away: The Compelling Case For The Workplace.* Retrieved on 27 July 2020 from https://www.forbes.com/sites/tracybrower/2020/06/07/why-the-office-simply-cannot-go-away-the-compelling-case-for-the-workplace/#70213d385baf

Browning, M. H. E. M., Larson, L. R., Sharaievska, I., Rigolon, A., McAnirlin, O., Mullenbach, L., Cloutier, S., Vu, T. M., Thomsen, J., Reigner, N., Metcalf, E. C., D'Antonio, A., Helbich, M., Bratman, G. N., & Alvarez, H. O. (2021). Psychological impacts from COVID-19 among university students: Risk factors across seven states in the United States. *PLoS One, 16*(1), e0245327. Advance online publication. doi:10.1371/journal.pone.0245327 PMID:33411812

Bruner, R. F. (2004). Applied Mergers and Acquisitions. John Wiley and Sons.

Brynjolfsson, E., Horton, J., Ozimek, A., Rock, D., Sharma, G. & TuYe, H. (2020). *COVID-19 and Remote Work: An Early Look at US Data.* NBER Working Paper (No. 27344).

Brynjolfsson, E., Hu, Y. J., & Rahman, M. S. (2013). *Competing in the age of omnichannel retailing.* MIT Cambridge.

Budd, J., Miller, B. S., Manning, E. M., Lampos, V., Zhuang, M., Edelstein, M., & Short, M. J. (2020). Digital technologies in the public-health response to COVID-19. *Nature Medicine, 26*(8), 1–10. doi:10.103841591-020-1011-4 PMID:32770165

Buera, F. J., & Shin, Y. (2011). Finance and development: A tale of two sectors. *The American Economic Review, 101*(5), 1964–2002. doi:10.1257/aer.101.5.1964

Burmeister, E. (2000). The capital theory controversy. In H. Kurz (Ed.), *Critical Essays on Piero Sraffa's Legacy in Economics* (pp. 305–314). Cambridge University Press. doi:10.1017/CBO9781139166881.008

Burt, S. (1989). Trends and management issues in European retailing. *International Journal of Retail & Distribution Management, 17*(4). Advance online publication. doi:10.1108/EUM0000000002924

Carr, R. (2017). *Teleworking in corporate information technology departments* (Honours Empirical Report). University of Cape Town.

Carter, D. (2016). Hustle and Brand: The sociotechnical shaping of influence. Social Media þ. *Society, 2*(3), 1–12.

Caselli, F., & Feyrer, J. (2007). The marginal product of capital. *The Quarterly Journal of Economics, 122*(2), 535–568. doi:10.1162/qjec.122.2.535

Castenson, J. (2020). *How Working From Home Is Changing The Way We Think About Where We Live*. Retrieved on 17 June 2020 from https://www.forbes.com/sites/jennifercastenson/2020/06/08/value-of-home-life-is-back-and-has-land-buyers-moving-way-out/#3014ae71f1aa

Cellan-Jones, R. (2014). *Stephen Hawking warns Artificial Intelligence could end mankind*. BBC News. www.bbc.com/news/technology-30290540

Centeno, M. A., & Tham, A. (2012). *The emergence of risk in the global system*. Princeton, NJ: Princeton University working paper.

Centeno, M. A., Cinlar, E., Cloud, D., Creager, A. N., DiMaggio, P. J., Dixit, A. K., Elga, A. N., Felten, E. W., James, H., Katz, St. N., Keohane, R. O., Leonard, Th. C., Massey, W. A., Mian, A. R., Mian, Z., Oppenheimer, M., Shafir, E., & Shapiro, J. N. (2013). *Global systemic risk*. Unpublished manuscript for research community. Princeton Institute for International and Regional Studies, Princeton University.

Chen, Y., & Zahedi, F. M. (2016). Individuals' Internet Security Perceptions and Behaviors: Polycontextual Contrasts between the United States and China. *Management Information Systems Quarterly, 40*(1), 205–222. doi:10.25300/MISQ/2016/40.1.09

Cimpanu, C. (2020). *FBI says cybercrime reports quadrupled during COVID-19 pandemic*. Retrieved on 23 July 2020 from https://www.zdnet.com/article/fbi-says-cybercrime-reports-quadrupled-during-covid-19-pandemic/

Činčala, P. A. (2016). *Building a Vibrant, Healthy, Growing Church*. Faculty Publications. https://digitalcommons.andrews.edu/pubs/231

Cirruzzo, C. (2021). *Long COVID can be a disability, White House says: The Biden administration has released guidance and resources on long COVID and disability*. U.S. News. Retrieved at https://www.usnews.com/news/health-news/articles/2021-07-26/long-covid-can-be-a-disability-bidenadministration-says

Clancy, E. (1998). The tragedy of the global commons. *Indiana Journal of Global Legal Studies, 5*(2), 601–619.

Coghlan, S., Miller, T., & Paterson, J. (2020). Good proctor or "Big Brother"? AI Ethics and Online Exam Supervision Technologies. *Ml*, 1–14. https://arxiv.org/abs/2011.07647

Colley, L., & Williamson, S. (2020). *With management resistance overcome, working from home may be here to stay*. Retrieved on 24 August 2020 from https://theconversation.com/with-management-resistance-overcome-working-from-home-may-be-here-to-stay-144850

Collins, B. W., & Sturgill, A. (2013). The Effects of Media Use on Religious Individuals' Perceptions of Science. *Journal of Media and Religion, 12*(4), 217–230. doi:10.1080/15348423.2013.845043

Comin, D., & Hobijn, B. (2004). Cross-country technology adoption: Making the theories face the facts. *Journal of Monetary Economics*, *51*(1), 39–83. doi:10.1016/j.jmoneco.2003.07.003

Communicating with Disaster Affected Communities (CDAC) Network. (2018). *Resources for those responding to COVID-19*. Available at www.cdacnetwork.org

Corlatean, T. (2020). Risk, discrimination and opportunities for education during the times of COVID-19 pandemic. *Proceedings of the 17th RAIS Research Association for Interdisciplinary Sciences Conference on Social Sciences and Humanities*, 37-46. Retrieved at http://rais.education/wp-content/uploads/2020/06/004TC.pdf

CSEA Africa. (2020). *Africa's digital technology response strategy to COVID-19*. Centre for the Study of the Economies of Africa. Available at cseaafrica.org

Curcio, G., Ferrara, M., & De Gennaro, L. (2006). Sleep loss, learning capacity, and academic performance. *Sleep Medicine Reviews*, *10*(5), 323–337. doi:10.1016/j.smrv.2005.11.001 PMID:16564189

Currie, D. J., Smith, C., & Jagals, P. (2018). The application of system dynamics modelling to environmental health decision-making and policy - A scoping review. *BMC Public Health*, *18*(1), 1–11. doi:10.118612889-018-5318-8 PMID:29587701

Daniel, S. J. (2020). Education and the COVID-19 pandemic. *Prospects*, *49*(1), 91–96. doi:10.100711125-020-09464-3 PMID:32313309

Dash, S. (2020). *Work from home fun is over – now there are endless work hours, midnight calls from bosses and employees are not happy*. Retrieved on 27 July 2020 from https://www.businessinsider.in/careers/news/work-from-home-has-brought-with-it-a-new-set-of-problems-with-endless-calls-and-works-hours/articleshow/76637605.cms

Data, D. (2020). *Your employees are working from home. Can you manage their expenses?* Retrieved on 16 June 2020 from https://techcentral.co.za/your-employees-are-working-from-home-can-you-manage-their-expenses/98647/

Deaton, A. (2010). Understanding the mechanisms of economic development. *The Journal of Economic Perspectives*, *24*(3), 3–16. doi:10.1257/jep.24.3.3

Deloitte. (2020). *Cyber crime – The risks of working from home*. Retrieved on 24 August 2020 from https://www2.deloitte.com/ch/en/pages/risk/articles/covid-19-cyber-crime-working-from-home.html

Dendir, S., & Maxwell, R. S. (2020). Cheating in online courses: Evidence from online proctoring. *Computers in Human Behavior Reports*, *2*(October), 100033. doi:10.1016/j.chbr.2020.100033

Denzin, N. K., & Lincoln, Y. S. (2005). Introduction: The Discipline and Practice of Qualitative Research. In The Sage handbook of qualitative research (pp. 1–32). Sage Publications Ltd.

Deutsche, D. W. Bank überrascht mit hohem Gewinn. (2020). Retrieved at https://www.dw.com/de/deutsche-bank-%C3%BCberrascht-mit-hohem-gewinn/a-55417971

Dhaliwal, M. (2018). *To Achieve Universal Health Coverage, We Must Connect the Dots Between Innovation and Delivery.* UHC Coalition. Available online at: https://medium.com/health-for-all/to-achieve-universal-health-coverage-we-must-connect-the-dotsbetween-innovation-and-delivery-2446bf1498ca

DHET. (2020). *Zero-rated websites.* DHET Retrieved from https://www.dhet.gov.za/SiteAssets/05%20June%202020%20zero-rate%20publication.pdf

Dodd, D. (2020). COVID 19's corporate casualties. *Financial Times.* Retrieved at https://www.ft.com/content/eb6efc36-bf99-4086-a98a-7d121738b4b4

Donaldson, T., & Preston, L. (1995). The stakeholder theory of the modern corporation: Concepts, evidence and implications. *Academy of Management Review, 20*(1), 65–91. doi:10.2307/258887

Dowell, R. (2018). Fundamental protections for non-biological intelligences or: How we learn to stop worrying and love our robot Brethren. *Minnesota Journal of Law, Science & Technology, 19*(1), 305–336.

Dray, M., & Thirlwall, A. P. (2011). The endogeneity of the natural rate of growth for a selection of Asian countries. *Journal of Post Keynesian Economics, 33*(3), 451–468. doi:10.2753/PKE0160-3477330303

Dua, A., Ellingrud, K., Mahajan, D., & Silberg, J. (2020). *Which small businesses are most vulnerable to COVID-19: And when.* McKinsey & Co. Retrieved at https://www.mckinsey.com/featured-insights/americas/which-small-businesses-are-most-vulnerable-to-covid-19-and-when

Duarte, M., & Restuccia, D. (2006). The productivity of nations. *Federal Reserve Bank Richmond Economic Quarterly, 92*(3), 195–223.

Durmaz, Y., Ilhan, A., & Ilhan, A. (2015). A Theoretical Approach to Purpose and Type of Strategy. *International Journal of Business and Management, 10*(4). Advance online publication. doi:10.5539/ijbm.v10n4p210

EcoWellness Group. (2020). *Salzburg Declaration: Interdisciplinary Conference on 'System change?! The chance of transformation of the healthcare system: Analysis and chances of the coronavirus crisis.* Retrieved at https://www.oekowellness.de/laenderuebergreifende-konzerenz-zum-thema-system-change-die-chance-der-transformation-des-gesundheitswesens-14-07-2020/

EcoWellness Group. (2021). *Salzburg European Declaration from the Gasteinertal: Interdisciplinary Conference on 'System change?! The chance of transformation of the healthcare system.* Retrieved at https://www.oekowellness.de/wp-content/uploads/2021/07/Final-Stand-5.7.-2021.07.04_Programm-14.7.-und-15.07.2021-2.pdf

Edwardes, H. (2020). *How we at Vox are helping our customers.* Retrieved on 10 July 2020 from https://www.vox.co.za/content-hub/category/vox-4-thought/how-we-at-vox-are-helping-our-customers?page=34710

Elliott, C. (2021). When will it be safe to cruise again? These signs that will help you decide when to sail. *USA Today*. Retrieved at https://www.usatoday.com/story/travel/advice/2021/02/05/covid-when-will-it-be-safe-to-cruise/4386762001

Entertainment Software Association. (2019). *Essential facts 2019 report 1*. Author.

Ergüzen, A., Erdal, E., Ünver, M., & Özcan, A. (2021). Improving technological infrastructure of distance education through trustworthy platform-independent virtual software application pools. *Applied Sciences (Switzerland)*, *11*(3), 1–17. doi:10.3390/app11031214

Erosa, A., Koreshkova, T., & Restuccia, D. (2010). How important is human capital? A quantitative theory assessment of world income inequality. *The Review of Economic Studies*, *77*(4), 1421–1449. doi:10.1111/j.1467-937X.2010.00610.x

Etikan, I. (2016). Comparison of Convenience Sampling and Purposive Sampling. *American Journal of Theoretical and Applied Statistics*, *5*(1), 1. doi:10.11648/j.ajtas.20160501.11

European Commission-DIGIT. (2020). *Digital technology response to COVID-19*. Available at https://ec.www.ec.europa.eu/isa2/home_en

Farzin, M., & Fattahi, M. (2018). eWOM through social networking sites and impact on purchase intention and brand image in Iran. *Journal of Advances in Management Research*. doi:10.1108/JAMR-05-2017-0062

Feather, N. (2019). *How to Protect Your Remote Employees from Cyber Threats*. Retrieved on 24 August 2020 from https://www.inc.com/neill-feather/how-to-protect-your-remote-employees-from-cyber-threats.html

Featherman, M. S., & Pavlou, P. A. (2003). Predicting e-services adoption: A perceived risk facets perspective. *International Journal of Human-Computer Studies*, *59*(4), 451–474. doi:10.1016/S1071-5819(03)00111-3

Fernández-Bustos, J. G., Infantes-Paniagua, Á., Cuevas, R., & Contreras, O. R. (2019). Effect of Physical Activity on Self-Concept: Theoretical Model on the Mediation of Body Image and Physical Self-Concept in Adolescents. *Frontiers in Psychology*, *10*, 1537. doi:10.3389/fpsyg.2019.01537 PMID:31354570

Foster, V. (2020). Is eating meat from meatpacking plants with Covid-19 Coronavirus outbreaks safe? *Forbes*. Retrieved at https://www.forbes.com/sites/victoriaforster/2020/06/21/is-eating-meat-from-meatpacking-plants-with-covid-19-coronavirus-outbreaks-safe/?sh=5d2d5bcb7089

Fred, B. J. (2015). *The Development and Implementation of a Community-Based Evangelism Model in the Word of Life Seventh-day Adventist Church in Memphis, TN*. Academic Press.

Furnival-Marar, L. (2011). *Financial analysis of companies entering new markets: A case study in the mobile telephony sector* (Unpublished doctoral dissertation). University of S. Paulo.

Futagami, K., Morita, Y., & Shibata, A. (1993). Dynamic analysis of an endogenous growth model with public capital. *The Scandinavian Journal of Economics*, *95*(4), 607–625. doi:10.2307/3440914

Galor, O., & Moav, O. (2000). Ability biased technological transition, wage inequality and growth. *The Quarterly Journal of Economics, 115*(2), 469–498. doi:10.1162/003355300554827

Galor, O., & Moav, O. (2004). From physical to human capital accumulation: Inequality in the process of development. *The Review of Economic Studies, 71*(4), 1001–1026. doi:10.1111/0034-6527.00312

Galor, O., & Tsiddon, D. (1997). The distribution of human capital and economic growth. *Journal of Economic Growth, 2*(1), 93–124. doi:10.1023/A:1009785714248

Garegnani, P. (2008). On Walras's theory of capital. *Journal of the History of Economic Thought, 30*(3), 367–384. doi:10.1017/S1053837208000345

Gartner. (2020). *9 Predictions for the Post-COVID Future of Work*. Retrieved on 28 June 2020 from https://www.gartner.com/document/3985163?ref=solrAll&refval=259205666

Gates, B. (2015). The next epidemic—Lessons from Ebola. *The New England Journal of Medicine, 372*(15), 1381–1384. doi:10.1056/NEJMp1502918 PMID:25853741

Gates, B. (2020). Responding to Covid-19: A Once-in-a-Century Pandemic? *The New England Journal of Medicine, 382*(18), 1677–1679. doi:10.1056/NEJMp2003762 PMID:32109012

Gelter, M., & Puaschunder, J. M. (2021). COVID-19 and comparative corporate governance. *The Journal of Corporation Law, 46*(3), 557–629.

General, D. (2005). *Implementation of the international health regulations*. Report of the review committee on the functioning of the International Health Regulations.

Gharoie Ahangar, R., Pavur, R., Fathi, M., & Shaik, A. (2020). Estimation and demographic analysis of COVID-19 infections with respect to weather factors in Europe. *Journal of Business Analytics, 3*(2), 93–106. doi:10.1080/2573234X.2020.1832866

Ghazawy, E. R., Ewis, A. A., Mahfouz, E. M., Khalil, D. M., Arafa, A., Mohammed, Z., Mohammed, E.-N. F., Hassan, E. E., Abdel Hamid, S., Ewis, S. A., & Mohammed, A. E.-N. S. (2021). Psychological impacts of COVID-19 pandemic on the university students in Egypt. *Health Promotion International, 36*(4), 1116–1125. doi:10.1093/heapro/daaa147 PMID:33367587

Giannini, S., Jenkins, R., & Saavedra, J. (2020). *Reopening Schools: When, Where and How?* UNESCO Blogs. Retrieved May 20, 2020, from https://en.unesco.org/news/reopening-schools-when-where-and-how

Gill, R. (2000). Discourse analysis. *Qualitative Researching With Text, Image, and Sound, 1*, 172-190.

Global 500. (2022, May 10). *Fortune*. Retrieved from https://fortune.com/global500/

Goldberg, K., & Pavcnik, N. (2007). The distributional effects of globalization in developing countries. *Journal of Economic Literature, 45*(1), 39–82. doi:10.1257/jel.45.1.39

Gorlick, A. (2020). *The productivity pitfalls of working from home in the age of COVID-19*. Retrieved on 08 August 2020 from https://news.stanford.edu/2020/03/30/productivity-pitfalls-working-home-age-covid-19/

GRF. (2014). *Transport strategy of the Russian Federation until 2030*. Government of the Russian Federation Moscow.

Griffith, J. L., Voloschin, P., Gibb, G. D., & Bailey, J. R. (1983). Differences in eye-hand motor coordination of video-game users and non-users. *Perceptual and Motor Skills*, *57*(1), 155–158. doi:10.2466/pms.1983.57.1.155 PMID:6622153

Grossman, G. M., & Helpman, E. (1991a). *Innovation and growth in the global economy*. MIT Press.

Grossman, G. M., & Helpman, E. (1991b). Quality ladders in the theory of growth. *The Review of Economic Studies*, *58*(1), 43–61. doi:10.2307/2298044

Hadaway, C. K. (1993). Is evangelism related to church growth? In D. A. Roozen & C. K. Hadaway (Eds.), *Church and Denominational Growth* (pp. 169–187). Abingdon Press.

Hajli, N., Shanmugam, M., Powell, P., & Love, P. E. D. (2015). A Study on the Continuance Participation in On-line Communities with Social Commerce Perspective. *Technological Forecasting and Social Change*, *96*, 232–241. doi:10.1016/j.techfore.2015.03.014

Hall, R. E., & Jones, Ch. I. (1999). Why do some countries produce so much more output per worker than others? *The Quarterly Journal of Economics*, *114*(1), 83–116. doi:10.1162/003355399555954

Hancock, D., & Algozzine, B. (2016). *Doing case study research: A practical guide for beginning researchers*. Teachers Collee Press.

Harberger, A. (1998). A vision of the growth process. *The American Economic Review*, *88*(1), 1–32.

Harker, B., & MacDonnell, R. (2012). Is telework effective for organizations? A meta-analysis of empirical research on perceptions of telework and organizational outcomes. *Management Research Review*, *35*(7), 602–616. doi:10.1108/01409171211238820

Harrod, R. F. (1939). An essay in dynamic theory. *Economic Journal (London)*, *49*(193), 14–33. doi:10.2307/2225181

Hart, R. (2021). Long Covid has over 200 symptoms and leaves 1 In 5 unable to work, study finds. *Forbes*. Retrieved at https://www.forbes.com/sites/roberthart/2021/07/15/long-covid-has-over-200-symptoms-and-leaves-1-in-5-unable-to-work-study-finds/?sh=7f71338e5eb2

Hatmaker, T. (2017). *Saudi Arabia bestows citizenship on a robot named Sophia*. Techcrunch. Retrieved at https://techcrunch.com/2017/10/26/saudi-arabia-robot-citizen-sophia/

Hausmann, R., Pritchett, L., & Rodrik, D. (2005). Growth accelerations. *Journal of Economic Growth*, *10*(4), 303–329. doi:10.100710887-005-4712-0

Hayes, A. (2018). *Decentralized banking: Monetary technocracy in the digital age.* Social Science Research Network working paper. Retrieved at https://papers.ssrn.com/sol3/papers.cfm?abstract_id=2807476

Hayward, J. (1999). Mathematical modeling of church growth. *The Journal of Mathematical Sociology, 23*(4), 255–292. doi:10.1080/0022250X.1999.9990223

Hayward, J. (2002). A dynamic model of church growth and its application to contemporary revivals. *Review of Religious Research, 43*(3), 218–241. doi:10.2307/3512330

Hayward, J. (2005). A general model of church growth and decline. *The Journal of Mathematical Sociology, 29*(3), 177–207. doi:10.1080/00222500590889721

Helminen, V., & Ristimäki, M. (2007). Relationships between commuting distance, frequency and telework in Finland. *Journal of Transport Geography, 15*(5), 331–342. doi:10.1016/j.jtrangeo.2006.12.004

Hershner, S. (2020). Sleep and academic performance: Measuring the impact of sleep. *Current Opinion in Behavioral Sciences, 33*, 51–56. doi:10.1016/j.cobeha.2019.11.009

Hester, A. J. (2011). A Comparative Analysis of the Usage and Infusion of Wiki and Non-wiki-based Knowledge Management Systems. *Information Technology Management, 12*(4), 335–355. doi:10.100710799-010-0079-9

He, W., Zhang, J., & Li, W. (2020). Information Technology Solutions, Challenges, and Suggestions for Tackling the COVID-19 Pandemic. *International Journal of Information Management, 102287*. Advance online publication. doi:10.1016/j.ijinfomgt.2020.1022 PMID:33318721

Hill, C., Jones, G., & Schilling, M. (2014). *Strategic management: Theory & cases: An integrated approach.* Cengage Learning.

Hill, G., Mason, J., & Dunn, A. (2021). Contract cheating: An increasing challenge for global academic community arising from COVID-19. *Research and Practice in Technology Enhanced Learning, 16*(1), 24. doi:10.118641039-021-00166-8 PMID:34345307

Hitt, M., Ireland, R., & Hoskisson, R. (2014). *Strategic management: Concepts: Competitiveness and globalization.* Cengage Learning.

Hoang, A. T., Nickerson, R. C., Beckman, P., & Eng, J. (2008). Telecommuting and corporate culture: Implications for the mobile enterprise. *Information Knowledge Systems Management, 7*(1-2), 77-97.

Hodge, G. L. (2002). Enterprise resource planning in textiles. *Journal of Textile and Apparel. Technology and Management, 2*(3), 1–8.

Hodges, C., Moore, S., Lockee, B., Trust, T., & Bond, A. (2020). *The difference between emergency remote teaching and online learning.* Educause Review. https://er.educause.edu/articles/2020/3/the-difference-between-emergency-remote-teaching-and-online-learning

Homer, J. B., & Hirsch, G. B. (2006). System dynamics modeling for public health: Background and opportunities. *American Journal of Public Health*, *96*(3), 452–458. doi:10.2105/AJPH.2005.062059 PMID:16449591

Hossain, M. A., & Quaddus, M. (2012). Expectation–Confirmation Theory in Information System Research: A Review and Analysis. *Information Systems Theory*, *28*, 441–469. doi:10.1007/978-1-4419-6108-2_21

Hsieh, C. T. (2002). What explains the industrial revolution in East Asia? Evidence from the factor markets. *The American Economic Review*, *92*(3), 502–526. doi:10.1257/00028280260136372

Hsieh, C. T., & Klenow, P. (2005). Relative prices and relative prosperity. *The American Economic Review*, *98*(3), 562–585. doi:10.1257/aer.97.3.562

Hsieh, C. T., & Klenow, P. (2010). Development accounting. *American Economic Journal. Macroeconomics*, *2*(1), 207–223. doi:10.1257/mac.2.1.207

Huang, C., Wang, Y., Li, X., Ren, L., Zhao, J., Hu, Y., Zhang, L., Fan, G., Xu, J., Gu, X., Cheng, Z., Yu, T., Xia, J., Wei, Y., Wu, W., Xie, X., Yin, W., Li, H., Liu, M., ... Cao, B. (2020). Clinical features of patients infected with 2019 novel coronavirus in Wuhan, China. *Lancet*, *395*(10223), 497–506. Advance online publication. doi:10.1016/S0140-6736(20)30183-5 PMID:31986264

Hui, L., Weiguo, F., & Chau, P. Y. K. (2014). Determinants of Users' Continuance of Social Networking Sites: A Self-regulation Perspective. *Information & Management*, *51*(5), 595–603. doi:10.1016/j.im.2014.03.010

Hussain, S., Hussain, Z., & Sheeraz, M. I. (2021). Challenges of the COVID-19 During Pandemic Situation, The Possible Solutions Using Information Technology. *Journal of Legal. Ethical and Regulatory Issues*, *24*, 1–14.

ICTwork. (2022). *Artificial Development and Human Development. Towards a Research Agenda.* Author.

Idemudia, E. C. (Ed.). (2020). *Handbook of Research on IT Applications for Strategic Competitive Advantage and Decision Making.* IGI Global. doi:10.4018/978-1-7998-3351-2

Idemudia, E. C. (Ed.). (2020b). *Handbook of Research on Social and Organizational Dynamics in the Digital Era.* IGI Global. doi:10.4018/978-1-5225-8933-4

IDI. (2020). *Security Challenges of Remote Workforce.* Retrieved on 24 August 2020 from https://www.identitymanagementinstitute.org/security-challenges-of-remote-workforce/

Ifenthaler, D., Gibson, D., Prasse, D., Shimada, A., & Yamada, M. (2021). Putting learning back into learning analytics: Actions for policy makers, researchers, and practitioners. *Educational Technology Research and Development*, *69*(4), 2131–2150. doi:10.100711423-020-09909-8

International Development Research Centre (IDRC) Canada. (n.d.). Available at https://www.ictworks.org/wpcontent/uploads/2022/01/Artificial-Intelligence-Human-Development.pdf iPass. (2017). *2017 Mobile Security Report*. iPass.

Ireland, S. (2020, May 16). The World's 100 Best-Performing Companies, 2020. *CEO World Magazine*. Retrieved from https://ceoworld.biz/2020/05/16/the-worlds-100-best-performing-companies-2020/

Islam, A. A. (2016). Development and Validation of the Technology Adoption and Gratification (TAG) Model in Higher Education: A Cross-cultural Study between Malaysia and China. *International Journal of Technology and Human Interaction*, *12*(3), 78–105. doi:10.4018/IJTHI.2016070106

Issar, G., & Navon, L. (2016). Operational excellence. *Manufacturing Overhead (MOH) and Departmental Expense Control*, 91–93.

Jackson, L. A., Von Eye, A., Witt, E. A., Zhao, Y., & Fitzgerald, H. E. (2011). A longitudinal study of the effects of Internet use and videogame playing on academic performance and the roles of gender, race and income in these relationships. *Computers in Human Behavior*, *27*(1), 228–239. doi:10.1016/j.chb.2010.08.001

Jacoby, H. G. (2008). Food prices, wages, and welfare in rural India. *Economic Inquiry*, *54*(1), 159–176. doi:10.1111/ecin.12237

Jameson, E., Trevena, J., & Swain, N. (2011). Electronic gaming as pain distraction. *Pain Research & Management*, *16*(1), 27–32. doi:10.1155/2011/856014 PMID:21369538

Jay, A. (2019, December 20). *Top 10 richest companies in the world in 2019 by revenue*. Retrieved from https://financesonline.com/top-10-richest-companies-in-the-world-in-2018-by-revenue/

Jones, Ch. I. (2004). *Growth and ideas*. National Bureau of Economic Research working paper. Retrieved at https://www.nber.org/papers/w10767

Jones, B. F. (2014). The human capital stock: A generalized approach. *The American Economic Review*, *104*(11), 3752–3777. doi:10.1257/aer.104.11.3752

Jones, B. F., & Olken, B. A. (2008). The anatomy of start-stop growth. *The Review of Economics and Statistics*, *90*(3), 582–587. doi:10.1162/rest.90.3.582

Jones, Ch. I. (1999). Growth: With or without scale effects. *The American Economic Review*, *89*(2), 139–144. doi:10.1257/aer.89.2.139

Kahneman, D., & Tversky, A. (1979). Prospect Theory: An Analysis of Decision Under Risk. *Econometrica*, *47*(2), 263–291. doi:10.2307/1914185

Kaldor, N. (1961). Capital accumulation and economic growth. In F. A. Lutz & D. C. Hague (Eds.), *The Theory of Capital* (pp. 177–222). St. Martin's Press. doi:10.1007/978-1-349-08452-4_10

Karahanna, E., Straub, D., & Chervany, N. (1999). Information Technology Adoption Across Time: A Cross-Sectional Comparison of Pre-Adoption and Post-Adoption Beliefs. *Management Information Systems Quarterly*, *23*(2). Advance online publication. doi:10.2307/249751

Katz, R.L., Callorda, F.M., & Jung, J. (2020). Can Digitalization Mitigate COVID-19 Damages? Evidence from Developing Countries. *Evidence from Developing Countries.*

Keough, M. (2018). Experience API. *Training & Development, 45*(1), 18–19.

Kgatle, M. S. (2018). Social media and religion: Missiological perspective on the link between Facebook and the emergence of prophetic churches in southern Africa. *Verbum et Ecclesia, 39*(1).

Khan, A. H., Sultana, S., Hossain, S., Hasan, M. T., Ahmed, H. U., & Sikder, T. (2020). The impact of COVID-19 pandemic on mental health & wellbeing among home-quarantined Bangladeshi students: A cross-sectional pilot study. *Journal of Affective Disorders, 277,* 121–128. Advance online publication. doi:10.1016/j.jad.2020.07.135 PMID:32818775

King, D. L., Delfabbro, P. H., Billieux, J., & Potenza, M. N. (2020). Problematic online gaming and the COVID-19 pandemic. *Journal of Behavioral Addictions, 9*(2), 184–186. Advance online publication. doi:10.1556/2006.2020.00016 PMID:32352927

Klenow, P. (2008). Discussion of 'Big Answers for Big Questions: The Presumption of Growth Policy' by A.V. Banerjee. In Brookings Institute (Ed.), What Works in Development? Thinking Big and Thinking Small. Washington, DC: Brookings Institute.

Klenow, P., & Rodríguez-Clare, A. (1997). Economic growth: A review essay. *Journal of Monetary Economics, 40*(4), 597–618. doi:10.1016/S0304-3932(97)00050-0

Knoop, M. S., de Groot, E. R., & Dudink, J. (2020). Current ideas about the roles of rapid eye movement and non-rapid eye movement sleep in brain development. *Acta Paediatrica (Oslo, Norway).* Advance online publication. doi:10.1111/apa.15485 PMID:32673435

Koetsier, J. (2020). *6 Reasons Most Want To Work From Home Even After Coronavirus.* Retrieved on 27 June 2020 from https://www.forbes.com/sites/johnkoetsier/2020/06/13/6-reasons-most-want-to-work-from-home-even-after-coronavirus/#4900e2ad38fa

Kolik, A., Radziwill, A., & Turdyeva, N. (2015). *Improving transport infrastructure in Russia.* Academic Press.

Korstjens, I., & Moser, A. (2018). Series: Practical guidance to qualitative research. Part 4: Trustworthiness and publishing. *The European Journal of General Practice, 24*(1), 120–124. doi:10.1080/13814788.2017.1375092 PMID:29202616

Kortum, S. S. (1997). Research, patenting, and technological change. *Econometrica, 65*(6), 1389–1420. doi:10.2307/2171741

Kovess-Masfety, V., Pilowsky, D. J., Goelitz, D., Kuijpers, R., Otten, R., Moro, M. F., Bitfoi, A., Koç, C., Lesinskiene, S., Mihova, Z., Hanson, G., Fermanian, C., Pez, O., & Carta, M. G. (2015). Suicidal ideation and mental health disorders in young school children across Europe. *Journal of Affective Disorders, 177,* 28–35. doi:10.1016/j.jad.2015.02.008 PMID:25745832

Kowalski, K. B., & Swanson, J. A. (2005). Critical success factors in developing teleworking programs. *Benchmarking, 12*(3), 236–249.

Kremer, M. (1993). Population growth and technological change: One million B.C. to 1990. *The Quarterly Journal of Economics, 108*(3), 681–716. doi:10.2307/2118405

Kremer, M., Rao, G., & Schilbach, F. (2019). Behavioral development economics. In D. Bernheim, St. DellaVigna, & D. Laibson (Eds.), *Handbook of Behavioral Economics: Foundations and Applications* (pp. 345–458). Elsevier. doi:10.1016/bs.hesbe.2018.12.002

Krueger, A. O. (1997). Trade policy and economic development: How we learn. *The American Economic Review, 87*(1), 1–22.

Kumar, N., & Haydon, D. (2020). *Industries most and least impacted by COVID-19 from a probability of default perspective: March 2020 update.* S&P Global Market Intelligence. Retrieved at https://www.spglobal.com/marketintelligence/en/news-insights/blog/industries-most-and-least-impacted-by-covid-19-from-a-probability-of-default-perspective-march-2020-update

Kundu, A., & Bej, T. (2021). COVID 19 response: An analysis of teachers' perception on pedagogical successes and challenges of digital teaching practice during new normal. *Education and Information Technologies, 26*(6), 1–24. doi:10.100710639-021-10503-5 PMID:33897267

Kuznets, S. (1973). Modern economic growth: Findings and reflections. *The American Economic Review, 63*(3), 247–258.

Kwak, J. (2020). The end of small business. *The Washington Post.* https://www.washingtonpost.com/outlook/2020/07/09/after-covid-19-giant-corporations-chains-may-be-only-ones-left/?arc404=true

Lagakos, D., Moll, B., Porzio, T., Qian, N., & Schoellman, T. (2014). *Life-cycle human capital accumulation across countries: Lessons from U.S. immigrants.* Cambridge, MA: National Bureau of Economic Research Working Paper 21914. Retrieved at https://www.nber.org/papers/w21914

Langa, G., & Conradie, D. (2003). Perceptions and attitudes with regard to teleworking among public sector officials in Pretoria: Applying the Technology Acceptance Model (TAM): Research case studies. *Communicatio: South African Journal of Communication Theory and Research, 29*(1-2), 280-296.

Laton, D. (2016). Manhattan_Project.Exe: A nuclear option for the digital age. *Catholic University Journal of Law & Technology, 25*(4), 94–153.

Lautsch, B. A., & Kossek, E. E. (2011). Managing a blended workforce: Telecommuters and non-telecommuters. *Organizational Dynamics, 40*(1), 10–17.

Lavelle, J. (2020). *Gartner CFO Survey Reveals 74% Intend to Shift Some Employees to Remote Work Permanently.* Retrieved on 13 August 2020 from https://www.gartner.com/en/newsroom/press-releases/2020-04-03-gartner-cfo-surey-reveals-74-percent-of-organizations-to-shift-some-employees-to-remote-work-permanently2

Leprince-Ringuet, D. (2020). *Remote working: How the biggest change to office life will happen in our homes.* Retrieved on 02 August 2020 from https://www.zdnet.com/article/remote-working-how-the-biggest-change-to-office-life-will-happen-in-our-homes/

Lerner, S. (2020). Big pharma prepares to profit from the Coronavirus: Pharmaceutical companies view the Coronavirus pandemic as a once-in-a-lifetime business opportunity. *The Intercept.* Retrieved at https://theintercept.com/2020/03/13/big-pharma-drug-pricing-coronavirus-profits

Lie, S. (2018). How best to evangelize to nonbelievers: Cultural persuasion in American and Chinese Indonesian evangelical Christian discourse on relational evangelism. *Journal of International and Intercultural Communication, 11*(1), 42–57. doi:10.1080/17513057.2017.1349920

Lincoln, Y. S., & Guba, E. G. (1985). Naturalistic Inquiry. In *The A-Z of Social Research.* Sage. doi:10.4135/9781412986281.n232

Link, S. C., & Ancoli-Israel, S. (1995). Sleep and the teenager. *Sleep Research, 24,* 184.

Lin, P., Abney, K., & Bekey, G. A. (2012). *Robot ethics: The ethical and social implications of robotics.* The MIT Press.

Liu, S. (2020). *Number of daily active users (DAU) of Microsoft Teams worldwide as of April 30.* Retrieved on 15 June 2020 from https://www.statista.com/statistics/1033742/worldwide-microsoft-teams-daily-and-monthly-users/

Loayza, N. V., & Pennings, S. (2020). *Macroeconomic Policy in the Time of COVID-19: A Primer for Developing Countries.* World Bank. doi:10.1596/33540

Long, T., & Johnson, M. (2000). Rigour, reliability and validity in qualitative research. *Clinical Effectiveness in Nursing, 4*(1), 30–37. doi:10.1054/cein.2000.0106

Lordan, O., & Sallan, J. M. (2017). Analyzing the multilevel structure of the European airport network. *Chinese Journal of Aeronautics, 30*(2), 554–560. doi:10.1016/j.cja.2017.01.013

Louraoui, S. M., Rghioui, M., & El Azhar, A. (2020). Letter to the editor: Medical Student concerns Relating to Neurosurgery Education During COVID-19: An African Experience. World Neurosurgery, 142, 553.

Lucas, R. E. (1999). Why doesn't capital flow from rich to poor countries? *The American Economic Review, 80*(5), 92–96.

Lucas, R. E. (2004). The industrial revolution: Past and future. *Annual Report of the Federal Reserve Bank of Minneapolis,* (May), 5–20.

Lucas, R. E. Jr. (1988). On the mechanics of economic development. *Journal of Monetary Economics, 22*(1), 3–42. doi:10.1016/0304-3932(88)90168-7

Lucas, R. E. Jr. (2009). Ideas and Growth. *Economica, 76*(301), 1–19. doi:10.1111/j.1468-0335.2008.00748.x

Lucas, R. E. Jr, & Moll, B. (2014). Knowledge growth and the allocation of time. *Journal of Political Economy, 122*(1), 1–51. doi:10.1086/674363

Magezi, V. (2015). Technologically Changing African Context and Usage of Information Communication and Technology in Churches: Towards Discerning Emerging Identities in Church Practice (A Case Study of Two Zimbabwean Cities). In HTS Teologiese Studies / Theological Studies (Vol. 71, Issue 2). doi:10.4102/hts.v71i2.2625

Mamelund, S. E. (2017). Social inequality–a forgotten factor in pandemic influenza preparedness. *Tidsskrift for Den Norske legeforening*.

Mankiw, N. G., Romer, D., & Weil, D. N. (1992). A contribution to the empirics of economic growth. *The Quarterly Journal of Economics*, *107*(2), 407–437. doi:10.2307/2118477

Männikkö, N., Billieux, J., Nordström, T., Koivisto, K., & Kääriäinen, M. (2017). Problematic gaming behavior in Finnish adolescents and young adults: Relation to game genres, gaming motives and self-awareness of problematic use. *International Journal of Mental Health and Addiction*, *15*(2), 324–338. doi:10.100711469-016-9726-7

Manuelli, R. E., & Seshadri, A. (2014). Human capital and the wealth of nations. *The American Economic Review*, *9*(9), 2736–2762. doi:10.1257/aer.104.9.2736 PMID:30443048

Marino, L. (2006). *Quality management and knowledge management: key factors for business productivity and competitiveness*. XIII SIMPEP.

Marks, G. (2020). *We're not all going to be working from home, nor should we. Here's why.* Retrieved on 18 June 2020 from https://www.theguardian.com/business/2020/jun/11/were-not-all-going-to-be-working-from-home-nor-should-we-heres-why

Marston, H. R., & Kowert, R. (2020). What role can videogames play in the COVID-19 pandemic? *Emerald Open Research*, *2*, 34. doi:10.35241/emeraldopenres.13727.2

Martin, L. A. (1997). *The First Step*. Massachusetts Institute of Technology. https://ocw.mit.edu/courses/sloan-school-of-management/15-988-system-dynamics-self-study-fall-1998-spring-1999/readings/step.pdf

Masoom, K. (2022, February). A Study of Influencers' Marketing and its Impact on Brand Engagement. *IJRESM*, *5*(2), 49–51.

Matobobo, C., & Bankole, F. (2020). Is the Impact of Human-Computer Interaction in Religious Organisations a Hype or Crossword? *UK Academy for Information Systems Conference Proceedings 2020*, 12. https://aisel.aisnet.org/ukais2020/12

Matobobo, C., & Bankole, F. (2021b). Evaluating eWOM in Social Media: Religious Leaders vs Religious Organizations: Functionality Approach. *UK Academy for Information Systems Conference Proceedings 2021*.

Matobobo, C., & Bankole, F. (2021a). Customizing and Implementing e-Dashboard in Religious Organisations. *Academic Journal of Current Research*, *8*(10), 1–15.

Matsuyama, K. (2000). Endogenous inequality. *The Review of Economic Studies*, *67*(4), 743–759. doi:10.1111/1467-937X.00152

Matsuyama, K. (2008). Structural change. In S. Durlauf & L. E. Blume (Eds.), *The New Palgrave Dictionary of Economics, pp.* Palgrave-Macmillan. doi:10.1057/978-1-349-95121-5_1775-2

Matsuyama, K. (2011). Imperfect credit markets, household wealth distribution, and development. *Annual Review of Economics, 3*(1), 339–362. doi:10.1146/annurev-economics-111809-125054

Mattern, F., Staake, T., & Weiss, M. (2010). ICT for green: How computers can help us to conserve energy. *Proceedings of the 1st international conference on energy-efficient computing and networking.*

Mauss, M. (1979). A category of the human mind: The notion of the person, the notion of 'self. In M. Mauss (Ed.), *Sociology and Psychology* (pp. 81–103). Routledge.

Mayer-Schönberger, V. (2009). *Delete: The virtue of forgetting in the digital age.* Princeton University Press.

Meghdari, A., & Alemi, M. (2018). Recent advances in social & cognitive robotics and imminent ethical challenges. In *Proceedings of the 10th International RAIS Conference on Social Sciences and Humanities.* The Scientific Press. 10.2991/rais-18.2018.12

Melone, N. P. (1990). A Theoretical Assessmenot f the User-Satisfaction Construct in Information Systems Research. *Management Science, 36*(1), 76–91.

Microsoft. (2020). *Remote work trend report: Meetings.* Retrieved on 13 May 2020 from https://www.microsoft.com/en-us/microsoft-365/blog/2020/04/09/remote-work-trend-report-meetings/?wt.mc_id=AID2409697_QSG_SCL_424041&ocid=AID2409697_QSG_SCL_424041

Milanovic, B. (2013). Global income inequality in numbers: In history and now. *Global Policy, 4*(2), 198–208. doi:10.1111/1758-5899.12032

Min, H. (2006). The applications of warehouse management systems: An exploratory study. *International Journal of Logistics: Research and Applications, 9*(2), 111–126. doi:10.1080/13675560600661870

Moavenzadeh, J. (2015). *The 4th industrial revolution: Reshaping the future of production.* World Economic Forum.

Moore, R. L., & Fodrey, B. P. (2018). Distance education and technology infrastructure: Strategies and opportunities. In A. A. Piña, V. L. Lowell, & B. R. Harris (Eds.), *Leading and Managing e-Learning* (pp. 87–100). Springer International Publishing. doi:10.1007/978-3-319-61780-0_7

Morrison, J. (2017). *Explaining the Intention of IT Workers to Telework: A South African Perspective* (Masters Dissertation). University of Cape Town.

Morrison, J. (2017). *Explaining the intention of IT workers to telework: A South African perspective.* University of Cape Town.

MS. (2013). *From cost center to growth center: Warehousing 2018* (Tech. Rep.). Motorola Solutions.

Mumford, A. (2001). *Taxing culture.* Ashgate.

Murphy, C. (2020). *Facebook employees could receive pay cuts as they continue to work from home.* Retrieved on 10 June 2020 from https://www.usatoday.com/story/tech/2020/05/21/facebook-pay-cuts-employees-could-have-reduced-salaries-if-they-move/5239532002/

Murphy, K. M., Riddell, W. C., & Romer, P. M. (1998). *Wages, skills, and technology in the United States and Canada.* Cambridge, MA: National Bureau of Economic Research (NBER) Working Paper 6638. Retrieved at https://www.nber.org/papers/w6638.pdf

Nabavi, E., Daniell, K. A., & Najafi, H. (2017). Boundary matters: The potential of system dynamics to support sustainability? *Journal of Cleaner Production, 140,* 312–323. doi:10.1016/j.jclepro.2016.03.032

Naidoo, R. (2020). A multi-level influence model of COVID-19 themed cybercrime. *European Journal of Information Systems, 29*(3), 1–17. doi:10.1080/0960085X.2020.1771222

Nayar, K. B., & Kumar, V. (2018). Cost benefit analysis of cloud computing in education. *International Journal of Business Information Systems, 27*(2), 205. doi:10.1504/IJBIS.2018.089112

Neirotti, P., Paolucci, E., & Raguseo, E. (2011). *Diffusion of telework: Myth or reality? Some stylized facts on telework diffusion in Italian firms.* Paper presented at the Mobile Business.

Ngai, L. R., & Pissarides, Ch. A. (2007). Structural change in a multi-sector model of growth. *The American Economic Review, 97*(1), 429–443. doi:10.1257/aer.97.1.429

Nie, N. H., & Hillygus, D. S. (2002). Where does Internet time come from? A reconnaissance. *ITandSociety, 1*(2), 1–20.

Nilles, J. M. (1975). Telecommunications and organizational decentralization. *IEEE Transactions on Communications, 23*(10), 1142–1147.

Nilles, J. M. (1991). Telecommuting and urban sprawl: Mitigator or inciter? *Transportation, 18*(4), 411–432.

Noble, H., & Smith, J. (2015). Issues of validity and reliability in qualitative research. *Evidence-Based Nursing, 18*(2), 34–35. doi:10.1136/eb-2015-102054 PMID:25653237

Novaes, D. R., Souza, D. C., de Veras Filial, M. A., Giordano, C. V., & Gonçalves, L. C. (2016). Implementation of wms technology in a 3pl. *Eniac, 5*(2), 223–239. doi:10.22567/rep.v5i2.386

Novotny, A. (2004). The Present and Future of Teleworking. *6th International Conference on Applied Informatics.*

Noyes, K. (2016). 5 things you need to know about A.I.: Cognitive, neural and deep, oh my! *Computerworld.* Retrieved at www.computerworld.com/article/3040563/enterprise-applications/5-things-you-need-toknow-about-ai-cognitive-neural-anddeep-oh-my.html

Offstein, E. H., Morwick, J. M., & Koskinen, L. (2010). Making telework work: Leading people and leveraging technology for competitive advantage. *Strategic HR Review,* (9), 32–37.

Olu, O., Muneene, D., Bataringaya, J. E., Nahimana, M. R., Ba, H., Turgeon, Y., & Dovlo, D. (2019). How can digital health technologies contribute to sustainable attainment of universal health coverage in Africa? A perspective. *Frontiers in Public Health*, *341*, 341. Advance online publication. doi:10.3389/fpubh.2019.00341 PMID:31803706

Owoyemi, A., Owoyemi, J., Osiyemi, A., & Boyd, A. (2020). Artificial intelligence for healthcare in Africa. *Frontiers in Digital Health*, *2*, 6. doi:10.3389/fdgth.2020.00006 PMID:34713019

Palinkas, L. A., Horwitz, S. M., Green, C. A., Wisdom, J. P., Duan, N., & Hoagwood, K. (2015). Purposeful sampling for qualitative data collection and analysis in mixed method implementation research. *Administration and Policy in Mental Health*, *42*(5), 533–544. doi:10.100710488-013-0528-y PMID:24193818

Parente, St. & Prescott, E. (1993). Changes in the wealth of nations. *Quarterly Review of Economics, 17*(2), 3-16.

Pee, L. G., Pan, S. L., Wang, J., & Wu, J. (2021). Designing for the future in the age of pandemics: A future-ready design research (FRDR) process. *European Journal of Information Systems*, *30*(2), 157–175. doi:10.1080/0960085X.2020.1863751

Peigneux, P., Laureys, S., Delbeuck, X., & Maquet, P. (2001). Sleeping brain, learning brain. The role of sleep for memory systems. *Neuroreport*, *12*(18), A111–A124. doi:10.1097/00001756-200112210-00001 PMID:11742260

Pervin, N., Fang, F., Datta, A., Dutta, K., & Vandermeer, D. (2013). Fast, Scalable, and Context-sensitive Detection of Trending Topics in Microblog Post Streams. *ACM Transactions on Management Information Systems*, *3*(4), 1–24. doi:10.1145/2407740.2407743

Petri, F. (2009). *On the recent debate on capital theory and general equilibrium*. Quaderni del Dipartimento di Economia Politica, Università di Siena.

Pfleeger, S. L., & Caputo, D. D. (2012). Leveraging behavioral science to mitigate cyber security risk. *Computers & Security*, *31*(4), 597–611. doi:10.1016/j.cose.2011.12.010

Philipsen, B., Tondeur, J., Pareja Roblin, N., Vanslambrouck, S., & Zhu, C. (2019). Improving teacher professional development for online and blended learning: A systematic meta-aggregative review. *Educational Technology Research and Development*, *67*(5), 1145–1174. doi:10.100711423-019-09645-8

Piketty, Th. (1997). The dynamics of the wealth distribution and the interest rate with credit rationing. *The Review of Economic Studies*, *64*(2), 173–189. doi:10.2307/2971708

Piketty, Th. (2016). *Capital in the Twenty-First Century*. Harvard University Press.

Piña, A. A. (2018). An Educational Leader's View of Learning Management Systems. In A. A. Piña, V. L. Lowell, & B. R. Harris (Eds.), *Leading and Managing e-Learning* (pp. 101–113). Springer International Publishing. doi:10.1007/978-3-319-61780-0_8

Posso, A. (2016). Internet usage and educational outcomes among 15-year old Australian students. *International Journal of Communication, 10*, 26.

Price, L. (2020). *Impact of COVID-19 on small businesses: Where is it worst?* Small Business Trends. Retrieved at https://smallbiztrends.com/2020/04/impact-of-coronavirus-on-small-businesses.html

Pritchett, L. (1997). Divergence, big time. *The Journal of Economic Perspectives, 11*(3), 3–17. doi:10.1257/jep.11.3.3

Puaschunder, J. M. (2018a). *Artificial Intelligence Evolution: On the virtue of killing in the artificial age.* Social Science Research Network working paper. https://papers.ssrn.com/sol3/papers.cfm?abstract_id=3247401

Puaschunder, J. M. (2019b). *Artificial Intelligence, big data, and algorithms in healthcare.* Report on behalf of the European Parliament European Liberal Forum in cooperation with The New Austria and Liberal Forum. Retrieved at https://papers.ssrn.com/sol3/papers.cfm?abstract_id=3472885

Puaschunder, J. M. (2020b). Economic growth in times of pandemics. *Proceedings of the ConScienS Conference on Science & Society: Pandemics and their Impact on Society*, 1-9. 10.2139srn.3679359

Puaschunder, J. M. (2020c). The future of the city after COVID-19: Digitionalization, preventism and environmentalism. *Proceedings of the ConScienS Conference on Science & Society: Pandemics and their Impact on Society*, 125-129.

Puaschunder, J. M. (2021a). Alleviating COVID-19 inequality. *ConScienS Conference Proceedings*, 185-190.

Puaschunder, J. M., Gelter, M., & Sharma, S. (2020b). COVID-19 shock: Considerations on socio-technological, legal, corporate, economic and governance changes and trends. *Proceedings of the 18th International Research Association for Interdisciplinary Studies Conference on Social Sciences & Humanities*, 82-93. Retrieved at http://rais.education/wp-content/uploads/2020/08/011JPB.pdf

Puaschunder, J.M. (2016). Putty capital and clay labor: Differing European Union capital and labor freedom speeds in times of European migration. *The New School Economic Review: A Journal of Critical Economics at The New School, 8*(3), 147-168.

Puaschunder, J. M. (2017a). Nudging in the digital big data era. European Journal of Economics. *Law and Politics, 4*(4), 18–23.

Puaschunder, J. M. (2017b). Nudgital: Critique of Behavioral Political Economy. *Archives of Business Research, 5*(9), 54–76. doi:10.14738/abr.59.3623

Puaschunder, J. M. (2017c). Nudgitize me! A behavioral finance approach to minimize losses and maximize profits from heuristics and biases. *International Journal of Management Excellence, 10*(2), 1241–1256. doi:10.17722/ijme.v10i2.957

Puaschunder, J. M. (2018b). Nudgitize me! A behavioral finance approach to minimize losses and maximize profits from heuristics and biases. *Journal of Organizational Psychology, 18*(1), 46–66.

Puaschunder, J. M. (2019a). Artificial diplomacy: A guide for public officials to conduct Artificial Intelligence. *Journal of Applied Research in the Digital Economy, 1*, 39–45. doi:10.2139srn.3376302

Puaschunder, J. M. (2019c). Towards a utility theory of privacy and information sharing and the introduction of hyper-hyperbolic discounting in the digital big data age. In E. Idemudia (Ed.), *Handbook of Research on Social and Organizational Dynamics in the Digital Era* (pp. 157–200). IGI Publishing.

Puaschunder, J. M. (2020a). *Behavioral Economics and Finance Leadership: Nudging and Winking to make Better Choices.* Springer Nature. doi:10.1007/978-3-030-54330-3

Puaschunder, J. M. (2021b). Generation COVID-19 Long Haulers. *Scientia Moralitas Conference Proceedings*, 99-104.

Puaschunder, J. M. (2021c). *Verhaltensökonomie und Verhaltensfinanzökonomie: Ein Vergleich europäischer und nordamerikanischer Modelle.* Springer Gabler. doi:10.1007/978-3-658-32474-2

Puaschunder, J. M. (forthcoming). The future of Artificial Intelligence in international healthcare: Integrating technology, productivity, anti-corruption and healthcare interaction around the world with three indices. *Journal of Applied Research in the Digital Economy.* Advance online publication. doi:10.2139srn.3633951

Puaschunder, J. M., & Gelter, M. (2021). The law, economics and governance of generation COVID-19 Long-Haul. *Indiana Health Law Review / [Indiana University School of Law-Indianapolis], 19*(1), 47–126. doi:10.18060/26085

Puaschunder, J. M., Gelter, M., & Sharma, S. (2020a). Alleviating an unequal COVID-19 world: Globally digital and productively healthy. *Proceedings of the 1st Unequal World Conference: On Human Development.*

Pyöriä, P. (2011). Managing telework: Risks, fears and rules. *Management Research Review, 34*(4), 386–399.

Rajan, R. G., & Zingales, L. (1998). Financial dependence and growth. *The American Economic Review, 88*(3), 559–586.

Restuccia, D., & Rogerson, R. (2017). The causes and costs of misallocation. *The Journal of Economic Perspectives, 31*(3), 151–174. doi:10.1257/jep.31.3.151

Restuccia, D., & Urrutia, C. (2001). Relative prices and investment rates. *Journal of Monetary Economics, 47*(1), 93–121. doi:10.1016/S0304-3932(00)00049-0

Rikunoa, S. E. A. (2015). Conditions and factors of economic growth in russia at the present stage of development. Voronezh State Industrial and Economic College, 194(5), 81–88.

Robinson, A. (2020). *Working from home: hello space as a service*. Retrieved on 01 August 2020 from https://www.iol.co.za/business-report/economy/working-from-home-hello-space-as-a-service-50294773

Rogers, F. H., & Sabarwal, S. (2020). *The COVID-19 pandemic: Shocks to education and policy responses*. Academic Press.

Romer, P. M. (2019). *Nobel Lecture: On the possibility of progress*. Retrieved at https://paulromer.net/prize/

Romer, P. M. (1986). Increasing returns and long-term growth. *Journal of Political Economy, 94*(5), 1002–1037. doi:10.1086/261420

Romer, P. M. (1987). Growth based on increasing returns to specialization. *The American Economic Review, 77*(2), 56–62.

Romer, P. M. (1990). Endogenous Technological Change. *Journal of Political Economy, 98*(5), 71–102. doi:10.1086/261725

Romer, P. M. (1993). Idea gaps and object gaps in economic development. *Journal of Monetary Economics, 32*(3), 543–573. doi:10.1016/0304-3932(93)90029-F

Romer, P. M. (1994). New goods, old theory, and the welfare costs of trade restrictions. *Journal of Development Economics, 43*(1), 5–38. doi:10.1016/0304-3878(94)90021-3

Rosenbaum, E. (2019, April 9). *Tech spending will near $4 trillion this year. Here's where all the money is going and why*. CNBC. Retrieved from https://www.cnbc.com/2019/04/08/4-trillion-in-tech-spending-in-2019-heres-where-the-money-is-going.html

Roy, S., & Covelli, B. (2020). COVID-19 induced transition from classroom to online mid semester: Case study on faculty and students' preferences and opinions. *Higher Learning Research Communications, 2020*(0), 10–32. doi:10.18870/hlrc.v11i0.1197

Rubinstein, C. (2020). *Beware: Remote Work Involves These 3 Cyber Security Risks*. Retrieved on 24 August 2020 from https://www.forbes.com/sites/carrierubinstein/2020/04/10/beware-remote-work-involves-these-3-cyber-security-risks/#2df630c661c4

Russell, St., & Norvig, P. (1995). *Artificial intelligence a modern approach*. Simon & Schuster.

Ryan, G. (2018). Introduction to positivism, interpretivism and critical theory. *Nurse Researcher, 25*(4), 14–20. doi:10.7748/nr.2018.e1466 PMID:29546962

Saffari, E., Meghdari, A., Vazirnezhad, B., & Alemi, M. (2015). Ava (a social robot): Design and performance of a robotic hearing apparatus. LNCS: Social Robotics, 9388, 440-450.

Sahay, B. S., Mohan, R., & Maini, A. (2004). Strategies for building a sustainable competitive edge. *International Journal of Innovation and Learning, 1*(3), 209. doi:10.1504/IJIL.2004.004879

Said, B., Hajar, E., & Amine, S. (2020). The COVID-19 outbreak: A catalyst for digitalization in African countries. *The Journal of the Egyptian Public Health Association, 95*(1).

Sargeant, K. H. (2000). *Seeker Churches: Promoting Traditional Religion in a Nontraditional Way*. Rutgers University Press.

Saunders, M., Lewis, P., & Thornhill, A. (2019). *Research methods for business students*. Pearson Education.

Schumpeter, J. A. (1934). *The theory of economic development*. Harvard University Press.

Schumpeter, J. A. (1943/1976). *Capitalism, socialism and democracy*. Allen & Unwin.

Schumpeter, J. A. (1989). *Essays on entrepreneurs, innovations, business cycles, and the evolution of capitalism*. Routledge.

Schwab, K., & Forum, W. E. (2013). *The global competitiveness report 2013-2014*. World Economic Forum.

Sein, M. K. (2020). The serendipitous impact of the COVID-19 pandemic: A rare opportunity for research and practice. *International Journal of Information Management*, *55*, 102164. doi:10.1016/j.ijinfomgt.2020.102164 PMID:32836630

Shao, G. (2009). Understanding the Appeal of User-generated Media: A Uses and Gratification Perspective. *Internet Research*, *19*(1), 7–25. doi:10.1108/10662240910927795

Sigarev, A. V., Kosov, M. E., Buzdalina, O. B., Alandarov, R. A., & Rykova, I. N. (2018). *The role of chains in the Russian retail sector*. Academic Press.

Silva, M. (2018). *Fashion retail: Branding and marketing strategies communication* (Unpublished master's thesis). University of Beira Interior, Portugal.

Smith, C. (2001). Sleep states and memory processes in humans: Procedural versus declarative memory systems. *Sleep Medicine Reviews*, *5*(6), 491–506. doi:10.1053mrv.2001.0164 PMID:12531156

Sofge, E. (2015). Bill Gates fears A.I., but A.I. researchers know better. *Popular Science*. Retrieved at www.popsci.com/bill-gates-fears-ai-ai-researchers-know-better

Solow, R. (1956). A contribution to the theory of economic growth. *The Quarterly Journal of Economics*, *70*(1), 65–94. doi:10.2307/1884513

Solum, L. (1992). Legal personhood for Artificial Intelligences. *North Carolina Law Review*, *70*(4), 1231–1287.

Speed, R. (2021, April 7). *How big might IT spending get in 2021? Gartner: How about $4 trillion. And no, you can't have a new MacBook*. The Register. Retrieved from https://www.theregister.com/2021/04/07/gartner_worldwide_it_spend/

Squire, L. R. (1992). Declarative and nondeclarative memory: Multiple brain systems supporting learning and memory. *Journal of Cognitive Neuroscience*, *4*(3), 232–243. doi:10.1162/jocn.1992.4.3.232 PMID:23964880

Statista. (2020) *Increase in video game sales during the coronavirus (COVID-19) pandemic worldwide as of March 2020.* https://www.statista.com/statistics/1109977/video-gamesales-covid/

Sternam, J. D. (2002). System Dynamics: Systems Thinking and Modeling for a Complex World. MIT Sloan School of Management.

Stiglitz, J. (1998). The private uses of public interests: Incentives and institutions. *The Journal of Economic Perspectives*, *12*(2), 3–22. doi:10.1257/jep.12.2.3

St-Onge, C., Ouellet, K., Lakhal, S., Dubé, T., & Marceau, M. (2021). COVID-19 as the tipping point for integrating e-assessment in higher education practices. *British Journal of Educational Technology*. Advance online publication. doi:10.1111/bjet.13169 PMID:34898680

Stroebe, W., & Frey, B. S. (1982). Self-interest and collective action: The economics and psychology of public goods. *British Journal of Social Psychology*, *21*(2), 121–137. doi:10.1111/j.2044-8309.1982.tb00521.x

Sturm, M., Junghanns, J., & Eichstedt, M. (2014). *Next stop digital: How logistics service providers can rethink operating models to benefit from emerging technology.* Verfügbar. https://www. accenture. com/t20150523T030128__w__/my-en/_acnmedia/Accenture/Conversion-Assets/DotCom/Documents/Global/PDF/Dualpub_4/Accen ture-Digital-Future-For-LSPs. pdf

Swiecki, T. (2017). Determinants of structural change. *Review of Economic Dynamics*, *17*(24), 95–131. doi:10.1016/j.red.2017.01.007

Tafesse, W., & Wood, B. P. (2020). Followers' engagement with instagram influencers: The role of influencers' content and engagement strategy. *Journal of Retailing and Consumer Services*, *58*, 102303. doi:10.1016/j.jretconser.2020.102303

Takahashi, Y. (2015). System Dynamics. In *Encyclopedia of Information Science and Technology* (3rd ed., pp. 1261–1272). IGI Global. doi:10.4018/978-1-4666-5888-2.ch120

Tan, W. J., Zhao, X., & Ma, X. J. (2020). A novel coronavirus genome identified in a cluster of pneumonia cases—Wuhan, China 2019–2020. *China CDC Weekly*, *2*, 61–62. doi:10.46234/ccdcw2020.017 PMID:34594763

Taro, L. (1999). *Baltic economies in 1998-1999: effects of the russian financial crisis.* Bank of Finland.

Tartaro, M. (2003). Best practices for supporting home users. *Network Computing*, *14*(11), 73–76.

Tcherneva, P. (2011). Bernanke's paradox: Can he reconcile his position on the federal budget with his charge to prevent deflation? *Journal of Post Keynesian Economics*, *3*(33), 411–434. doi:10.2753/PKE0160-3477330301

The Economist. (2019, Jan. 26). The steam has gone out of globalisation: Slowbalisation. *The Economist*, 17-20.

The White House of The United States of America. (2021). *Fact Sheet: Biden-Harris Administration Marks Anniversary of Americans with Disabilities Act and Announces Resources to Support Individuals with Long COVID.* https://www.whitehouse.gov/briefing-room/statements-releases/2021/07/26/fact-sheet-bidenharris-administration-marks-anniversary-of-americans-with-disabilities-act-and-announces-resources-tosupport-individuals-with-long-covid/

The White House of The United States of America. (2021). Retrieved at https://www.whitehouse.gov/briefing-room/legislation/2021/01/20/president-biden-announces-american-rescue-plan/

The World Economic Forum. (2021). *The World Economic Forum Great Reset.* https://www.weforum.org/great-reset/

Themistoklis, T. (2018). Artificial intelligence as global commons and the "international law supremacy" principle. In *Proceedings of the 10th International RAIS Conference on Social Sciences and Humanities.* The Scientific Press.

Thilakarathne, N. N., Kagita, M. K., Gadekallu, T. R., & Maddikunta, P. K. R. (2020). *The adoption of ICT-powered healthcare technologies towards managing global pandemics.* arXiv preprint arXiv:2009.05716.

Thomas, D. R. (2017). Feedback from research participants: Are member checks useful in qualitative research? *Qualitative Research in Psychology, 14*(1), 23–41. doi:10.1080/14780887.2016.1219435

Thompson, C. (2020). *What If Working From Home Goes on … Forever?* Retrieved on 20 June 2020 from https://www.nytimes.com/interactive/2020/06/09/magazine/remote-work-covid.html

Thong, J. Y. L., Hong, S.-J., & Tam, K. Y. (2006). The effects of post-adoption beliefs on the expectation-confirmation model for information technology continuance. *International Journal of Human-Computer Studies, 64*(9), 799–810.

Thornton, A., & Koech, J. (2018). Building an e-learning center from the ground up: The challenges and lessons learned. In A. A. Piña, V. L. Lowell, & B. R. Harris (Eds.), *Leading and Managing e-Learning* (pp. 73–85). Springer International Publishing. doi:10.1007/978-3-319-61780-0_6

Tomalin, E. (2018). Religions, poverty reduction and global development institutions. *Palgrave Communications, 4*(1), 132. Advance online publication. doi:10.105741599-018-0167-8

Top 10 company in the corporate world. (2021, July 5). *InnovativeZone.* Retrieved from https://innovativezoneindia.com/top-10-company-in-the-world/

Townsend, R. M., & Ueda, K. (2006). Financial deepening, inequality, and growth: A model-based quantitative evaluation. *The Review of Economic Studies, 73*(1), 251–293. doi:10.1111/j.1467-937X.2006.00376.x

UNESCO. (2020). *Education from disruption to recovery.* UNESCO Blogs. Retrieved May 20, 2020, from https://en.unesco.org/covid19/educationresponse

UNESCO. (2020, April). *Distance learning strategies in response to COVID-19 school closures* (Programme and Meeting Document ED/2020/IN2.1/REV). Retrieved from the United Nations Educational, Scientific, and Cultural Organization website: https://unesdoc.unesco.org/ark:/48223/pf0000373305/PDF/373305eng.pdf.multi

United Nations Department of Economic and Social Affairs. (2017). *Will robots and AI cause mass unemployment? Not necessarily, but they do bring other threats.* https://www.un.org/development/desa/en/news/policy/will-robots-and-ai-cause-mass-unemployment-not-necessarily-but-they-do-bring-other-threats.html

Uzawa, H. (1965). Optimum technical change in an aggregate model of economic growth. *International Economic Review, 6*(1), 18–31. doi:10.2307/2525621

Valdes, M., Rios, D., Rocha, A., & Rodriquez, K. (2021). Sleep Irregularity and Academic Performance. *Optometric Education, 46*(2).

Van der Merwe, F. (2012). Enablers and moderators of telework: assessing the maturity of telework practices in organisations (Honour). University of Cape Town.

Van Neuss, L. (2019). The drivers of structural change. *Journal of Economic Surveys, 33*(1), 309–349. doi:10.1111/joes.12266

Venkatesh, V., Morris, M. G., & Davis, F. D. (2014). Individual-level technology adoption research: An assessment of the strengths, weaknesses, threats, and opportunities for further research contributions. In H. Topi & A. Tucker (Eds.), Computing Handbook: Information Systems and Information Technology (3rd ed., pp. 38-1-38–25). CRC Press.

Ventura, L. (2021, August 3). *World's Largest Companies 2021.* Global Finance. Retrieved from https://www.gfmag.com/global-data/economic-data/largest-companies

Ventura, J. (1997). Growth and interdependence. *The Quarterly Journal of Economics, 112*(1), 57–84. doi:10.1162/003355397555127

Vivek, K., & Bhattacharjee, P. (2021). *Use of information and communication technologies in education: Effectively integrating technology in under-resourced education systems.* World Bank. doi:10.1596/35423

Voskoglou, M. G. (2016). Problem-solving in the forthcoming era of the third industrial revolution. *International Journal of Psychological Research, 10*(4), 361–380.

Walker, C. L. (1989). Correlational Research. *Journal of Pediatric Oncology Nursing, 6*(1), 21–22. doi:10.1177/104345428900600108 PMID:2921740

Walters, J. P., Archer, D. W., Sassenrath, G. F., Hendrickson, J. R., Hanson, J. D., Halloran, J. M., Vadas, P., & Alarcon, V. J. (2016). Exploring agricultural production systems and their fundamental components with system dynamics modelling. *Ecological Modelling, 333*, 51–65. doi:10.1016/j.ecolmodel.2016.04.015

Wang, C., Jin, X. L., Zhou, Z., Fang, Y., Lee, M. K. O., & Hua, Z. (2015). Effect of Perceived Media Capability on Status Updates in Microblogs. *Electronic Commerce Research and Applications*, *14*(3), 181–191. doi:10.1016/j.elerap.2014.11.006

Wang, L., Wang, Y., Ye, D., & Liu, Q. (2020). A review of the 2019 Novel Coronavirus (COVID-19) based on current evidence. *International Journal of Antimicrobial Agents*, *105948*(6), 105948. Advance online publication. doi:10.1016/j.ijantimicag.2020.105948 PMID:32826129

Wease, G., Boateng, K., Yu, C.-J., Chan, L., & Barham, H. (2018). Technology assessment: Cloud service adoption decision. In T. U. Daim, L. Chan, & J. Estep (Eds.), *Infrastructure and Technology Management: Contributions from the Energy, Healthcare and Transportation Sectors* (pp. 447–471). Springer. doi:10.1007/978-3-319-68987-6_16

Wee, D., Kelly, R., Cattel, J., & Breunig, M. (2015). Industry 4.0-how to navigate digitization of the manufacturing sector. McKinsey & Company.

Westerlund, M., & Leminen, S. (2012). Categorizing the Growth Strategies of Small Firms. *Technology Innovation Management Review*, 5–9. https://doaj.org/article/37533f7a928d48dc85294090f648f8ff

White, P., Tella, F., & Ampofo, M. D. (2016). A missional study of the use of social media (Facebook) by some Ghanaian pentecostal pastors. *Koers*, *81*(2), 1–8. doi:10.19108/KOERS.81.2.2250

WHO. (2020). *Protect yourself and others from the spread COVID-19*. Retrieved on 27 July 2020 from https://www.who.int/emergencies/diseases/novel-coronavirus-2019/advice-for-public

Wijman, T. (2019) *The global games market will generate $152.1 billion in 2019 as the U.S. overtakes China as the biggest market.* https://newzoo.com/insights/articles/theglobal-games-market-will-generate-152-1-billion-in-2019-as-the-u-s-overtakes-china-as-the-biggest-market/

Wilson, B. R. (2017). The Depiction of Church Growth in Acts. *Journal of the Evangelical Theological Society*, *60*(2), 317–332. https://search-proquest-com.ezproxy.regent.edu/docview/1964553500/fulltextPDF/D5E30159B0CE4128PQ/1?accountid=13479

Wilson, O. W. A., Holland, K. E., Elliott, L. D., Duffey, M., & Bopp, M. (2021). The impact of COVID-19 pandemic on US college students' physical activity and mental health. *Journal of Physical Activity & Health*, *18*(3), 272–278. doi:10.1123/jpah.2020-0325 PMID:33601332

Winnie Byanyima. (2022). *How to beat pandemics*. Accessed at https://blogs.lse.ac.uk/covid19/2022/04/06/the-uns-winnie-byanyima-how-to-beat-pandemics/

World Economic Forum. (2015). *Managing the risk and impact of future epidemics: Options for public-private cooperation*. Industry Agenda reports. Available at: https://www3.weforum.org/docs/WEF_Managing_Risk_Epidemics_report_2015.pdf

World Economic Outlook. (2018). *Groups and Aggregates Information*. World Economic Outlook, Database—WEO. Available at https://en.wikipedia.org/wiki/Developing_country#cite_note-107

World Health Organization. (2011). *Implementation of the International Health Regulations (2005): report by the Director-General*. World Health Organization.

World Health Organization. (2020). Coronavirus disease (COVID-19): Situation report. WHO.

World Health Organization. (2022). *Novel coronavirus (2019-nCoV) situation reports*. https://www.who.int/emergencies/diseases/novel-coronavirus-2019/situation-reports

Wright, J. (2011). The effects of video game play on academic performance. *Modern Psychological Studies, 17*(1), 37–44.

Wu, A. H. (2018). Gendered language on the economics job market rumors forum. *American Economic Association Papers and Proceedings, 108*, 175–179. doi:10.1257/pandp.20181101

Xie, X., Siau, K., & Nah, F. F.-H. (2020). COVID-19 pandemic – online education in the new normal and the next normal. *Journal of Information Technology Case and Application Research, 22*(3), 175–187. doi:10.1080/15228053.2020.1824884

Xing, Y., Grant, D. B., McKinnon, A. C., & Fernie, J. (2010). Physical distribution service quality in online retailing. *International Journal of Physical Distribution & Logistics Management, 40*(5), 415–432. doi:10.1108/09600031011052859

Yasmin, N., & Grundmann, P. (2019). Pre- and Post-Adoption Beliefs about the Diffusion and Continuation of Biogas-Based Cooking Fuel Technology in Pakistan. *MDPI*, 16.

Yilmazkuday, H. (2020). Coronavirus Disease 2019 and the Global Economy. *Transport Policy, 120*, 40–46. doi:10.1016/j.tranpol.2022.03.003 PMID:35280846

Young, J. (2020). *Scenes from college classes forced online by COVID-19*. Available at https://www.edsurge.com/news/2020-03-26-scenes-from-college-classes-forced-online-by-COVID-19

Yu, K. H., Beam, A. L., & Kohane, I. S. (2018). Artificial intelligence in healthcare. *Nature Biomedical Engineering, 2*(10), 719–731. doi:10.103841551-018-0305-z PMID:31015651

Zambrano-Monserrate, M. A., Ruano, M. A., & Sanchez-Alcalde, L. (2020). Indirect effects of COVID-19 on the environment. *The Science of the Total Environment*.

About the Contributors

Dr. Efosa C. Idemudia, an internationally known scholar, is a Professor of Business Data Analytics/Information Systems at Arkansas Tech University. In addition, Dr. Idemudia is the Program Coordinator for Business Data Analytics and Marketing at Arkansas Tech University. Dr. Idemudia holds degrees from universities located on three different continents: a PhD in Management Information Systems from Texas Tech University, a Master's in Computer Information Systems from the University of Texas at El Paso, and an MBA in International Business from the Helsinki School of Economics and Business Administration; he completed his Fulbright at the Lagos Business School and Carnegie Fellow at Covenant University.He participated as a member of the University System of Georgia's Academic Advisory Committee for Computer Disciplines for five years and is a member of Strathmore Who's Who of Professionals. Dr. Idemudia taught both graduate and undergraduate students as a visiting scholar in the Computer Information Systems (CIS) Department at Georgia State University, which the U.S. News & World Report ranked within the top ten CIS departments in the United States.

Tiko Iyamu holds a PhD in Information Systems. He is currently a Research Professor at the faculty of Informatics and Design, Cape Peninsula University of Technology, Cape Town, South Africa. He was previously with the Tshwane University of Technology, South Africa and the Namibia University of Science and Technology, Windhoek, Namibia. Prior to his fulltime appointment in academic in 2009, Professor Iyamu held several positions in both Public and Private Institutions in South Africa. Professor Iyamu has authored books, and research articles in book chapters, journals, and conference proceedings.

Patrick Ndayizigamiye obtained his PhD (Information Systems and Technology) from the University of KwaZulu-Natal in South Africa. Patrick is currently employed as a Senior Lecturer at the University of Johannesburg in South Africa and is the ICT4D research cluster leader at the University of Johannesburg. He has more than 8 years of experience in teaching information systems modules and has published in international journals and conference proceedings. He has also presented his research outputs at many local and international conferences. He is currently an associate editor for the African Journal of Information Systems and has been a Track Program Committee (TCP) member of many reputable international conferences. Patrick is also a member of the Association for Information systems (AIS) and the South African Institute of Computer Scientists and Information Technologists (SAICSIT). His current research interest is in the design and deployment of ICT-led interventions to provide healthcare services in Resource-Limited Settings. He is also conducting research in ICT4D and Cybersecurity.

Irja Naambo Shaanika holds a Master's degree in Informatics from Namibia University of Science and Technology (NUST) formerly known as polytechnic of Namibia. Research areas include health informatics, information systems, IT, enterprise architecture.

* * *

Abiodun (Abbey) Alao obtained her Doctor of Philosophy in Information Systems at the University of Cape Town. She has been an active researcher and teaching fellow at various South African Universities. Abiodun is passionate about research and keen to demonstrate her academic capabilities in academia. She is currently a research associate at the University of Johannesburg. She has mentored and supervised projects that focus on Management Information Systems, Information and Communication Technology for Development, Sustainable ICT, Development Communication, Innovative Management, Health Informatics, Information Learning, and Work Integrated Learning (WIL). She has written journals, chapters, and conference papers using a multidisciplinary investigative approach, and Information Communication Technology (ICT) as a pathway to information and knowledge management on various issues related to the social implications of ICTs that affect the well-being of people and society.

Simon Bourdeau is an Associate Professor of MIS at ESG-UQAM, Montreal, Canada since 2012. He holds a Ph.D. in information systems from HEC Montreal and is an active member of several research groups and centers, including CIRANO and GReSI. His research interests focus on IS project management, project team dynamics, operational risk, strategic planning and innovation. Since 2013, he has been a Serious Play ™ certified Lego Facilitator © and he uses Serious Play methodologies in teaching and in research, as well as in trainings offered to private and public organizations.

Leigh Breda holds an Honours degree in Information Systems from UCT. He is currently completing his Masters in Information Systems. He has work in both the private and public sector specialising in End User Computing. His research interests include Teleworking, Cloud computing and their impact on Society

Roelien Brink is the Deputy Head of Department: (CEP, SLPs, and Online) and lectures in the Department of Applied Information Systems. She holds a Ph.D. from the University of Johannesburg, South Africa, with a focus on information management for the work-integrated learning process. She is a member of Universities South Africa (USAF), World of Work Strategy Group, and Partner of Work-Integrated Learning South Africa (WILSA) under the auspices of THE NSA. She has been involved in Work Integrated Learning for 13 years and obtained her Ph.D. in Information Management with the title: An Information Management Framework for the Work-Integrated Learning Process. Prof Roelien Brink is currently involved in research on Work Integrated Learning (WIL), which is conducted in Ireland and South Africa. She is the lead researcher for WILSA on environmental scan research of the Work-Integrated Learning landscape in South Africa. She is the Vice Chair of Africa on the International Research Group for the World Association for Cooperative Education (WACE) – Research work-integrated learning. She was part of the advisory board for the World Association for Cooperative Education (WACE) Second International Research Symposium 2016. She is also part of the international review team for the WACE 2nd International Research Symposium, the WACE 20th World Conference, and the WACE 4th International Research Symposium. She is also part of the Emerald Insight Editorial Guest Team for the PCL International WIL Unconference, Higher Education Skills, and Work-Based Learning Journal.

Reza Gharoie Ahangar is an Assistant Professor of Business Analytics at Lewis University. He holds a B.Sc. in Business Management, an MBA in Finance, an MSc in Finance, an MSc in Business Analytics, and a Ph.D. in Management Science with a minor in Economics from the University of North Texas. He is a member of the American Finance Association (AFA), Production and Operations Management Society (POMS), Institute for Operations Research and the Management Sciences (INFORMS), Decision Sciences Institute (DSI), and Association of Scientists, Developers, and Faculties (ASDF). Mr. Ahangar has been a teaching assistant at UNT for seven years and has authored eight books and book chapters as well as several journal and conference publications in business analytics and operations journals, including Journal of the Operational Research Society, with more than fifty technical publications, and over 500 google scholar citations. His research works are cited by the top 0.1% of most-read authors in academia. He serves as an editorial board member & reviewer for several scientific journals.

Hakan Islamoğlu is a professor of Computer Education and Instructional Technology at Recep Tayyip Erdogan University. He has authored several book chapters, articles, and conference presentations. His research interests include mobile learning, technology integration in education, technology acceptance model, computational thinking skill development, and meaningful learning.

Tobias Jung is a consultant at Deloitte Consulting in Cologne, Germany. He holds a M.Sc. degree in IS from University of Muenster, Germany.

Michael Kyobe is a Professor of Information System. He holds a PhD in Computer Information Systems from the University of Freestate, South Africa and an MBA from the University of Durham, UK. Prior to joining academia in 2000, Michael worked as a project manager and IT manager for several years and has consulted extensively with the public and SMEs sectors in various fields of Information Technology. His research interests include Cybercrime, Cyberbullying, IT Management and governance and Computer security.

Kaneez Masoom is an Assistant Professor of Business Management at BBD University, Lucknow, India. Her research and publications address digital marketing and branding. She is currently working on a series of publications and conference presentations addressing digital marketing, entrepreneurship, brands and consumer behavior. She is perusing PhD from Khawaja Moinuddin Chishti language university, Lucknow, India. Her dissertation briefly examines impact of social media marketing on Consumer's purchase intention. Her research concerns broadly fall under the larger field of digital media and entrepreneurship and extend into certain questions about the nature of digital marketing and consumer behavior.

Mickaël Ringeval is a PhD Candidate in IT at ESG-UQAM in Montreal, Canada. His research interests are in IT use, IT Project management, Artificial Intelligence and Health Informatics.

Dragos Vieru is a Full Professor at TELUQ University of Quebec. He holds a Ph.D. degree in Information Technology from HEC Montreal and a M.Sc. degree in Management of Information Systems from John Molson School of Business, Montreal, Canada. His research interests are in the areas of IT-enabled organizational change, knowledge sharing, and IT governance. Dragos has published papers in the International Journal of Information Management, Information Systems Management, Journal of Knowledge Management, and Journal of Information Technology Teaching Cases. He has over 15 years of professional experience in IT project management in the healthcare sector. Dr. Vieru is also a LEGO® Serious Play® Facilitator since 2013.

Index

3IR 48, 64
4IR 48, 51, 64

A

Access to information 66, 74, 80
adoption 5, 9, 19, 38, 42, 49, 52-54, 56-57,
    63, 101, 115, 131, 148-149, 152, 192,
    195-197, 200-205, 207, 209, 211, 213,
    216-217, 219-220, 224
algorithms 23, 44, 54, 66-68, 70-71, 73,
    78-80, 88-89, 108, 112
Artificial Intelligence (AI) 22, 45, 48-49,
    53-54, 58, 67-68, 70, 112
Artificial Intelligence Ethics 112

B

Balanced Scorecard 146
Balancing Loop 169-170, 176
big data 22, 44, 48, 68, 71-74, 78-81, 92-96,
    99, 107-108, 112, 127
blackhat strategies 112-113
brand 1-5, 7-20, 135, 140, 172
brand awareness 1-2, 4-5, 7-10, 13-17,
    19-20
Brand impact 3, 10, 20

C

case study 23, 28, 37-38, 40, 43, 127, 129,
    143, 171-173, 194, 201, 220
Center-of-Gravity (COG) 146
Chatbots 21-22, 39-40, 42-43
church members 148, 151, 154, 157-158,
    160, 164-166, 169-171
Church membership growth 148-149, 176
churches 149, 151-152, 154, 164, 166, 171,
    173-174, 176
client computer 197-198
cloud computing 22, 180-181, 188, 194, 197
Collaboration tools 205, 224
college students 114-122, 126, 128
Consumer behaviour 14, 20
continued use 199-202, 204, 209, 216-217,
    223-224
COVID-19 2-4, 6-7, 14, 19, 22, 43-44,
    47-48, 50, 52, 58, 61-64, 66-67, 70-
    73, 91-93, 95, 99-103, 105, 107-109,
    112-128, 149, 152, 177, 181, 189,
    193-194, 196, 199-201, 210, 213,
    218-221, 223-224, 226-228, 232-237
COVID-19 pandemic 2, 6, 14, 19, 43, 48,
    50, 63, 66, 91, 101, 114-128, 177,
    181, 189, 199-201, 219, 223, 226-
    228, 232-237
COVID-19 Preparedness 64
CSEA 48, 52, 61, 64
Customer-Supplier Partnership 146

D

Dashboard 146
democratization 66, 71, 96
DH 64
digital education 177, 193
Digital Innovation 22, 26-27, 42, 45
digital marketing 7, 12, 20
digitalization 26, 48, 53, 62-63, 66-68,
    70-74, 80, 93, 96, 98, 113, 132, 138

digitalization disruption 66, 71, 96, 98

distribution 38, 59, 76-77, 90, 103, 106-107, 130-133, 137, 139, 143, 145-146, 156-157, 184

Distribution Channels 131, 146

Distribution Requirements Planning (DRP) 146

E

ease of use 202-203, 217, 223-224

economic growth 67-69, 74-76, 78-79, 87-88, 90-91, 98-100, 103-106, 108, 110-111, 113, 141, 144

Economics 64, 67-69, 74, 77, 89-90, 92, 97, 100-112, 171

E-Ethics 113

electronic word of mouth 13, 152, 169-170, 176

Enterprise Resource Planning (ERP) System 146

evangelism 148, 152, 157-158, 162-164, 166, 168-173, 176

Experience API (xAPI) 197

F

FDI 67, 113

FRDR 63-64

Free on Board (FOB) 146

future pandemics 47-50, 56, 58-61, 64

G

GDP 67-68, 81, 91, 113, 134

global pandemic 1-2, 6, 9, 17, 47, 66, 115, 120, 152, 227-228

Global Strategy 146

H

healthcare institutions 47-60, 64-65

healthcare systems 53-54, 61, 64, 153

higher education 19, 177, 180, 182, 184, 186, 192-194, 196, 228, 235-236

Human Resource Management 27, 39-41, 43-45, 90, 133, 208, 218

I

ICT 47-48, 60, 151-152, 157-160, 163, 176, 205, 221, 225

Inbound Logistics 146

influencer marketing 1-3, 5-7, 10, 12-13, 16, 19-20

influencers 1-3, 5-7, 9-10, 12-13, 16-17, 19-20

Information and communications technology 176

information technology 18, 40, 44, 47-49, 56, 60, 62, 65, 114-116, 123, 126, 128-129, 131, 133, 139, 177, 179, 192, 195, 217-218, 220, 222-223, 226-229, 232, 237

innovation 19, 22-23, 26-27, 42, 45, 49, 53-54, 58, 61, 69, 76, 88, 103, 115, 139, 141-142, 174-175, 200-204, 216, 224

innovative technologies 47-53, 55-58, 60, 65

Inorganic growth 151, 176

international company 129-132, 134-137, 139-140

IoT 51, 53-54, 65

it 1-17, 20-29, 31-39, 45, 47-49, 53-55, 65, 67-69, 71-74, 77, 80-81, 87-90, 93, 100,'102, 107, 113, 116, 118-119, 121-122, 128, 131-134, 136-142, 149-152, 154, 158-169, 176, 178-193, 200-201, 204-205, 211, 214-215, 218, 221, 230, 233-234, 237

J

job market 111

Just-in-Time (JIT) 146

L

learning analytics 185, 194, 196-197

learning management system (LMS) 193, 197-198

Long COVID or Post-COVID Conditions 113

M

Manufacturing Lead Time 146
Master Production Schedule (MPS) 146
ML 42, 65, 193
Model Church Growth 148

N

NATO 50, 65
NLP 49, 58, 65

O

Online Course Contents/Components Model 237
online education 54, 126, 178, 195, 226-227, 229, 231-233, 235-237
Online Education and Virtual Collaboration Model 226-227, 229, 231-232, 237
Online Meeting Tool (OMT) 197
Online persona 9, 20
online proctoring 188-189, 193, 198
Organic growth 151, 153, 176
Original Equipment Manufacturer (OEM) 146

P

pandemics 1, 47-54, 56, 58-61, 63-64, 108, 117
perceived benefits 202-203, 224
Perceived Cost 204, 224
Perceived Risk 204, 219, 224
Perceived Satisfaction 224
Perceived Trust 203, 224
perceived usefulness 202, 204-205, 217, 223-225
perception 5, 9, 20, 36-37, 54, 201, 203, 211, 224, 234, 236
Performance Measures 146
phenomenon 6, 19, 23, 29, 31, 93, 95, 97, 119, 155, 201, 224
Plagiarism Detection System 198
product 3, 8, 10, 13, 15-16, 20, 26, 36, 55, 65, 69, 89, 100, 113, 129, 139, 142, 146, 150, 176

R

Radio Frequency (RFID) 146
Reinforcing Loop 168-169, 176
religious leaders 149, 151, 153, 155, 174
religious organisations 148-153, 155, 157, 161, 163, 165, 168-171, 174, 176
Remote Work 199, 218, 221-222
Resilient Healthcare 61, 65
Right to Deletion 113
Right to Not be Forgotten 113
robotics 42, 51, 66, 71, 78, 80, 89, 93, 99, 105-106, 110, 112
Russia 130-134, 136, 138-139, 141-144

S

SDGs 65
searchplace discrimination 98, 113
Secondary resources 201, 225
Server Computer 198
Seventh-day Adventist Church (SDA) 148-149
Sharable Content Object Reference Model (SCORM) 185, 197-198
social distancing 16, 64, 70, 72-73, 200, 215, 224-226
social media 1-7, 9-20, 26, 55, 71, 78, 92-94, 148-149, 151-159, 161-166, 169-171, 173-176, 229
social media environment 4, 10, 20
social media information systems 1, 5
social media marketing 1, 3, 6, 9, 15, 20
South Africa 47, 64, 148, 154, 159-160, 171, 199, 206, 218
SPRP 58, 65
stakeholder theory 226, 231, 233, 237
Statistical Process Control (SPC) 146
stress 28, 118, 128, 206, 208, 215
supply chain 129, 138, 145-146
Sustainable healthcare service 65
system dynamics 148-150, 152-153, 172-176

T

technology affordances 21, 23, 26-27, 36-

38, 41, 44-45

Telework 199-205, 207, 209-217, 220-223, 225

trainee management software 21, 23, 27, 36-37, 45

Transportation Requirements Planning (TRP) 147

U

UNHCR 58, 65

Unified systems 205, 225

Universal Healthcare Coverage 65

University 1, 21, 39-40, 43, 47, 60, 66, 77, 98-101, 105-107, 109-110, 112, 114, 123, 128-129, 143, 145, 148, 174, 177-178, 180-183, 186-187, 189, 191, 199, 218, 221-222, 224, 226-227, 229-230, 232-233, 235, 237

University Information Technology Applications Model 229, 237

University Infrastructure 177

University IT Competitive Advantages Model 230, 237

V

value 2, 5, 9, 13, 15-16, 69, 72, 78-81, 90, 92, 113, 133, 138, 147, 168, 176, 182, 199-203, 216-217, 224-225, 228

value chain 147, 228

video conferencing 181-182, 191

video games 114-122, 128

Video Games Industry 117, 128

Virtual Assistant 22, 26, 29, 45

Virtual Assistants 21-25, 37

Virtual Collaboration 44, 226-227, 229, 231-232, 237

Virtual Desktop Infrastructure (VDI) 190, 198

Virtual Private Networking (VPN) 183, 198

Virtualization 179-180, 189-190, 193, 195, 198

W

warehouse management systems 129, 144-145

WEF 63, 65

who 3, 6-7, 9-10, 14, 16-17, 20, 26, 35-36, 50, 63, 65, 73-75, 78, 93-94, 97-98, 112, 115, 118, 126, 128, 152, 155, 158, 160-164, 166, 169-170, 186, 189, 191, 200, 204, 209, 212, 223, 232

 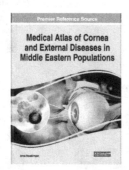 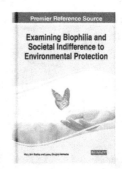 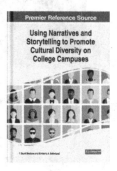

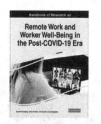